OXFORD MODERN LANGUAGES
AND LITERATURE MONOGRAPHS

Editorial Committee

C. GRAYSON M. JACOBS

A. J. KRAILSHEIMER C. N. J. MANN A. W. RAITT

G. C. STONE R. W. TRUMAN

BRECHT'S POETRY

A critical study

by

PETER WHITAKER

CLARENDON PRESS · OXFORD

Oxford University Press, Walton Street, Oxford OX2 6DP
Oxford New York Toronto
Delhi Bombay Calcutta Madras Karachi
Petaling Jaya Singapore Hong Kong Tokyo
Nairobi Dar es Salaam Cape Town
Melbourne Auckland
and associated companies in
Beirut Berlin Ibadan Nicosia

Oxford is a trademark of Oxford University Press

Published in the United States
by Oxford University Press, New York

© Peter Whitaker 1985

First published 1985
Reprinted 1987

All rights reserved. No part of this publication may be reproduced, stored in a retrieval system, or transmitted, in any form or by any means, electronic, mechanical, photocopying, recording, or otherwise, without the prior permission of Oxford University Press

British Library Cataloguing in Publication Data
Whitaker, Peter
Brecht's poetry: a critical study.—(Oxford
modern languages and literature monographs)
1. Brecht, Bertolt—Poetic works
I. Title
831'.912   PT2603.R397Z/
ISBN 0–19–815541–7

Library of Congress Cataloging in Publication Data
Whitaker, Peter, 1952–
Brecht's poetry.
(Oxford modern languages and literature monographs)
Bibliography: p.
Includes index.
1. Brecht, Bertolt, 1898–1956—Criticism and
interpretation. I. Title II. Series.
PT2603.R397Z898 1985   832'.912   84-27204
ISBN 0–19–815541–7

Printed in Great Britain by
Antony Rowe Ltd.,
Chippenham

For my parents

ACKNOWLEDGEMENTS

I am grateful for their help and encouragement to Mr F. J. Lamport, Dr K. O. Gore, Professor S. S. Prawer, Mr G. W. McKay, and my generously patient supervisor, Dr R. C. Ockenden. Professor Hans-Albert Walter, formerly of the Hamburger Arbeitsstelle für deutsche Exilliteratur, provided much invaluable assistance and advice. I have gained much from working with pupils and fellow students, particularly from a period of collaboration with Wolfgang Vietrich in Hamburg. The staff of the Bertolt-Brecht-Archiv were unfailingly welcoming and helpful; I am especially grateful to Frau Lisa Kiel, Frau Herta Ramthun, and the Director, Dr Gerhard Seidel, for their indispensable assistance. My research was supported in part by grants from the Department of Education and Science, London, and the Stiftung FVS, Hamburg.

CONTENTS

ABBREVIATIONS	xi
INTRODUCTION	1
CHAPTER 1 THE EARLY POETRY	4
Materialism against Metaphysics	8
Sense-experience: Things as they are	14
Hauspostille	18
A Typology	24
CHAPTER 2 EXPERIMENTS IN REALISM	33
Aus einem Lesebuch für Städtebewohner	39
CHAPTER 3 ALIGNMENT AND EXILE 1926–1934	62
Types of Poetry: A Survey	62
Songs and Ballads	63
Die drei Soldaten	65
Poems in Free Rhythms	71
Exile: *Lieder Gedichte Chöre*	79
CHAPTER 4 EXILE (2) 1934–1939	98
Taking Stock	99
'Daß er ohne seine Hörer nichts ist'	102
The Dialectics of Defiance	105
Botschaften	113
Svendborger Gedichte	114
CHAPTER 5 EXILE (3) 1939–1947	150
The Epigram	152
Landscapes	162
Materialism	164
Lehrgedicht von der Natur der Menschen	169
Satires	181
CHAPTER 6 THE POST-EXILE POETRY 1948–1956	183
Brecht and Germany	183
New Poems	184
'Kinderlieder 1950' and Warnings of Crisis	194
Buckower Elegien	201

The Last Poems	216
APPENDIX	222
NOTES	225
BIBLIOGRAPHY	265
COPYRIGHTS	275
INDEX	277

ABBREVIATIONS

GW	Bertolt Brecht, *Gesammelte Werke* (followed by volume and page-number)
GW Supp.	Bertolt Brecht, *Gesammelte Werke, Supplementbände III, IV* (followed by page-number)
AJ	*Arbeitsjournal* (followed by date of entry)
Brief	Bertolt Brecht, *Briefe* (followed by letter-number)
TAA	*Tagebücher: Autobiographische Aufzeichnungen* (followed by page-number)
bba	Bertolt-Brecht-Archiv photocopies (followed by file- and leaf-number)

INTRODUCTION

In organization as in conception the study attempts to conform to its object; hence its chronological plan and also its disruptions of chronology in treating the collections *Hauspostille, Lieder Gedichte Chöre,* and *Svendborger Gedichte*. Similarly, in discussing the highly deliberate poetry written after 1925, the study does not attempt to disclose hidden relationships or to interpret 'against the grain'. Rather, 'practical' readings of Brecht's texts are constructed, which seek to combine a reasonably precise estimate of what could have been, and can be, expected of readers, with thorough analysis and clear presentation: the latter in particular demands that a certain artificiality be accepted, that the readings constructed should be, in some measure, ideal.

In this undertaking paraphrase is an indispensable instrument: not the goal of analysis, but its aid. The value of paraphrase rests on its formulation of what otherwise may remain nebulous: it constitutes a useful critical test of a particular direction of reading, since it tends immediately to highlight any disparity between text and reading.[1] Close analysis of texts provides material for commentary which endeavours to locate texts within Brecht's literary production and in their historical context, and to establish their specific character and effectiveness. Generalizations are derived from collation of individual cases, and it is the intended general scope of the study which necessarily limits the extent of individual analyses. There is so much material of importance that a single text cannot properly claim more than a few pages; many readings and commentaries must be concise to the point of allusion and understatement.

A comprehensive survey of Brecht's poetry must concern itself above all with the poems written after 1925. These poems, which constitute three-quarters of Brecht's lyric production, have so far been neglected, both in comparison with the attention which continues to be lavished on the early poems, and absolutely, in terms of their proper significance.

Esslin and Arendt, who agree on the division of Brecht into poet and Marxist, both show a marked preference for the pre-1925 poems and postulate a radical division at, or about, this date.[2] It is paradoxical that Schuhmann, who sets out to disprove the poetry-politics dichotomy, himself adopts a much more emphatic system of divisions in the conclusion of his book.[3]

The dialectic of continuity and discontinuity is not simple: the opposition is relativistic, and subjective. It depends, for example, on the question of scale and interpretation: how substantial a break or transformation is to be regarded as discontinuity—and is not transformation itself a kind of continuity? In a historical account of literary production, it seems reasonable not to insist dogmatically on the primacy of either continuity or discontinuity: elements of both are frequently evident. Schuhmann's criticism of Esslin and Arendt would have been more convincing had he concentrated less on his alternative distinctions; Walter Benjamin, writing in the late thirties, offered a better argument:

solchen Leuten, welchen der Kommunismus das Stigma der Einseitigkeit zu tragen scheint, mag die genauere Lektüre einer Gedichtsammlung wie der Brechts eine Überraschung bereiten. Man darf sich freilich um eine solche Überraschung nicht selber bringen, wie es geschähe, wenn man nur die 'Entwicklung', welche die Lyrik Brechts von der 'Hauspostille' bis zu den 'Svendborger Gedichten' genommen hat, betont. Die asoziale Haltung der 'Hauspostille' wird in den 'Svendborger Gedichten' zu einer sozialen Haltung. Aber das ist nicht gerade eine Bekehrung. Es wird da nicht verbrannt, was zuerst angebetet wurde. Eher ist auf das den Gedichtsammlungen Gemeinsame zu verweisen.[4]

This study, though far from wishing to ignore significant distinctions, seeks to apply Benjamin's recommendation productively, by adopting a chronological sequence as the basis for its critical analysis of the poems both synchronically and diachronically: only the first (and the shortest) of its six chapters is devoted to the early poems; it offers a summary account of their specific character, concentrating primarily on their potential for development and transformation, on their continuity with the later work. The concept of materialism, which corresponds closely to elements of Brecht's own analysis, was applied to the early poems principally in order to illuminate their fundamental relatedness to Brecht's later production; the basis of this relatedness appears to be central to the poems.

Comprehensiveness was a basic criterion; there is now a substantial body of secondary literature covering an abundance of primary texts of, or about, poetry. There are books and dissertations (Schuhmann, Schlenstedt) which adopt, and others (e.g. Steffensen) which claim, a comprehensive approach, but most of the secondary literature consists of small-scale studies of sources and influences, or of interpretations of individual poems.[5] It is true that there many unanswered questions about the poetry, some of them of the most basic kind: this should be a limiting factor on any large-scale view, but not an inhibiting one. The lack of a general model for the development of the poetry itself limits the scope of individual studies.

In the framework of this general view, there are also detailed studies of many poems not previously discussed. The analysis of the poems is itself a large undertaking; a full-scale examination of the literary theory as it relates to the poems would extend far beyond the prescribed bounds of this work. Nevertheless, some treatment of theoretical questions is often suggested by the poems themselves, and to this extent forms an integral part of the present study.

The edition of Brecht's works referred to is the most recent and most widely used collected edition: Bertolt Brecht, *Gesammelte Werke in 20 Bänden* (Frankfurt am Main, 1967). This is not an ideal edition, but it is the best available at present. Unpublished manuscripts were consulted in preparation of the study, and are referred to where appropriate; no general attempt can be made to anticipate the work of the critical edition. Some poems can now be dated precisely, the majority with a high degree of probability, and others only approximately: texts in the latter category, where a probable year of origin is given, are indicated by a question-mark.

Chapter 1

THE EARLY POETRY

BRECHT'S juvenilia, mostly epigonal texts concerned with the First World War (GW 8, 3–15), have been examined in detail by Klaus Schuhmann.[1] They are of little literary value and will not be discussed here. The early poetry has attracted most critical attention to date, though it has not been treated exhaustively. The standard work on the poems written before 1933, indeed the pioneering large-scale study of Brecht's poems, is Schuhmann's book; it places the poems, sometimes a little too mechanically, in their historical context and collects valuable material on first publication, early versions, and theoretical reflection. Its interpretations of individual poems are, however, occasionally disappointing, the specifically literary text being neglected. This study is none the less the necessary point of departure for any analysis of the poems.

P. P. Schwarz approaches a much smaller body of poems (1914–22): probably too limited a selection for his purpose, which is to define and illustrate a unifying core within the early poetry.[2] This core, it is suggested, may be termed Nihilism. Jan Knopf[3] has criticized this approach energetically, condemning its lack of rigour in applying extraneous concepts to Brecht's work; and Schwarz's method does indeed involve some surprising consequences. The *Baal*-complex, of central importance for Brecht's entire career, above all for the early work, is relegated to the status of a mere Vitalist exception. This is a distortion which is not justified by the insights offered in Schwarz's book. Schwarz does respond to important elements of these poems, their frequent ironic coloration, their reflective and 'philosophical' orientation; these characteristics account for the inadequacy of some of Schuhmann's attempts to link the poems to historical background: the texts are often more introspective, more limited in scope than such an approach assumes. Nihilism, on the evidence of the poems themselves, is not the central point of the early poetry, and this, in spite of useful studies of individual texts, undermines the book.

THE EARLY POETRY 5

The triad of large-scale studies is completed by Carl Pietzcker, who examines the poems (chiefly those written before 1925) with the aid of concepts from many strands of psychoanalysis and from a Marxism manipulated by the Critical Theory of the Frankfurt School.[4] This is a problematic methodological organization and does not lead to any significant illumination of the poems as literary artefacts. The value of the book, which revives, in a modified and restricted form, the Nihilism thesis, rests principally on the considerable detail of its analyses, rather than on its general conclusions. At its worst, Pietzcker's book becomes an indirect psychological study of Brecht, viewing Brecht's poetry 'als Ausdruck eines Heilungsprozesses';[5] such a view completely fails to grasp the degree of self-consciousness and irony inherent in Brecht's treatment of death and sexuality.

The endeavour to define the central orientation of the early poetry, whose coherence is intuited by many critics, is worth while: but this general definition should not be tied to any single narrow abstraction. If it is to embrace a significant number of poems, it should remain flexible and relatively open, to accommodate nuances and developments.

The early poetry presents a chaotic picture. It is characterized by a high degree of ironic mobility, by an elusiveness which operates against definition. Nevertheless, the poems have a common source and stand in ultimate relationship with one another.[6]

One of the earliest poems, 'Das Beschwerdelied', is both representative of the period and important in its own right.

> So mancher rennt sich müd
> Weil er die Ruh zu sehr
> Liebt. Alle rennen nach dem Glück:
> Das Glück rennt hinterher.
> Wer sich lang zermartert
> Kommt zu spät zum Fraß.
> Wer sich kurz zermartert
> Rennt die falsche Straß. (1916, GW 8, 16)

The poem of which this forms the first strophe was produced only months after the last of the war poems, 'Soldatengrab', published in February 1916:

> Hat einst gekämpft und gesungen
> Mit allen in einer Reih,

> Hat mit allen den Säbel geschwungen
> Und ist mit allen verklungen
> Und liegt nun drunten dabei.[7]

The sharp distinction between this typical example of Brecht's self-imposed juvenile laureateship and the 'Beschwerdelied' is evident. The latter is more representative of the main body of early poetry than 'Das Lied der Eisenbahntruppe von Fort Donald', which was suggested by Schuhmann as a marker for this division.[8] This ballad, though it is the first poem to dispense with Brecht's pseudonym, is close to the war poems, and shares their images and motifs; the motif of the wind's song, for example, is common to the 'Eisenbahntruppe' ballad and to 'Soldatengrab'. The laconic and superior voice of 'Das Beschwerdelied' delivers a series of apodictic sentences, modified by the paradoxes they contain. The ironic collision of sense produced in the first strophe requires the reader to reconstruct the meaning so that some delicate balance between exertion and inertia is proposed as the means to happiness. This theme is elaborated in the direction of salutary humility and resignation, culminating in the admonition not to waste time in futile worry:

> Sind zu kurz die Brücken
> Was das Herz beschweren!
> Ob viel oder wenig fehlt
> Daß sie lang g'nug wären! (GW 8, 17)

The poem's conclusions mock its title: it is in fact a song against complaint. This is clearly not philosophy in any rigorous or academic sense; the term here signifies the general reflections which constitute *Lebensweisheit*. The poem does not expound any philosophy of life with direct seriousness, it does not simply describe the ironies of life and man's helpless inadequacy before them: it participates in this irony, inviting the reader to recognize and indulge himself in the world's mockery of man. Its mood is one of enthusiastic disillusion. A complex of attitudes rich in ambiguity is presented here: in so far as it can be made to render any fixed sense, it seeks an equilibrium between scepticism and acquiescent adaptation. If life is beautiful, it is precisely so beautiful and no more:

> Schön ist das Leben
> Wenn du schöner bist:

THE EARLY POETRY

Dann bleibst du dran kleben
Weil es schmutzig ist.

The poem invokes and celebrates the 'Gott der Dinge, wie sie sind'. This richly ambiguous phrase which mixes empiricism with metaphysics has its origins in the shorter form: 'die Dinge, wie sie sind'. A diary entry for 8 July 1920 records that Brecht had been reading the letters of Van Gogh; the reflections which these letters occasioned are concluded by the sentence: 'Ausschlag gibt... die Unerschrockenheit des menschlichen Herzens, das die Dinge zeigt, wie sie sind, und sie so liebt' (TAA, 18). This is the attitude of 'Das Beschwerdelied'.

Michael Morley has identified Kipling's poem 'When Earth's last picture is painted' as the source of the later phrase.[9] J. K. Lyon lists this as one of the poems translated for Brecht in 1925-7 by Elisabeth Hauptmann.[10] If the phrase of 1920 signified primarily honest recognition, '"heroischer Realismus" (Sehen der Dinge, wie sie sind)' (GW 18, 167), its later transformation via the Kipling translation emphasized more strongly the aspect of reconciliation, of passive acceptance: things as they are being not merely recognized, but worshipped as God-given. This negative perspective is illuminated by the ironic usage in *Die Ausnahme und die Regel:* 'Der Gott der Dinge, wie sie sind, schuf Herr und Knecht!/ Und das war gut so' (GW 2, 808). Finally a later series of notes ('Die dialektische Dramatik', 1931) attempts to construct a critique of early post-war literature, including Brecht's own work; here too the phrase plays an important part in defining a central attitude:

die Welt, wie sie ist, sollte gezeigt und anerkannt, ihre eigene Schonungslosigkeit als ihre Größe schonungslos aufgewiesen werden: ihr Gott sollte sein 'der Gott der Dinge, wie sie sind'. Dieser Versuch, eine neue Ideologie zu schaffen, die mit den Tatsachen direkt zusammenhängen sollte, war gegen das Bürgertum gerichtet. (GW 15, 218.)

This passage is preceded by the assertion that such a new ideology would be 'völlig idealistisch und völlig kapitalistisch'. This rebellion against bourgeois ideas itself remained safely within the sphere of ideas and ultimately allowed itself to be neutralized and accommodated by bourgeois society: 'das gegen ihn gespritzte Gift verwandelt der Kapitalismus sogleich und laufend in Rauschgift und genießt dieses' (GW 20, 37).

The poem's verbal wit is supplemented by prosodic features: the grotesque enjambement of ll. 2-3 and the departure from the general rhyme scheme in the first four lines of the second strophe. Its sardonic tone limits the poem's conceptual horizon; the satisfaction it proposes is of a non-transcendent kind. 'Fraß' in the first strophe indicates unambiguously that the fruits referred to in the poem are material, immanent gratifications, rather than spiritual rewards. The second strophe makes this reduced horizon explicit when it suggests that the stars are so distant that they are practically unattainable and directs the reader's attention instead to the 'Baum des Lebens'. Its fruits are only to be won by the abandonment of self-denial and righteousness: they must be seized, or stolen, in the knowledge that violence and pain may ensue. They must also be seized at precisely the right moment ('man pflückt sie nur im Fall'), when they are ripe for enjoyment, but equally ready to fall and rot. Wine and women figure amongst the fruit of this secular and materialistic tree; the highest reaches of attainment, it is implied, are in coitus—the fifth strophe is laden with sexual metaphor. The ambivalence of 'höchstens' implies that this peak of achievement is itself an anti-climax. Finally, such enjoyment is seen as a mere 'Zeitvertreib' and, moreover, an inescapably commercial arrangement.

To paraphrase the light wit and energy of this poem is to weigh it down; but this is necessary in order to make clear how the text operates. This should not obscure the fact that the poem invites the reader to share in its cynical and indulgent pose and enables him to do so with enjoyment.

'Das Beschwerdelied', formally typical of much of the early poetry, is representative in two further senses. First, generally, it embodies existential reflection—it is a philosophizing poem. Secondly, it introduces the specific modes of reflection which are common to the majority of the early poems. The poetry is in tension between extreme scepticism on one side and the exploration of areas of reliable solidity on the other. These diametrically opposed directions are susceptible to different positions of balance in individual texts.

Materialism against Metaphysics

The dominant element in the early poetry is negative, reductive, employing scepticism and ironic destruction. One reason for this is the importance, in the poems written before 1920, of the death theme. The consciousness of mortality becomes a fundamental truth, in the face of which metaphysical speculation fades into meaninglessness. Christian doctrine (in particular the idea of the resurrection of the body) is found to be an inadequate response to this great existential question, and is attacked.

'Man feiert die Auferstehung des Fleisches' (GW 8, 242): this line, from one of the 'Psalmen', is typical of them in its appropriation of the high tone of biblical language for a secular and physical celebration, its reference is made immediate and literal. Similarly, in 'Die Legende der Dirne Evlyn Roe' (GW 8, 18) the legend is inverted, so that a Christian pilgrim is made a prostitute in the service of a God who no longer exists. The concluding strophes of the ballad show that Evlyn Roe is fitted for neither heaven nor hell, being too fallible for the former and too virtuous for the latter. The received categories of doctrine are insufficient to accommodate the complex reality of humanity. This quasi-theological argument is on the periphery of the poem, whose main interest is centred on the narrative moment. Nevertheless, it is in this argument that the poem's unifying motivation lies. The text does not stop at the point of Evlyn Roe's double rejection; its final lines evoke a transcendence which is a 'poetic' version of Christian doctrine. In a ghost-like vision where there is no longer any trace of physical reality, the heroine is made to wander endlessly through the skies.

Other poems are more decidedly and bluntly opposed to the Christian faith: 'Von der Kindesmörderin Marie Farrar', relating how Marie prayed and hoped for help, comments dismissively 'Doch die Gebete hätten, scheinbar, nichts genützt./ Es war auch viel verlangt' (GW 8, 176). The problem, in the realm of material reality, is inaccessible to prayer.

'Vom Brot und den Kindlein' presents a cautionary tale in which the warnings given to children are made real; having refused to eat the bread offered to them, the children are in defiance of parental and religious authority. They do indeed suffer hunger, but they have left the narrow limits of home and religion, and are situated in the real world:

> Es sind die Kindlein gangen
> Viele Straßen weit.
> Da mußten sie ja gelangen
> Außer die Christenheit. (GW 8, 172)

Its heathen inhabitants do not offer food to innocent wanderers. The repetition in str. 6 of the moralistic warning given in the third—the warning is now literal fact—exemplifies the poem's basic structure: 'Sie würden sich gerne stürzen/ Auf ein Stückelein Brot'. It is a cautionary tale, but an ironic one, which implies the invalidity of the traditional tale: it cautions the reader against the dangerous distractions of Christianity. The prayer which concludes the poem is also ironic; the preceding strophes demonstrate that the idea of heaven is an irrelevance. Children who starve in the real world will find no sufficient nourishment in an imaginary heaven. The unreality of the notion is underlined in the final strophe by the significant reference to material fact: the bread of which the first strophes spoke has grown mouldy and has been fed to the animals. The phrase 'ein kleines Gewürzlein' suggests a misleading and superficial sugaring of the bitterness of starvation and increases the ironic force of the concluding lines.

Christianity is attacked, not only (as principally in the above examples) for its inadequacy, for its failures, but also for what it achieves. If its indication of possible transcendence means that it ignores real problems, Christianity also helps actively to spoil mortal existence. 'Bericht vom Zeck' (GW 8, 187) describes the influence of the 'Mann in Violett', identified as the author of a book of forty-nine commandments. God appears as a ghost in the dreams of children; he is otiose and self-indulgent, demanding and jealous of his pleasures, a leech preying on his victims until they can yield no more. He negates all human pleasure:

> Und hast du eine Freude
> Und lachst du noch so leis—
> Er hat eine kleine Orgel
> Drauf spielt er Trauerweis'. (GW 8, 188)

God may be an imagined figure, but the damage inflicted in his name is none the less real. As the final strophe makes clear, his aim is the destruction of life. The believer dies, robbed and defeated by a phantom of his own fabrication. The satiric theology of the eighth strophe is typical of the poetry of this period: 'Und hat doch auch die Säue/ Nach seinem Bild gemacht.'

'Gegen Verführung' (1920, GW 8, 260) adopts the verbal gestures of the Christian hymn to contradict Christian doctrine. The poem's argument and its received model intersect in its exhortation against being led astray. A stable construction of sense is made possible by the second line in its denial of transcendence: 'Es gibt keine Wiederkehr.' The text reflects on the precious brevity of life, it is a *carpe diem*; life's short span is at the same time its greatness, its proper definition and the condition of its reality: 'Das Leben ist am größten:/ Es steht nicht mehr bereit.' The closing strophe warns against the enslaving bonds of fear; there is, it suggests, no ultimate sanction—man is free and has, literally, nothing to fear after death, which he shares with all other animals. There is a momentary sense of rebellion in the first lines of this strophe, which express what is implicit throughout the poem: the promise of a life beyond death is a mere ruse to cheat men into despising the life which precedes it—'Laßt euch nicht verführen/ Zu Fron und Ausgezehr!'. This element of social criticism remains general and abstract, it is bedded firmly in the dominant existential argument, even partially neutralized by the poem's impartial and dignified tone, suggesting the wisdom of knowledge and resignation. The limits set by the poem's model mean that it is ultimately not so far removed from the very meekness and acceptance which it set out to challenge. Most of its energy is expended in the corrective statement of facts, leaving little for the suggestion of defiant action.

The knowledge of physical reality, of mortality, is similarly the central focus of 'Großer Dankchoral' (1920); like 'Gegen Verführung' it is a serious parody, a poem of contradiction. Far from praising the Lord Creator of an ordered universe, the poem invites the reader to recognize the indifference of the cosmos, and to be glad of it.

> Lobet den Baum, der aus Aas aufwächst jauchzend zum Himmel!
> Lobet das Aas
> Lobet den Baum, der es fraß
> Aber auch lobet den Himmel. (GW 8, 215.)

The image of the tree growing out of the body's decay has, even at this early stage, a considerable history in Brecht's poetry. It is employed for its intimation of a mediated transcendence in the 1918 version of 'Der Tod im Wald'[11] ('Tod im Walde'), in the patriotic war poem 'Der belgische Acker' (1915, GW 8, 9), and, here somewhat less mystically, in 'Die Geburt im Baum' (1920, GW 8, 85). In 'Großer Dankchoral' the image is used directly and simply to describe in real material terms the mechanism of life. The tree may appropriate the corpse, but does not offer any continuity of individual existence: what continues is the natural process.

Other poems attack Christianity with aggressive satire: 'Und immer wieder gab es Abendröte' (GW 8, 73) resurrects the figure of God as the tormentor of mankind, but the resurrection is accomplished with such irony that it demands immediate destruction. 'Lied der Schwestern' (GW 8, 64) examines the mechanism of the Christian myth. The search for God, lacking all material foundation, is forced to concentrate on the vague and ethereal. Apparently a gentle, sympathetic poem, it requires ironic reading for its full effect. 'Hymne an Gott' (GW 8, 54) presents a satiric theodicy. After a twelve-line indictment of God's failings (were he to exist), the poem recognizes the force of illusion: how can so effective a deceit be countered by the mere fact of its falsehood? Here, characteristically, the idea of decay is used to undermine metaphysical superstition by reference to material fact:

> Ließest die Armen arm sein manches Jahr
> Weil ihre Sehnsucht schöner als dein Himmel war
> Starben sie leider, bevor mit dem Lichte du kamst
> Starben sie selig doch — und verfaulten sofort.

The poems do, however, have other targets besides Christianity. They oppose metaphysical ideals in general. In contrast to the credulous and pious tone of 'Karfreitag' (GW 8, 7–8):

> Daß es Menschen gibt, die für Menschen sterben können!
> Und er fühlte Staunen (als er weiterspann):
> Und daß es Dinge gibt, für die man sterben kann.

the post-1916 poems are sceptical, disillusioned, based on a consciousness of the limits and value of life. Where the immature poems had been patriotic, the majority of the early poetry is unambiguously pacifist: 'Legende vom toten Soldaten' (GW 8, 256), 'Caspars Lied mit der einen Strophe' (GW 8, 29), 'Larrys Ballade von der Mama Armee' (GW 8, 39), 'Ballade vom Weib und dem Soldaten' (GW 8, 239), and 'Gesang des Soldaten der roten Armee' (GW 8, 41).

This anti-metaphysical orientation is central to the early poetry; Christianity is its most obvious target and is the object of a remarkably consistent technique in these poems. Ideas whose general indebtedness to the Christian body of thought is apparent are understood in a completely literal way and tested against concrete examples. This is a simple procedure and Brecht executes it with considerable wit and elegance. The application of physical fact is the negative aspect of what may be termed the 'materialism' of these poems. It is, as was suggested earlier, demonstrably the dominant aspect. If there is an accompanying positive aspect, what does it affirm and how? These questions become acute when it is recalled that the sense of mortality, itself negatively charged, is a principal determinant in the anti-metaphysical stance. 'Gegen Verführung' suggested that the recognition of mortality potentially and paradoxically implied the affirmation of physical life, by setting material limits to it and therefore making it real. This paradox is also the basis of 'Von der Freundlichkeit der Welt' (1922), which examines the extent and quality of human life in a cold and indifferent world. It is noticeable that the context of human life is now not seen as simply biological, as in 'Gegen Verführung' or the 'Großer Dankchoral'; in this later text the social element of this context appears in the shape of fellow human beings. This does not significantly alter the overall picture, since these fellow men are as indifferent as the rest of nature. Nevertheless, after its brief survey of the 'kindness' of the world, the poem concludes with the formulation of an enigma:

> Von der Erde voller kaltem Wind
> Geht ihr all bedeckt mit Schorf und Grind.
> Fast ein jeder hat die Welt geliebt
> Wenn man ihm zwei Hände Erde gibt. (GW 8, 205.)

This too refers back to 'Gegen Verführung': 'Es wird euch nicht genügen/ Wenn ihr es lassen müßt!'.

The early poetry offers little progression beyond the crystallization of such paradoxes, and the continuous recourse to the statement of material fact. If man is placed among the animals in an implicitly Darwinian scheme of evolution, his non-intellectual, instinctual characteristics must be recognized as part of his reality. In Baal's words: 'nichts versteht man. Aber manches fühlt man' (GW 1, 48). An equivalent intellectual pessimism is exhibited in 'Über die Anstrengung', where evolution is seen as degeneration:

> Der Geist hat verhurt die Fleischeswonne
> Seit er die haarigen Hände entklaut

> Es durchdringen die Sensationen der Sonne
> Nicht mehr die pergamentene Haut. (GW 8, 207.)

Similarly in *Mahagonny* civilization is presented as a disease ('Zivilis', GW 8, 244).

Sense-experience: Things as they are

Experience of material reality is through the senses: what is experienced directly, felt immediately, is reliable to a degree unattainable by mediated intelligence. It is, after all, abstract reflection which produces false and inadequate metaphysical ideals. Much of Brecht's early poetry is concerned with the attempt to establish an area of material fact on the basis of sense-experience.

The functions of colour adjectives, which are frequently employed in these poems, have been briefly examined by Sträter and Steffensen; Schuhmann discusses them in detail and concludes: 'die frühen Gedichte sind undenkbar ohne die Farbtypologie'.[12] Schuhmann links the colours green, red, and blue to specific themes, and this is generally convincing. There are, however, other colours, and Brecht is far from entirely consistent in his application of colour epithets, so that there is no fixed code to which each instance can be referred. Such adjectives are limited as an expressive device by their low degree of semantic specificity, they operate by association. Colour may indeed be a totally arbitrary marker:

> Neher Cas malt den violetten Himmel über Petschawar weiß:
> weil er kein Blau mehr in der Tube hat. (GW 8, 31.)

The frequency and variety of colour adjectives have the cumulative effect of evoking a rich and changing visual environment. The impression of movement is a visual element, at least peripherally. It is common to many poems, from 'Ballade vom Mazeppa' (GW 8, 233) to 'Das Schiff' (GW 8, 179).

The areas of sound and smell do not figure significantly here, though in the case of smell there are important exceptions: 'Apfelböck oder Die Lilie auf dem Felde' (GW 8, 173) and 'Die Ballade vom Liebestod' (GW 8, 253) record smells as an accompaniment to the imagery of decay. Smells which are not thus negatively marked are described in 'Von dem Gras und Pfeffer-

THE EARLY POETRY 15

minzkraut' (GW 8, 84) and 'Der Fluß lobsingt die Sterne im Gebüsch' (GW 8, 74).

Taste sensations occur in conjunction with those of smell in 'Von dem Gras und Pfefferminzkraut'; they are also present as pleasurable sensations in 'Lied der Galgenvögel' ('Dein Rahm der Milch schmeckt schließlich nicht ganz übel', GW 8, 36) and 'Vom François Villon', where they form the refrain: 'François Villon, den nie ein Bett bedeckte/ Fand früh und leicht, daß kühler Wind ihm schmeckte' (GW 8, 38). Taste does, however, normally occur as a negative property in these poems, emphasizing the bitterness of a hostile environment: 'Über die Anstrengung' (GW 8, 207)—'Auch finden wir oft auf der Zunge beim Gähnen/ Einen bitterlichen Orangegeschmack'.

The most important area of sense experience is that of touch; material contact is used in a generally illustrative way to express contrasts:

> Evlyn Roe war so scheu und so weich:
> Sie waren härter als Stein. (GW 8, 18.)

> Der Füße Bluten und des Steißes Beißen
> Lehrt ihn, daß Steine spitzer sind als Felsen. (GW 8, 38.)

Corresponding to the dominant bitter taste is the sensation of coldness, which is also frequently described, particularly in conjunction with the wind. 'Die Kälte der Welt' (GW 8, 117) is a basic and recurrent existential image: life as exposure.

The hardness–softness contrast noted above itself leads to a further general distinction within the area of contact imagery: that between pleasure and pain. Sensations of pain are dominant, conspicuous examples being 'Das Lied vom Geierbaum', 'Ballade vom Mazeppa' and 'Prometheus' (GW 8, 87).

> Und die peitschenden Flügel, die auf ihn gezückt
> Zerhauen im Sturz ihm den zitternden Leib und
> zerstücken ihm Knospe und Glied. (GW 8, 31.)

These lines, from the 'Geierbaum' poem, contain one of the key words of the early poetry, 'Leib'. Besides the birth–death paradigm described by poems such as 'Von der Freundlichkeit der Welt' (GW 8, 205), 'Vom Mitmensch' (GW 8, 190), 'Der Choral vom Manne Baal' (GW 8, 249), the consciousness of the body constitutes an important element of material reality. The 'Exerzitien'

(GW 8, 209), 'Vom Klettern in Bäumen' and 'Vom Schwimmen in Seen und Flüssen', evoke a sensuous self-consciousness by exploring the boundary area between autonomous individual existence and absorption into the biological environment. The limits of the body are defined in terms of this boundary: 'Wenn kühle Blasen quellen/ Weiß man: ein Fisch ist jetzt durch uns geschwommen' (GW 8, 210). Any distinction between the body and its surroundings has here been suspended; the poem implies that this transient unity of man and nature is pleasurable.

Such exercises are, however, the exception; they may be seen as an attempt to conquer the sense of extreme vulnerability which commonly accompanies the imagery of the body:

> Ich füllte mich mit schwarzen Asphalttieren...
>
> Sie schlugen Löcher wohl in meine Wände
> Und krochen fluchend wieder aus von mir...
>
> Leis und feierlich
> Lief jetzt der Wind schneller durch meine Wände
> Es schneite noch. Es regnete in mich.
>
> ('Lied am schwarzen Samstag', GW 8, 213.)

Skin, similarly, is seen as a fragile covering easily penetrated by the violence of the world: 'Der Felsen wächst durch rohe Fetzen meiner Haut' (GW 8, 87). It may be hardened: ''s ist besser/ Wir gerben die köstlichen Häute mit Schnee!' (GW 8, 208).

The physical processes of life also play a part in these poems. Mankind is seen as a consumer, in a literal biological sense, and eating is identified as a source of pleasure:

> Habe verschlungen, was da war, mit Appetit. (GW 8, 111.)
>
> So einer kann noch lange leben.
> Er kann sich den Leib voll mit Hühnern und Brombeeren
>   schlagen. (GW 8, 114.)
>
> Fröhlich machet das Haus den Esser: er leert es. (GW 8, 262.)

'Satte Fresser' (GW 8, 85) is a synonym for the dead. In spite of its pleasurable associations, reference to eating also has a predominantly reductive function: it situates man among the animals, as a carnivore:

> Viele Weiber trollten mit mir in Lumpen
> Aber seit ich diese verfaulten Stumpen

THE EARLY POETRY

> Im Maul hab, bin ich für sie kein Mann
> Der Fleisch einfach zerreißen kann. (GW 8, 49.)

The consumption theme also includes the frequent references to alcohol, tobacco, and opium, and to some extent sexual activity. This is apparent in 'Vom schlechten Gebiß' in the strophe quoted above.

If 'Leib' usually denotes the living body, the matrix of sensation, ('ich spüre mein rotes Herz', GW 8, 120), the knowledge of mortality still intrudes, suggesting that the body is merely a quick corpse:

> Zartes Lammfleisch du, in steifem Linnen.
> Ach, schon sucht dich wild der gute Hirt!
> Ja, noch weidest du, und rot darinnen
> Sitzt ein Herz, das bald verfaulen wird. (GW 8, 50.)

Indeed, 'Aas' and 'Leiche' appear as frequently as 'Leib'.

The positive establishment of material fact is a mechanism which underlies many early poems: it surfaces most clearly in the form of the simple statement— 'meine Hand ist aus Fleisch' (GW 8, 243). But it is often accomplished by the reductive approach used to destroy metaphysical illusion. The solid, real base of existence is the cold world with its pains and bitter tastes. Some poems intimate the possibility of an affirmation of pleasurable life—the 'Exerzitien' referred to above, 'Vom Gras und Pfefferminzkraut' and 'Der Fluß lobsingt die Sterne im Gebüsch', though even these exceptions are characterized by an obliqueness which qualifies the affirmation. In 'Der Fluß lobsingt . . .', for example, happiness is partly defined negatively: 'das Weib ohn Bitternis' (GW 8, 74). In this sense the early poetry offers 'Propaganda für Lebenslust' (GW 8, 242) of a very special kind.

It was noted in reference to 'Gegen Verführung' that the confrontation with material reality may appear to point towards resignation, simple acceptance. If the poetry celebrates the 'Gott der Dinge, wie sie sind', this celebration consists in a passive response, an inner recognition: in practical terms, complicity and concurrence. This attitude, however different its foundation in existential perception, has its equivalent in the humility of Christian doctrine:[13]

> Und wenn wir's überlegen
> Wir konnen nicht lang groß sein
> Der Wind kommt und der Regen

> Und machen uns eilig klein
> Elendiglich und klein
> Muß der Mensch dürfen sein. (?1926, GW 8, 159)

This resigned humility is directly connected with the *memento mori* theme in 'Ich beginne zu sprechen vom Tod' (GW 8, 65): 'Die Dinge sind, wie sie sind/ Ein Daumen ist immer ein Daumen' and, similarly, in 'Karl Hollmanns Sang'(GW 8, 60): 'Ich sag' nur: man findet sich ab!'. This was prefigured in the resigned conclusion of the 'Beschwerdelied'.

In order to make these philosophical undercurrents clear it was necessary to abstract statements from their contexts and construct an artificially coherent argument. This process involves some distortion: in context, many of the statements quoted are less serious, less monoemphatic than has been implied. The early poems are ironic; they philosophize with mock seriousness, preferring to touch real concerns in passing. For this reason the extraction of significant phrases is an appropriate and legitimate method of exposition. Irony here is not stable: statements do not signify the opposite of their explicit sense; instead it is a means of toying with the possibilities of a question, while keeping all options open.

The question of how the poetry affirms anything while relying so heavily on reductive materialism may be answered by taking this (in the early poems) almost universal ironic perspective into account. The poems' affirmation of pleasurable existence is implicit in the enjoyment generated by their superior and immune attitude. The hard reality which has been so carefully prepared in all its physical detail by individual poems is made anodyne by ironic distance: it is ultimately only a potential reality, from whose full impact the poetic speaker is insulated. Under these conditions, almost anything is acceptable and the mild philosophic acquiescence which follows the definition of the real becomes comprehensible.

Hauspostille

Besides the limited private circulation of early poems in manuscript, many were published, singly or in small series, in newspapers and magazines. Brecht also collected his own poems; the first result, the *Klampfenfibel,* exists as a set of manuscripts. Its full title was *Lieder zur Klampfe von Bert Brecht und seinen*

THE EARLY POETRY

Freunden 1918.[14] The half-dozen texts of this collection circulated amongst the Brecht clique in Augsburg and, as the full title indicates, originated there. Some of the references of these typical early poems would have been unintelligible to readers outside this select group; 'Lied von den Kavalieren der Station D',[15] for example, is a result of Brecht's experiences as a conscript medical orderly in the venereal diseases ward and depends partly on this biographical basis for its piquancy.

Two years after this first, unpublished, anthology Brecht considered the possibility of preparing a more substantial collection of poems for publication. According to Münsterer the title 'Hauspostille' also dates from 1920.[16] The history of the edition of this collection is a complex one and has been described by Schuhmann. A summary will suffice here. In 1922 the project had become more clearly defined; a list of contents had been drawn up, notices of publication had appeared, and it might have been assumed that the collection would soon be in print. In fact it was four years before Kiepenheuer published the collection—in a limited edition of twenty-five copies, not for sale, under the title *Bertolt Brechts Taschenpostille*. The collection finally appeared early in 1927 in the Propyläen-Verlag, this time once again with the original title: *Bertolt Brechts Hauspostille*. The project had been neglected between 1922 and 1925, when Brecht began serious work on the selection, revision, and organization of the texts, half of which had already appeared in newspapers and periodicals.[17]

This was, even in 1925, a retrospective collection, a selection of representative poems from the early work; although it is true that, as Hans Mayer suggests, many poems of particularly private reference are excluded, others are included which are considerably less clear in their allusions than 'Lied von den Kavalieren der Station D'.[18] This is especially true of the poem 'Von den Sündern in der Hölle' (GW 8, 20) and 'Vom schlechten Gebiß' (GW 8, 48), from the 'Anhang' of the 1927 edition. (These poems were excluded from the later editions made in Brecht's lifetime, presumably for this reason.) This was the first attempt to make the poems known to a wider public; they had proved successful in performance in Munich and Berlin, and it was reasonable to expect an edition to continue the trend of financial success started by *Baal* and *Trommeln in der Nacht*. It seems likely that such considerations played a significant part in Brecht's mercurial treatment of the collection; in general he seems not to have been eager to publish the poems. His dramatic work was the first priority and although poems of quality were produced throughout the period in question, Brecht apparently was content to file them away. In an interview conducted in 1926 Brecht refers to his poetry as a 'Privatsache' and later remarks in a note to Döblin ruefully conclude that the poems are a weak point, at which attacks on his literary practice can be aimed.[19]

Publication, then, was carried out with both reluctance and determination, in the knowledge that the poems represented a creative phase which was now finished. The 'Anleitung zum Gebrauch der einzelnen Lektionen' (GW 8, 169–71) was probably written in, or after, 1925; this introduction and the organization of the poems in chapters reflect what the collection's title indicates: that the book is liberally dressed in irony. The transparent disguise as a book of devotions in which the poems appear is an appropriate one, in view of their anti-metaphysical stance: this external irony amplifies that internal to the poems. These are devotions, not to the Christian deity, whose existence they deny and whose worship they ridicule, but to the 'Gott der Dinge, wie sie sind'. This superimposed and unifying ironic clash was conceived in 1922 or earlier, when both the idea of the collection and most of the titles concerned already existed. In 1925, however, Brecht had developed a critical attitude towards his early work, and this new element produces a further layer of ironic coloration in the 'Anleitung', which both augments the irony of the poems and, at least partly, undermines it. The first sentence of the 'Anleitung' makes this critical ambivalence clear, the first two sentences were added in 1927: they do not appear in the *Taschenpostille*.[20]

Diese Hauspostille ist für den Gebrauch der Leser bestimmt. Sie soll nicht sinnlos hineingefressen werden.
Die erste Lektion (Bittgänge) wendet sich direkt an das Gefühl des Lesers. Es empfiehlt sich, nicht zuviel davon auf einmal zu lesen.

This is partly arbitrary and anarchic irony of the kind illustrated later in the same text:

das zweite Kapitel (Von den verführten Mädchen) ist zu singen unter Anschlag harter Mißlaute auf einem Saiteninstrument. Es hat als Motto: Zum Dank dafür, daß die Sonne sie bescheint, werfen die Dinge Schatten. (GW 8, 169–70)

What is evoked here is substantive or objective irony, *l'ironie du sort*, on which 'Das Beschwerdelied' and many other poems of the period reflect.

At the same time, the warning with which the introduction to the collection begins is a serious one: from Brecht's newly developing viewpoint of social criticism, from an austerely sceptical standpoint, these poems could only appear excessively indulgent, tending to metaphysics themselves, in their celebration of materialism. This nuance of criticism is not developed explicitly in the introduction; its most obvious focus is the ironic description of bankruptcies together with rain and snow, as 'rohe Naturgewalten', which anticipates the provocative use of this definition in *Die heilige Johanna der Schlachthöfe* and 'Lied des Stückeschreibers'. The poems tend to present as natural and absolute events and conditions which are social and historical: such fundamental self-criticism is latent in the 'Anleitung', but is in the shadow of its generally sympathetic account of the poems.

The 'Anleitung' supports the view of the early poems which was presented above: it recognizes their 'philosophical' tendency—'aus den darin verborgenen Sprüchen sowie unmittelbaren Hinweisen mag mancher Aufschluß über das Leben zu gewinnen sein'—and their materialism—'das Bewußtsein des Fleisches' is mentioned in connection with the songs from *Mahagonny*. It becomes a more apposite remark in the mid fifties, when the 'Psalmen' are added to this section of the *Hauspostille*.

Hans Mayer suggests that *Hauspostille* is not simply a collection, but rather a cycle, whose composition is precisely organized.[21] This view is rightly criticized by Hans Sträter, who points to the considerable divergences between the three main editions of the collection in selection and organization.[22] Any cyclic composition of the kind posited by Mayer would undoubtedly be altered in the later editions, but Mayer does not claim that only the 1927 version is acceptable. Sträter's argument is convincing: if the sections of the work are so closely unified, how could a poem be transferred from one section to another without destroying this unity? (The poem 'Der Herr der Fische', which had belonged to the 'Chroniken' in 1938, became one of the 'Exerzitien' in 1955 (GW 8, 192). A. C. Baumgärtner, apparently in ignorance of Sträter's work, writes of 'in sich geschlossenen Textgruppen'—presenting texts in 'wohldurchdachte[r] Reihenfolge'.[23] This double assertion is open to criticism independently of the developmental objections raised by Sträter; it becomes questionable when tested against any of the different versions of the collection. The first claim, that the 'Lektionen' are fixed and closed sets of poems seems untenable; most attempts to define the common denominator of the texts in any one section are extremely inadequate. Single texts sometimes stand in obvious relationship to the title of their section, as, for example, the poems 'Vom Klettern in Bäumen' (GW 8, 209) and 'Vom Schwimmen in Seen und Flüssen' (GW 8, 209–10), in the section 'Exerzitien'. In general, nevertheless, this relationship is a loose, even an arbitrary one. The second claim is similarly exaggerated; if the poems' order in a given version seems appropriate, this does not mean that no other order is conceivable. Regine Wagenknecht deals with both these questions in her essay on the *Hauspostille:* her tentative suggestions for the logic behind the composition of the 'Lektionen' are the most convincing offered to date.[24]

Wagenknecht takes up the suggestions made by Rotermund and Lerg-Kill in her discussion of the complex intersection of attitudes and intentions which make up the *Hauspostille*. Her sensitive account of the ironic nuances of the work represents an important advance in the understanding of the text, but the conclusion of her essay seems slightly off balance.

Wenn das 'Schlußkapital' als ernsthaftes Lehrgedicht gedacht wäre, dann müßten alle in ihm enthaltenen Lehren sinnvoll sein, auch die Aufforderung aus der ... Strophe 'Schlürft es in vollen Zügen ...'. In dem Kontext der *Hauspostille* erweist sich dieser Imperativ als bare Ironie; 'Bitternisfrohsinn der Welt' gibt es zu schlürfen; ein Leben zwischen verfaulenden Planken ist zu haben; aber ungetrübter Genuß ist weder innerhalb noch außerhalb der Christenheit mehr möglich.[25]

This passage recognises clearly what was identified as the dominantly negative orientation of these poems; but this recognition is one-sided, dwelling on the 'Bitternis' and all but ignoring the 'Frohsinn' which is at least potentially a defiant and easy response to it. Unalloyed pleasure may be impossible: pleasure itself, the poems show, is not.

The poems which Brecht collected in the *Hauspostille* are representative of the early period and were therefore not separated from the poems in general in the above discussion. The collection does, nonetheless, introduce a new emphasis by its selection of texts: there are, amongst the early poems, significant traces of social criticism—'Legende vom toten Soldaten' (GW 8, 256) and the other pacifist poems are obvious examples, but there are others: 'Von der Kindesmörderin Marie Farrar' (1922, GW 8, 176), 'Liturgie vom Hauch' (1924, GW 8, 181), and the 'Mahagonny-gesänge' (1925, GW 8, 243). The challenge which had concluded the important poem 'O Falladah, die du hangest': 'so helfet ihnen doch! Und tut es in Bälde!' (GW 8, 61) is taken up by 'Liturgie vom Hauch' which envisages the possibility of active struggle against oppression, albeit in a coyly allusive manner.

> Da kamen einmal drei bärtige Männer einher...
> Da kamen mit einemmal viele rote Männer einher...
> Da kam einmal ein großer roter Bär einher...
> Und der fraß die Vöglein im Walde.[26]

The *Hauspostille* of 1927 is the most important early publication, though individual texts published in newspapers may have reached a larger readership. There was, however, a further project, contemporary with this collection: *Augsburger Sonette*. This was to be a private edition of erotic sonnets, but was never printed.

Much of Brecht's early poetry was written with a specific and limited audience in mind.[27] This early awareness of the social functions of poetry is explicitly, if peripherally, thematized in 'Der Dichter, der ihn manchmal geliebt' (1919, GW 8, 45): the poem implies a relationship of patronage, which makes the poet a kind of servant, to whom his master gives bread and wine in exchange for 'schöne Worte'. The poet is far from being an unwilling servant: he speaks of his master, a merchant, in tones of admiration and approval. The merchant is at home in the world: 'Ihn fesseln die Dinge, die da sind.../ [Er] will die Dinge nicht verbessern, die er liebt, wie sie sind'. This social perspective, here explicitly connected with the central materialism of the early poetry, might have had far-reaching consequences for Brecht, had he developed the point theoretically. The portrait of the merchant is a historical one, he is a bourgeois, interested in exchange-values, in profit. He does not seek to change the state of things in a general way, merely to exploit the opportunities presented: 'er will das Schicksal lenken, nicht es halten'. It would be a short step from this reflection to a view of the 'Dinge, wie sie sind', not as an absolute, but as historical reality. Brecht does not take this step in 1919; the idea of the poet-servant is simply a fascinating perspective (it is not how Brecht sees himself, and indeed his poetry, like that of the dramatic figure Baal, is not capable of fulfilling this simple decorative function). The poem as a whole is an exercise, a conceit: it is one of the rare examples of Brecht's use of iambic pentameters in the poetry.

A Typology

An examination of thematic strands and dominant imagery transects all the poetry, and reveals the astonishing variety of forms which characterizes the production of this period. The nature of this variety can be properly described if a simple typology is constructed.

The first category is that of the *Lied*: its characteristics are a three or four-stress line, with considerable variation in the number of unstressed syllables. These poems employ a simple rhyme scheme, abab, abba, abac . . . ., and are strophically arranged, the typical strophe being of four lines. There are multiples and sub-multiples of this model, and frequent examples of the addition of a refrain to the basic strophe, probably an influence from Kipling or Villon. Brecht uses genre-terminology as a poet, and many texts entitled 'Ballade', 'Gesang', 'Song' and 'Moritat' belong to the *Lied* category as far as formal characteristics are concerned. (So also do many poems under titles such as 'Legende', 'Chronik' and 'Hymne'.) The *Lied* type, of which 'Das Beschwerdelied' is an example, predominates in the early poetry.

Secondly, there is the category of prose-poetry, where the rhythmic unit is not the line but the sentence. Groups of lines often form pseudo-strophes, but there is no strophic model to which each group adheres. This is a small category in the early period and indeed throughout Brecht's work; it includes the later 'Visionen' appended to the *Steffinische Sammlung*, and the 'Psalmen', written in 1920.

oh, warum sagen wir das Wichtige nicht, es wäre so leicht und wir werden verdammt darum. Leichte Worte waren es, dicht hinter den Zähnen, waren herausgefallen beim Lachen, und wir ersticken daran in unsrem Halse. (GW 8, 79.)

'Von einem Maler', which was quoted from above, is a peripheral case: it is basically a prose-poem (and as such it is the earliest—

1917), but occasionally employs the 'artificial' line divisions characteristic of the poems in free rhythms:

> Neher Cas reitet auf einem Dromedar durch die Sandwüste
> und malt mit Wasserfarben eine grüne Dattelpalme
> (unter schwerem Maschinengewehrfeuer).[28] (GW 8, 30.)

The third category is that of the free rhythms, 'reimlose Lyrik mit unregelmäßigen Rhythmen'. These, like the prose-poems, are often divided into line-groups which are more closely related to paragraphs than to strophes; but their principle of organization is the individual line, which may sometimes be a single word. Unlike the 'Psalmen', which make up for their lack of metrical organization by the intensive use of rhetorical figures, the free rhythms adopt basically colloquial patterns; though they too employ rhetoric. One of the earliest poems, probably written in 1913, is in free rhythms: 'Der brennende Baum' (GW 8, 3) shows strong Expressionist influence, however, and is hardly related to the latter applications of the form. The earliest typical example of the relaxed, reflective colloquialism of the free rhythms is 'Wie ich genau weiß' (GW 8, 56), of 1919 or 1920. There are many poems in this category, though significantly fewer than in that of the *Lieder*: poems like 'Jene verloren sich selbst' (GW 8, 67), 'Deutschland, du blondes, bleiches' (GW 8, 68), 'Der Nachgeborene' (GW 8, 99), all of 1920, 'Epistel' (GW 8, 106) of 1921, and 'Ein pessimistischer Mensch' (GW 8, 117) of 1922 or 1923, are important examples of this formal development.

These categories do not correspond to general divisions of theme and attitude; they may be regarded as experiments in the treatment of a consistent thematic complex. Brecht himself offered a similar general categorization: the *Lieder,* comprising the ballads and 'Songs' ('Schlager'), are differentiated from the free rhythms, which, he suggests, were primarily developed in his dramatic work. The psalms are recalled as experiments which anticipated the use of free rhythms in the poetry.[29]

There is also one other small group of texts which do not belong to these categories: the stichic metrical compositions. 'Tarpeja' (GW 8, 24) and 'Von des Cortez Leuten' (GW 8, 222) are poems in blank verse, the epistolary monologue 'Brief an einen Freund' (GW 8, 43), like 'Der Dichter, der ihn manchmal geliebt' (GW 8, 45) is composed in rhymed iambic pentameters.

The specific character of the principal strand of Brecht's poetry can be demonstrated by the contrastive study of representative texts. The first poem quoted below is typical of the majority of early poems, the second represents an exploratory direction.

AUSLASSUNGEN EINES MÄRTYRERS

Ich z.B. spiele Billard in der Bodenkammer
Wo die Wäsche zum Trocknen aufgehängt ist und pißt.
Meine Mutter sagt jeden Tag: Es ist ein Jammer
Wenn ein erwachsener Mensch so ist
Und so etwas sagt, wo ein anderer Mensch nicht an so etwas denkt.
Bei der Wäsche, das ist schon krankhaft, so was macht ein Pornografist!
Aber wie mir dieses Blattvordenmundnehmen zum Hals heraushängt
Und ich sage zu meiner Mutter: Was kann denn ich dafür, daß die Wäsche so ist!
Dann sagt sie: So etwas nimmt man nicht in den Mund, nur ein Schwein
Dann sage ich: Ich nehme es ja nicht in den Mund
Und: Dem Reinen ist alles rein
Das ist doch ganz natürlich, wenn einer sein Wasser läßt, das tut doch jeder Hund.
Aber dann weint sie natürlich und sagt: Von der Wäsche! Und ich brächte sie noch unter die Erde
Und der Tag werde noch kommen, wo sie ich werde mit den Nägeln auskratzen wollen
Aber dann sei es zu spät, und daß ich es noch merken werde
Was ich an ihr gehabt habe, aber das hätte ich dann früher bedenken sollen
Da kannst du nur weggehen und deine Erbitterung niederschlucken
Wenn mit solchen Waffen gekämpft wird, und rauchen, bis du wieder auf der Höhe bist.
Dann sollen sie eben nichts von der Wahrheit in den Katechismus drucken
Wenn man nicht sagen darf, was ist. (1918, GW 8, 37.)

The poem takes as its subject a moment of conflict between mother and son; it is an archetypal situation, the complexities of which are delicately explored in the replies and counter-arguments recorded in direct speech. The mother's sense of order and propriety is outraged by her son's anarchic and provocative association of ideas. The poem is autobiographical in its basis. Such genetic detail is, however, far from essential to an understanding of the text. As the first line indicates, ('Ich, z.B. ...'), the purely personal element is of little importance and the poem's speaker is a representative, not a unique individual.

This fictional speaker confronts the conventions of politeness and propriety with psychological and physical observation, with experienced fact. The conventions are found wanting. It is nevertheless the mother who has the final word; she resorts to an emotional argument to which there is no imaginable witty reply. The speaker reflects on this and similar confrontations, and concludes that only tobacco can restore good humour after such an onslaught. He also formulates a more abstract and general conclusion, taking up the position from which he had originally argued: 'Dann sollen sie eben nichts von der Wahrheit in den Katechismus drucken/Wenn man nicht sagen darf, was ist'. If politeness is all, why should truth be officially elevated to such a degree of importance? The poem presents its argument in a mediated, semi-dramatic form as a long-lined ballad. The title suggests an ironic perspective: the seeker after truth as a martyr. The final lines quoted above summarize the poem's argument in an attitude characteristic of the early poetry: doctrine is taken at its word. 'Auslassungen ...' advocates the recognition and honest acceptance of material reality, and the early poems in general are concerned, in however oblique and uncritical a way, to state the truth, 'sagen ... was ist'.

The views proposed in this typical example of the first major creative period are attributable to fictitious speakers, lyric personae whose function is representation; they do not dissolve into their factual autobiographical components, even when these are apparent, but remain specifically impersonal. Irony is a means of adding tonal nuance and aesthetic interest, by increasing ambiguity. In association with distance produced by narrative perspective, it is also a defensive measure: every statement is attributable to some third person, every position is made relative, and potential.

MAN SOLLTE NICHT ZU KRITISCH SEIN

Man sollte nicht zu kritisch sein.
Zwischen ja und nein
Ist der Unterschied nicht so groß.
Das Schreiben auf weißes Papier
Ist eine gute Sache, auch

Schlafen und abends essen.
Das frische Wasser auf der Haut, der Wind
Die angenehmen Kleider
Das Abc
Der Stuhlgang!
Im Hause des Gehenkten vom Strick zu reden
Ist nicht schicklich.
Und im Dreck
Zwischen Lehm und Schmirgel einen
Scharfen Unterschied finden
Das geziemt sich nicht.
Ach
Wer von einem Sternenhimmel eine
Vorstellung hat
Der
Könnte eigentlich sein Maul halten. (1922/3, GW 8, 118.)

This is a concise, spare poem, using colloquial diction. Here there is no integral, distancing perspective, no persona present in the text to assume authorship of its statements. Brecht has taken a different, but equally effective step towards self-effacement, by simply retiring behind the text. This is, none the less, a persona-poem, a *Rollengedicht*. Representation is here signified by anonymity of attribution; the reader's attention is focused, not on the speaker, but on his statements, which the poem lists in loose, but coherent order.

The poem is (apparently) a protest against criticism, perhaps against pedantry. It is surprising to read that there is no significant difference between yes and no, and it is not clear why this should be so. Perhaps nothing really matters, or it may be that the possibility of real choice is in doubt. After this sceptical and melancholy beginning, marked by the abandonment of rhyme in the third line, the poem turns, with an implicit adversative, to positive statements:

Das Schrieben auf weißes Papier
Ist eine gute Sache, auch
Schlafen und abends essen.

At this point, an autobiographical connection again becomes possible: this is a poet's list of pleasures, with writing at its head—the formal alphabet of didacticism has a lower position. This list places the poem firmly in the mainstream of the early work; it refers to sensation, to physical function, partly motivated reductively, though by an ascetic modesty: it is materialistic in conception.

The list occupies seven lines of the text, which then proceeds to a new critical position. It adopts the normative and conventional usages 'schicklich sein' and 'sich geziemen', and by confirming their validity in extreme situations makes their relevance exceptional, rather than normal. In general, it is implied, such restrictive taboos should be ignored. Delicacy and politeness are less important than the truth (as in 'Auslassungen . . .'), and minute pedantry is improper if it excludes the recognition of more important and general facts. 'Im Hause des Gehenkten . . .' also suggests that criticism is useless if it comes too late.

The poem's attitude here is at once critical and resigned: in attacking detailed analyses of a situation which is described as a mess (a reading as social metaphor is very strongly implied, here), it appears to dismiss all analysis, and point only to the bald, hopeless honesty of the statement: things are in a mess. This attitude connects with the enigmatic scepticism of the poem's opening lines, and transforms it to cynicism. The five lines which conclude the poem emphasize the priority of immanent reality: talk of the starlit heavens is a mere distraction and should be treated with the contempt exemplified in the last line. This last argument has a double target in poetic and religious metaphysics. Read in this direction, the enigma of the poem's beginning would be soluble: if the only criticisms and distinctions allowed are verbal ones, the real difference between them would indeed be negligible. To state the truth is apparently no longer enough.

On this reading the poem appears to be engaged in a dialogue concerning literary art: the original statement that writing is 'eine gute Sache', becomes a hypothesis. However critical its attitudes on paper, writing may be reduced to abstract pedantry. The poem is for effective criticism ('Man sollte nicht zu kritisch sein' would require ironic negation by the reader), and thus against mere critical posturing. It is important that the value of literary production be made dependent, not on internal, but on contextual factors: if things were not in a mess the most extreme pedantry would presumably be acceptable. The principle of judgement in social context which emerges here makes the materialism of the poem's constituent attitudes relative: given that writing is good, what is it good for? is it good enough? and however good, is it adequate?

The elliptic style of the text, and its ironic mobility, mean that it offers only the framework of an argument, which the reader, in the course of overcoming the poem's problems, reconstructs. Its conclusions can only be open, hypothetical. The poem is cool and urbane in manner, relying not on association, but on logical progression. Apparently simple, it is able to support a complex structure of meaning. It is technically sophisticated, an advanced experimental text.

The two poems examined demonstrate (by their similarities and their differences) the extent and nature of the development which Brecht's poetic production underwent during the period after 1916 (when the 'Beschwerdelied' was written). Economy dictates that a small number of examples be used to illustrate the development; such limited selection tends to simplify the complex history of Brecht's experimentation. The process is not linear, nor is it composed of one continuous strand. New themes and techniques nevertheless build upon earlier ones, and would be impossible without them.

It was shown that the general analysis offered by Müller is confirmed by empirical study of the texts; Ernst Schumacher's concise diagnosis is in agreement with these findings:

der junge Brecht zeigte sich als mechanischer Materialist, Naturalist, in der ethischen Konsequenz Vitalist und Vulgärmaterialist . . . er erledigte den Transzendentalismus mit materialistischer Metaphysik.[30]

The criticism implicit in the formulations 'mechanischer Materialist', 'materialistischer Metaphysik' is aimed at the tendency described above, for the apparently absolute state of things as they are to be contemplated with acquiescence, or celebrated as if in worship of a 'Gott der Dinge, wie sie sind'.

Brecht's own reflections on his early poetry are similarly critical (AJ 20.8.40). He reads his poems as documents of alienation, emphasizing their reductive attitude, and the celebratory element which accompanies it:

die poesie folgt der zugrundegehenden gesellschaft auf den grund. die schönheit etabliert sich auf wracks, die fetzen werden delikat. das erhabene wälzt sich im staub, die sinnlosigkeit wird als befreierin begrüßt.

Brecht's criticisms are directed against the predominantly negative

THE EARLY POETRY

orientation of the early poetry, its general lack of effective rebelliousness ('der dichter solidarisiert nicht einmal mehr mit sich selber'), and concludes that the most generous view of the poems which the *Hauspostille* collects would be the modest: 'aber kraftlos ist das nicht'. Brecht's dialectic could be widened, however, by a more positive view; the celebration of material reality at least implies its attempted recognition—as Brecht himself remarks, the poems penetrate 'auf den grund'. This determination to destroy illusion, however confused and inadequate its results, is a productive attitude.[31] Brecht's view of the *Hauspostille* remained, in spite of such fundamental criticisms, a sympathetic one; the collection was to be included in the 1938 *Gesammelte Werke*, it was reprinted in its original (1927) form in 1951 and was to have been published, probably in the same form, in 1949. Brecht himself was preparing the collection for publication in the parallel edition of *Gedichte, 1* in 1955–6, and carried out considerable revision of some texts. The capacity of the early poems to provoke their author's critical interest had still not been exhausted.[32]

Between 1918 and 1925 there is a gradual reorientation, discernible in both the *Lied* poems and those in free rhythms, towards a poetry increasingly interested in social reality. This shift in focus signifies both a widening and a narrowing of the poems' field of vision: widening because the objective social field is larger than that of subjective, individual reflection, however devoted to material reality; and narrowing because the social interest is specifically defined, less ambiguous than the ontological philosophizing of many early poems. Verbal gestures of provocation give way to subtle, but insistently provocative argument. Anarchic play is superseded by controlled inventive wit. Irony, part play and part defence in the early poems, assumes the placing function of distance, defining poetry as mediated quotation. This social orientation makes possible the externalization of philosophical, reductive materialism: the poetry moves towards realism, not as a dominant theme, but as the basis of technique.

DAS ENTSETZEN, ARM ZU SEIN

Ich streiche aus
(Mit einem dünnen Strich ohne Erbitterung)

Alle, die ich kenne, mich eingeschlossen.
Über alle diese wird man mich in Zukunft
Nicht mehr
Erbittert sehen.

Das Entsetzen, arm zu sein![33]   (1925/6, GW 8, 156.)

Chapter 2

EXPERIMENTS IN REALISM

As part of the revision of *Hauspostille* undertaken in 1938, Brecht added the poem 'Über die Städte' to the second lesson.[1] The poem was probably written in 1927, and thus falls in the period from which the original selection was made. It is, however, the latest 'contemporary' text in the final version of the collection, and is a departure from the general character of the other poems; only 'Vom armen B. B.' displays similarities of theme and tone.

Unter ihnen sind Gossen
In ihnen ist nichts, und über ihnen ist Rauch.
Wir waren drinnen. Wir haben nichts genossen.
Wir vergingen rasch. Und langsam vergehen sie auch. (GW 8, 215.)

The poem's cold sobriety at once distinguishes it from its context; it is a series of simple statements, giving the impression that the cities are regarded with numb distaste. They are defined as the emptiness situated between subsidiary functions, which are at least evidence of processes of consumption. Even this modest comfort is disposed of by the third line, which insists that nothing was enjoyed: in terms of the ideas of the early poetry, this is an extremely negative assertion. Indeed, far from being the agents of pleasurable consumption, the poem's collective speakers have apparently themselves been consumed, used up in a process which evidently will devour the cities themselves. It is precisely the controlled reticence of the poem which gives it the force of an indictment: it provides only the facts, on which the reader's evaluation must follow.
  'Bidis Ansicht über die großen Städte' (GW 8, 128) was written two years before 'Über die Städte', which is apparent in its more energetic and freely imaginative treatment. Confronted with the 'Petrefakt' of the spreading cities, Bidi (Brecht) concludes that they cannot last long; his hope that they will not is clearly the dominant motivation; the notion of the city as a transient phenomenon is evi-

dently an encouraging one. Referring to the 'Große Stadt', the final strophe concludes:

> Sie steht nicht mehr lang da
> Der Mond wird älter.
> Du, der sie sah
> Betrachte sie kälter. (GW 8, 129.)

Brecht appears to temper his annoyance and follow this advice in the later city poems of which 'Über die Städte' is a representative example.

The city is a dominant theme in the poetry of the mid twenties, and not only in the poetry.[2] There is probably a significant personal element in this development; Brecht's childhood and adolescence were spent in Augsburg, a small provincial town. Open countryside was never far away, and the town itself was prosperous, and for Brecht, living at home in considerable comfort, not disagreeable. His experiences of city life in Munich and Berlin were thus a rude awakening. It is true that he first lived in Munich in 1917, when he began his studies there: but weekends were regularly spent in Augsburg, and this undoubtedly had a cushioning effect. Brecht was, however, less insulated from 'die Kälte der Welt' on his subsequent visits to Berlin, in 1920 and 1921–2. The contrast with his accustomed semi-rural environment was a sharp one, and must have been acute on the occasion of the second visit, when Brecht was admitted to the Charité suffering from malnutrition.[3] Later, in an unnumbered strophe of the second version of 'Vom armen B. B.' (perhaps written in 1925 as a revision of the 1922 original for *Hauspostille*), Brecht commented:

> aber ich habe nicht genug zu essen bekommen
> denn die tiere die ich jagte waren schon matt
> und das fleisch das ich aß war: wie schon gegessen
> und ich esse und esse und werde nicht satt.[4]

The point of departure for Brecht's literary preoccupation with the city was thus a negative one and the idea that the cities might disappear soon was comforting. One possibility of their disappearance would be the partial apocalypse imagined in 'Vom armen B. B.' The idea of natural disasters sweeping away the accumulated weight of civilization is one which Brecht shares with the Expressionist poets; in the poems before 1920 there is a further parallel in the concept of the New Man evoked in 'Jene verloren sich selbst aus den Augen' (GW 8, 67), 'Unsere Erde zerfällt' (GW 8, 69), for example. Its inspiration is probably Nietzschean. In later poems ('Vom armen B. B.', 'Jetzt ist alles Gras aufgefressen' (GW 8, 154)), the new species is no longer mentioned; attention rests instead on the defects of present generations, and their replacement by anything better is not envisaged.

Und auf den Kontinenten spricht es sich herum, daß das Leben nicht mehr Wert ist, gelebt zu werden.
Die Rassen sind alt, man darf nichts mehr von ihnen erwarten.
(1925, GW 8, 154.)

The view of the cities presented in the poems of the mid twenties is in accordance with this historical pessimism, which the apparently sceptical attitudes of 'Vom armen B. B.' seem to reinforce. The sense of transience ('Wir wissen, daß wir Vorläufige sind') which is one of the grounds for pessimism, *may* equally point to a historical process which endows this transitional phase with significance: 'Von der zermalmenden Wucht der Städte' (?1925, GW 8, 129) commences in a familiar way with an analysis of the inhospitality of the city, its devastation of its inhabitants' personalities: 'Viele gesammelt/ Gaben ein Loch/ Das sehr groß war'. This criticism is followed by a pause and a remark which limits the reference of the analysis by relating it to an implied historical scheme:

> Immer jetzt rede ich nur
> Von der stärksten Rasse
> Über die Mühen der ersten Zeit.

Here, for the first time, the cities are seen as a potentially progressive development, part of a temporary problem faced by the strongest elements of humanity. The lines which follow this remark return to the emphasis on the negative features of the development, but the decisive modification has been made.

'Über den Einzug der Menschheit in die großen Städte zu Beginn des dritten Jahrtausends' (GW 8, 143), probably written in 1925, takes the argument considerably further in the direction indicated by 'Von der zermalmenden Wucht...'. The poem belongs to the fragmentary drama *Joe Fleischhacker,* a complex of central importance in the work of 1925–30.[5] The construction and growth of the cities is seen as part of a historical process which is gathering momentum, a process which has a high cost in the destruction it causes, but which is inexorable and ultimately positive, if short-lived:

> Diese neue Zeit dauert vielleicht nur vier Jahre
> Sie ist die höchste, die der Menschheit geschenkt wird
> Auf allen Kontinenten sieht man Menschen, die fremd sind
> Die Unglücklichen sind nicht mehr geduldet, denn
> Menschsein ist eine große Sache.[6]   (GW 8, 143)

Brecht's appreciation of the importance of the city was well founded, not simply in his own experience of city life. The development of large cities in Germany had occurred very rapidly during the nineteenth century: an urban population of a mere 20 per cent of the total in 1830 had grown to 80 per cent by 1895; and by 1900 there was a German proletariat of thirty-five millions, largely concentrated in the cities.[7] *Joe Fleischhacker* was set in Chicago, and other American settings were common in Brecht's work of this period; but America is simply an epitomized Germany, chosen because it is an additional, and more highly developed example. Berlin is characteristically referred to as 'das kalte Chikago'.

'Diese babylonische Verwirrung' (GW 8, 149) was written in 1926; it reflects the shift in Brecht's understanding of the city, from the anarchic-apocalyptic gesture of resigned protest to the recognition of the city as belonging to a historical phase of significance. The poem takes account of the linguistic confusion, the difficulty of communication which the poet sees as accompanying this phase; here once again the concept of catastrophe is introduced ('babylonisch'). It is explained in the poem by the assurance that the general development is, after all, one of decline: but a further perspective brings another, quasi-utopian phase into the argument. Here, then, an additional complication is presented: the positive vision offered by 'Über den Einzug...' is modified, placed at some more distant date in the future. Curiously, 'Diese babylonische Verwirrung' is a poem about the very play to which 'Über den Einzug...' belongs; the play remained a fragment, though an extremely fertile one—

> Neulich wollte ich euch
> Erzählen mit Arglist
> Die Geschichte eines Weizenhändlers in der Stadt
> Chikago. Mitten im Vortrag
> Verließ mich meine Stimme in Eile   (GW 8, 150.)

During his work on the *Joe Fleischhacker* drama Brecht experienced what he later referred to as a 'Betriebsunfall'. The drama was set in the city, and it was decided to collect material about the details of city life, including its economic character; the difficulty of questions concerning the organization and function of the Chicago stock market caused Brecht to suspend work on the drama and read about economics. By October 1926 he was 'acht Schuh tief' in *Das Kapital*.[8]

In order to understand how such an accident could occur in July 1926 it is necessary to review Brecht's work during the preceding years. *Im Dickicht der Städte* (1921-3) was itself a powerful reflection on the city as a jungle; it was followed by the tangential experiment of *Das Leben Eduards des Zweiten,* and by *Mann ist Mann* (1924-5), a drama whose conception reaches back at least six years (to the 'Galgei' project). While *Im Dickicht der Städte* presented a vivid picture of chaos, of the impossibility of communication in the context of the modern city, *Mann ist Mann* is not set in the city at all; it is a cool, detached parable on determinist lines, and demonstrates with wit and clarity that people are the products of their social environment. In the *Fleischhacker* drama, the general model constructed in the parable was to be tested in a specific case; particular mechanisms of determination were to be examined.

The history of Brecht's literary production is the history of experimentation; within this general framework the mid twenties were a period of especially intense experimentation. Besides the preparation of the premiere of *Mann ist Mann,* Brecht was at work on the *Fatzer* complex, on *Inflation* and on the *Fleischhacker* drama. Klaus Völker writes that the cycle of plays referred to by Elisabeth Hauptmann in her work-notes for 1927 consisted of *Im Dickicht der Städte* (for which a basic revision must have been planned), the *Fatzer* drama and *Joe Fleischhacker*.[9]

Brecht did not commit himself to any extensive theoretical statement on literature until the late twenties, but the ideas finally presented pointed to a considerable background of reflection. Much of this was undoubtedly carried out privately, in discussion with friends and collaborators, only occasional traces being recorded in newspapers and periodicals. In July 1926, for example, in an interview already quoted from, Brecht discussed his work with Bernard Guillemin.[10] His remarks reinforce the impression given by the dispassionate observations of *Mann ist Mann:* 'die Ansichten der Leute interessieren mich überhaupt mehr als ihre Gefühle'. Five months later, in *Das Tagebuch* his answer to an enquiry about the books he considered best of the year began: 'ich selber mag keine Bücher lesen, in denen nicht entweder Information oder Methode steckt'. Klaus Schuhmann has described the significant, if transient influence of 'Neue Sachlichkeit' on Brecht's work of this period, and the above remarks illustrate a degree of coincidence between Brecht's thoughts and the emphasis on functionalism and rationality typical of the movement.[11]

Brecht's report as judge of the 1927 poetry-competition organized by the *Literarische Welt* provides similar evidence; referring to the dominant fashion in poetry, which took Rilke, George, and Werfel as its models, he noted:

gerade Lyrik muß zweifellos etwas sein, was man ohne weiteres auf den Gebrauchswert untersuchen können muß.... Von einigen... Ausnahmen abgesehen, werden solche 'rein' lyrischen Produkte überschätzt. Sie entfernen sich einfach zu weit von der ursprünglichen Geste der Mitteilung eines Gedankens oder einer auch für Fremde vorteilhaften Empfindung. Alle großen Gedichte haben den Wert von Dokumenten. (GW 18, 55.)

The aesthetic principle was to be replaced by a new order of priorities; in 1926 Brecht wrote:

praktisch gesprochen: *Wünschenswert ist die Anfertigung von Dokumenten.* Darunter verstehe ich: Monographien bedeutender Männer, Aufrisse gesellschaftlicher Strukturen, exakte und sofort verwendbare Information über die menschliche Natur und heroische Darstellung des menschlichen Lebens, alles von typischen Gesichtspunkten aus und durch die Form nicht, was die Verwendbarkeit betrifft, neutralisiert.

(GW 18, 51.)

Here, too, a distinct emphasis on the functions of literature, in the service of which formal aspects are to be subordinated. More specifically, Brecht proposes the introduction of what might be termed the documentary principle; documents being defined as exact, informative texts, offering general and representative material on primarily social matters. Literature, it appears, is to become the medium of a science of society; and such a science would not cease with the collection of knowledge, but would imply its immediate dissemination and active application in society. It is in this theoretical sphere that the controversial 'Behaviourist' element in Brecht''s work belongs.[12] Given the difficulty of extracting the 'Behaviourist' orientation from the first traces of Marxism, and the generally analytical, 'scientific' attitude of the period, it is right that the idea of 'influence' from this direction be treated sceptically. Brecht was informed about the basic assumptions of the theory, but his references to it suggest critical interest, nothing more.

Brecht's excursions into theory are small-scale, notes and glosses or remarks made in reponse to specific questions: his preference was for immediate, practical experimentation.

A note of Elisabeth Hauptmann's makes the complexity of this process clear:

> um Ostern herum hatte Brecht eine neue Leihbibliothek entdeckt. 'Der arme Weiße' von Sherwood Anderson macht einen großen Eindruck auf ihn; er schreibt danach das Gedicht 'Kohlen für Mike'. Um dieselbe Zeit ungefähr 'Das Grab des unbekannten Soldaten unter dem Triumphbogen' (über den metaphysischen Soldaten) und 'Vier Aufforderungen an einen Mann zu verschiedenen Zeiten von verschiedener Seite'. (Die Großstadt= Das Dickicht, der Dschungel, der Kampfplatz.) Diese Gedichte will Brecht in die 'Hauspostille' aufnehmen. Das Gedicht '8000 arme Leute kommen vor die Stadt' (für den 'Knüppel') 'müßte aber in eine andere Sammlung' sagt Brecht 'die sich mit dem neuen Menschen befaßt'.[13]

The plans outlined here were never realized; the 'andere Sammlung' was not produced (not until *Svendborger Gedichte* did 'Kohlen für Mike' appear in a collection), and the other poems referred to were included neither in *Taschenpostille* nor in *Hauspostille*. On the contrary, 'Vier Aufforderungen...' appeared with nine other poems in *Versuche 2* in 1930, in a collection titled *Aus einem Lesebuch für Städtebewohner*. This was a new title, first used in 1927 when two of the poems (7 and 8) were published separately.[14]

Aus einem Lesebuch für Städtebewohner

This was a series of experimental poems which developed gradually. At least five texts from the series existed by January 1927, when the idea of a collection is first recorded; but 'Vier Aufforderungen...' was almost certainly written before this plan had been evolved. The collection grew, eventually comprising thirty-two texts, most of which originated in the years 1926 and 1927. The title is a significant one: it does not announce the 'Lesebuch für Städtebewohner' itself, only selected extracts, as if it were Brecht's intention to keep the collection open in order to accommodate additional material. This was a period of experimentation and fragments; individual works of whatever genre are assembled in large thematic complexes, which often intersected, sharing elements of plot, general theme, or even whole texts.[15] Elisabeth Hauptmann mentions the dramatic complex 'Einzug der Menschheit in die großen Städte' and it seems likely, as Schuhmann suggests, that the *Lesebuch* complex was closely associated with it.

Because of the extreme complexity of these strands of Brecht's work and because many of the dramatic fragments have not yet been fully (critically) edited, the precise limits of the works involved are very difficult to define. It is not known exactly when it was decided to collect texts for a *Lesebuch,* nor which poems were already in existence; and the poems identified in *Gesammelte Werke* as belonging to the series probably do not represent a complete list. It is, however, clear that the poems *Aus einem Lesebuch für Städtebewohner* span the important months of 1926 and 1927 during which Brecht's interest in Marxism began.

The series *Aus einem Lesebuch für Städtebewohner* emerges at the coincidence of Brecht's scientific-analytical and historical reflections: social determinism, the concept of the 'New Man', the prognosis of catastrophe or progress, the city, the organization of labour. The city is a setting which is important for personal and for objective, historical reasons: it is the specific mode of concentration of labour. This constellation makes the 'Betriebsunfall' appear rather less accidental than Brecht suggests; the questions arising out of his literary production make a fundamental enquiry into economic and social processes almost inescapable. Brecht did not seek to escape it: Marxism indicated the possibility of answering the questions which crystallized for him in 1926. *Aus einem Lesebuch für Städtebewohner* records some of the exercises and explorations undertaken by Brecht in this decisive period.

The texts to be discussed are in two groups; the first (GW 8, 267–76) contains the poems published under the title quoted in *Versuche,* the second (GW 8, 277–95) related texts, mostly unpublished, and never published as a series, by Brecht. The nineteenth text from the second section records some of the questions Brecht may have asked: it was probably written in 1926.

> Warum esse ich Brot, das zu teuer ist?
> Ist nicht das Getreide zu teuer in Illinois?
> Wer hat mit wem ausgemacht
> Daß die Traktoren nicht haben soll
> der Mann in Irkutsk
> Sondern der Rost?
> Ist es falsch, daß ich esse? (GW 8, 293.)

At first sight this might seem a banal and arid poem compared with those of the *Hauspostille*. The formal character of the text is made to support the reflective process which it records and has no other function. Technique serves efficiency of communication; its primary aim is clarity. The four questions listed are offered to the reader for his use; such questions are the starting-point of a large enquiry, and the poet's only implicit claim is that these are productive questions. The first is an easy question to ask; it is based on an experience accessible to many readers (though not all: there is an implied definition of intended readership here). The second line assumes a reply to the first: the grain from which bread is made is too expensive—and the enquiry 'why?' is surely also assumed. The third line proposes a shift in focus from effects to causes; prices are high because they have been agreed at such levels by certain people. And, as the following three lines indicate, such people are able to reinforce their agreements by the exercise of power; technology which would enable increased productivity and cheaper produce is withheld in order to maintain present (too expensive) levels. Already the picture of the originators of the price of bread is clearer; they are economically defined as those for whom bread prices are hardly high enough. The poem is built of contradictions: the first line enshrines one in its question, which may also be answered by reference to basic metabolic requirements. Bread is the cheapest food: if one eats nothing else, one must eat bread, even if to do so means having no money for shoes. It is also a contradiction that the means of production are not permitted to produce; the rust may have what is denied to the peasant in Irkutsk. The final line takes up this line of argument and links it to the first line; its enquiry is rhetorical, it assumes and demands an answer in the negative. It cannot be humanly wrong to eat: but it may seem wrong, and in this sense the question is also a serious one.

The poem is an open-ended one, which presents exploratory questions in order to provoke a wide-ranging enquiry. In terms of the clarity and economy with which this is executed, the poem attains a modest perfection. Its connection with the *Fleischhacker* drama (and Brecht's 'Betriebsunfall') is apparent.

The ten texts published as a cycle in 1930 were thereby given a certain prominence by Brecht; with three exceptions, the poems published separately were also taken from this cycle. The first text, 'Verwisch die Spuren' (GW 8, 267), also belongs to the *Fleischhacker* material.[16]

The poem presents a set of instructions, as if to a newcomer, a stranger to the cities; in particular, the recommendations are isolation and the abandonment of social ties and obligations of friendship, family, and property. Individual personality is superfluous, or dangerous, as is spontaneous and independent action. There is no suggestion that these measures are addressed to a hunted criminal; on the contrary, this is the normal state of affairs, and it is the ordinary inhabitant of the cities who must avoid danger by covering his tracks. The danger is not specified, but it is apparent from the severity of the measures suggested that it is extreme.

These instructions are not addressed by the poet to his readers; the narrative structure of the poem is more complex than that. The concluding line, printed in parentheses to distance it from the preceding text, introduces a speaker, thus dramatizing the poem. This speaker does not, however, voice his own opinions; he reports what he was told. This he does quite impartially and without comment, his function being to mark the text as a recording, as quotation. It is evident that this is not a poem which invites identification with its speaker: attention is drawn to the text itself.

There is, even on a first reading, something puzzling about the final line-group, though its structure, mirroring that of the preceding groups, conceals this effectively. The suggestions made in the earlier sections do make sense, if they are also surprising. The exhortation to leave no trace even in death follows neatly from the preceding lines, but it makes no literal, real sense: it is impracticable. In fact, it recalls the theme of 'Legende vom toten Soldaten': 'man gräbt schon die Toten aus für den Kriegsdienst'. How else could the poem's addressee be threatened in his grave? The final section is thus ironic; it depends on the restrained use of the *reductio ad absurdum*, which is here accomplished by exaggeration, by the addition of excessive weight, so that the *prima facie* meaning of the poem collapses like an overladen house of cards. Instead of simply repeating instructions, the speaker makes a sly but insistent protest about the conditions in which the real instructions given are appropriate: he abandons his impartiality for a critical position. This is an important addition to the poem's documentary value, its accuracy as a recording of social reality.

Walter Benjamin provides an unhistorical but illuminating commentary on the poem, in which he suggests that it be seen as a prophetic picture of work with the outlawed opposition after 1933, a position which he describes as 'Krypto-Emigration'. 'Der Kämpfer für die ausgebeutete Klasse ist im eigenen Lande ein Emigrant.' This is an insight to which the poem may assist the reader: it is not an interpretation of the poem, which might be better glossed by a reminder that the proletarian is like a stranger in his own land.[17]

The poem does not explicitly define either the social group exposed to danger or the nature of the danger. Nevertheless, it makes sense only if read as referring to the proletariat, subject to exploitation and oppression, recognizing its anonymity as its defence.

In some respects the first poem is representative of the cycle; there is a similar use of the indirect narrative persona in the succeeding five texts. In the final four the structure is implicit, the reader has acquired the habit of setting imagined quotation marks before and after the text, so that an explicit marker would be superfluous.

The text of the fourth poem (GW 8, 270) is a monologue; the anonymous 'internal' speaker is a woman, whose words are recorded by an intermediary. The tone in which she speaks is one of defiant assertion ('Ich weiß, was ich brauche'), but implicitly also of complaint. This element of complaint emerges in the form of factual statements: 'der Mann, den ich habe, schädigt mich'. The speaker's image of herself is as an object, susceptible to damage by the man whom she, in turn, possesses. Her pleasures are not appreciated in their own right but have a functional character: 'Heute bin ich lustig; das ist gut für/ Den Teint'. Her complexion too must be functional, to be so important. Indeed, as the following lines make clear, her appearance is the object of considerable effort—never too much, however, since excessive exertion would show, thus defeating its own purpose.

The nervous intensity of the final section emphasizes the sense of delicate and precarious balance evoked in the poem. The speaker's life is viable: she survives, but only just, and in an agony of moderate circumspection. She expends most of her energy in an attempt to stand still. The 'external' speaker is thus giving an accurate summary of the woman's position when he contradicts her, commenting: '(So habe ich Leute sich anstrengen sehen)'.

P. V. Brady ascribes 'great ruthlessness' to the woman whose words the poem records.[18] It is difficult to share this view, unless it is adapted to mean introverted ruthlessness. Her image of herself is a linear extension of her economic and social situation, of a ruthlessness which does not have its origins in individual personality. The attitudes she adopts are her strategy for survival in society, her equivalent to the anonymity advocated in 'Verwisch die Spuren'. The comment in parentheses is an entirely sympathetic contradiction, painfully aware of the imperative to live in a way which is less than human.

In this case, as in the first poem, there is no explicit social definition of the subject; but the fourth poem does include a clear economic description. The woman may be a secretary, she may work in a factory: if she is not already of the proletariat, she is in constant danger of joining it. The danger is lessened, however, if she finds a partner to support her; hence her concern for her appearance, on which such an arrangement would depend.

The two poems from the cycle discussed above may at first appear to be simple documents, selected recordings from the city. If this were so, they might be termed realistic in the sense that a photograph may be so described, or a sound-recording. (Such a description would be superficial: both photographs and sound-recordings select, and allow the registration of attitude and point of view; what is meant here is their apparent neutrality.) They would be impartial, true reproductions of selected portions of reality.

Wir haben uns (provisorisch) damit geholfen, die Motive überhaupt nicht zu untersuchen (Beispiel: *Im Dickicht der Städte*...), um wenigstens nicht falsche anzugeben, und haben die Handlungen als bloße Phänomene dargestellt. (1929, GW 15, 197.)

Such cautious restraint would be a possible approach to the writing of poems about the city: but it does not appear to be the approach adopted in the texts *Aus einem Lesebuch für Städtebewohner*. Both the first and the fourth poem were shown to offer distinctly critical perspectives on the material they present, and both imply some degree of analysis, of examination of motives. In this sense they are not neutral.

The literary techniques which produce such critical attitudes are themselves at some distance from the passive reproduction defined above as one species of realism. The fourth text is perhaps closest to it; much of it could be direct, unedited quotation. Much, but not all: the final section does not simply transcribe, it transforms its colloquial raw material.

> Ich habe nichts zum Verschenken, aber
> Ich reiche aus mit meiner Ration.
> Ich esse vorsichtig; ich lebe
> Langsam; ich bin
> Für das Mittlere. (GW 8, 271.)

The short lines render the line divisions conspicuous: they are artificial, artistic. They underline the syntactic parallelisms on which the section is based, generating a controlled emotiveness which less rhetorical, more 'natural' speech scarcely achieves.

Similarly, 'Verwisch die Spuren' contains elements of colloquial language ('sonstwo', 'wie soll der zu fassen sein') which might be read as direct quotation. But here, to a much greater degree than in the fourth text, colloquial diction is artificially organized; the entire poem is constructed on the principle of syntactic parallelism, both within and between line-groups:

> Trenne dich von deinen Kameraden...
> Gehe am Morgen in die Stadt...
> Suche dir Quartier...
>
> wenn dein Kamerad anklopft...
> wenn du deinen Eltern begegnest...
> wenn es regnet...

If this is quotation, it derives its material, not from colloquial speech, but from the Bible, where such rhetorical figures are common. Within the general pattern of repetition and reflection, there are verbal gestures which precisely mirror biblical sentences in attitude and rhythm: 'Ich sage dir: Verwisch die Spuren!'. This apodictic style employs elements of colloquial speech; but it filters out all traces of colloquial syntax, arranging these elements so that the ultimate effect is far removed from a Naturalistic use of language. The poem evokes a sense of didactic authority through emphatic repetition and discipline, but also through its biblical associations.[19]

It was noted in the discussion of the first and fourth texts that despite their apparent neutrality, both poems allow readings which at least modify this impartiality. In the fourth poem this modification takes the form of suggested sympathy of the narrator for the woman whose statements he conveys; in 'Verwisch die Spuren' a more evident departure from neutrality is accomplished by the ironic provocation of the final line-group. These findings are complemented by an examination of the style of the texts concerned, which indicates that Brecht's technique was not neutral or Naturalistic, but artificial and literary. These poems, which in this respect are representative of the published selection, are not documents in the simple sense of recordings; their structure incorporates distance and (more or less clearly) suggests points of view.

P. V. Brady suggests that the relationships between texts and their order in the published series are of significance.[20] The series does form a cycle of texts so closely related in theme and technique that they illuminate one another, and the specific order of their arrangement does lead to a fixed sequence of interaction between texts.

The first three texts form the exposition; they present the reader with a paradox—the poems are easy to understand, they seem to record direct speech, their language is simple, yet they are also difficult to understand, to construe fully, since it is not immediately clear who is speaking, nor what the speakers intend by their words. This difficulty is made greater by the fact that there are mostly two speakers, the interposed narrator and the third persons whose words he employs. It is this paradox which Brady characterizes as the 'obliqueness' of the collection: local clarity is combined with general ambiguity. In this way, then, the first three poems provoke the reader's incomprehension; but the third text, 'An Chronos', as Brady points out, makes an unambiguous attribution: '(So sprechen wir mit unseren Vätern.)' Incomprehension is displaced by the emphatic *tua res agitur* of this line, which, though it refers explicitly only to the third text, equally modifies the reader's impression of the preceding two, suggesting that he is immediately included in their generality. This dramatic moment of explicitness concludes the exposition. The following six texts constitute the extension and development of the theme introduced in poems one to three; they return to the provocative paradox. The final (tenth) text provides a conclusion. It does so because it is placed at the end of a primary sequence; it may operate as an introduction for any subsequent readings, which would not necessarily be bound to the sequence as printed. The same would apply to any sound recording made of the series; a gramophone record can be played from any point in the microgroove to any other. The significance of the order of texts in the collection can be maintained only within these limits.

Whether it operates as conclusion or introduction, the tenth poem stands alone in the series. It refers to its companion poems and provides an apology for them:

> Wenn ich mit dir rede
> Kalt und allgemein
> Mit den trockensten Wörtern
> Ohne dich anzublicken
> (Ich erkenne dich scheinbar nicht
> In deiner besonderen Artung und Schwierigkeit)
>
> So rede ich doch nur
> Wie die Wirklichkeit selber
> (Die nüchterne, durch deine besondere Artung unbestechliche
> Deiner Schwierigkeit überdrüssige)
> Die du mir nicht zu erkennen scheinst. (GW 12, 498.)

The poem has only one speaker, who may be identical with the narrator present or implied in the other poems; he appears to represent the poet, and addresses the reader directly. Like most of the texts in the *Lesebuch* complex it employs the familiar form, which here indicates both the fundamentally friendly disposition of the speaker and his refusal to observe polite formalities. The poem's description of the *Lesebuch* texts is accurate; their primary impartiality has already been noted. It is also evident that the texts, though presenting individual cases, exploit them for their typicality. The second section proceeds to justify this attitude of cold generality by referring to an equally sober and impersonal reality; it is implied that the poems' attitude is appropriate to the reality with which they are concerned. The final line extends this argument by implying that it is the function of these texts to bring the reader to recognize this reality, and that their characteristics are also explicable in terms of this function. The justification is thus a double one, resting on accuracy of reflection and effectiveness of portrayal. Simply, it is claimed that the poems are realistic.[21]

Jürgen Jacobs explicitly denies that it is possible to portray reality itself, stating that Brecht's collection presents: 'nur eine bestimmte Interpretation der Wirklichkeit, nicht diese selber'.[22] This seems to contradict his assertion in the same article that the collection constitutes an attempt 'eine brutale Wirklichkeit "mit den trockensten Wörtern" ohne Wertung und Kritik zu zitieren'. Or perhaps Jacobs means only that Brecht believed a 'kommentarlose Zitierung der Realität' to be possible. His confused article throws little light on the complexities of the poem. The confusion arises partly from the separation of the first two lines of the second section from their context: 'So rede ich doch nur/ Wie die Wirklichkeit selber'. Jacobs reads this sentence as if it signified that reality could speak and could therefore be quoted: he corrects this mistake of his as if Brecht had made it. These words form a sentence only when removed from their context: in the poem they are dependent on two series of epithets, describing the narrator's speech ('kalt . . . allgemein . . . trocken'), and comparing it, on the basis of these characteristics, with reality ('nüchtern'). There is no suggestion that what is intended is simple reproduction of reality, indeed, the above poem may be understood as an apology for a provocative and artificial mode of realism which generates 'Wertung und Kritik', in a subtle, exploratory way. The poem is itself provocative, in its combination of strictness and benevolence; the reader is made to reflect on the simple statements which it presents.

The key to such reflection is offered by the final line, which implicitly states the speaker's intentions: the perception and understanding of reality on the part of the reader. This aim accounts for many of the difficulties of this and the accompanying texts; reality is comprehensive, general, and to dwell on individual detail would make an overview too complex to be useful. If reality takes no account of the individual moment, it is also impersonal and impartial, inaccessible to pleading. These qualities of reality are imitated in the poems *Aus einem Lesebuch für Städtebewohner;* but not for the sake of appropriateness and verisimilitude. As the final line implies, the aim is not to imitate reality in any illusionistic

EXPERIMENTS IN REALISM

way, but to exhibit it so that it becomes the object of cognition which it is normally not ('die du mir nicht zu erkennen scheinst'). This is why the texts concerned are fundamentally sympathetic (they set out to accomplish something for and with the reader), and at the same time cold, strict, impersonal (since this is an accurate, and above all an effective mode). The poems' primary coldness is intended to awaken the reader's critical attention; their imitation of reality does not offer him an aesthetic experience, but demands his critical questioning.

Given that the collection of poems is intended to be an exhibition of reality, it may be established by examination of the texts what 'reality' signifies. In each case the reader is offered an implicitly familiar and representative document. 'Verwisch die Spuren' presents a picture of human isolation, in which others are a liability or a danger; this is echoed by the third poem, 'An Chronos' (GW 8, 269), describing the enmity of parents and children, and by the seventh, which records a situation of extreme danger, where anonymity and isolation are demanded. The second poem, 'Vom fünften Rad' (GW 8, 268), shows that there are too many people (some are superfluous), the fourth text demonstrates that people may become objects for themselves (GW 8, 270), the fifth that they may become objects for others (GW 8, 271). The sixth poem illustrates isolation from the standpoint of the others (GW 8, 273): a man who is lost, who has nothing to fall back on, is one competitor fewer. The eighth poem may be read as a direct statement made by the speaker, or as a reported speech to which the speaker appends an ironic comment (GW 8, 274). It is, in either case, an important summary of the situation which defines the dangers to which people are exposed; it is made clear that what is said has general relevance. Dreams, agreements, rights, and aspirations are worth nothing; the provision of food is dependent on labour. The general principle is 'man wird mit euch fertig werden'; this has the primary sense that all objections are futile, that adaptation and compliance are the only feasible course of action. But, in conjunction with the sinister assertion: 'Die Esser sind vollzählig/ Was hier gebraucht wird, ist Hackfleisch', it acquires the additional meaning of people being consumed, used up in the completion of an unspecified operation. This is an extremely hostile environment, which could only be discouraging—and yet it is the only environment, and must be endured. Reading the final line ironically, however, suggests that discouragement is to be replaced, not by resignation, but (perhaps) by rebellion. In contrast to the hostility described in the eighth poem, the ninth 'Vier Aufforderungen an einen Mann von verschiedener Seite zu verschiedenen Zeiten' concerns varieties of hospitality. The four sections of the poem offer material for an analysis of one of the modes of isolation: the division of society into classes.

The poems present a coherent view of a reality which might be termed alienation or inhumanity: people are alienated from themselves, from others, from their labour, and from its products. The State, social classes, the economic system of capitalism, are all forms of human alienation. The concept of alienation, as developed by Marx, is appropriate on interpretative and possibly (in some texts) directly genetic grounds.[23]

It is not claimed that *Aus einem Lesebuch für Städtebewohner* provides an explicit or fully developed Marxist analysis; it is established that some of these poems were written before Brecht was in a position to make such an analysis. At the same time, it has been demonstrated that Brecht was experimenting with literary methods of exhibiting things as they are in such a way that they are exposed to the reader's critical attention; his findings display a high degree of coincidence with those of Marx.

Marx's concept of alienation also illuminates Brecht's attitude and technique. As the tenth poem implies, the reality of alienation is usually not perceived, but must be artificially impressed on the reader's consciousness. Alienation embraces the concepts of ideology and false consciousness, which at least coincide, if they are not identical; if alienation is material loss of human reality, ideology is the equivalent of this loss in human thought. The effects of alienation are perceived, while its precise nature and its causes remain obscure. This problem seems to underlie Brecht's reflections, and his writing, in the mid twenties. If the reality of alienation includes a high degree of mystification, neutral, illusionistic reproduction of reality can only reproduce in this mystified form, and contributes nothing to an analytical and critical understanding of reality. Brecht's technique includes a twofold departure from such neutrality. Firstly, the poems in the collection are given a dramatized narrative structure in the form of the interposed narrator (whether present or implicit), whose function is the distancing of the text from the reader, so that each text seems to present mere testimony, requiring careful assessment. This device is employed in combination with local disturbances generally classifiable as ironic; paradox, exaggeration, ambiguity set problems for the reader, forcing him to ask questions. The result of such questions is the destruction of one reading of the text (for example, as a neutral document), and the construction of a new reading (as provocative criticism, perhaps) which involves a definite decision about the assessment of the poem's evidence.

Such a technique might be defined as 'Verfremdung gegen Entfremdung' (Mitscherlich);[24] it appears to anticipate much of the thinking which was later formulated in the theory of the 'Verfremdungseffekt', and in the discussion of realism. The extent and detail of the anticipation of theory by practical experiment can be demonstrated by quoting representative elements of the later theoretical argument:

die Lage wird dadurch so kompliziert, daß weniger denn je eine einfache 'Wiedergabe der Realität' etwas über die Realität aussagt. Eine Photographie der Kruppwerke oder der AEG ergibt beinahe nichts über diese Institute. Die eigentliche Realität ist in die Funktionale gerutscht. Die Verdinglichung der menschlichen Beziehungen, also etwa die Fabrik, gibt die letzteren nicht mehr heraus. (1930, GW 18, 161–2.)

Es müssen die Gesetze sichtbar werden, welche den Ablauf der Prozesse des Lebens beherrschen. Diese Gesetze sind nicht auf Photographien sichtbar. Sie sind aber auch nicht sichtbar, wenn der Zuschauer nur das Auge oder das Herz einer in diese Prozesse verwickelten Person borgt. (1939, GW 16, 520.)

The second group of poems, published in the *Gesammelte Werke* under the title *Zum Lesebuch für Städtebewohner gehörige Gedichte*, was not published as a collection by Brecht. A third or more of these texts represent the extension of the alienation theme which is dominant in the published collection. Thus the third and fourth poems (GW 8, 278–9) describe a sense of disjunction which connects with 'Verwisch die Spuren' in its view of the city as a foreign environment. The seventh poem pursues this point further, adding an economic perspective:

> Oft in der Nacht träume ich, ich kann
> Meinen Unterhalt nicht mehr verdienen.
> Die Tische, die ich mache, braucht
> Niemand in diesem Land. Die Fischhändler sprechen
> Chinesisch. (GW 8, 281.)

This, the first line-group of the poem, suggests a causal basis for the threatened loss of identity which the succeeding lines describe. The fifth poem, 'Über die Städte (2)' (GW 8, 279), also illustrates the fragility and arbitrariness of identity, the ease with which personal contact may be lost. The thirteenth, fourteenth, and fifteenth texts appear to form a series with the fourth and fifth poems of the published collection, with which they share a direct, confidential quality. These poems describe disturbances in human relations. These relations have the character of a struggle in which the parties concerned continually adopt new strategies of war:

> Es war leicht, ihn zu bekommen.
> Es war möglich am zweiten Abend.
> Ich wartete auf den dritten (und wußte
> Das heißt etwas riskieren)   (GW 8, 288.)

As the first line indicates, people are treated as objects; and human affairs are the subject of the same cold calculation which economic matters demand: they are economic matters. This too is part of the condition of alienation; the displacement of use-value by commodity-value penetrates all human behaviour more or less fully.

The poems of this second group are, however, more than a simple expansion of the themes and techniques identified in the collection. The collection was shown to have coherence and a certain unity; this is probably the result of Brecht's selection. As a whole the collection aims at critical perception; it does so in a reticent, exploratory manner, and stops short of explicit recommendation which might follow its analysis. Schuhmann sees this fact as limiting the poems' significance:

er [Brecht] hat zwar den ökonomischen Mechanismen des Kapitalismus nachgespürt und ihre Auswirkung auf den Menschen sinnfällig machen können, aber er unterschlägt die Existenz der Arbeiterklasse und läßt sie nicht auf dem 'Kampfplatz' der Großstadt erscheinen.[25]

It is true that the collection is limited, that it does not explicitly demonstrate the existence of the proletariat, still less describe it as an organized political force. These limitations are the result of the specialization of the poems concerned. Schuhmann, while implicitly recognizing this, apparently does not think it worth close critical attention at the level of the individual text; he does not show the analysis which the poems offer but takes it for granted. Close examination does, however, reveal that the analysis is a detailed and serious one which deserves more than the condescending and dismissive treatment given it by Schuhmann. The question of technique is also dismissed with the assertion that it is Brecht's concern merely to register certain aspects of reality. In accordance with this assumption (which careful reading of the texts should at once dispel) Schuhmann reads the tenth poem of the collection in the same way as Jacobs: 'der Lyriker glaubt, der Wahrheit am nächsten zu sein, wenn er wie die Wirklichkeit selber spricht'.[26] It was argued above that this is a superficial reading: Brecht suggests that in order to make the truth visible it is necessary to provoke critical attention; this is achieved by the imitation of the cold, impersonal generality of reality. Such a process is far removed from passive registration: its aim is activation.

Schuhmann's criticisms appear particularly unreasonable when he suggests that the *Lesebuch* collection is 'der Versuch, den Weg zur Überwindung des Kapitalismus an der Seite der Arbeiterklasse zu finden',[27] an attempt whose failure is easy to maintain, since it was never made. Schuhmann here proceeds in a normative and unhistorical way; in his eagerness to criticize he undervalues the cycle as an experimental work of considerable thematic and technical importance.

The second group of texts includes poems which proceed beyond the specialized range of the published cycle. The first and second texts seem to form a pair; like the eighth poem of the first cycle, with which they share a high degree of explicitness, they demonstrate the gap separating the expectations of the city-dwellers from their experiences. The second text makes an ironic revision of the first:

> Da man eure Wünsche nicht genauer kannte
> Erwartet man natürlich noch eure Verbesserungsvorschläge
> (GW 8, 277.)

This passage from the first poem is mocked by the brutality recorded in the second:

> Zeigt dem Mann mal, auf was es hier ankommt.
> Wenn er meint, er kann brüllen bei jeder Kleinigkeit
> Immer auf das Maul ... (GW 8, 278.)

The indistinct threat implied, for example, in 'Verwisch die Spuren', is here brought into focus; voluntary adaptation to the conditions of the city is preferable to the violent mutilation which is described here:

> So, wenn ihr mit ihm fertig seid, könnt ihr
> Hereinbringen, was von ihm noch da ist, das
> Wollen wir behalten. (GW 8, 278.)

The concept of dehumanization is here made immediate and concrete.

Where the published cycle remains reticent and subtle, some of these related texts resort to open provocation. The eighth poem begins with a casual, conversational manner, which, together with its use of the polite form, clashes with the astonishing opinions voiced:

> Von selber stirbt doch niemand!
> Und was hat der Krieg genützt?
> Ein paar Leute haben wir natürlich angebracht
> Und wie viele sind erzeugt worden?   (GW 8, 282.)

Behind these reflections is the idea that there are too many people, and that this is the basic cause of the social malaise. This view was also proposed in 'Vom fünften Rad': 'Nicht schlecht ist die Welt/ Sondern/Voll'. This is a provocative idea; it challenges the reader to correct it. This mechanism is especially clear in the lines quoted above, where the theory of the full world is subjected to reductive exaggeration. A similar satiric device was employed by Swift in the *Modest Proposal,* which Brecht knew; confronted with error in an extreme form, the reader is forced to correct it. Nevertheless, the concept of superfluity is not entirely fantastic: just as capitalism has a use for only part of each person ('was von ihm noch da ist'), so also it can exploit only part of the proletariat, making those who remain superfluous. Hurricanes, as the poem shows, are an inadequate solution to the problem of unemployment.

The ninth text is similarly generous in its application of wit; in spite of its use of the polite 'Sie', the poem insults the addressee with sustained condescension, repeating the assertion 'Sie sind ein Plattkopf'. This seems at first to be a simple synonym for 'Dummkopf', but the carefully placed emphases of the poem suggest that a more specialized sense is intended. A 'P' has no

EXPERIMENTS IN REALISM 55

responsibilities, a fact which is convenient both to him and to others:

> Ist ja auch gar nicht schlimm
> Damit können Sie achtzig werden.
> Geschäftlich ist es direkt ein Vorteil. (GW 8, 284.)

He is easily manipulated, easily exploited. The poem seeks to undermine the attitude of compliance which it describes.

The twelfth text employs the related expression 'ein breiter Kopf' in its less energetic exposition of a similar attitude. In this case, however, the attitude which attracts ironic interest is less passive: apparently a 'breiter Kopf', although he does little ('viel weniger, als Sie annehmen!'), does have some responsibilities. He is informed about the state of things, at least up to a point ('er ist im Bilde'). His actions follow the line of least resistance, but despite his relative powerlessness he is optimistic. As the concluding lines imply, only an irrational optimist could cheerfully envisage the growth of the cities, the flourishing of business, and a rising population. If the 'Plattkopf' signifies the proletarian, the 'breiter Kopf' refers to the petty bourgeoisie.

The tenth poem invites further reflection in the same area; it introduces the term 'Dummkopf', appearing to employ it in its colloquial sense. Rockefeller, it is conceded, was no fool. Subsequent sections imply an additional significance, suggesting that the failure to prevent the establishment of Standard Oil defines all concerned as fools. The poem proposes questions and indicates points of view (the category 'Interesse' for example); but its final lines are explicit:

> Hoffentlich glauben Sie nicht
> Ein Dummkopf ist
> Ein Mann, der nachdenkt. (GW 8, 286.)

The text itself provides only the starting-point for a process of reflection in which the reader is asked to engage. This is the mode of operation of the nineteenth poem, 'Warum esse ich Brot, das zu teuer ist?', which introduced the discussion of the *Lesebuch* complex. Unlike the nineteenth poem, however, the tenth is long-winded and mechanical, the clarity of the final lines appearing as a necessary corrective to the confused questions of the preceding sections.

The series of poems belonging to the *Lesebuch* complex could not constitute a reader in any simple sense; it was not Brecht's intention to instruct his readers how to live in the cities. The examples collected are negative ones, calculated to provoke criticism; in this complex way the series is an instructive reader. Its chief lesson is that life as organized at present is, or should be, unbearable for most people. But this lesson is principally critical, negatively determined: the poems describe alienation, the resigned adaptation of those who suffer most. The reader's criticisms may end in mere scepticism and disillusion.

Here, the eighteenth poem, 'Über das Mißtrauen des Einzelnen', becomes relevant. The poem takes issue with the mutual distrust between people which was illustrated in the sixth text of the published cycle ('er ging die Straße hinunter, den Hut im Genick'): competition makes solidarity impossible. The first two sections of the poem argue against this vicious circle:

> Sage mir nicht, dein Mißtrauen
> Sei im Verbrechen der andern begründet.
> Woher immer das Mißtrauen kommt, der Mißtrauische
> Neigt zu Verbrechen. (GW 8, 292.)

The following sections define the limits within which distrust is appropriate. Natural events are first distinguished from historical ones (attributable to the actions of men):

> Manche, ins Wasser gefallen, erreichen spielend das Flußufer
> Andere mit Mühe und wieder andere gar nicht.
> Dem Fluß ist dies gleichgültig.

Natural catastrophes affect everyone equally and can scarcely be influenced. Accidents must be dealt with by those to whom they happen. In such cases, blame and mistrust are misplaced. As the final lines assert, the distrust between social classes is a different matter. This is an abrupt conclusion; the poem corrects error, but characteristically makes no detailed recommendations. Nevertheless its closing words are important: distrust is as inappropriate on an individual level as it is when applied to earthquakes; its proper sphere of operation is the class struggle. The implications of this argument are indeed positive: the poem recommends solidarity in the proper, active application of protest and distrust—conscious participation in class conflict. This critical attitude towards the purely personal is another aspect of the position described in the programmatic tenth poem of the published collection ('kalt und allgemein'). The social system is independent of individual volition. The twentieth poem, also entitled 'Gesänge des Proletariats', takes the argument further in this direction. The speaker, a proletarian, announces his intention to take by force what he has been denied:

> Wenn ich wiederkehre
> Unter roherem Mond, meine Lieben
> Dann komme ich in einem Tank
> Rede mit einer Kanone und
> Schaffe euch ab. (GW 8, 294.)

Once again the concluding lines are highly significant; the speaker's brother is to be spared (this should probably be understood in a social, collective sense, as class brotherhood), but rewarded for his passivity by a punishing blow.

The sixth poem, 'Bericht anderswohin', also describes political conflict. It employs the form of the negative example: like the brother of the speaker in the 'Gesänge des Proletariats', those who ought to be active participants remain passive observers, watching from the safety of the walls. Rather than fight, they have accomplished a new, grotesque adaptation:

> Was sie aßen, waren Steine
> Und ich sah, sie hatten schläulich
> Neue Speis zu essen grad noch
> Rechtzeitig gelernt. (GW 8, 280.)

The speaker of the poem also falls prey to this (in the Marxian, negative sense) ideological reconciliation between opposing interests; this is where distrust has its proper function:

> Alsbald gingen wir hinab, um
> Miteinander, Freund und Feind jetzt
> Wein zu trinken und zu rauchen.

The reader's corrective criticism is thus almost explicitly invited.

Schuhmann quotes Marx's *Thesen über Feuerbach* in defining what he sees as a major fault of the *Lesebuch* poems:

auch Brecht erkennt, daß 'die Menschen Produkte der Umstände' sind, aber er läßt noch außer acht, 'daß die Umstände eben von den Menschen verändert werden' und die Arbeiterklasse angetreten ist, einen menschenunwürdigen Gesellschaftszustand aufzuheben.[28]

This is patently inaccurate in the case of the *Lesebuch* complex as a whole, a fact which is sufficiently attested by the poems discussed above. In the case of the published cycle, which is less explicit than some unpublished poems, Schuhmann's criticisms are less easily refuted; but his argument is weakened by the fact that he sees these poems as closed objects, which require the reader's assent or disagreement. The preceding analysis sought to show that the poems are, on the contrary, open, argumentative, provocative; they do not mean what they at first seem to say. It is doubtful whether such an attitude is reconcilable with a simple, passively deterministic view of society; the understanding of the proletariat as a potentially active, conscious social and political force seems implicit both in the published cycle, and in the complex as a whole.

In contrast to the predominantly oblique mode of the complex, to the persona-poems which depend on irony, the seventeenth poem is direct and explicit, its instructions are literal. Like the tenth text of the cycle it addresses the reader immediately: 'Du, der das Unentbehrliche/ Wenige machen sieht, verlaß sie nicht!' (GW 8, 291). This urgent theme is developed throughout the poem, which seeks to persuade the addressee of his important place in a reciprocal relationship which is part of a vitally necessary operation. Though explicit, the poem works at a high level of abstraction, the specific reference of which is assumed as common ground between speaker and listener. This reference is not difficult to infer from the context of the poems described above: what the poem refers to as 'das Unentbehrliche', 'das Richtige' is conscious, active participation in class conflict. Once this preliminary identification has been made, the poem develops its meaning without resistance. Such active participation is practised by a small group, whose effective operation is the primary imperative. Individual interests are subordinate. Here, once again, the ideas formulated in 'Wenn ich mit dir rede' are implicit: the reality of political conflict is 'Nüchtern, durch deine besondere Artung unbestechlich/ Deiner Schwierigkeit überdrüssig'. In spite of such strictness and the hardships involved in the struggle, participation honours the participant: 'Wie immer du behandelt wurdest, so eben/ Wurden die Geachtetsten behandelt'. The concluding lines repeat the injunction against apostasy with which the poem began. This is in no sense a neutral poem.[29]

EXPERIMENTS IN REALISM

As the preceding discussion sought to show, the cycle *Aus einem Lesebuch für Städtebewohner* and the larger series of poems related to it extend over a considerable range of themes and attitudes. This variety, especially conspicuous in the case of the poems not published by Brecht, is explicable in terms of the genesis of the texts in what Schuhmann describes as the transitional phase of Brecht's work. These poems do illustrate some of the intellectual processes which constitute this decisive period; but it is a mistake to see them as purely experimental, a mistake made by Schuhmann and Brady.[30] Many of these texts seem significant as literary works, not simply as literary-historical documents. Moreover, within the historical perspective itself the *Lesebuch* complex does not appear as a mere transition; it is not, as Brady suggests, 'an abandoned experiment'. The experiment was not abandoned in the years which intervened between the first publication of individual texts and the publication of the cycle of ten poems in *Versuche* (1930). The project was mentioned as one of a number of experimental undertakings in the *Dreigroschenprozeß* of the same year. It was thus placed firmly amongst the Marxist writings forming a critique of intellectual life in the Weimar Republic, literature, the press, the theatre and radio. The poems were themselves introduced in *Versuche* as 'Texte für Schallplatten'; they are implicitly directed towards the 'Umfunktionierung' of the media in the same way as the *Versuche* as a whole.

die Publikation der 'Versuche' erfolgt zu einem Zeitpunkt, wo gewisse Arbeiten nicht mehr so sehr individuelle Erlebnisse sein (Werkcharakter haben) sollen, sondern mehr auf die Benutzung (Umgestaltung) bestimmter Institute und Institutionen gerichtet sind (Experimentalcharakter haben) und zu dem Zweck, die einzelnen sehr verzweigten Unternehmungen kontinuierlich aus ihrem Zusammenhang zu erklären.[31]

As Brady himself notes, the *Gesammelte Werke* edition of 1938 was to include a volume devoted to poetry. Its third section was titled 'Aus dem "Lesebuch für Städtebewohner"'; this suggests anything but abandonment.

Similarly, the *Lesebuch* complex should not be seen as an isolated phase in the development of Brecht's poetry. Examination of the early poem 'Man sollte nicht zu kritisch sein' showed that a reflective, exploratory mode of writing did not commence with the *Lesebuch*; though most of the poems were written in 1926 or 1927, the fourth poem of the second section, 'Früher dachte ich ...', is taken from a diary of 1921.[32] The biblical tone that is part of Brecht's technique in some of the *Lesebuch* texts is similarly not a new development in the mid-twenties. The 'Psalmen' of 1920 anticipate this use of biblical syntax.

Within this general view of the *Lesebuch* complex as belonging to a continuous development, some differentiation is possible between experimental directions which are restricted to this complex, and those which provide the bases for Brecht's later practice. A degree of reticence, despite their explicitness a characteristic of many of these poems, is a special feature of the complex, while obliqueness and an increasingly controlled ironic provocation remain a fundamental part of Brecht's technique. In terms of the poems themselves, 'Verwisch die Spuren' and 'Setzen Sie sich' might be cited as typical of the *Lesebuch* project, while the seventeenth and eighteenth texts of the second section anticipate the later poetry.

The significant differences between these two categories depend on explicitness, on closeness to direct instruction; later poems tend to provoke reflection without employing the interposed persona which gives many *Lesebuch* poems their apparent neutrality. The specific development anticipated by texts such as those suggested above is of central importance in Brecht's poetry: the *Lehrgedicht*. The term will be defined in more detail below, in the discussion of later developments, but some general remarks are appropriate here.

The *Lehrgedicht* is a poem of instruction, a didactic poem. It is reflective, argumentative, rather than flatly dogmatic, seeking to open a dialogue with the reader, to engage him in criticism, rather than feed him with statements. It has more or less pure, abstract forms, and is also realized in texts which proceed from specific, concrete cases. The seventeenth and eighteenth poems of the second section, but also 'Wenn ich mit dir rede', (and perhaps 'Laßt eure Träume fahren ...') are examples of the *Lehrgedicht* in its pure, theoretical form. Such poems mark the beginning of a strand of literary practice, but also the culmination of another strand of Brecht's early poetry.

'Das Beschwerdelied', it was suggested, is a reflective, 'philosophical' poem, and may be adopted as marking the beginning of this strand. It is a relatively closed, fully formulated lyric, which states its position explicitly. 'Man sollte nicht zu kritisch sein' no longer presents finished reflection; it is an open poem, suggesting directions of thought for the reader to pursue. The early *Lehrgedichte* of the *Lesebuch* develop this orientation: they too are open poems, which provoke thought rather than simply recording it. Their distinctive features are a higher degree of control and definition, they are more explicit in their attribution and intention, and more general in their reference than the poems represented by 'Man sollte nicht zu kritisch sein'. The balance of exploration and exposition shifts towards expository emphasis.

Analysis of the *Lesebuch* poems demonstrates that Brecht's programmatic statement concerning the 'Anfertigung von Dokumenten' (GW 18, 51), quoted above, finds only partial correspondences in his literary practice. The poems may be understood as 'Monographien bedeutender Männer', though not in the original sense of the phrase; they imply, but do not present, 'Aufrisse gesellschaftlicher Strukturen'. Similarly, the information provided by the poems may be exact, but it seems to concern not 'die menschliche Natur', but its unnatural distortion in alienation. The phrase 'heroische Darstellung des menschlichen Lebens' is applicable to these poems only in a secondary, ironic sense. The final words of the statement do, however, directly anticipate important characteristics of the poems: 'alles von typischen Gesichtspunkten aus und durch die Form nicht, was die Verwendbarkeit betrifft, neutralisiert'. It was argued that Brecht's provocative technique was adopted in order to prevent such neutralization, that it constitutes a 'Verfremdungseffekt' *avant la lettre*.

If the reflective orientation of the early poems finds its equivalent in the experimental *Lehrgedichte* of the *Lesebuch,* the simple materialism of the early poems corresponds to the informative, documentary, and selective approach of these later poems. The attitude of acquiescence and resignation characteristic of many early poems is also present in the *Lesebuch* texts, where, however, as passive adaptation, it is exhibited and made accessible to criticism. The *Lesebuch* poems illustrate the development of Brecht's commitment to a position from which such criticism can be practised.

Chapter 3

ALIGNMENT AND EXILE 1926-1934

Types of Poetry: A Survey

The formal typology suggested in Chapter 1 is also applicable to the poems written between 1926 and 1934; the basic division between rhymed, strophic texts and those in free rhythms becomes a more equal one in the mid twenties, with the *Lesebuch* poems, and the free rhythms are the dominant strand in the following two decades. The work of this period does not include prose-poems.

This categorization in terms of prosody may be supplemented by a typology based on poetic attitude and thematic orientation. Its central point of reference, the *Lehrgedicht*, was introduced in the analysis of the *Lesebuch* complex. The term denotes an abstract category, susceptible of many different realizations: besides the theoretical didactic poems which are a kind of *Gedankenlyrik*, the category also includes the *Chroniken*, which proceed from a concrete and specific historical case to more general and abstract reflection. A third sub-group is formed by the autobiographical *Chronik*, in which the poet reflects on his own situation, exploring its representative significance.

A tentative prehistory of the theoretical *Lehrgedicht* was suggested at the end of Chapter 2; the other sub-groups also correspond to early texts. The *Chronik* is anticipated in the early *Hauspostille* poems presenting typical cases and life-histories ('Von der Kindesmörderin Marie Farrar', 'Der Choral vom Manne Baal') and, more immediately, in the chronicle 'Liturgie vom Hauch'. 'Ich sage ja nichts gegen Alexander' and 'Der gordische Knoten' (1924, GW 8, 141), both sceptically critical in their treatment of historical subjects, also belong to the line of antecedents of the *Chronik*. The autobiographical *Chronik* finds antecedents in early poems such as 'Auslassungen eines Märtyrers' and 'Vom armen B. B.'

This second typology intersects the primary formal one; in general, the *Lehrgedicht* category (in all three sub-groups) is realized in free rhythms, metrical forms being reserved for more immediate, less reflective writing (which is none the less didactic: the distinction rests on the degree of abstraction). There are important exceptions to this general rule: *Die drei Soldaten* of 1930 and *Lehrgedicht von der Natur der Menschen* of 1945-55, are metrical, though not strophic texts; the attitudinal characteristic (both are *Lehrgedichte*) is more important than the formal one (they are not in free rhythms). They are clearly distinct from the strophic songs and ballads.

Songs and Ballads

'Achttausend arme Leute kommen vor die Stadt' (GW 8, 148), contemporary with many of the *Lesebuch* poems, was first viewed by Brecht as a more important work, indicating the way forward. The 'andere Sammlung, die sich mit dem neuen Menschen befaßt',[1] in which this poem was to be included, was replaced by the *Lesebuch* project; examination of the poem does not make Brecht's original high opinion easy to understand. It is a documentary poem in the simplest sense: its source, probably from a newspaper, is recorded in the text, which presents a dramatized commentary. The events from which the poem proceeds are an episode of oppression, against which it formulates a restrained protest. It is much more specific, but less immediate and forceful than the grotesque humour of 'O Falladah, die du hangest' or the satire of 'Legende vom toten Soldaten'. The poem's most significant feature is its description of political action based on collective solidarity: this may be what Brecht found so important. In this case, however, political action ends in defeat and the poem, like the similar 'Dreihundert ermordete Kulis berichten an eine Internationale' (GW 8, 296), has nothing to celebrate.

Later poems of the period were more energetic in their expression of political commitment: the 'Ballade vom Stahlhelm' (GW 8, 304) was written in 1927, probably in immediate response to the militaristic nationalism of the 'Stahlhelmtag' in Berlin.[2] This direct relevance is not apparent in the poem, which draws on historical material to support its argument that aggressive imperialism ultimately will be defeated:

>Nichts half Stahlhelm und Kanone
>Und die weißen Bataillone

> Kamen nie bis Leningrad
> Nie hält Stahlhelm und Kanone
> Halten weiße Bataillone
> Auf der Weltgeschichte Rad.

Brecht exploits the historical identification of the nationalistic forces in Germany with the counterrevolution in the Soviet Union; the political position of the 'Stahlhelm' organization in the Weimar Republic is thus defined and the socialist state functions as a positive model for comparison.

There are many other poems concerned with social and political affairs of the Republic: 'Diese Arbeitslosigkeit!' (GW 8, 330). 'Der Führer hat gesagt' (GW 8, 374), 'Drei Paragraphen der Weimarer Verfassung' (GW 8, 378), and 'Herr Doktor...' (GW 8, 382). These were all written in the period 1930–1 and were designed for immediate application, as agitprop material. They were published in satirical periodicals, *Simplizissimus*, and above all *Der Knüppel*, and in the *Arbeiter-Illustrierte-Zeitung* and *Die Rote Fahne*.[3] Some were produced for use in political revues. These are direct, simple poems, some of them of ephemeral value; their effective impact must have been increased by their use of rhyme to hold the attention and aid memory.

Kuhle Wampe, oder Wem gehört die Welt? (1931–2) also included important poems, among them the still popular 'Solidaritätslied' (GW 8, 369), a modern addition to the repertoire of political songs beginning with the 'Marseillaise' and the 'Internationale'. This is a more general and abstract song than those discussed above, but it shares their directness and clarity. It is a song in the exact sense; Hanns Eisler's melody, once heard, clings persistently to the words which it carries and emphasizes. Both words and music mix fierceness with friendliness, seriousness of intention with graceful optimism:

> Auf, ihr Völker dieser Erde!
> Einigt euch in diesem Sinn:
> Daß sie jetzt die eure werde
> Und die große Nährerin.
>   Vorwärts und nicht vergessen
>   Worin unsre Stärke besteht!
>   Beim Hungern und beim Essen
>   Vorwärts, nie vergessen
>   Die Solidarität!

The poem recommends conscious, active participation in the class struggle on the basis of unity in the political organization of the proletariat. This had urgent relevance in the context of the Weimar Republic, where the proletariat was divided between the SPD and the KPD. Relations between the parties were bad, intermittently hostile; and the ruling SPD pursued a policy of appeasement which meant that there was no effective opposition to the fascist movement at higher levels of the political machinery.[4] Brecht's 'Solidaritätslied' opposes this passivity, but insists that only a united front can act effectively.

Also in the screen play of *Kuhle Wampe* is the 'Ballade vom Tropfen auf den heißen Stein' (GW 8, 370). In spite of its title, this is no ordinary ballad; apart from the four-line rhymed refrain the poem is composed in free rhythms and thus conveniently illustrates the two fundamental approaches characteristic of Brecht's writing: on the one hand the metric, strophic texts, songs, ballads, usually rhyming, on the other the more reflective and abstract free rhythms. Since it combines both strands the poem also demonstrates that they are not opposing orientations, polarities, but positions on a scale, which may (as in this case) coincide.

Die drei Soldaten

This series of thirteen loose *Knittelvers* poems (GW 8, 340ff.), was written in 1930 and first published in 1932, in the experimental *Versuche* (Heft 6). It carries the sub-title 'Ein Kinderbuch' and was originally accompanied by line-drawings by Georg Grosz, and by the note: 'das Buch soll, vorgelesen, den Kindern Anlaß zu Fragen geben'.

The poem's bright, condescending tone reflects its stated function as a work for children; but this reflection, as if from a distorting mirror, mimics the familiar manner of patronizing instruction, rather than assuming it. The first section places the three soldiers firmly in the twentieth century; like many of their comrades they had been shepherded into the war and were disillusioned by their experiences. Unlike most others, however, their disillusion had a solid critical base:

> Als nun kam das vierte Jahr
> War es ihnen offenbar
> Daß es ein Krieg der Reichen war

> Und daß die Reichen den Krieg nur führten
> Damit die Reichen noch reicher würden. (GW 8, 341.)

Here the cheerful tone is temporarily abandoned: the argument is direct and serious. Finding no further response from the external military enemy, the soldiers turn about, directing their weapons instead towards their own country.

> Denn sie hatten beschlossen, jetzt alle zu erschießen
> Die sich etwas gefallen ließen
> Und es gab da viele, die nicht zu mucksen wagten
> Und zu allem Ja und Amen sagten
> Und die mußten eben alle erschossen werden
> Damit man sich endlich auskannte auf Erden. (GW 8, 341.)

As the final line indicates, the earnest tone of the argument is not matched by its logic, which is deliberately arbitrary, parodic. The three soldiers choose their new target with apparently senseless rage, killing others when they might as logically kill themselves; since, as is explicitly stated, they had tolerated no more or less than others. The idea that such slaughter would serve the purpose of clarifying the situation ('damit man sich endlich auskannte') implies still more extreme disproportion. At these points, where primary sense breaks down, the reader is forced to enquire what reconstruction of sense is intended; his attention is drawn to the following sections.

The second section shows that 'erschießen' is not to be understood literally; the soldiers appear in the forms of famine, disease and accident. As the section proceeds to explain, such a concealed kind of murder is appropriate to the agreement between the rich and their God that misery should be invisible. In the third section which completes the preamble to the main discourse, the narrator's deliberate *naïveté* and lack of expertise are demonstrated by the sudden transformation of the soldiers from invisible instances of misery into searchlights illuminating it. The transformation is accomplished by the transition from 'unsichtbar' to 'durchsichtig'; the latter denotes the real narrative function of the soldiers in the poem: they personify (and reveal) negative elements in its description of human society.

The long and elaborate introduction accomplishes two things: it sets the scene, displaying the background and elements of the narrative; and it acquaints the reader with the narrative mode, which is a complex one. Play is the primary constituent of the mode; it is apparent, for example, in the subtitle and note which declare that this is 'Ein Kinderbuch'. This is a fictional construction which the mobile tone of the poem both extends by imitation, and undermines by poor imitation, obvious mimicry. This mimicry is extended by further flaws in craftsmanship; both the explicit logic of the argument and the underlying logic of the narrative are faulty—hence the shifts and revisions in the function of the soldiers. These flaws are themselves a fiction: they are deliberate weak points, which puzzle the reader, and hold his attention, gaps which allow him to inspect the structure of the narrative. It is, paradoxically, precisely their 'incompetent' execution which allows the writer's intentions to become emphatically clear. The writer behaves as a clown in *Die drei Soldaten*; he invites, and depends on, the reader's complicity, his enjoyment of the clown's narrative antics. Here the 'incompetent writer' fiction supports that of the 'Kinderbuch': jokes are made and the writer's relationship to his reader is one of intimacy.

The poem's function, in spite of the playfulness of its construction, is not exhausted in the amusement offered to the reader; its real seriousness becomes clear in the following sections, but is anticipated in elements of the introductory triad.

There is, as Marsch remarks, a paradox in the decision of the three soldiers to attack, not the rich, in whose interests the original war was fought, but the poor like themselves, who tolerated this fatal servitude.[5] The paradox is crystallized in the phrase 'dulden kein Dulden' (GW 4, 1540), which identifies a recurrent theme of Brecht's work. It emerges in the 'Liturgie vom Hauch' of 1924, in which the quiet birds of the wood, who make no sound of protest at the murder committed in their sight, are themselves finally eaten by the avenging bear: 'da schwiegen die Vöglein nicht mehr' (GW 8, 186). The negative aspect of tolerance is illuminated here. *Die drei Soldaten* is, however, considerably more aggressive than this early poem, more so, too, than a *Lesebuch* poem with which it is thematically related: the revolutionary promises:

> Wo mein Tank durchfährt
> Da ist eine Straße
> Was meine Kanone sagt
> Das ist meine Ansicht
> Von allen aber

> Verschone ich nur meinen Bruder
> Indem ich ihn lediglich aufs Maul schlage. (GW 8, 294.)

His fellow proletarians are to be spared (but punished). *Die drei Soldaten* returns to the pre-revolutionary context, in which this negative tolerance must be actively opposed; the strategy proposed is closer to the attitude adopted in another *Lesebuch* text, where with Swiftian irony the inefficacy of natural disasters and wars in disposing of over-population is bemoaned ('Hätten Sie die Zeitungen aufmerksam gelesen wie ich'; GW 8, 282).[6] Draconian measures are needed, and the poem recommends them.

The dimensions of this theme may be illustrated by quoting from Brecht's theoretical writings, probably from 1926:

> ich will mich, um besser verstanden zu werden, lieber etwas undeutlich ausdrücken: von meinen Gegnern interessiert mich die Bourgeoisie gar nicht — trotz ihrer Bemühungen. Dagegen interessiert mich das Proletariat — trotz seiner Gleichgültigkeit. (GW 18, 15.)
>
> Den wirklichen Gegner kann ich mir nur im Proletarier erhoffen.
> (GW 15, 64.)

The at first enigmatic concept of the proletariat as an opponent becomes significant in connection with the poem, which suggests that a tolerant proletariat is its own worst enemy. The theme is also developed in Brecht's prose works *Geschichten vom Herrn Keuner* ('Der hilflose Knabe', GW 12, 381), and *Me-ti* ('Unrecht tun und Unrecht dulden', GW 12, 473).[7]

The introductory sections introduce another element directly connected with the 'dulden kein Dulden' theme. The three soldiers aim their weapons, after turning away from the foreign armies, at the enemy within: they become avenging angels. This reversal of aim anticipates the later important motif formulated most clearly in 'Der große Oktober' (GW 9, 675, 1937): 'O Soldaten, die ihr/ Endlich die Gewehre in die richtige Richtung gerichtet!' The proper direction, the real alternative to participation in imperialist wars, as cannon-fodder, is conscious participation in the class struggle. A further strand of parody is apparent here, since the three soldiers are clearly not engaged in the revolutionary struggle, and must be corrected by the reader. Anger at the passivity of the proletariat should clearly not lead to punishment, but to information about its real social position; this is provided in the following sections of the poem.

The third section had already described some manifestly critical features of capitalism; 'Den Maurer, der das Haus baut dann/ In dem er selber nicht wohnen kann'. Its analysis is supplemented by the evidence of accidents, inadequate housing, and medical care, the role of the church and the judiciary, and the fundamental economic organization of capitalism ('Die drei Soldaten und der Weizen', GW 8, 352). Among the major contradictions isolated is the discovery that capitalism fears abundance: corn is dumped in the sea in order to maintain prices. Here, Brecht returns to the major thematic complex of the mid twenties, bread as a model of capitalist economy (as in the *Fleischhacker* drama). Similarly, the proletariat is forced to produce the instruments of its own oppression and exploitation, as the eleventh section shows ('Die drei Soldaten und das Giftgas', GW 8, 356): 'Denn das Giftgas, wie man's nimmt/ Ist immer für Proletarier bestimmt.' These disparate pieces of information are conveyed in sections which share a common tone and structure; in accordance with the preparatory exercises of the first three sections, the three soldiers appear as the agents of the events and conditions described. The point of this transparent fiction is not simply wit: this device brings social phenomena out of the area of nature, into that of history. The question of agency itself is appropriate, and is not obscured by parodistic proposition.

In the concluding three sections of the poem, these isolated aspects are unified and the narrative structure previously established is gradually dissolved. The dismissal of God in the twelfth section signals a departure from the image of a passive proletariat, the victim of deception by institutions of the bourgeois state; the rejection of illusion indicates a willingness to see things as they are. The thirteenth section, 'Die drei Soldaten und der Klassenkampf', draws conclusions for the whole poem, defining the 'richtige Richtung':

> Als Gott aus der Welt war
> Da war auch nichts mehr unsichtbar.
> Und alsbald wurde laut, was schwieg
> Der Frieden wurde sichtbar als ein Krieg.

This is the 'Krieg im Frieden' of class conflict, in which the proletariat is defeated until it acts in conscious political unity. In the present context, where such organization has not been developed, social conflict appears as a chaotic and senseless struggle in the vision of the three soldiers:

> Es rangen Richter und Angeklagte
> Der Lehrer bekämpfte den, der ihn fragte.
> Der Schreiber mit dem Leser
> Der Verweste mit dem Verweser:
> Es war ein ungeheurer Krieg
> Der kannte Opfer, doch keinen Sieg. (GW 8, 361.)

As the final lines of the section make clear, the understandable desire to ignore all this, to make it invisible, does not solve the problem: indeed it prevents a real solution which lies in the proper conduct and conclusion of the struggle—revolution.

The fourteenth section introduces the Soviet Union as a contrastive example, where such proper conduct had been applied:

> Da war wohl Elend noch vorhanden
> Aber niemand war damit einverstanden. (GW 8, 362.)

This change of scene allows a neat ending to the poem: the fictional agents of oppression, the soldiers of the class war, are themselves at last despatched. In their final words the three soldiers express their approval of this new direction of conflict:

> Das sind Leute, die haben Verstand
> Die stellen uns einfach an die Wand. (GW 8, 363)

This conclusion should not be read as an exhortation to assassinate opposing participants in the class struggle. The poem's main burden is the demonstration that such antagonism exists, but it also shows in its treatment of different manifestations that general causality is not the same as individual blame. The patently false punishment of the oppressed which the poem describes equally excludes the punishment of their oppressors, laying the foundations for an understanding of social complexes as systematic and historical. The final section emphatically disposes of the soldiers' function as agents of a kind of 'natural' justice, by which the passive tolerance of the proletariat is properly rewarded by exploitation. This is the significance of the Soviet example; only a revolution is capable of removing the symptoms of exploitation.

In the last years of the Weimar Republic the conciliatory and reformist policies of the SPD had been an important factor in the neutralization of the political struggle in which Brecht had participated as a Marxist since 1926; hence the importance in *Die drei Soldaten* of the exhibition of typical symptoms of hidden antagonisms. As an analytical work the poem is restricted in scope and theoretical sophistication: it presents the starting points for a critical discussion, provokes questions.

Technically the poem is characterized by functional effectiveness, clear and incisive treatment of its subject. Its pretended crudity, its flaws and disproportions are the result of an extremely flexible and deliberate technique applied with considerable wit.

Poems in Free Rhythms

> Wer sich wehrt, weil ihm die Luft weggenommen wird
> Indem man ihm den Hals zupreßt, vor den stellt sich ein Paragraph
> Und schreit, er hat in Notwehr gehandelt. Aber
> Dieser selbe Paragraph wendet sein Gesicht weg und tritt auf die Seite
> Wenn ihr euch wehrt, weil euch das Brot weggenommen wird.
> Und doch stirbt, wer nicht ißt und wer zu wenig ißt
> Wenn auch langsam. Alle die Jahre, die er stirbt
> Darf er sich nicht wehren. (GW 8, 364.)

Like *Die drei Soldaten* this is a *Lehrgedicht;* it is representative of a large and important group of poems and, specifically, of the subgroup of abstract theoretical texts. Where *Die drei Soldaten* was extensive, this contemporary work is intensive, concentrating on an isolated contradiction; it proceeds from, and returns to, the recognition that the proletariat has limited rights in a bourgeois state and may need to exceed them in protecting itself. Implicitly, the poem refers to the familiar critique of reformism, the doctrine of the importance of legality: it opposes to this the doctrine of active self-defence, defence by attack. The poem does not offer comprehensive statements, nor does it record a discussion: it operates instead by indicating critical points which may refer the reader to previous discussion, or make new discussion necessary. This reticence and limitation is the basis of the poem's broad significance as a starting-point; it records only simple facts which become problematic through their combination. The text makes visible the permissible (legal) limits of self-defence, and at the same time considers whether immediate physical violence is the only kind.

Among the many similar and related poems the following are especially important: 'Wer keine Hilfe weiß' (GW 8, 364), 'Keinen

Gedanken verschwendet an das Unänderbare!' (GW 8, 390), 'Lob des Dolchstoßes' (1931, GW 8, 372). This last poem takes up the motif of the rifles turned against the generals, which *Die drei Soldaten* had employed. The motif is a reversal of the nationalistic 'Dolchstoßlegende', in which the Deutschnationale Volkspartei had argued that the Imperial army had been betrayed ('stabbed in the back') by the SPD in 1918. Brecht understands this 'betrayal', on the model of the Russian revolution, as the proper course of action.

> Bald
> Wißt ihr: der Krieg
> Ist nicht euer Krieg. Hinter euch erblickt ihr
> Den eigentlichen Feind.
> Die Gewehre werden umgedreht
> Es beginnt: der Kampf um die Suppe.

There are many poems belonging to this subgroup which are devoted to criticism, not of the bourgeois republic or its government but of the work of the communists and their allies. It is not overall policy which is criticized primarily, but tendencies at the political base in poems such as 'Die da wegkönnen' (GW 8, 398), 'Es gibt kein größeres Verbrechen als Weggehen' (GW 8, 399), and 'Wir haben einen Fehler begangen' (GW 8, 401), which were written in the crisis of 1932–3; Brecht insists that solidarity and unrelenting pursuit of the struggle are essential.[8] He does so in the knowledge that defeat is likely to precede victory; thus, in 'Wir hören: Du willst nicht mehr mit uns arbeiten' (GW 8, 404) of 1933:

> Wenn wir nicht das Übermenschliche leisten
> Sind wir verloren
> Wenn wir nicht tun, was niemand von uns verlangen kann
> Gehen wir unter.

These poems were anticipated in theme and technique by the *Lesebuch* text 'Du, der das Unentbehrliche ...' of 1927 (GW 8, 291).

The subgroup of abstract, theoretical *Lehrgedichte* may best be represented by two major poems 'Von allen Werken' (GW 8, 386) and 'Über die Bauart langdauernder Werke' (GW 8, 387). They are dated 1932. It was noted above that the *Lehrgedichte* are a form of *Gedankenlyrik;* this aspect is conspicuous in these poems, which at first appear to be records of their author's private reflections. As often, however, Brecht makes private thoughts open and public;

these texts present experiments in reflection, propose models for the reader to test and criticize. In 'Von allen Werken' Brecht proceeds as if he were airing personal tastes. In the first of two long line-groups, satisfaction is expressed with products of human labour which, in the dual sense implied by 'gebraucht', are both needed and used constantly, undergoing alteration and improvement in the process. Aesthetic nobility coincides with functional appropriateness. The second line-group summarizes the point:

> Eingegangen in den Gebrauch der vielen
> Oftmals verändert, verbessern sie ihre Gestalt und werden köstlich
> Weil oftmals gekostet.

Aesthetic quality is seen partly as a function of the capacity for change: its standard is not the classic stability of perfection, but an open, functional felicity, which enables the product's user to work with it and on it. Perfection is brittle, limited; it is significant that the materials referred to with approval are all relatively soft, easy to work: copper, wood, stone.

The second section continues to deal with objects more generally considered in relation to aesthetic categories, products of sculpture and architecture. The destruction of a work of art or part of it, usually viewed as sacrilege, is here contemplated with positive appreciation. This point of view is a logical consequence of the reflections considered above; like other products, works of art are objects of use and are capable of being changed in their use. In continued use, they maintain contact with their recipients, until they are exhausted, capable of no further application or modification. A broken statue thus states that someone at least was impelled to do something with it: 'wenn auch fallengelassen, wurden sie doch getragen'. This startling, positive theory of vandalism recalls Brecht's earlier notes on the 'Materialwert' of tradition, where 'use' has an equally generous breadth of reference (GW 15, 105f.; GW 15, 175 f.).

A half-ruined building serves as the focal point for a contemplation of history as alteration, as human labour: in the wit of the 'schon' 'noch' dialectic, the juxtapostion of past and future is made clear and immediate:

> Die halbzerfallenen Bauwerke
> Haben wieder das Aussehen von noch nicht vollendeten

> Groß geplanten: ihre schönen Maße
> Sind schon zu ahnen; sie bedürfen aber
> Noch unseres Verständnisses. Andrerseits
> Haben sie gedient, ja, sind schon überwunden. Dies alles
> Beglückt mich. (GW 8, 386.)

A ruin might be seen as the skeleton of a new building: more generally destruction and construction may be seen as points on a continuous line, activities differing only in detail and connected by logical necessity. Destruction of the old must precede construction of the new.

The poem's aesthetic reflections are grounded in economy; 'Werk' signifies both process and the products of human labour, which operates, in the first instance, on natural products. The resulting new 'worked' products are themselves operated on by natural and human forces, like the flagstones of the poem, worn to shape by usage and further ennobled by the grass growing between them. In this sense, 'Werk' as process is never completed: the 'Werk'—object—is constantly being altered. 'Gebrauch' designates that part of the operation which can be distinguished from primary production, the area of consumption or reception. The products of human labour described in the poem are useful: capable of fulfilling human needs (the dual sense of 'gebraucht' is a unity). The category 'Gebrauch' appears to be a purely economic, general one, pure, too, in the sense that it is free from class ties; but there are two points at which such abstract reference is modified. 'Eingegangen in den Gebrauch der vielen' suggests not simply frequent use, but use by the many; similarly, the broken sculptures were overrun precisely because they were not placed out of reach, they were not aloof, but accessible. Here 'use' develops a distinctly plebeian character.

Explicit development of the poem's theoretical dimensions tends towards dry abstraction: but the text condenses these reflections poetically and also explores their aesthetic potential. 'Werk' and 'Gebrauch' are repeated in the poem: so is the root 'glück'.

There is also an undercurrent of polemic in the connection made by the poem between aesthetics and economics; the conception of art as sacred, perfect, and untouchable is undermined by the placing of artistic production in the context of general human labour. Far from insisting that art can serve no purpose external to itself, the poem argues that aesthetic quality depends on the extent to which needs are fulfilled.

'Über die Bauart langdauernder Werke' adopts and extends the ideas of the above poem, and shares its programmatic and reflective character. The grand epic title introduces a poem full of classical features, rhetorical figures and tropes of the logical or grammatical kind. In spite of the title, however, the poem is not a discourse on the construction of lasting works from a neutral point of view. It offers an ambitiously critical analysis.

The first line-group examines the conditions affecting the 'duration' of works.[9] The awkwardness of the paraphrase indicates that here, as in 'Von allen Werken', the process/product ambivalence is exploited; 'Werke' seems to refer to pieces of work, but this reading is immediately negated by the answer to the introductory enquiry. Works last until they are completed, it is asserted: the reader's attention is focused on work as process. Duration is made a function of continuing labour. The question: whose labour? does not at first arise, it seems clear that the producer's labour is meant. Again, the poem demands that the reader revise a first reading: the lines 'Die nützlichen/ *Verlangen Menschen*' clearly refer to those who receive the products of primary labour. This revision in turn fixes the sense of 'Werk' in its original meaning, as product.

The ambivalence of 'fertig', inadequately expressed in its translation as 'completed', connects this poem with 'Von allen Werken' and its emphasis on 'Gebrauch', reception and use. Works are 'fertig' in the full sense (finished and exhausted, used up) when further application ceases to be possible; but this application and consumption is part of the work as process. The division between production and consumption is here dissolved in favour of a concept which emphasizes their continuity: its application alters the product, 'produces' a new one.

> Wie lange
> Dauern die Werke? So lange
> Als bis sie fertig sind.
> So lange sie nämlich Mühe machen
> Verfallen sie nicht. (GW 8, 387.)

A work is a problem, an object of labour for its user, as for its producer. Similarly, the old buildings of 'Von allen Werken' are said on one hand to have served, on the other to have been 'overcome': 'überwunden' too defines the work as a problem (formulated as a solution by the primary producer), elements of which are continually being solved in its application. The artefact is seen as a working hypothesis, useful so long as it demands that others work with it; once proved or disproved, it is exhausted.

The poem makes use of paradox in order to focus in sharp clarity on details of its argument: thus, it is not men who demand useful products, but vice versa: and the duration of works depends, like their completeness, on a finely pointed ambivalence—'einladend zur Mühe'.

The image of the wall and the ivy which makes up the fourth linegroup of the poem underlines the idea that the completion of a work combines the labour of production with that of application. The artefact is here finished by the ivy's work on it. Here again, the harmonious co-operation of human and natural forces is evoked.

> So gebaut sein muß
> Das Werk für die Dauer wie
> Die Maschine voll der Mängel. (GW 8, 388.)

'Mängel' should not be understood simply as faults causing malfunction. They are also productive incompletenesses which leave the work open to change and use, ultimately rendering it capable of being used up. The relative softness of wood is such an imperfection.

In the line-group marked as part 3 of section I, the transition from the artefact in general to the linguistic work is made. The incompleteness which should characterize such work is described in a series of paradoxes stressing the elements of design and communication. The continuity of production and consumption is implicit in the poem's assertion that the production of any work must include planning for its reception.

> Gehe nie vor, ohne zuvor
> Zurückzugehen der Richtung wegen!
> Die Frager sind es
> Denen du Antwort geben wirst, aber
> Die dir zuhören werden, sind es
> Die dich dann fragen. (GW 8, 388.)

The writer can only speak to those who read his work; it is thus part of his task to promote this possibility. A passage from the *Arbeitsjournal* illustrates Brecht's acute consciousness of the reciprocal basis of communication:

ich kann selten widerstehen, wenn hunde um ein kraulen betteln. es kommt mir vor, als dürfe ihr appell nicht abgeschlagen werden, da es eben ein appell ist, ein anruf, der, einmal enttäuscht, womöglich nicht mehr wiederholt würde, womit jede beziehung aufgehoben wäre, die vernunft selber abgeschafft wäre. keine antwort, keine frage. (AJ 23.1.42.)

In the context under discussion, the formula applies in reverse form: 'keine frage, keine antwort'. The writer must provoke the questions without which he can offer no answer: he must have an audience—the dictum 'die nützlichen verlangen Menschen' is valid for writers, too.

In a passage which recalls the biblical 'blessed are the meek' this audience is defined with dogmatic force, confirming the orientation implicit in 'Von allen Werken'.

> Deren Stellung gering erscheint
> Wenn man sie ansieht
> Das sind
> Die Mächtigen von morgen
> Die deiner bedürfen, die
> Sollen die Macht haben. (GW 8, 389.)

The duration of works depends on the needs of this public, needs which the writer must anticipate and stimulate.

The second major section locates the more or less abstract preceding discussion both socially and historically. It considers what general conditions make the construction of lasting works necessary, reaching conclusions which correspond to the situation of the Marxist writer in the decline of the Weimar Republic.

> Wenn etwas gesagt werden soll, was nicht gleich verstanden wird
> Wenn ein Rat gegeben wird, dessen Ausführung lang dauert
> Wenn die Schwäche der Menschen befürchtet wird
> Die Ausdauer der Feinde, die alles verschüttenden Katastrophen
> Dann muß den Werken eine lange Dauer verliehen werden

As these specifications imply, and as the final section confirms, duration is merely one variable in a complex situation. The poem describes metaphorically, but nonetheless materialistically, the conditions of production, literary production in particular. When the monumental ideal of artistic perfection ('exegi monumentum aere perennius') ceases to be an absolute criterion, the question of duration or endurance becomes secondary to that of function. The poem ends with an extended warning, indicating the dangers of producing lasting works: even an as yet unborn public must be adequately addressed, and the writer must be sure that its birth is not in jeopardy. In the unfavourable conditions outlined above, it is suggested, literary production should be directed to the posterity which may outlast the enemy, but also to the more immediate goal of opposition to that enemy. Without such duality of direction there might never be a posterity to use and complete enduring works: the wall of the literary work would be permanently bare of the ivy which should flourish on it—the continuous work of reception.

This long poem attains impressive theoretical richness and sophistication: it is at the same time an aesthetic object and incorporates an awareness of the limitations of theory. Its argument is developed in a logical, but not linear manner, generating not fixed conclusions, but a set of paradigmatic positions. The poem operates with complex, contradictory unities: its method is dialectic. Where Brecht's own production is concerned, the poem's immediate relevance consists in the dual orientation of the poetry in relation both to the future and to the daily struggle of the present; also, in the attention paid to reception design and publicistic effectiveness. 'Über die Bauart langdauernder Werke' belongs to the first phase of theoretical development, whose first results appeared in 1930, with the 'Anmerkungen' to *Mahagonny*, the 'Erläuterungen' to the *Ozeanflug*, and the *Dreigroschenprozeß*: all these dealt critically with artistic production in the context of modern capitalism, and were, like the *Versuche* series, aimed at the 'Umfunktionierung' of its institutions. In its insistence on the use-value of literary production, the poem is no less radical than these contemporary works: use-value is reinstated against the dominance of exchange-value precisely through the conscious application of literature, its function in the revolutionary cause.[10]
'Von allen Werken' and 'Über die Bauart langdauernder Werke' demonstrate with particular clarity the typical mode of Brecht's *Lehrgedichte*, their refined, noble, and rhetorical style which combines intellectual and aesthetic effectiveness. Far from being indiscriminately iconoclastic, these poems are avant-garde in a complex sense: their literary antecedents include the free rhythms of Goethe, Klopstock, and Hölderlin, as well as the apodictic sentences of the Bible.

Besides a major subgroup of abstract *Lehrgedichte* there are those of the *Chroniken* and autobiographical *Chroniken*. 'Die

Internationale' (1932, GW 8, 394), 'Die Bolschewiki entdecken...' (1932, GW 8, 392), 'Als der Faschismus immer stärker wurde' (1932, GW 8, 400) and 'Dimitroff' (1932, GW 8, 420) all are examples of this subgroup in which general conclusions are derived from specific historical material. 'Die Nachtlager' (1931, GW 8, 373) is typical: the poem begins as a report, followed by a discursive commentary:

> Einige Menschen haben ein Nachtlager
> Der Wind wird von ihnen eine Nacht lang abgehalten
> Der ihnen zugedachte Schnee fällt auf die Straße
> Aber die Welt wird dadurch nicht anders
> Die Beziehungen zwischen den Menschen bessern sich dadurch nicht
> Das Zeitalter der Ausbeutung wird dadurch nicht verkürzt.

Here, the dialectic method finds a structural correspondence in the composition of the poem; after a one-line axis, the same passage is repeated, its two halves reversed to emphasize the two directions of sight which constitute the dialectic. First, humane and generous action is acknowledged, then it is criticized; Brecht's opposition to reformism does not prevent his recognition of humane action—the age of exploitation is not shortened if the homeless are ignored. Thus, in the mirrored form, approval and acknowledgement have the final word. Such deliberate and rational manipulation of complex situations towards a practical and useful goal is precisely the role of the dialectic.[11]

The minor subgroup of autobiographical *Chroniken* includes poems written in 1933, at the beginning of Brecht's exile: 'Verhalten in der Fremde' (GW 8, 407), 'Ich habe lange die Wahrheit gesucht' (GW 8, 414), 'Als ich ins Exil gejagt wurde' (GW 8, 416) and 'Zeit meines Reichtums' (GW 8, 418). These poems make Brecht's own experience generally significant in the same way as the *Chroniken* employ historical material. Both these subgroups become more important in the subsequent development of Brecht's poetry; in the period 1926–33 the abstract *Lehrgedicht* is dominant.

Exile: *Lieder Gedichte Chöre*

Exile was, in 1933, a consequence of political commitment.[12] Brecht's attitude to exile was appropriately polemic: he was determined to continue active participation in the anti-fascist struggle.

> Unsere Feinde sagen: die Wahrheit ist vernichtet.
> Aber wir sagen: wir wissen sie noch.
> Unsere Feinde sagen: auch wenn die Wahrheit noch gewußt wird
> Kann sie nicht mehr verbreitet werden.
> Aber wir verbreiten sie. (GW 8, 420)

The optimism of this attitude (considerably exceeded by that of the KPD at this period) was productive, but had little foundation in the reality of the German political context.[13] In exile, Brecht was safer and freer than he had been for several months; his financial situation, if precarious, was not a matter for serious concern during the first years of exile. Brecht was, however, separated from his German-speaking public, in particular from the theatre, which had been his most important sphere of activity. Though he produced many dramatic works during the fifteen years of exile, few could be tested in practice; lyric poetry became an area of central importance in Brecht's work.

It is necessary to depart from chronological organization in the treatment of the two collections of poetry published in exile. It is more important to analyse the collections as such than to examine individual poems in the context of the general history of the poetry. Such an analysis illuminates several aspects of Brecht's work, in particular publicistic ones, which are relevant not simply on the level of the single text.

Lieder Gedichte Chöre was published in Paris in 1934 by Willi Münzenberg's company 'Éditions du Carrefour', in an edition of three thousand. Even for the early years of exile when the financial situation was not yet desperate, this must be regarded as a large edition for a volume of poems.[14] There is no evidence of any of these copies reaching Germany, and it may be assumed that they found a market among German speaking exiles in Europe. Attempts were made to smuggle anti-fascist literature into Germany, in the form of camouflaged editions, which included several poems by Brecht. Other poems, for which no such evidence has been found, also became known inside Germany. Before the collection had appeared, a number of poems were published as previews in exile periodicals.[15]

There were, as Brecht knew, immense difficulties operating against any attempt to import oppositional literature into Germany: the regime's terrorism was a powerful deterrent.

Nevertheless, successful smuggling did occur, and Brecht's defiant optimism in producing a collection which was not intended only for fellow exiles is not without foundation.

Lieder Gedichte Chöre (GW 9, 425-88) is a selection from Brecht's poetry containing a majority of texts produced in the early thirties, with some earlier texts. The poems were selected, not simply to provide representative samples of Brecht's work, but as the contribution of a political exile to the anti-fascist struggle. The aim which governs the choice of texts also determines their organization in the collection, which has a coherent, carefully designed structure. It may conveniently be divided into five sections.

The first contains the early poems 'Legende vom toten Soldaten' (GW 8, 256), 'Gedicht vom unbekannten Soldaten unter dem Triumphbogen' (1926), 'Zweites Gedicht vom unbekannten Soldaten unter dem Triumpbogen' (1927/8) and 'Zu Potsdam unter den Eichen' (1927). All are anti-war poems of a general kind and constitute an admonitory introduction to the collection.

The second section begins with 'Grabschrift 1919' (1929) which marks the transition from the subject of open war to that of the 'Krieg im Frieden' of class conflict. Rosa Luxemburg is remembered as one of its many casualties. The 'Wiegenlieder' of 1932 elaborate on this theme. The contemporary form of class conflict, in particular the opposition to national socialism, is examined in two poems, 'Das Lied vom SA-Mann' (1929) and 'Das Lied vom Klassenfeind' (1931).

Introduced by 'Das Lied vom Anstreicher Hitler', the third section contains the satirical 'Hitler-Choräle' and 'Die Ballade vom Baum und den Ästen'. They are followed by a series of poems attacking obvious weak points in the regime's ideological armour: concentration camps ('Sonnenburg', 'Ein Bericht', 'An die Kämpfer in den Konzentrationslagern'), institutional terror ('Begräbnis des Hetzers im Zinksarg') and rigged trials 'Adresse an den Genossen Dimitroff'). These poems were written in 1933.

Section four is a collection of songs and choruses from the dramas *Die Mutter* and *Die Maßnahme,* written between 1929 and 1931. These poems link the anti-fascist position expressed in section three with the preceding two sections: they are concerned with the active opposition of the organized proletariat.

The fifth section, the 'Anhang', contains four poems of wider

scope, presenting a critique of capitalism as the context of fascism.
   The collection is constructed with rigorous logic to form a consistent and forceful argument.
   'Legende vom toten Soldaten', written in 1918, is the earliest text of the collection. A 'historical' text when published in *Hauspostille* in 1927, it became actual once again in 1933 when militarism and large-scale rearmament began to flourish. The ironically titled poem commences in the voice of feigned innocence: the sense of naive wonder evoked permeates the first six strophes. In the third, ingenuousness extends as far as prosody:

> Der Sommer zog über die Gräber her
> Und der Soldat schlief schon
> Da kam eines Nachts eine militär-
> ische ärztliche Kommission.

In the seventh strophe material reality ('in den halb verwesten Leib') introduces a tone of hard seriousness into the grotesque ballad. With bitterly aggressive satire, the poem erodes the ideals of militarism and empire, reveals the church's function as cosmetic deceit, and attacks the nationalism of the bourgeoisie, and the gullible obedience of the people. The renewed actuality of the poem penetrates as far as its detail: the black–red–gold of the republic, the object of hatred from the military and the monarchist bureaucracy, was now deposed by the colours of the empire:

> Sie malten auf sein Leichenhemd
> Die Farben Schwarz-Weiß-Rot
> Und trugen's vor ihm her; man sah
> Vor Farben nicht mehr den Kot.   (GW 8, 258.)

'Legende vom toten Soldaten' had aroused the nationalistic anger of a shareholder in the Gustav Kiepenheuer Verlag in 1926, as a result of which the *Hauspostille* was published by Propyläen.[16] In June 1935 Brecht was deprived of German nationality: National Socialist commentaries recalled that he was the author of a poem displaying lack of proper respect for the heroism of the German soldier. This heroism was soon to be called upon again.
   The following two poems stand in sharp contrast to the affective, energetic ballad, though they are also satirical. The poems on the Unknown Soldier belong to the experimental strand of the *Lesebuch*, and are, typically, persona-poems. The first poem has a mythic dimension; it adopts the symbol of the Unknown Soldier,

integrating it into a narrative. This is presented as a confession and is delivered in a conspicuously unemotional manner, which is disturbed only when the speaker recalls that the soldier's mother was among those who brought about his death:

> Dabei war eine Frau, die ihn geboren hatte
> Und die geschwiegen hatte, als wir ihn holten.
> Der Schoß sei ihr ausgerissen!
> Amen! (GW 9, 425–6.)

This mode of ironic provocation is familiar from *Die drei Soldaten*; here, too, passivity is criticized: whoever declines to oppose a murderer is an effective accessory to murder. The satirical strand of the poem is evident in its final lines, where the received public myth of the Arc de Triomphe is undermined by the practical function newly attributed to the monument.

The second poem announces itself as a revision of the first; it confirms the factual basis of the preceding poem (the murder of the Unknown Soldier), but strips it of its mythic elements and locates the discussion in present times. The speakers live their lives in peace, the soldier has been forgotten; here, however, myth has been replaced by social definition: the speakers introduce an implicit distinction between themselves and the soldiers' murderers (in the sixth section), at the same time stressing their own close relation to him ('unser Bruder ist tot'). This distinction produces a refinement in the question of responsibility; where the first poem ends in extravagant satire, the second is concluded by a crescendo of anger, addressed not to the people, despite their acquiescence, but to those who (it is implied) exercise real power and hence carry active responsibility: the owners and administrators of armaments industries, and the governments and generals who are their allies. Still, the final lines enquire how such acquiescence is possible:

> ... Dieses Triumphgeheul
> Ist doch nicht nötig und macht
> Uns Kummer, denn uns
> Die wir den Erschlagenen
> Schon vergessen hatten, erinnert er
> Täglich aufs neue an euch, die ihr noch
> Lebt und die ihr
> Immer noch nicht erschlagen seid—
> Warum denn nicht? (GW 9, 428.)

The concept of the class struggle as the right war is latent in these lines.

'Zu Potsdam unter den Eichen' is a simple poem, more direct than the preceding pair. The ballad shows, in its ironic reading of the patriotic slogan 'jedem Krieger sein Heim', that obedience leads the soldier to be slaughtered, and that disobedience occasions prompt oppressive measures ('da kam die grüne Polizei/ Und haute sie zusamm' GW 9, 429).

The four-line epitaph for Rosa Luxemburg takes up this point, completing the transition in theme from external to class war:

> Weil sie den Armen die Wahrheit gesagt
> Haben die Reichen sie aus der Welt gejagt. (GW 9, 429.)

It introduces the 'Wiegenlieder', persona-poems in which a proletarian mother addresses her son. The four sections of the poem provide a direct, exemplary account of class conflict as it is enacted at a basic level. Where economic questions intervene brutally in human decisions, there is no room for maternal sentimentality:

> Als ich dich trug all die Monate
> Sprach ich mit deinem Vater über dich.
> Aber wir hatten das Geld nicht für den Doktor
> Das brauchten wir für den Brotaufstrich. (GW 9, 430.)

Such conditions make the mother's attitude to her son, a defiant and pragmatic kind of love, the more remarkable. This is not a neutral account and could not be so; the mother is aware of her situation in an immediate, real way:

> Brot und ein Schluck Milch sind Siege!
> Warme Stube: gewonnene Schlacht!
> Eh ich dich da groß kriege
> Muß ich kämpfen Tag und Nacht. (GW 9, 431.)

This perception is accompanied, not by despair, but by determination; where theoretical speculation has no value, where there is no prospect of material assistance or guidance from above, self-defence is the only possible hope. It depends on the organized solidarity of the proletariat in the revolutionary struggle, and is thus an active role. The mother instructs her son with tender strictness in the poem's final strophe:

Du, mein Sohn, und ich und alle unsresgleichen
Müssen zusammenstehn und müssen erreichen
Daß es auf dieser Welt nicht mehr zweierlei Menschen gibt.
(GW 9, 433.)

The 'Wiegenlieder' offer a positive alternative to the attitude of acquiescence which the poetry of this period repeatedly criticizes. Clearly, if active participation is to be recommended, it is vital that the struggle should have a proper goal, and appropriate means to achieve it. This problem, in its most basic form, underlies 'Das Lied vom SA-Mann' and 'Das Lied vom Klassenfeind'; the National Socialist movement adopted, in its name and in its declared policies, elements which were calculated to engage the interest of a proletariat eager for action (an eagerness for which massive unemployment adequately accounts). These poems attempt to show that the 'socialism' of the movement was an empty phrase, that it concealed the real aims of the movement's leaders, which were opposed to the workers' interests.

Ich wollte nach links marschieren
Nach rechts marschierte er
Da ließ ich mich kommandieren
Und lief blind hinterher. (GW 9, 434.)

The simple allegory portrays the inevitable contradictions which follow the socialist aspirations of those who were persuaded to support fascism; the final strophe of 'Das Lied vom SA-Mann', in which the proletarian supporter of National Socialism murders his brother, provides a warning, a negative example to contrast with the positive model of the 'Wiegenlieder'.

This point is reinforced in the extensive 'Lied vom Klassenfeind' which relates the idea of brotherhood to real social categories. The speaker, unequivocally identified as proletarian in the first strophe, reviews the history of the Weimar Republic: a history of illusion and deception of the proletariat. A refrain is appended to each strophe, providing a distancing commentary on the preceding text. The refrain refers to the natural image of the rain, which has a central function in the poem's argument. In the first two strophes the image appears as a proverb, enshrining 'obvious' common sense: exploitation and poverty have always existed, are natural and inevitable. The third strophe transforms the proverb into a complaint, while the fourth and fifth employ the apparently immutable principle as an anchor of political realism, a positive model of scepticism as a defence against reformist promises:

> Sie gaben uns Zettel zum Wählen
> Wir gaben die Waffen her
> Sie gaben uns ein Versprechen
> Und wir gaben unser Gewehr...
> Da ließ ich mich wieder bewegen
> Und hielt, wie's verlangt wurd, still
> Und dachte: das ist schön von dem Regen
> Daß er aufwärts fließen will. (GW 9, 436-7.)

The seventh strophe completes the range of significance of the image by placing it in relation to a wider context: though rain can never fall upwards into the clouds (though factory-owners will never be exploited by their employees), it may stop (changes in relations of production may produce a classless society, where exploitation is abolished).

> Der Regen kann nicht nach aufwärts
> Weil er's plötzlich gut mit uns meint.
> Was er kann, das ist: er kann aufhörn
> Nämlich dann, wenn die Sonne scheint. (GW 9, 438.)

Here, the absolute 'natural' principle of the proverb is made to act as the basis of a historical view, in which it is only valid in relation to a specific phase. With the eighth strophe the poem returns to the urgent problems of Germany under the fascist regime. It insists that, in spite of all the National Socialist slogans, the class war has not been (and cannot be) abolished; the poem is concluded by the polemic assertion that, on the contrary, it must be deliberately pursued 'Das Lied vom Klassenfeind' is a lively, skilful *Lehrgedicht*, tending towards the more immediate and limited political *Kampfgedicht*.

The series of poems which follows is still closer to such a direct and practical orientation. The 'Hitler-Choräle' are based on Protestant hymns, not principally for parodistic ends, but because the new words fit patterns already familiar to the reader, and are thus easier to learn. At the same time, this traditional model was a safety-factor for performance: the original words could be reverted to in case of danger, providing a perfect disguise for illegal propaganda. Besides the functional advantage offered by the dogmatic manner of the Lutheran hymn, the wit inherent in the undertaking was probably an important attraction for Brecht. The dangerous illusions propagated by the church were replaced by strict materialism; the poems' basic opposition to ideology leads to the appearance of the church as an ally of fascism (which it was not, at least not always): 'Nun danket alle Gott/ Der uns den Hitler sandte' (GW 9, 442). Hitler and his regime are represented as liars, as the whitewashers of the German sepulchre. Their solutions are cosmetic, they exist only in the realm of propaganda. The comic elements employed in these poems, far from making fascism appear harmless, trivially quixotic, strip it of its mythic grandeur and reveal the flaws which such grandeur effectively concealed. In this sense, their comic elements are integrated into a profound seriousness of intention.

The poems attack National Socialism where it is inextricably involved in the contradictions of German capitalism: promises made are confronted with the hard reality to which they refer. It is demonstrated that fascism can offer no significant, lasting improvements to the proletariat, because it operates on the base of capitalist economic organization:

> Mög er der Löhne der Arbeiter gnädig gedenken!
> Sorg er für sie!
> Doch auch für die Industrie!
> Mög er den Arbeitslohn senken! (GW 9, 445)[17]

Sung with studied innocence, these poems are corrosively satirical. In the lines quoted, Brecht does not simply isolate the contradiction, but shows which direction its avoidance must take: the rhyme emphasizes the contrast 'gedenken'/'senken', stressing that it is the capitalist who has the last word.

The poems which follow the 'Hitler-Choräle' explore the specific and obvious faults of the regime. 'An die Kämpfer in den Konzentrationslagern' takes up the theme of 'Sonnenburg' and 'Ein Bericht'; a *Lehrgedicht* in the form of an epistle, it describes the exemplary behaviour of the interned communists. The style is classical, rhetorical: the poem is a political ode.

> Unbelehrbar, heißt es, seid ihr der proletarischen Sache ergeben
> Unabbringbar davon, daß es immer noch in Deutschland
> Zweierlei Menschen gibt: Ausbeuter und Ausgebeutete
> Und daß nur der Klassenkampf

Die Menschenmassen der Städte und des Landes aus dem Elend befreien
kann ...
Also seid ihr ...
Zusammen mit allen unverbesserbar Weiterkämpfenden
Unbelehrbar auf der Wahrheit Beharrenden
Weiterhin die wahren
Führer Deutschlands. (GW 9, 456.)

'Begräbnis des Hetzers im Zinksarg' (GW 9, 457) is an aggressively satirical poem; aping the regime's accusations of its victim, it relentlessly examines the aims for which he had agitated and been silenced. Such humane, reasonable aims are a threat to the regime and a danger to all who share them. The third section of the collection is closed by a further poem in the grand heroic style, concerning the example set by Dimitrov, who succeeded brilliantly in transforming a rigged trial into a public tribunal for the indictment of fascist crimes. This was both a significant political victory and an important moral one for the resistance movement inside and outside Nazi Germany.

These positive examples of resistance against overwhelming odds are followed by the songs and choruses from *Die Mutter* and *Die Maßnahme*, which relate opposition to the regime to the proletarian struggle in general. This reiterates elements from the second and third sections, concerning the class struggle and its particular anti-fascist form in Germany; but it implies a return to first principles in order to confirm the previous progression of the argument. 'An die Frauen' proceeds, like the 'Wiegenlieder', from a specific situation; it records the experiences of a proletarian woman who has learnt that the most desperate efforts of labour and economy are limited and cannot make clothes out of rags:

> Wenn der Pfennig fehlt
> Ist die Suppe nur Wasser. (GW 9, 460.)

Such truths are concrete, incontrovertible; they were empirically verifiable for millions in the early thirties. The poem proceeds with the same logical solidity:

> Über das Fleisch, das euch in der Küche fehlt
> Wird nicht in der Küche entschieden ...
> So geht es nicht weiter
> Aber was ist der Ausweg? (GW 9, 461.)

Acquiescence provides no solution to an unbearable situation; since politics affects even those without political power, such power must be seized. 'Das Lied von der Suppe' completes the transition from individual to general reference:

> Wenn du keine Suppe hast
> Wie willst du dich da wehren?
> Da mußt du den ganzen Staat
> Von unten nach oben umkehren. (GW 9, 461)

On this positive and hopeful note the introduction to the more detailed discussion in the *Lehrgedichte* is concluded. While the two poems examined above stand in the *Lied* tradition, the following eight poems in free rhythms should be seen in relation to the classical ode. Brecht substitutes a less formal discipline of his own for the strict prosodic prescriptions which otherwise govern the ode; this should not distract from the similarity in attitude. Just as the polemic, dogmatic energy of the Protestant hymn had attracted Brecht in the 'Hitler-Choräle', so the calm, precise authority, the controlled enthusiasm of the ode attract him here.

The fact that Brecht has not preserved the original order of texts, the order in which they appear in the dramas, indicates the attention he paid to the organization of the collection. 'Lob des Lernens' which follows 'Lob des Kommunismus' in the play, precedes it here because this suits the process of the argument. The reader has been told that the structure of society must be changed 'Lob des Lernens' instructs him in this undertaking. To learn is both the necessary beginning and the constant orientation of the task:

> Scheue dich nicht zu fragen, Genosse!
> Laß dir nichts einreden
> Sieh selber nach!
> Was du nicht selber weißt
> Weißt du nicht. (GW 9, 463.)

The repeated imperative 'du mußt die Führung übernehmen' on which the poem rests is not part of any vague conception of necessity as an absolute principle; revolution is not the historic mission of the proletariat. Rather it is derived (this is clear both in the drama and in the collection of poems) from specific material conditions, and is necessary only in a particular and limited sense.

'Lob des Kommunismus' introduces an analytic body of teaching which is placed in the service of proletarian revolution. The political movement of communism is here fully integrated with its theoretical dimension, Marxism. This is a dogmatic poem, a series of responses to familiar anti-communist utterances; it emphasizes that communism is a rational and practical method, and a partisan one. Its fundamental attitude is one of corrective assertion built on a series of oppositions: 'Keine Tollheit, sondern/ Das Ende der Tollheit'.[18] Its final formulation is the illuminating paradox: 'Er ist das Einfache/ Das schwer zu machen ist' (GW 9, 463). Here too Brecht operates at a material level: the revolution is not an abstract historical necessity which automatically occurs, but the result of organized human actions. A revolution which might have fulfilled the needs of the German proletariat had been prevented by the actions of other classes and sections of society.

In 'Lob der Partei' forms of organization of such conscious action are recommended; they are examined in detail in 'Wer aber ist die Partei?'. The party is defined as the collective organization of its members; its relationship to individual members is thus one of reciprocal dependence. The poem's central concern is the exhortation to maintain solidarity: an erring party should be corrected, not abandoned:

> Zeige uns den Weg, den wir gehen sollen, und wir
> Werden ihn gehen wie du, aber
> Gehe nicht ohne uns den richtigen Weg
> Ohne uns ist er
> Der falscheste   (GW 9, 464–5.)

This is an abstract statement of principle, but it is not merely idealism. The poem's assertions contain challenges, both to the individual and to the collective; the former must be able to demonstrate that a change of course is appropriate, while the party must remain flexible, accessible to such correction, which, once demonstrated, must be accepted. Such fine critical nuances were more apparent to readers who had observed the bitter political struggles of the Weimar Republic, in which the SPD and the KPD (as well as publicly denigrating one another) were quick to expel members critical of party policy. Discipline, the poem implies, is not the same as obedience.[19]

At this point, treatment of fundamental principles is concluded; the progression from the particular to the general (from 'An die Frauen' to 'Lob des Kommunismus') now approaches a new level of particularity. 'Lob der illegalen Arbeit' attains a new actuality in the context of this collection. Since March 1933 the KPD had been an outlawed party; its funds had been seized and much of its organization destroyed. In its continued illegal work it needed support. The poem contrasts the attractions of open battle with the secret toil of illegal resistance, at the same time implying that such work is no less important, and that it, too, has heroic dimensions. Lerg–Kill notes that the first lines of the poem contain echoes of Horace and Klopstock;[20] it is typical of the *Lehrgedichte* in its classical syntax, its rhetorical parallelisms and repetitions, which produce a text of expressive strength and aesthetic interest in balance. 'Bericht über den Tod eines Genossen' follows with a warning of the dangers which accompany illegal work; it is a lament of an unsentimental style appropriate to those who must continue their work as they speak.

Und die Gewehre, gerichtet auf seine Brust, und die Kugel
Waren von seinesgleichen gemacht. Nur fortgegangen
Waren sie also oder vertrieben, aber für ihn doch da
Und anwesend im Werk ihrer Hände. Nicht einmal
Die auf ihn schossen, waren andere als er und nicht ewig auch unbelehrbar.
(GW 9, 466.)

The vision of the growing army of the proletariat suggests that the struggle, however difficult and dangerous, serves a purpose, 'Lob des Revolutionärs' extends the exemplary function of this poem, stressing the attitude of defiant persistence:

Wo immer geschwiegen wird
Dort wird er sprechen
Und wo Unterdrückung herrscht und von Schicksal die Rede ist
Wird er die Namen nennen. (GW 9, 467.)

The fourth section closes with 'Lob der Dialektik', which consolidates the immediate point of the argument that the struggle must continue, however desperate the situation. For the dialectic thinker, defeat means delay, and a lesson:

Wer niedergeschlagen wird, der erhebe sich!
Wer verloren ist, kämpfe!
Wer seine Lage erkannt hat, wie soll der aufzuhalten sein? (GW 9, 468.)

With characteristic dogmatic emphasis (derived partly from the use of the biblical cursus), Brecht presents the long-term revolutionary perspective.[21] In the dialectic compression of the poem:

> ... Die Besiegten von heute sind die Sieger von morgen
> Und aus Niemals wird: Heute noch!   (GW 9, 468.)

Here the argument of the collection, which reached its highest level of sophistication and detail in the fourth section, has been concluded. It has offered information in three major categories; the possibility of action, (action which, in a specific sense, is necessary), its prescription, and appropriate methods for its execution. These abstract categories are often combined in individual texts, but they determine, on a larger scale, the organization of the collection.

Lieder Gedichte Chöre was a collection intended to fulfil functions of agitation and propaganda, to provide texts which, individually and collectively, would contribute to the anti-fascist struggle. There was, in 1934, only a relatively small number of political exiles outside Germany: their efforts were directed to influencing the situation within their country.[22] This appears to be true of Brecht; to address the collection to this small, exiled public would have meant preaching to the converted, or relying on sympathetic exiles as mediators between the writer and the larger public inside Germany. It is unlikely that this would have satisfied Brecht. Much more likely, as was suggested above, is that he hoped somehow to reach this public directly; there were several possibilities, besides simple smuggling of undisguised copies of the book. The use of radio is an apparent solution, though at this early stage it was probably impossible. Consideration of the practical means to which Brecht hoped to resort remains speculative.

Whatever his understanding of the political situation and its implications, Brecht is likely to have retained in these first years of exile a conception of his public based largely on his last experiences of contact with it. On this assumption, the addressees of *Lieder Gedichte Chöre* would have included the organized political groups, communist above all, but social democratic too, and their sympathizers. If there were any grounds for hoping that the fascist regime might soon be overthrown, they rested on the extent of co-operation between the illegal cells of the SPD and the KPD (with those of the numerous smaller groups). Brecht had argued for such co-operation in 1932, and this hope seems also to underlie the collection;[23] assuming that the didactic poems of the fourth section would encourage the communists, they might also persuade workers with SPD allegiances that a united front was necessary, and possible. The hope that it would contribute to the unified solidarity of the German proletariat would explain both the selection of poems, and their organization in the collection: individual texts and the collection itself argue and instruct insistently: effective opposition to fascism depended on the organized proletariat and its revolutionary party. In retrospect, such intentions appear impossibly optimistic: the extent and intensity of the terrorist dictatorship could not be foreseen.

The fifth section, which concludes the collection, has an emphatic function. Its first three texts present a general critique of aspects of capitalism, while the final poem returns to its development of fascism in Germany. The 'Ballade von der Billigung der Welt' is a satire based on the negative example; the speaker confesses that he was an observer who assented to what he saw. Like the patient proletarians of *Die drei Soldaten* he was tolerant: tolerant of brutal exploitation. Where the proletarians had simply been passive victims, however, the speaker is active in voicing his approval for all he sees. Here, the sphere of reference of the collection has been widened to include those who are potential allies of the proletariat: the petty bourgeoisie (whose desperate opportunism the poem imitates) and the intellectuals, the teachers, doctors, and journalists. The final crises of the Weimar Republic, when even the formerly safe professions had seen their members reduced to poverty, had made possible the critical positions on which an allegiance to the workers' movement would have been possible: but national socialism, *par excellence* the mass movement of the petty bourgeoisie, had offered easy and opportunistic solutions on the line of least resistance (it had revived chauvinistic nationalism, along with crude mythology and emotive slogans).[24] Its appeal to these social groups was more direct, and was successful.

The poem seizes on the points at which criticism suggests itself to these groups peripheral to the basic processes of society. The choice is shown to be between the risks of protesting and a safe, but implicating acquiescence:

> Ich sah die Mörder und ich sah die Opfer
> Und nur des Muts und nicht des Mitleids bar

Sah ich die Mörder ihre Opfer wählen
Und schrie: Ich billige das, ganz und gar! (GW 9, 474.)

Such acquiescence means complicity, not blameless innocence; similarly, it is argued, sympathy without action is mere self-indulgence.

'Verschollener Ruhm der Riesenstadt New York' consolidates the critical position recommended by examining the American model of capitalism. America had been widely admired in the twenties, for its fashions and customs, as for its advanced technology and designs; here it is firmly dismissed as a positive example. The satirical elegy on the lost glory of New York makes use of the grand style, deliberately inflated to convey the sense of vain ambition and unfulfilled promise. Satire does not, however, exclude admiration for the real technical and social advances which had been achieved. The Wall Street crash of 1929 destroys any illusions about the fundamental nature of American society, however, and it is the critical account of the effects of the crisis which carries most weight. The ultimate disillusion is of epic proportions:

In den Eisenbahnzügen, die rollenden Hotels gleichen, heißt es
Wohnt jetzt oft kein Mensch.
Er fährt nirgends hin
Mit einer unvergleichlichen Schnelligkeit!
Was ist das mit den Brücken? Sie verbinden
(Die längsten der Welt!) Schuttplätze jetzt mit Schuttplätzen ...

Welch ein Bankrott! Wie ist da
Ein großer Ruhm verschollen! Welch eine Entdeckung:
Daß ihr System des Gemeinlebens denselben
Jämmerlichen Fehler aufwies wie das
Bescheidenerer Leute! (GW 9, 481–3.)

'Lied der preiswerten Lyriker' extends the critique of capitalism from the viewpoint of the artist. Taking up the observation of the final strophe of 'Ballade von der Billigung der Welt': 'Da Niedrigkeit und Not mir nicht gefällt/ Fehlt meiner Kunst in dieser Zeit der Schwung' (GW 9, 475), the poem analyses the role of the artist. Proceeding from the decline in demand for art, the poem enquires what the artist had done to deserve such neglect; its conclusions differ from those quoted. Art suffers, not from an unwillingness or incapacity to fulfil its functions in barbarous times, but rather from the inadequacy of these functions.[25] As in the early poem 'Der

Dichter, der ihn manchmal geliebt', the artist's position is seen in clear economic terms: he is a servant. In its details, this is an analysis which describes the feudal situation better than that of capitalism, but the central relationship is preserved in the abstract structure implied. From the apparently neutral admission that artists must enquire not only simply who will use their work, but also who will pay for it, the analysis continues to show that artists serve those social groups who have economic power. This service implies that the artist is a literary courtesan, an intellectual mercenary:

> Aber warum nur? so fragt er, was habe ich verbrochen
> Hab ich nicht immer getan, was verlangt wurd von denen, die zahlen? ...
> Haben wir nicht, wenn wir genügend im Magen
> Hatten, euch alles besungen, was ihr auf Erden genossen?
> Daß ihr es nochmals genösset: das Fleisch eurer Weiber!
> Trauer des Herbstes! Den Bach, und wie er durch Mondlicht geflossen...
> (GW 9, 484.)

Besides celebrating the pleasures of their masters, the artists are expected to consolidate their position by comforting those who suffer at their masters' hands (str. 8), and by attacking their opponents (str. 13). Where it was accessible to those without power, art was a placative diversion, a drug which rendered the exploited less capable of resistance:

> Wir haben die Wörter studiert und gemischt wie Drogen
> Und nur die besten und allerstärksten verwandt.
> Die sie von uns bezogen, haben sie eingesogen
> Und waren wie Lämmer in eurer Hand! (GW 9, 486.)

The decline of art occurs, as the final stanza explains, when the established social organization is in crisis. The support of the arts is no longer enough; while more drastic measures are sought, the arts are redundant. Here, the abstract, sweeping generality of the analysis is made particular, located 'im ersten Drittel des 20. Jahrhunderts', by its implicit reference to fascism, which Brecht convincingly interprets as an attempt to restore an ailing capitalism.[26] The poem addresses itself to the artists and intellectuals who were taken by surprise by fascism's suppression of intellectual freedom. The conditions under which such freedom was possible are defined by reference to the model of patronage described in the poem. When the poem was written (probably between 1927 and

1929), it was a programmatic, critical analysis of a social activity which amounted to 'Billigung' of the bourgeois world. Thomas Mann, as the 'Ballade von der Billigung der Welt' reveals, was seen as representative of this position. In the context of an open fascist dictatorship in 1934, Brecht may have hoped that his analysis would have greater force; it implies that the artist or intellectual must find a new function, and suggests that this would be achieved by the integration of opposition to fascism in their specialized activity. To adopt the terms of Walter Benjamin's argument: after its 'Ästhetisierung des politischen Lebens' fascism had no use for independent artistic enterprise. The artists' response, provided in exemplary fashion by Brecht (with *Lieder Gedichte Chöre* as a substantial witness) was the 'Politisierung der Kunst'.[27]

'Deutschland' concludes the collection. It is an elegy, a partial revision of 'Deutschland, du blondes, bleiches', conspicuously more controlled and serious, less extravagantly concerned with imagery. The poem's emotions are honest, direct: the 'bleiche Mutter' from whose house he was expelled is Brecht's reply to the rhetoric of the 'Vaterland'. Sadness mingles with anger:

> O Deutschland, bleiche Mutter!
> Wie haben deine Söhne dich zugerichtet
> Daß du unter den Völkern sitzest
> Ein Gespött oder eine Furcht! (GW 9, 488.)

This is both a summary and a challenge.

Lieder Gedichte Chöre is not simply a representative selection of Brecht's poetry, but a meticulously organized series of poems. It was shown that the basis of its organization was the development of an argument. The collection as collection is also a piece of work.[28] It is evident that many of these poems, which were produced independently of the collection, have a scope considerably broader than that defined by their position in the series. Most of them are discussed in Ulla Lerg-Kill's study, which is especially useful for its close attention to publicistic aspects of individual texts and for its analysis of their use of rhetorical devices. Precisely because the individual poems exist as texts in their own right, the principle of repetition operates beside that of development in the collection; consolidation of the argument complements its elucidation.

It is possible that the entire collection (with the exception of the more extensive 'Anhang') was intended for use as 'Agit-Prop' material at illegal meetings. The texts, in their given order, would have served as provocative introductory matter for discussion and information which could have been interposed. Many of the poems had been used in the last years of the Republic, in revues and other meetings: 'Gedicht vom unbekannten Soldaten unter dem Triumphbogen' was used in the *Berliner Requiem* of 1929, an anti-war work with music by Kurt Weill. The songs and choruses from *Die Mutter* and *Die Maßnahme* had enjoyed much more extensive use in settings by Hanns Eisler. It is likely that Brecht wished to re-establish this direct contact with his public as his only hope of any immediate influence, of contributing to anti-fascist resistance in Germany.

The collection presents a wide range of poems: from the parodied hymn to the satirical elegy in free rhythms, from the directness of the *Lobgedichte* to the obliqueness of the ironic negative example in the satirical poems. The fundamental attitude of the collection as a whole, and of its constituent texts, is didactic; it contains no poem which would serve well as a *Kampflied* or *Massenlied*. Its dominant tone is defiant optimism. The general target group has been tentatively defined above; the 'Anhang' may be seen as appealing to a wider and more disparate (if smaller) group of professional people, artists and intellectuals, or indeed, as far as it is concerned with literature especially, also as a personal appendix, a public dialogue concerning Brecht's understanding of his work.

Chapter 4

EXILE (2) 1934–1939

THE first year of Brecht's exile was a period of intense activity and almost continuous travel. Immediate products of this furious labour were *Lieder Gedichte Chöre* and the satirical novel *Dreigroschenroman* (1933–4). Not until December 1933 did Brecht move into the house he had purchased in Skovsbostrand, where he was to be based for the next five years. Although he travelled extensively throughout this period, attending international congresses, assisting in productions of his works and visiting friends, Brecht was acquainted after 1933 with the relative isolation which exile implied. The first months of his residence in Denmark offered time, and demanded reflection.

> Ausschließlich wegen der zunehmenden Unordnung
> In unseren Städten des Klassenkampfs
> Haben etliche von uns in diesen Jahren beschlossen
> Nicht mehr zu reden von Hafenstädten, Schnee auf den Dächern, Frauen
> Geruch reifer Äpfel im Keller, Empfindungen des Fleisches
> All dem, was den Menschen rund macht und menschlich
> Sondern zu reden nur mehr von der Unordnung
> Also einseitig zu werden, dürr, verstrickt in die Geschäfte
> Der Politik und das trockene 'unwürdige' Vokabular
> Der dialektischen Ökonomie
> Damit nicht dieses furchtbare gedrängte Zusammensein
> Von Schneefällen (sie sind nicht nur kalt, wir wissen's)
> Ausbeutung, verlocktem Fleisch und Klassenjustiz eine Billigung
> So vielseitiger Welt in uns erzeuge, Lust an
> Den Widersprüchen solch blutigen Lebens
> Ihr versteht. (1934, GW 9, 519.)

The poem is an elegy; but while it declares the poet's regret at the loss of breadth and complexity forced upon him by politics, it is itself able to avoid one-sidedness. A sense of human roundness is here produced, even if, as the poem suggests, it is now to be abandoned. It is characteristic of this period that the poem's reflections are retrospective; the order of priority which its programmatic sentences define had in fact been established (certainly in Brecht's work) some eight years previously. In recalling his decision, Brecht produces a prescriptive model for other writers and artists: he does not forget what the decision costs. Exile itself was a constant reminder.

In this phase of Brecht's production of poetry, the position of the *Lehrgedicht* as a central focus is consolidated. Besides the *Lehrgedicht* as theoretical exposition, there are *Chroniken*; the third subgroup, the autobiographical chronicle, is absorbed into the group of abstract theoretical poems, which employ an increasing proportion of autobiographical material. It is as if, conscious of the introversion to which exile constantly invited him, Brecht sought to avoid the danger of excessive concern for his own experiences by integrating them more rigorously and analytically into general, theoretical discourse. The strophic forms, the *Lied*, ballad, and song, occur much less frequently; an increasing realization of the distance and obstacles separating him from an audience for such 'collective' works may explain the partial inhibition of Brecht's production in this area. Nevertheless, the 'Moritat vom Reichstagsbrand' (GW 8, 408) was followed by 'Ballade vom 30. Juni' (GW 9, 520), and the earlier political songs by 'Das Saarlied' (GW 9, 542), published in *Unsere Zeit* in 1934, and widely known in the Saar. Brecht wrote two series of poems for children, in 1933-4 (GW 9, 507-14), and in 1937 (GW 9, 583-5); these were mostly songs. Two groups of sonnets were written in the same years (GW 9, 536-41 and GW 9, 608-17).

Within the dominant sphere of production, that of poetry in free rhythms, there is a tendency of approximation to the epigram. Many longer poems are sectionally constructed, so that they could conceivably be divided to form short autonomous texts.

Publication of poems continued through the medium of exile journals; it may reasonably be assumed (though it cannot be demonstrated) that their readership was extended by the circulation of duplicated copies, and indeed that they were transmitted by word of mouth. Radio transmission from Moscow and by the 'Deutscher Freiheitssender' is documented in some cases.[1]

Taking Stock

Like the poem quoted above, many others of this period record fundamental reflections, summarizing arguments and taking stock of positions. This is true of 'Der Kommunismus ist das Mittlere'

(GW 9, 503) written in 1934: replying to familiar criticisms of communism, the poem insists that what it seeks to overthrow is itself mere chaos, in contrast to which revolutionary violence appears unremarkable. More important, communism is not extreme; it demands not the maximum but the minimum necessary for humane social existence:

> Der Kommunismus ist nicht das Äußerste
> Was nur zu einem kleinen Teil verwirklicht werden kann, sondern
> Vor er nicht ganz und gar verwirklicht ist
> Gibt es keinen Zustand, der
> Selbst von einem Unempfindlichen ertragbar wäre
> Der Kommunismus ist wirklich die geringste Forderung
> Das Allernächstliegende, Mittlere, Vernünftige.

There is a sense in which much of this is repetition: for example, the poem overlaps considerably with 'Lob des Kommunismus', 'Wer sich wehrt' and 'Viele sind für die Ordnung'. This is part of Brecht's literary strategy: far from striving for perfection in his treatment of a given theme, Brecht approaches it from different sides, altering the emphasis of his argument in an experimental process. Important elements of this strategy form the theme of 'Der Gedanke in den Werken der Klassiker' (GW 9, 568):

> Nackt und ohne Behang
> Tritt er vor dich hin, ohne Scham, denn er ist
> Seiner Nützlichkeit sicher.
> Es bekümmert ihn nicht
> Daß du ihn schon kennst, ihm genügt es
> Daß du ihn vergessen hast.

The qualities ascribed to the works of Marx, Engels, and Lenin are models for literary production, which Brecht's work did not always observe: clarity and directness are sometimes subordinated to artistry and force of argument. The term 'Nützlichkeit' adopts the concept of usefulness which Brecht had introduced in his verdict on the 1927 poetry competition, and increases the emphasis on its positive prescriptive aspect. Social usefulness, specific necessity determine the spare, undecorated language of the typical *Lehrgedicht,* in which literary art is apparent, but in syntax, shape, and pattern, rather than in lexis, colour.

'Er spricht/ Mit der Grobheit der Größe' recalls the *Lesebuch* poem 'Wenn ich mit dir rede' which Brecht himself took up once again (probably in the late thirties) and placed in the context of *Me-ti* under the new title 'Me-tis Strenge' (GW 12, 498). Marxist thought is partisan, but impersonal, because of the general scale on which it operates. Brecht later compared this lack of politeness, this crudity of focus, with the scientific problem described by Planck and Heisenberg:

aus DETERMINISMUS ODER INDETERMINISMUS (1938) von PLANCK: '... es ist unmöglich, das innere eines körpers zu sondieren, wenn die sonde größer ist als der ganze körper'.
auch der historische materialismus weist diese 'unschärfe' in bezug auf das individuum auf. (AJ 26.3.42.)

The basis of this partisanship is located in necessity; in the specific imperative which confronts those whom Brecht, like the classical writers of Marxism, addresses: the proletariat.

Sein Hörer ist das Elend, das keine Zeit hat.
Kälte und Hunger wachen
Über die Aufmerksamkeit der Hörer. Die geringste Unaufmerksamkeit
Verurteilt sie zum sofortigen Untergang. (GW 9, 568.)

In the final seven lines of the poem there is a transition from concern for the needs of the listeners to insistence that everything depends on precisely this desperate audience, including Marxist thought. The sovereignty of Marxism itself is derived from recognition of the urgency of its work and of its total dependence on its audience: 'Tritt er aber so herrisch auf/ So zeigt er doch, daß er ohne seine Hörer nichts ist' (GW 9, 569). This in the context of a poem which relies largely on provocative exaggeration is certainly partly a conceit, an invitation to the proletariat to take pity, and listen to what Marxism has to say. At the same time it is a hard theoretical insight, relevant to political history in general and to Brecht's work in particular. He too is engaged in the propagation of Marxist thought and is ultimately dependent on an audience: 'keine frage, keine antwort'. This concern for the relationship between producer and recipient was anticipated in 'Über die Bauart langdauernder Werke', where, as here, it was defined as a reciprocal relationship. The final lines of 'Der Gedanke in den Werken der Klassiker' recall the earlier 'Wer aber ist die Partei?' in their declaration that the individual does not simply stand in relation to a superior authority, that the proletariat is not the errand-boy of historical materialism, but its employer and improver:

> Ja, von ihnen nicht belehrt
> Den gestern noch Unwissenden
> Verlöre er schnell seine Kraft und verkäme eilig.[2]

This, written in 1936, is not a private poem. Nevertheless, it has, as a *Lehrgedicht*, more private aspects which become clear when the text is considered in relation to Brecht's situation and to contemporary works. The conception of literature as dialogue, the emphasis on the importance of the work of reception, become critical under the conditions of exile. Brecht, far from trying to exclude this area of experience, exploits it persistently, making his difficulties as an author symptomatic, and thereby productive. Exile is a determinant theme in Brecht's poetry at this time.

'Daß er ohne seine Hörer nichts ist'

This theme, potential isolation, the interruption of all communication, which the reduced access of exile suggested, recurs frequently. 'Das Neujahr der Verfolgten' (GW 9, 494) and 'Die Auswanderung der Dichter' (GW 9, 495) describe the facts of exile and place Brecht in a long tradition of exiled poets, of great men fallen on hard times.

> Ich las ein unbeschriebenes Blatt
> Und schrieb in ein bedrucktes Buch
> Da bekam ich in meiner Kerkerstatt
> Sehr erlauchten Besuch.   (GW 9, 494.)

This, the second strophe of 'Das Neujahr der Verfolgten' (1933), makes the sense of disjunction, of isolation and imprisonment clear; the entire poem is a dream in which figures of history appear, ghostlike, and as fugitives. This imaginative, mythologizing approach may have been a defence against despair, its bold comparisons are gestures of defiant self-assertion. 'Im Überfluß' (GW 9, 496) employs the same mode in its portrayal of exile as purification, as the path to knowledge. 'Die Auswanderung der Dichter' is a more sober and modest poem, content to refer to literary tradition:

Den François Villon suchte nicht nur die Muse
Sondern auch die Polizei.
'Der Geliebte' gennant
Ging Lukrez in die Verbannung
So Heine, und so auch floh
Brecht unter das dänische Strohdach. (GW 9, 495.)

'Exil' (GW 9, 555) of 1935 is more critical and pessimistic; it considers the faults of the exiles, their inadequate responses to their situation:

> Da sie keine Gegenwart haben
> Suchen sie sich Dauer zu verleihen ...
> Mit ihren Vorfahren
> Haben sie mehr Verbindung als mit ihren Zeitgenossen.

The poem lists the pitfalls which threaten political exiles; there is no reason to suppose that Brecht considered himself exempt from such criticism, which often seems derived from reflection on his own case. In 'Über das Lehren ohne Schüler' (GW 9, 556) for example.

> Dort spricht der, dem niemand zuhört:
> Er spricht zu laut
> Er wiederholt sich
> Er sagt Falsches:
> Er wird nicht verbessert. (1935, GW 9, 557.)

Dialogue continually risks decay into soliloquy, condemning the exile to isolation and innocuous gesturing. Exile was a time between times, devoid of its own reality. Consciousness of this crisis was inescapable and was based, as the poems imply, not only on the greatly increased problems of production and transmission or distribution, but more seriously and painfully, on those of reception. If Brecht had written (in the 'Wiegenlieder' of 1932) that the hope of the proletariat rested only with Marx and Lenin, the general correctness of his analysis had been eclipsed by the skilful manipulation of these hopes by National Socialism. The poem was published in 1934, in *Lieder Gedichte Chöre*, and again in 1935 in a camouflaged edition, specifically for circulation in Germany; but if Brecht had hoped, with the KPD, that German fascism would soon be bankrupt, disillusion on his part was perhaps swifter than in the case of the party. In 1934 *Dreigroschenroman* was published;

in its attention to the problems of the petty bourgeoisie, it creates the basis for an understanding of National Socialism as a mass movement, an understanding which did not penetrate to the KPD in the mid thirties. At the same time, the movement appealed to the proletariat, with its simple promise of employment; the hopes of the proletariat became fatal. Recognition of this situation, which clearly also meant the partial loss of Brecht's audience, lies behind another aspect of the satirical novel: its rejection of hope—Fewkoombey's dream begins:

Nach Jahren des Elends kam der Tag des Triumphes. Die Massen erhoben sich, schüttelten endlich ihre Peiniger ab, entledigten sich in einem einzigen Aufwaschen ihrer Vertröster, vielleicht der furchtbarsten Feinde, die sie hatten, gaben alle Hoffnung endgültig auf und erkämpften den Sieg. (GW 13, 1152.)

Lack of hope accelerates what hope itself postpones: the revolution. Increasingly, from the mid thirties onward, Brecht's own work represents a recurring act of defiance, scorning the deceptions of hope, rescuing productive labour from despair.

Fünf Schwierigkeiten beim Schreiben der Wahrheit (GW 18, 222–39), written in 1934–5, offers a classic summary of Brecht's attitude in the precise formulations of its challenging propagandistic thesis:

wir können die Wahrheit über barbarische Zustände nicht erforschen, ohne an die zu denken, welche darunter leiden, und während wir, immerfort jede Anwandlung von Feigheit abschüttelnd, die wahren Zusammenhänge im Hinblick auf die suchen, die bereit sind, ihre Kenntnis zu benützen, müssen wir auch noch daran denken, ihnen die Wahrheit so zu reichen, daß sie eine Waffe in ihren Händen sein kann, und zugleich so listig, daß diese Überreichung nicht vom Feind entdeckt und verhindert werden kann.[3] (GW 18, 239.)

The essay identifies the 'Ton der Wahrheit' as polemic ('etwas Kriegerisches', GW 18, 230); literary technique is understood as a tactical problem (style may be the camouflage which fools the censor). More generally, aesthetic elements may contribute to the effectiveness of the literary work as argument: 'der große Lukrez betont ausdrücklich, daß er sich für die Verbreitung des epikureischen Atheismus viel von der Schönheit seiner Verse verspreche' (GW 18, 233). This, as an examination of the early experimental poems was able to show, was a point of view highly relevant to Brecht's own practice. Other propositions are equally illuminating; the acute awareness of the problem of reception which Brecht had acquired since the early thirties is here made public:

ich will hier nur hervorheben, daß aus dem 'jemandem schreiben' ein 'schreiben' geworden ist. Die Wahrheit aber kann man nicht eben schreiben; man muß sie durchaus *jemandem* schreiben, der damit etwas anfangen kann. (GW 18, 230.)

By far the longest section of the essay is the fifth, that devoted to 'Die List, die Wahrheit unter vielen zu verbreiten'. Brecht's polemic literary efforts were aimed at the destruction of ideology; this is achieved by stripping words of their 'faule Mystik' (GW 18, 231), referring them to material fact ('Volk' is to be read as 'Bevölkerung', for example, which dissolves its spurious dignity and prevents it being taken for granted). Irony has a dual function which makes it doubly valuable to Brecht's production; besides being too mobile and subtle to be easy prey for censorship, it demands, even from its intended readers, especially careful attention and deliberate reflection. As Brecht notes (placing his observation in italics): '*die Propaganda für das Denken, auf welchem Gebiet sie immer erfolgt, ist der Sache der Unterdrückten nützlich*' (GW 18, 235). Brecht defines the special mode of thought which he considers of most relevance to the struggle of the proletariat:

eine Betrachtungsweise, die das Vergängliche besonders hervorhebt, ist ein gutes Mittel, die Unterdrückten zu ermutigen. Auch, daß in jedem Ding und in jedem Zustand ein Widerspruch sich meldet und wächst, ist etwas, was den Siegern entgegengehalten werden muß. (GW 18, 237.)

The Dialectics of Defiance

The theoretical method thus described is the dialectic, the 'Lehre vom Fluß der Dinge'. One of its principal applications in Brecht's work is the treatment of defeat as an interruption of the struggle, but not its conclusion. *Die Horatier und die Kuriatier* (1934), subtitled 'Ein Lehrstück über Dialektik', is devoted to this theme, which was also anticipated in 'Lob der Dialektik'.

'In finsteren Zeiten' (GW 9, 587), written in 1937, registers, in a series of antitheses, the simple practical component of this attitude of defiance. Exile was a consequence of defeat; but it was the writer's task to ensure that this was not the last word. Silence was emphatically not an adequate response. 'Zitat' (GW 9, 601), a contemporary poem, defines Brecht's position more closely:

> Wie soll ich unsterbliche Werke schreiben, wenn ich nicht berühmt bin?
> Wie soll ich antworten, wenn ich nicht gefragt werde?
> Warum soll ich Zeit verlieren über Versen, wenn die Zeit sie verliert?
> Ich schreibe meine Vorschläge in einer haltbaren Sprache
> Weil ich fürchte, es dauert lange, bis sie ausgeführt sind.

It is clear that the conditions described in 'Über die Bauart langdauernder Werke' are here fulfilled: 'Zitat' consciously echoes the earlier poem, but having adopted the long-term view, it is silent on the question raised in the earlier text, concerning the demands of the present. This question is left to other poems to answer. Though the difficulties of the present situation are frankly acknowledged, the poem refuses to admit the possibility of final defeat.

The poetry of defiance is a strand which reaches back into the pre-exile period, to the early *Lehrgedichte*; it surfaces throughout the years of exile, in admonitory poems:

> Unsere Niederlagen nämlich
> Beweisen nichts, als daß wir zu
> Wenige sind
> Die gegen die Gemeinheit kämpfen.
>
> ('Gegen die Objektiven', GW 9, 493.)

'Was nützt die Güte' (GW 9, 553), also written in 1935, proceeds from the assertion that good will and kind words, like 'objectivity' are valueless unless transformed into action. There is no abstract virtue outside the struggle:

> Was nützt die Güte
> Wenn die Gütigen sogleich erschlagen werden, oder es werden erschlagen
> Die, zu denen sie gütig sind?

Similarly, in 'Wer zu Hause bleibt, wenn der Kampf beginnt' (GW 9, 503) it is insisted that there is no position of safe impartiality: 'Denn/ Es wird kämpfen für die Sache des Feinds/ Wer für seine eigene Sache nicht gekämpft hat.' In a perspective which transcends the exigencies of the immediate context, 'Was nützt die Güte' makes kindness, freedom, and reason relative. However necessary they may be to the revolutionary struggle, they do not represent absolute categories, and it is the purpose of that struggle to make them superfluous:

> Anstatt nur gütig zu sein, bemüht euch
> Einen Zustand zu schaffen, der die Güte ermöglicht, und besser:
> Sie überflüssig macht! (GW 9, 553.)

This is a major theme in Brecht's mature work. In the 'Unordnung' of modern capitalism, such virtues, and indeed all human qualities, are inappropriate and dangerous to those who possess them: *Die Ausnahme und die Regel, Der gute Mensch von Sezuan* and *Der Kaukasische Kreidekreis* all demonstrate this. *Leben des Galilei*, in which the protagonist is likewise the victim of his own productivity, illuminates the point from a different side, in Galileo's exclamation: 'unglücklich das Land, das Helden nötig hat' (GW 3, 1329). In the later *Flüchtlingsgespräche*, virtue is defined as a deficiency disease.

As the very large number of theoretical poems written in these years suggests, exile was conducive to the learning of abstract lessons, rather than to direct polemic intervention. 'Auf einen Emigranten' conveys, in its short angry sentences, the difficulty of accepting this role:

> Nützlich
> War er. Gefährlich
> Ist er nicht mehr. Kaum wird er es werden ...
> Der die Sprache beherrschte
> Sucht die Wörter zusammen, sich zu entschuldigen. Selbst die
>   Dummheiten
> Muß er hier lernen erst. In solcher Lage
> Ist es Zeit, zu wissen, daß Lernen nützlich ist. (GW 9, 622.)

This poem remains a fragment, perhaps because the brave proposition of the final lines quoted is outweighed by the predominantly negative view given in the preceding sentence. In the later poem 'Bericht über einen Gescheiterten' (GW 9, 623), the substance of 'Auf einen Emigranten' is compressed into the last words of the title, while the remaining text demonstrates the usefulness of learning. This poem is a fictional *Chronik*; its plot is a variation on the Robinson Crusoe theme. The shipwrecked man arrives on the island as if it had been his destination; accepting the unalterable facts, he is prepared to deal with the next practical challenge.

> Ich glaube fast: uns erblickend
> Die zur Hilfe herangeeilt waren
> Fühlte er sogleich Mitleid mit uns.

The wit of paradox is an appropriate mode for the exposition of the dialectic, which is the poem's central function. The terms of the dialectic are condensed in the dual significance of the title: 'gescheitert' means shipwrecked, but also failed. The first sense is clearly present on the explicit level of narrative in the poem, but the text also operates parabolically and here the general meaning, failure, is relevant. This complex title contains the argument of the poem: Brecht plays on the tension between these two levels of meaning, indicating that, in spite of their verbal proximity, an instance of failure, such as a shipwreck, and final defeat are not identical.

The shipwrecked man has learnt from his experiences, and has much to teach:

> Aus den Erfahrungen seines Schiffbruchs
> Lehrte er uns das Segeln. Selbst Mut
> Brachte er uns bei. Von den stürmischen Gewässern
> Sprach er mit großer Achtung, wohl
> Da sie einen Mann wie ihn besiegt hatten. Freilich
> Hatten sie dabei viel von ihren Tricks verraten.   (GW 9, 623.)

The interdependent imperatives of survival and learning meet in practice in the exercise of this defiant cunning. The force of the poem is derived from its considerable elegance of language and thought, but also significantly from the way in which the experience of exile is made typical, accessible to critical thought, and ultimately productive. The epigrammatic conclusion of 'Der Lernende' (GW 9, 558) would serve as a motto for this strand of poetry:

> Die Narben schmerzen
> In der kalten Zeit.
> Aber ich sagte oft: nur das Grab
> Lehrt mich nichts mehr.

The dialectic offers a way of extracting defiance from defeat; once continued action has been decided upon, it is again the dialectic which regulates the specific mode of action. The general lesson of defeat is crystallized in an acutely critical attitude, which demands reappraisal of each step in any argument or plan. This reflective attitude is embodied in the figure of 'Der Zweifler' in the poem of that name. Consulted after the conclusion of a piece of work, he asks:

> Ist alles belegbar?
> Durch Erfahrung? Durch welche? Aber vor allem
> Immer wieder vor allem andern: Wie handelt man
> Wenn man euch glaubt, was ihr sagt? Vor allem: Wie handelt man?
>
> (GW 9, 588)

The ability to learn means that defeat can be made to produce more than simply despair; doubt itself, as the poem insists, is a positive factor in the determination of the appropriate course of action, to the ultimate force of which it thus contributes.

Doubt is also the subject of another poem of the period, the ode of 1939, 'Lob des Zweifels' (GW 9, 626). The critical, testing attitude exemplified in the questions of 'Der Zweifler' is not an invention of Brecht's, but a borrowing from scientific method. It is thus intimately connected with the origins of Marxism, and with its modern reception by Brecht and others. Karl Korsch, who in spite of all controversy concerning details is recognized as an important collaborator and friend of Brecht's, stated in 1934: 'Marxismus ist nicht positiv, sondern kritisch'.[4] The scientific connections of this theme are apparent when 'Lob des Zweifels' is placed in the context of the first version of *Leben des Galilei*, written in late 1938. In the drama, the considerable social significance of the critical attitude is examined at one of its points of origin.

The poem itself connects doubt to the central method of Marxist thought, the dialectic; as 'Lob der Dialektik' had announced, 'Das Sichere ist nicht sicher': 'Lest die Geschichte und seht/ In wilder Flucht die unbesieglichen Heere' (GW 9, 626). For all its controlled modesty this invitation displays a confident equanimity which is remarkable; Brecht had no illusions about the imminent war, nor about the position of strength from which the fascist regime was able to begin it. If these lines have specific contemporary relevance, the poem as a whole does not omit to define the general revolutionary perspective:

> Schönster aller Zweifel aber
> Wenn die verzagten Geschwächten den Kopf heben und

> An die Stärke ihrer Unterdrücker
> Nicht mehr glauben! (GW 9, 626.)

As in 'Der Zweifler', doubt has a positive function in the definition of action; it must inform, but not inhibit.

> Freilich, wenn ihr den Zweifel lobt
> So lobt nicht
> Das Zweifeln, das ein Verzweifeln ist! (GW 9, 628)

The final section of the poem is reminiscent of 'Lob der Partei' in its rejection of absolute authority. Leadership, it implies, depends on responsiveness to criticism, not on the ability to suppress it.

The poems examined so far belong to the category of the *Lehrgedicht*; they are poems of abstract theoretical exposition. In general, these poems were not written for immediate publication and may be understood as contributions to a theoretical debate which had been indefinitely postponed, and whose practical relevance was not foreseeable: 'Ich schreibe meine Vorschläge in einer haltbaren Sprache/ Weil ich fürchte, es dauert lange, bis sie ausgeführt sind' (GW 9, 601). Brecht's commitment to the long-term perspective of 'Über die Bauart langdauernder Werke' is very clear: but that poem is careful to warn against the danger of an attitude of confident expectation: 'Wer sich an die Ungeborenen wendet/ Tut oft nichts für die Geburt' (GW 8, 389). Writing for the future thus clearly demands some form of assurance that the envisaged future will arrive: in practice, that the writer should work to that end. This leads, finally, to the adoption of a dual perspective: the present-for-the-future complements the future itself as an orientation. Brecht, in writing the *Lehrgedichte,* is not simply taking refuge in theory; the volume of production in this area is adequately explained by the extreme difficulty of direct literary participation. Nevertheless, Brecht was repeatedly able to defy these obstacles, thus putting into practice his frequently declared conviction that the most urgent immediate concern was: 'der umfassende, mit allen Mitteln geführte unermüdliche Kampf gegen den Faschismus auf breitester Grundlage' (GW 18, 251).

The *Lehrgedichte* are accompanied by poems of more direct and immediate reference, by the *Chroniken*. That the theoretical poems are not exclusively governed by the aspect of postponement is, however, indicated by the choice of texts for publication in *Svendborger Gedichte,* and by poems like 'Gebt keinen euresgleichen auf' (GW 9, 570). This, though it is certainly a general theoretical poem, has a specific contemporary meaning in the context of the united front strategy which Brecht supported. The dual orientation is manifested not only in the two principal strands of poetry in this period, but in many individual texts; the *Chroniken*, though inviting interpretation as immediate appeals, equally have the force of models from which it is possible to generalize. The *Chronik*, as was insisted above, is defined as a species of didactic poetry, and is related to the theoretical *Lehrgedicht*. A rather later note of Brecht's emphasizes the importance of this quality of perspective within individual texts; here again the reflections of 'Über die Bauart langdauernder Werke' are taken up:

werken eine lange dauer verleihen zu wollen, zunächst nur eine'natürliche' bestrebung, wird ernsthafter, wenn ein schreiber grund zu der pessimistischen annahme zu haben glaubt, seine ideen ... könnten eine sehr lange zeit brauchen, um sich durchzusetzen. die maßnahmen, die man übrigens in dieser richtung hin trifft, müssen die aktuelle wirkung eines werks keineswegs beeinträchtigen. (AJ, 24.4.41.)

Considerable emphasis has been placed on the poetry as argument; it is also literary art, and a number of poems of this period bear witness to Brecht's concern for technique and aesthetic quality in their explicit treatment of theoretical questions. Brecht's cultivation of an economical, but effective artistry in practice has been demonstrated above. The reference to Lucretius in *Fünf Schwierigkeiten beim Schreiben der Wahrheit* suggested that aesthetic quality should be seen, not as an incidental addition to the primary function of exposition, but as integral to the writer's purpose; far from being autotelic, it contributes to the effectiveness of argument. 'Der Zweifler' defines the relationship between artistry and argument as one based on mutuality:

Ich zweifle, ob
Die Arbeit gelungen ist, die eure Tage verschlungen hat.
Ob was ihr gesagt, auch schlechter gesagt, noch für einige Wert hätte.
Ob ihr es aber gut gesagt, und euch nicht etwa
Auf die Wahrheit verlassen habt dessen, was ihr gesagt habt.
                                                                (GW 9, 588.)

This literary principle clearly matches Brecht's work as a poet; and, theoretically, there is no question of Brecht's advocating crude functionalism—he is committed to literary excellence. In the context of the prolonged debates on questions of tradition and experimentation in literature which took place in the late thirties, Brecht found it necessary to defend his position, both against the charge of self-indulgent, decadent experimental writing (in the essay *Über reimlose Lyrik mit unregelmäßigen Rhythmen)*, and against that of an excessive interest in literary values, in tradition.[5] 'Sonett vom Erbe' provides an apologia in reply to this claim:

> Als sie mich sahn aus alten Büchern schreiben
> Saßen sie traurig mürrisch bei mir, die Gewehre
> Auf ihren Knien und folgten meinem Treiben:
> Gehst du bei unsern Feinden in die Lehre?
> Ich sagte: Ja. Sie wissen, wie man schreibt.[6] (GW 9, 615.)

'Da das Instrument verstimmt ist' (GW 9, 624) introduces a dual system of governing factors; recognizing that, in such barbarous times, the arts have fallen into disrepute, the poem concludes that 'einige neue Griffe' are required. Its following sections imply that artistic experiment must avoid mere decorativeness ('wäre nicht auch Dummes klug zu sagen') on one hand, and condescending artlessness on the other ('Das Volk/ Ist nicht tümlich'). It is recommended that literary technique should serve the oppressed, by conveying the truth:

> Versschreiber, bedenkt
> Daß der Unterdrückten sehr viele sind:
> Da auch sie zahlen
> Wenngleich wenig, lohnt es doch
> Die Wahrheit zu schreiben. (GW 9, 624–5.)

This constitutes at least a partial reply to the critical questions posed in 'Lied der preiswerten Lyriker': everything depends on the writer's audience, but the writer in turn may select his audience (in terms of intention and design at least), and the appropriate mode of addressing it. Finally, the major comprehensive statement of Brecht's general conception of literature is 'Die Literatur wird durchforscht werden' of 1939 (GW 9, 740). The poem evokes a historical perspective to predict that literature will find critical readers in future generations (after the revolution); mere excellence will be viewed with suspicion:

> Aber in jener Zeit werden gepriesen werden
> Die auf dem nackten Boden saßen, zu schreiben

> Die unter den Niedrigen saßen
> Die bei den Kämpfern saßen. (GW 9, 740.)

The poem proceeds to place artistic quality firmly in the context of the social struggle:

> Die von den Leiden der Niedrigen berichteten
> Die von den Taten der Kämpfer berichteten
> Kunstvoll. In der edlen Sprache
> Vordem reserviert
> Der Verherrlichung der Könige. (GW 9, 741.)

In the intellectual, as in the material sphere, an act of appropriation is demanded.[7] The penultimate section of the poem considers the prospect of reception, of active appropriation by the proletariat, with wishful confidence. It is clear from these poems that the limitations imposed on his art by politics, the one-sidedness regretted by Brecht in 'Ausschließlich wegen der zunehmenden Unordnung' did not signify lack of attention to aesthetic quality. Only in the question of theme is there evidence of the strict order of priority established in that poem; and this recognition must itself be modified by reference to the peripheral, but important area of production which includes the sonnets. Here the poet devotes undivided attention to 'Empfindungen des Fleisches/ All dem, was den Menschen rund macht und menschlich'.[8]

Botschaften

> Und die Botschaft, meine Lieben
> Billig ist sie nicht gewesen!
> Vor die Meinung sie geschrieben
> Hat der Zweifel sie gelesen. (GW 9, 745.)

The *Chroniken* are, in their immediate aspect, messages; propaganda. They record specific contemporary events from the viewpoint of the anti-fascist struggle. These poems describe exemplary instances of solidarity in opposition to the regime ('Rapport von Deutschland', GW 9, 545), above all in the form of individual, but public action: 'Die Käuferin' (GW 9, 496), 'Was zersetzt' (GW 9, 497), 'Die sechzehnjährige Weißnäherin Emma Ries vor dem Untersuchungsrichter' (GW 9, 546) and 'Der letzte Wunsch' (GW 9, 547). Two poems, 'Die Macht der Arbeiter' (GW 9, 557) and 'Kantate erster Mai' (GW 9, 563), refer to solidarity outside the German context. The *Chroniken* recognize that there is little individuals can do; they nonetheless insist that even when collective organization is not possible, individual action must not be abandoned. 'Die Käuferin' demonstrates that even the weakest victims of the regime need not remain passive:

> Ich sagte mir:
> Wenn wir alle, die nichts haben
> Nicht mehr erscheinen, wo das Essen ausliegt
> Könnte man meinen, wir brauchten nichts
> Aber wenn wir kommen und nichts kaufen können
> Weiß man Bescheid. (GW 9, 497.)

This, like the other cases recorded in these *Chroniken*, is only a gesture: significant but powerless. These poems, which were probably based on material collected from newspapers and pamphlets, all belong to the first three years of exile; by the mid thirties it was clear that the regime had been able to consolidate its position sufficiently to make resistance within Germany a hopeless endeavour. Brecht's own awareness of this situation is indicated by the fact that the poems which record active opposition are supplemented (and ultimately outnumbered) by those which themselves attack the regime satirically. 'Tödliche Verwirrung' (GW 9, 498) and 'Stärke des dritten Reiches' (GW 9, 549) are examples of this satirical strand, as is 'Über den enthaltsamen Kanzler' (GW 9, 602).

In the satirical mode, between the polarities of gentle, disingenuous elegance, and the destructive brilliance of anger openly expressed, Brecht continues a major creative line of his poetry, from 'Legende vom toten Soldaten' to the 'Hitler-Choräle':

> Viele rühmten am Anfang die Stärke der neuen Regierung
> Taten folgten den Worten; Morde der Drohung. (GW 9, 549.)

The determination to write, to reach his public, to continue the struggle with all means, including literary art, is expressed in the third and last collection of poems made and published by Brecht himself.

Svendborger Gedichte

The collection appeared in mid 1939, published in London, by Wieland Herzfelde's Malik-Verlag, in an edition of a little over one thousand. Planned from 1937 onward as the final section of the volume of Brecht's *Gesammelte Werke* (1938) devoted to poetry, this was conceived as a definitive collection of poems written since the publication of *Lieder Gedichte Chöre*.[9] The first section is headed 'Deutsche Kriegsfibel'; it contains a series of epigrams. The epigram represents, not an autonomous strand in Brecht's work, but part of the development of poetry in free rhythms. Elisabeth Hauptmann notes (GW 10 Anmerkungen 27) that Brecht's interest in the epigram is an early one, and in its origins not restricted to free rhythms; early epigrams include: 'Auch der Himmel' (GW 8, 89), written in 1920; 'Der Nachgeborene' (GW 8, 99), probably of 1922; 'Sintflut' (GW 8, 147) and 'Und wenn wir's überlegen' (GW 8, 159), both of 1926. Nevertheless, the epigram only becomes a major part of Brecht's work during the later thirties. The close connection between the epigrams and the poetry in free rhythms is evident, for example, in the 'Dankgedicht an Mari Hold' (GW 9, 527): after a long narrative and descriptive passage, the poem ends with an epigrammatic envoi, an abstraction from the particular case described:

> Der Nützliche ist immer in Gefahr
> Allzu viele brauchen ihn.
> Wohl ihm, der der Gefahr entrinnt
> Nützlich bleibend.

Similarly, 'Seht ihr nicht, daß ihr zu viele seid?' (GW 9, 524), like the first poem of the 'Deutsche Kriegsfibel' section, is constructed of a set of line-groups, each of which is potentially autonomous, but which are integrated into a single argument. This poem, written in the mid thirties, is one of the earliest direct antecedents of the 'Deutsche Kriegsfibel', and anticipates the latter's critical attitude towards the fascist solution to the problem of unemployment:

> Viele bereiten jetzt den Krieg vor
> So sind sie von der Straße
> Aber da sind immer noch viele, die zu viel sind.
>
> Im Kreig
> Werden sie beschäftigt werden.
> Nach dem Krieg
> Werden sie nicht mehr da sein.

This is the 'volle Welt' motif of the *Lesebuch* made clear and direct in its reference.

The epigram is the result of careful excision; in its pointed economy and wit it is also the continuation, through more disciplined application, of the ironic mode of the early poetry. The epigram's concentration of material tends to give more prominence to figures of thought than the more extensive texts. This is not to say that the epigram is purely analytical or reductive in approach; Brecht's mastery of the technique is such that he attains a relaxed and reflective manner even within these confines. The second section of 'Bei den Hochgestellten', for example, is elegiac in tone. Walter Benjamin identifies the style of these poems as 'lapidar', and Brecht had himself expressed his approval of the concise polished manner appropriate to inscriptions in stone:

> Wenn sie der Steinmetz nach den Wörtern fragt
> Dann werden sie ihm nur die besten schreiben:
> Sie sehn, 's ist mühsam, sie in Stein zu treiben.
>
> ('Vorschlag, die Architektur mit der Lyrik zu verbinden',
> 1935, GW 9, 552.)

Characteristically, Benjamin defines the situation of the epigrams in terms of a paradox: 'der Dichter belehnt mit dem Horazischen aere perennius das, was, dem Regen und den Agenten der Gestapo preisgegeben, ein Proletarier mit Kreide an eine Wand warf'.[10] The elegance of the paradox is matched by its accuracy: these poems are derived from the political *Volksmund*, the chalked slogan, but they transform such utterances into specifically literary texts. The slogan's qualities of brevity and attack are enhanced in the more ordered and artificial epigram, which is built to last. Durability depends partly on the fact that these are well-made poems, partly on the quality retained from the slogan, of being easily memorized and transmitted. The function of these poems should not, however, be seen in their potential for outlasting the catastrophic situation in which they were produced; however effective they appear as documents for posterity, they constitute, in their immediate context, an attempt to continue the struggle by extending its basis: the anti-fascist gestures of the proletariat are adopted (or anticipated) and endowed with the emphasis of artistry.[11]

'Deutsche Kriegsfibel': the title underlines the didactic function of the poems which it introduces. The lessons imparted are connected by the destruction of ideology which they all effect; they extend the line of attack selected in the 'Hitler-Choräle'. These classically organized, lexically spare poems are small-scale models of critical thought:

> Der Anstreicher spricht von kommenden großen Zeiten.
> Die Wälder wachsen noch.
> Die Äcker tragen noch.
> Die Städte stehen noch.
> Die Menschen atmen noch. (GW 9, 634.)

Irony supplies a minute amount of extra weight, but sufficient to bring about the collapse of illusion; however loudly the regime's leaders denied their interest in war, their massive expansion of war industry was a louder contradiction. Brecht, following the mode of operation suggested in *Fünf Schwierigkeiten beim Schreiben der Wahrheit*, makes this contradiction vocal, thereby effecting what the title of another essay termed 'Die Wiederherstellung der Wahrheit'.[12] The regime's lies are unmasked and corrected. In the example quoted above, the collision of the first line with the following four is made all the more powerful by the absolute simplicity of language; but the poem is not direct: it exploits the sense of threat generated by the four reticent statements: today the cities still stand—and tomorrow? The 'große Zeiten' of Hitler's promises, it is implied, will be measured only by the extent of the destruction they involve.

'Die Oberen sagen' proceeds from the same idea to relate the impending war to the 'peace' in which it is planned:

> Die Oberen sagen: Friede und Krieg
> Sind aus verschiedenem Stoff.
> Aber ihr Friede und ihr Krieg
> Sind wie Wind und Sturm.
>
> Der Krieg wächst aus ihrem Frieden
> Wie der Sohn aus der Mutter
> Er tragt
> Ihre schrecklichen Züge
>
> Ihr Krieg tötet
> Was ihr Friede
> Übriggelassen hat. (GW 9, 635.)

Here again a longer text is constructed from what could be a series of epigrams. The devastating logic compressed into the final sentence reminds the reader that war is the continuation of the class struggle by other means; Brecht was concerned to damage the ideological mechanism of nationalism, which assisted in the neutralization of opposition to the regime. This is the basis of 'Der Krieg, der kommen wird' (GW 9, 637) and 'Wenn es zum Marschieren kommt' (GW 9, 638), which insists that the only allegiance of the proletariat is to its real interests: these are not identical with those of the regime: 'Der da vom Feind spricht/ Ist selber der Feind'. The final text makes this completely explicit: 'Wenn der Trommler seinen Krieg beginnt/ Sollt ihr euren Krieg fortführen' (GW 9, 639).

The immediate audience is thus clearly defined as the proletariat ('Mann mit der zerschlissenen Jacke'); the entire section relies on a duality simply expressed in the opposition 'die Oberen': 'die Niedrigen', which is understood even when not directly referred to. In these poems, Brecht appears to maintain the position denoted by the 'Einheitsfront' in stressing the primary importance of material interests; the political alliance from above which the later 'Volksfront' policy envisaged is seen as an unreliable base from which to resist.

The poems articulate suspicions and doubts accessible to the proletariat; they present models for critical argument as the theoretical basis for resistance. Their critical operation is that of the dialectic: admission is followed by qualification. Recognizing that expansion of armaments production has allowed a decline in unemployment, Brecht modifies this argument for fascism by noting that it did not mean a dramatic rise in the workers' standard of living:

> Der Arbeitslose hat gehungert. Nun
> Hungert der Arbeitende.
> Die Hände, die im Schoße lagen, rühren sich wieder:
> Sie drehen Granaten.[13]   (GW 9, 634.)

Having isolated the underlying economic factors, Brecht extends his attack on Nazi ideology by producing a further contradiction: the workers fortunate enough to find employment were producing, not goods for consumption, but means of destruction, which, moreover, above all were the means of their own destruction. As *Die drei Soldaten* had declared: 'Denn das Giftgas, wie man's nimmt/ Ist immer für Proletarier bestimmt' (GW 8, 357).

The strength of these poems is their simplicity, a quality which is the result of careful work; it is strikingly illustrated by two poems not included in *Svendborger Gedichte* (they do, however, belong to the group of poems from which the 'Deutsche Kriegsfibel' section was selected, and are included in the *Gesammelte Werke* as 'Deutsche Kriegsfibel II'):

> Wozu Märkte erobern für die Waren
> Welche die Arbeiter herstellen?
> Die Arbeiter
> Würden sie gerne übernehmen. (GW 9, 736.)

This is the simplicity which Brecht had attributed to communism: 'das Einfache, das schwer zu machen ist'. It implies sweeping aside the entire complex of ideology to recognize that fascism solves Germany's economic and social problems within what Brecht, borrowing the term from theoretical physics, described as the 'capitalist field'.[14] Only in capitalism is there a lack of effective demand from the producers, 'over-production' which turns to foreign markets, prepared to conquer them militarily if necessary. The poem opens a new, communist perspective on this situation, revealing a solution of concise directness, based on material fact. The legal category of property, and its accompanying economic interest (profit), stand between the proletariat and the products capable of fulfilling its, and mankind's needs. None of this is mentioned explicitly in the text, but is nonetheless made conspicuous by it: the poem demands to know why its simple solution is not already in practice. The line of enquiry thus initiated also produces a materialistic argument against any objectivist belief in historical necessity; the historical field is conceived as one in which real political forces engage in conflict on the basis of opposing interests.[15] This theoretical richness is impressive in a text of such small dimensions.

> Es ist Nacht
> Die Ehepaare
> Legen sich in die Betten. Die jungen Frauen
> Werden Waisen gebären. (GW 9, 735.)

This too is a poem of sovereign simplicity; its force, at once rational and emotional, is derived from the sudden transition of the final lines. The domestic idyll becomes an urgent and agonized warning.[16]

The second section of *Svendborger Gedichte* collects songs and ballads, including songs for children. It is introduced by an epigraph formulating the determination to continue, even in such dark times, to write appropriate poetry: 'Da wird auch gesungen werden./ Von den finsteren Zeiten' (GW 9, 641). The first poem of the section, 'Deutsches Lied', is a bridging poem, connecting the 'Deutsche Kriegsfibel' with the songs which follow; it employs the familiar gesture of correction. Public claims made by the leaders of the regime are referred to the real experience of the 'kleiner Mann', and are shown to be inadequate lies. The ballads 'Von der "Judenhure" Marie Sanders' and 'Von den Osseger Witwen' (GW 9, 641 and 642), both written in 1935, are examples of a strand of songs of agitation which originated in the last years of the Republic. To a large extent, this area of Brecht's production depended on immediate contact with active recipients, with the proletarian organizations in whose meetings songs like these were used collectively; *Svendborger Gedichte* nevertheless includes six poems of this type, which became progressively rarer after 1935, as the possibility of its application became more remote.

'Lied der Starenschwärme' (GW 9, 644), of 1932, is at first a puzzling poem, apparently nothing more than a melancholy lyric. This first impression collides so evidently with the tenor of Brecht's collection that the reader is ultimately obliged to read it ironically as a tentative allegory, warning the addressees in Germany (!) against the false hopes engendered by the decrease in unemployment. The workers were earning a living by preparing for their own destruction, a situation which the final strophe of the poem adequately parallels:

> Wir sehen unter uns große Netze und wissen
> Wohin wir geflogen sind fünf Tage lang:
>   Die Ebenen haben gewartet
>   Die Wärme nimmt zu und
>   Der Tod ist uns sicher.[17]

'Lied gegen den Krieg' (GW 9, 651) takes up this warning, and translates it into specific demands, employing the familiar motif of the weapons reversed:

> Der Prolet steht Jahr und Tag im Kriege
> In der großen Klassenschlacht
> Und er blutet und zahlt bis zu seinem Siege
> Der ihn für immer zum Herren macht.
>   Dreck euer Krieg! So macht ihn doch allein!
>   Wir drehen die Gewehre um

Und machen einen andern Krieg
Das wird der richtige sein.

'Resolution der Kommunarden' (GW 9, 653) and 'Keiner oder alle' (GW 9, 649) extend the argument, insisting that the revolutionary struggle, which depends on the conscious action of the proletariat, is the only real solution. The 'Einheitsfrontlied' of 1934 (GW 9, 652) is more specific in its recommendations; although *Svendborger Gedichte* was published in the 'Volksfront' era, the poem states clearly where the basis of opposition to fascism is to be sought: 'reih dich ein in die Arbeitereinheitsfront'. The song seems crudely simple, though its direct argument is effective, especially with Hanns Eisler's astringent score. Closer examination reveals considerable subtlety in the categories with which the poem operates. The refrain, together with the explicitly admonitory third strophe, defines the intended audience as the proletariat; the impatient declaration of the first strophe is less strictly formulated. Like the second strophe it refers to mankind, thus apparently appealing to a much wider range of interests: but the abstract ideals of humanity are at once confronted with their material base. Without the satisfaction of elementary needs, there is no humanity: as the *Dreigroschenoper* had proclaimed—'erst kommt das Fressen, dann kommt die Moral'. Since the general satisfaction of these needs is among the fundamental interests of the proletariat, it represents mankind as a whole. The material motive is more effective than moral ideals; the first lines of the poem undermine such abstract ideals by their ironic logic: 'Und weil der Mensch ein Mensch ist/ Drum will er was zu essen, bitte sehr!' (GW 9, 652). From the proclamation suggested by the first line, there is a sudden, almost bathetic descent to the material reality of the second; the logic is superficial and might be contradicted by the assertion that the food requirement defines man as an animal, but that his humanity commences only after its fulfilment. This is an important constituent of the poem's argument, and the basis of its appeal to potential allies outside the proletariat itself. Once the salutary warning against metaphysical ideals has been issued ('es macht ihn ein Geschwätz nicht satt'), the second strophe may properly make an appeal to moral sensibility which contributes to the poem's general movement.

The 'Einheitsfrontlied' was commissioned by the International Music Bureau (Moscow) in December 1934;[18] it rapidly became a popular song, even outside Germany: the melody was used by Jean Renoir in his film *La vie est à nous* (1936), commissioned by the PCF. Later it became as ubiquitous as the 'Solidaritätslied'.

These poems are didactic in a propagandistic, rather than a reflective sense; as the preceding analysis sought to show, they are nonetheless more sophisticated than a first reading reveals. They stimulate critical reflection by gradual insinuation.

It is at first surprising that the section also includes six 'Kinderlieder'; but the contrast between them and the other songs discussed above is less marked than might be expected. Indeed, Brecht's first children's poems, the 'Kranlieder' of 1927 (GW 8, 299–302) were explicitly political, as were the verses of *Die drei Soldaten*. These later poems are distinguished by their makeshift perfection: their rhythms move naïvely between delicate hesitancy and strong stressing; they include a consistent element of play ('Und er stieg mit so 'nen Dingen/ Die aussahn wie Schwingen/ Auf das große, große Kirchendach' GW 9, 645). Far from being merely playful, however, the poems provoke thought; 'Der Schneider von Ulm', for example, conveys a basic lesson in historical thought. Glancing with mild irony at a traditional story, the poem shows that the category of truth is itself historical and implies that received beliefs may be mere superstition. Like 'Lob des Zweifels', the 'Kinderlied' recommends an attitude of sceptical enquiry. Beyond the primary historical view, the poem also intimates that a single instance of failure does not demonstrate the impossibility of an undertaking; both strands of significance are easily accessible through the reversal of the bishop's confident statement: 'es wird nie ein Mensch fliegen' (GW 9, 646).

'Vom Kind, das sich nicht waschen wollte' (GW 9, 646) mingles the banal with the fantastic in order to demonstrate the unreality of an authoritarian imperative: 'der Kaiser persönlich kommt zu Besuch, so daß für das Kind, das ihn gern gesehen hätte, ein wirklicher Nachteil aus der Vernachlässigung seines Äußeren entsteht' (GW 19, 423).[19] Here, too, Brecht recommends the application of doubt to established custom: rules are to be examined critically for their functional basis. 'Kleines Bettellied' (GW 9, 646) extends the doctrine of scepticism by further appeals to the child's experience and observations: behaviour is referred to its social context.

'Der Pflaumenbaum' (GW 9, 647) is deceptively slight, modest and simple. In its studied *naïveté* each line accommodates a sentence or phrase, as if composed, one at a time, by a child whose whole attention is devoted to the maintenance of rhyme. The poem shows the influence of context on development, illuminating the gap between potential and realization. Thematically, it is closely related to an epigram which also employs the organic metaphor: 'Über die Unfruchtbarkeit' (GW 9, 602).

> Der Obstbaum, der kein Obst bringt
> Wird unfruchtbar gescholten. Wer
> Untersucht den Boden?
> Der Ast, der zusammenbricht
> Wird faul gescholten, aber
> Hat nicht Schnee auf ihm gelegen?

The extended metaphor admits a rich system of readings, from the general insistence on the determination of limits to possibility by economic life, to the individual reflections of a poet on the political burden which has been forced upon him. 'Der Pflaumenbaum' concentrates on the general plane of reference; the situation it describes is more acute than that of the above poem. Not only does the tree fail to bear fruit: its very existence as a member of the species is threatened, finding partial confirmation in isolated features:

> Den Pflaumenbaum glaubt man ihm kaum
> Weil er nie eine Pflaume hat
> Doch er ist ein Pflaumenbaum
> Man kennt es an dem Blatt. (GW 9, 647)

Somehow, the tree, in its dark back-yard, has survived; and even its miserable development is a major sign of defiance. Paradoxically, limitation signals the fulfilment of potential with confident determination. Like Blake's 'Tiger, Tiger, burning bright', 'Der Pflaumenbaum' presents simple images of immediate clarity and solidity; since it is not plain from the first that they are symbols, the ultimate leap of understanding is dramatic and convincing. The extreme distance between primary and secondary significance (produced by the poem's naïve manner) is a type of 'Verfremdungseffekt'. The meaning of the poem seems to rest on a transfer of reference from plant to human species: the reader is asked to consider the causes of human limitation. A text written five to ten years later proceeds more explicitly in this direction:

> Den Kindern der Armen
> Stopfen ermüdete Mütter ins Mäulchen was immer erschwinglich
> Langen den Schreienden müde den Bierkrug, sie schlafen zu machen

Oder sie schicken sie, größer geworden, in finstere Höfe.
Dorten dann wachsen sie auf mit den anderen Schattengewächsen.

Lehrgedicht von der Natur der Menschen, (GW 10, 901.)

'Mein Bruder war ein Flieger' (GW 9, 647) was written in 1937, three years later than its companion 'Kinderlieder', and is clearly a response to the events in Spain. The Spanish war was used as an exercise-ground for German armed forces; here, and in 'Die Sendlinge' (GW 9, 576), Brecht warns against participation. In the 'Kinderlied' the nationalistic 'Blut und Boden' ideology is eroded by examination of its real results.

The final children's song, 'Der Gottseibeiuns' (GW 9, 648), takes up the theme of sceptical criticism with which the series began; it pretends to adopt a traditional myth (the devil, here significantly reduced to the role of a miscreant goblin), only to demonstrate more clearly its inadequacy. The devil who is blamed for human error becomes an instrument of deception when invoked by the government; but the people have the last, ironic word. Besides the perspective of political action which it presents, the poem argues against idealism, confronting it with material causality (which includes human nature).

It is easily established that the 'Kinderlieder' are political poems and in this simple sense they belong with the other texts in the second section of *Svendborger Gedichte*. It is conceivable that these poems, like many which purport to be addressed to children (*Die drei Soldaten*, for example), employ this mode as a fiction, or mask. In the case of the above poems, this is not easy to decide; they are certainly accessible to older children, but equally capable of engaging the interest of adult readers. Whether it is understood literally or as fiction, the category 'Kinderlied' does not have an *a priori* place in a collection of songs by a political exile, still less in a section devoted to songs of the dark times.

One of Brecht's concerns in this phase, and indeed throughout the period of exile, was the 'one-sidedness' imposed on his art by the growing disorder of the European world. It was emphasized that there are areas of Brecht's poetic production which clearly escape the sterility which he sees as a danger (the sonnets were cited as an example). Brecht's advocacy of opposition to fascism with all available means clearly offers a theoretical justification for art within this struggle; the 'Kinderlied' would present a basis for a new equilibrium between political and artistic interests, specifically one which might be less one-sided. This view of the contextual appropriateness of the 'Kinderlieder' as redressing the balance in favour of literary art is supported by the evidence of Walter Benjamin's notes on conversations with Brecht (3 August 1938).[20] Benjamin felt that the 'Kinderlieder' should not be included in the collection, while Brecht, concerned to show that he was a '*mittlerer* Maniker', considered their contribution to be most important. Benjamin summarizes his argument thus:

> die Erkenntnis des Mittleren dürfe auch in dem Gedichtband nicht zu kurz kommen; daß das Leben, trotz Hitler, weitergeht, daß es immer wieder Kinder geben wird. 'In dem Kampf gegen die darf nichts ausgelassen werden. Sie haben nichts Kleines im Sinn. Sie planen auf dreißigtausend Jahre hinaus. Ungeheures. Ungeheure Verbrechen. Sie machen vor nichts halt. Sie schlagen auf alles ein. Jede Zelle zuckt unter ihrem Schlag zusammen. Darum darf keine von uns vergessen werden. Sie verkrümmen das Kind im Mutterleib. Wir dürfen die Kinder auf keinen Fall auslassen.'

This middle sphere, to which children belong, and which Brecht claims as the basis of his 'mania' may be understood as an area of non-alienated values. At this level of generalization, the connection between the freedoms of childhood and those of art (in its playful elements), becomes apparent. The above quotation also shows that this middle sphere is the focus of two distinct, though connected, approaches; firstly it is seen as a vulnerable and precious set of values, which demands protection from the massive destruction planned by the fascists. Secondly it appears, though fragile, as part of a polemic repertoire capable of mobilization against fascism.

This theoretical development should be understood, not as a basic revision of Brecht's thinking on art, but as a supplementary refinement. It does not constitute a repentant conversion to the doctrine of *l'art pour l'art*, nor a general acceptance of humanist values (for example, 'culture'), as the basis for opposition to fascism. Brecht's speeches for the International Writers' Congresses of 1935 and 1937 emphasize what *Fünf Schwierigkeiten beim Schreiben der Wahrheit* had made clear: that the basis of the anti-fascist struggle could only be economic and social—'Kameraden, sprechen wir von den Eigentumsverhältnissen!' (GW 18, 246). As analysis of the 'Einheitsfrontlied' suggested, rational humanist arguments might be adopted on that basis, in order to extend the fundamental line of attack. The materialist attitude was understood as a critical controlling factor, to which more abstract argument could be referred. With this provision, the 'Kinderlieder' represent Brecht's intention to broaden the front of opposition to the regime by means of a more extensive integration of free artistry. This too is an attitude of defiance.

In the *Svendborger Gedichte* there is no overall organization of texts to form a sustained argument. Its third section, 'Chroniken', does, however, display this kind of supra-textual composition.[21] The first poem, 'Fragen eines lesenden Arbeiters' (1934/5, GW 9, 656), provides a general introduction; its questions probe behind the heroic patina of historical tradition to reveal class structures, and economies based on exploitation. The *Chronik* was defined as a type of didactic poetry which moves from specific historical cases to more general reflection. This mechanism of abstraction is apparent in the reiterated enquiry of the poem, which refuses to accept received accounts as adequate. In this case, the general lesson concerns the conception of history itself; the reader is invited to adopt a sceptical attitude, to insist on the fundamental, material facts: to share the speaker's proletarian view.

The idea of correcting traditional history may be traced back to Brecht's early work, where it is associated with a more rudimentary concept of materialism: 'Maria' (GW 8, 122) of 1922 contrasts the simple facts of the familiar story with the later 'historical' version— 'Das rohe Geschwätz der Hirten verstummte/ Später wurden aus ihnen Könige in der Geschichte'. 'Sokrates' (GW 12, 392) and the prose pieces entitled 'Berichtigungen alter Mythen' (GW 11, 207– 9) are more sophisticated experiments in the same direction.

'So viele Berichte./ So viele Fragen' (GW 9, 657), the final lines of 'Fragen eines lesenden Arbeiters' are both a summary and a programmatic model; the second poem, 'Der Schuh des Empedokles' (1935), examines more closely what was identified as the materialistic orientation of the critical approach. The poem is relaxed, extensive, classical (there are, for example, dactylic phrases, and the poem also contains an epic simile in the passage beginning 'langsam, wie Wolken . . .'). Rival accounts of Empedocles' death, and the different conceptions of history they imply, are compared. The structure of the poem is such that the first account, itself a materialist, rational one, is accepted and apparently confirmed by comparison with the rumours of Empedocles' divinity, and by the discovery of his shoe:

> Geheimnis umgab ihn. Es wurde für möglich gehalten
> Daß außer Irdischem anderes sei, daß der Lauf des Menschlichen
> Abzuändern sei für den einzelnen: solches Geschwätz kam auf.
> Aber zu dieser Zeit ward dann sein Schuh gefunden, der aus Leder
> Der greifbare, abgetragene, der irdische! Hinterlegt für jene, die
> Wenn sie nicht sehen, sogleich mit dem Glauben beginnen.
>
> (GW 9, 658–9)

It is thus surprising, when in the second section of the poem this version is revealed to be, not established fact, but hypothesis. It is suggested that the proper, critical method is more important than the question whether Empedocles lost his shoe intentionally or not. The additional accounts recorded in the second part are reviewed in the same spirit of scepticism; though the writer's informed admiration of the philosopher influences his argument, his conclusion depends ultimately on the material evidence of the shoe. This is interpreted, far from all metaphysics, following the criteria of simplicity, economy, and rationality. The basis of this scientific reasoning is causal logic: 'suchen nach einem zureichenden Grund' (GW 9, 659).

This critical, materialistic understanding of history is the central theme of the poem; but besides the exercise in historical method, it has another peripheral, but important concern. The poem may be read as an allegory on the problem of personality and doctrine; the greatness of Empedocles is never in doubt, but it is seen as proper that he should one day cease to teach. Those who have learnt from him may respond to his disappearance in different ways: 'Immer noch stellten/ Einige ihre Fragen zurück bis zu seiner Wiederkehr, während schon andere/Selber die Lösung versuchten' (GW 9, 658). The kind of doctrine capable of such inheritance is that based upon method, rather than dogmatic principle: not a specific set of solutions, but a general mode for their definition. If the abstract insistence on sober, rational historiography has any immediate reference, it is to the cult of personality, fundamentally inappropriate to Marxism, and a poor substitute for the practical, critical appropriation of method which more effectively honours a former teacher and leader. This range of allusion is problematic for the non-contemporary reader, who is able to make a tentative reconstruction of the expectations and sensibilities of contemporary readers, but unable to prove its correctness.

The third poem of the 'Chroniken' Section, 'Legende von der Entstehung des Buches Taoteking auf dem Weg des Laotse in die Emigration' (1937/8 GW 9, 660) demonstrates that, even within the didactic strand, Brecht did not restrict himself to 'reimlose Lyrik mit unregelmäßigen Rhythmen': it is a rhymed, metrical poem. Brecht employs the traditional 'legend' as a vehicle for a rich complex of themes: exile, the teacher, wisdom and its communication, are central strands. The first two are inherent in the tradition itself, and, with the themes of wisdom, form a bridge between the Lao-tzŭ story and the concerns of the exiled Marxist in 1937; Brecht appropriates the wisdom of the Tao in a selective way, quoting one sentence only. In the poem this wisdom is not imparted spontaneously by the aged philosopher, but as his response to a direct enquiry.

> Eine höfliche Bitte abzuschlagen
> War der Alte, wie es schien, zu alt.
> Denn er sagte laut: 'Die etwas fragen
> Die verdienen Antwort'. (GW 9, 662.)

This insistence on the reciprocity of communication ('keine frage, keine antwort') is a familiar theme of the exile period; in this context, its specific and acute relevance to Brecht's work is played down in favour of clearer presentation as a general problem. The philosopher defines the problem more precisely, before making his generous statement 'Über seine Schulter sah der Alte/ Auf den Mann: Flickjoppe. Keine Schuh' (GW 9, 662). Questions alone are not enough, as Walter Benjamin observes: 'die Bitte des Zöllners mag noch so höflich sein. Laotse versichert sich erst, daß ein Berufener sie tut'.[22] Like the ancient wisdom adopted in the poem, this calling has acquired a new quality: material, social definition. The questioner, though a servant of the state, is poor and oppressed; he understands the philosopher's sentence from this position. Himself 'kein Sieger', he has everything to gain from knowledge of the laws of conflict.

> 'Daß das weiche Wasser in Bewegung
> Mit der Zeit den mächtigen Stein besiegt.
> Du verstehst, das Harte unterliegt.' (GW 9, 661.)

The philosopher's boy offers this summary of his master's discoveries: proceeding from apparent weakness, the aphorism reveals, paradoxically, a perspective of confident hope. The weakest forces may ultimately triumph, if they combine in persistent action; again, Brecht illuminates the element of defiance which belongs to the dialectic. The sovereign confidence which is the basis of the poem's dominant 'Heiterkeit' (Benjamin) depends on combined movement; the felicitous interaction, the 'Höflichkeit' here described, are appropriate to such a co-operative alliance—'wer das Harte zum Unterliegen bringen will, der soll keine Gelegenheit zum Freundlichsein vorbeigehenlassen'[23]

'Besuch bei den verbannten Dichtern' (1937, GW 9, 663) is an example of a familiar strand: the general theme of communication treated in the preceding poem is here examined as an immediate and specific crisis. Brecht locates himself in the long and honourable tradition of literary exiles in a attempt to exorcize the consciousness of his precarious situation: it was reasonable to consider the likelihood of few 'Berufene' being found to ask eager questions of him—

'Du, wissen sie auch
Deine Verse auswendig? Und die sie wissen
Werden sie der Verfolgung entrinnen?'—'Das
Sind die Vergessenen', sagte der Dante leise
'Ihnen wurden nicht nur die Körper, auch die Werke vernichtet.'
Das Gelächter brach ab. Keiner wagte hinüberzublicken. Der
Ankömmling
War erblaßt. (GW 9, 664.)

This melancholy reflection is followed by a contrastingly energetic text, 'Gleichnis des Buddha vom brennenden Haus' (1937, GW 9, 664). As in the 'Empedokles' poem, ancient tradition is treated with both scepticism and veneration. The poem is divided into two, its first, major section relating an episode from the Buddha's life, while the second part (the final eight lines) extract a modern lesson from the Buddha's parable. Before this 'Umfunktionierung', which retains the structure of thought of the original, applying it to new terms, the poem subjects the content of Buddhist doctrine to severe criticism. The apparent neutrality of the first lines, in which the central themes of Buddhism are summarized, is gradually undermined by irony. 'Alle Begierde abzutun und so/ Wunschlos einzugehen ins Nichts' may not at once arouse the reader's suspicions, but the following lines report the naïve questions of the Buddha's pupils with such iterative indulgence that they demand to be read as satire. However simple-minded their enquiries, these pupils are not themselves the chief objects of ridicule, which is directed rather against the body of teaching capable of provoking such questions:

> Ob dies Nichts also
> So ein fröhliches ist, ein gutes Nichts, oder ob dies dein
> Nichts nur einfach ein Nichts ist, kalt, leer und bedeutungslos.
> (GW 9, 665.)

The reader is asked to recognize that the substance of Buddhist teaching is itself 'leer und bedeutungslos', before being invited to observe that its figures of thought may none the less be translated fruitfully. This is a practical illustration of the critical dialectic on which Brecht's 'Materialwert' theory of tradition is grounded. The final section makes this corrective sympathy explicit, by defining the fundamental disagreement between the interests of a Marxist and those of Buddhism:

> Aber auch wir, nicht mehr beschäftigt mit der Kunst des Duldens
> Eher beschäftigt mit der Kunst des Nichtduldens und vielerlei Vorschläge
> Irdischer Art vorbringend und die Menschen lehrend
> Ihre menschlichen Peiniger abzuschütteln, meinen, daß wir denen, die
> Angesichts der heraufkommenden Bombenflugzeuggeschwader
>   des Kapitals noch allzulang fragen
> Wie wir uns dies dächten, wie wir uns das vorstellten
> Und was aus ihren Sparbüchsen und Sonntagshosen werden soll
>   nach einer Umwälzung
> Nicht viel zu sagen haben. (GW 9, 666.)

On this high point the abstract, more distantly historical part of the 'Chroniken' section is concluded; the poems which follow are historical in a contemporary sense, more concrete and direct. The sixth poem, 'Die Teppichweber von Kujan-Bulak ehren Lenin' (1929, GW 9, 666), takes up the theme of the teacher which recurred in the preceding poems, connecting them with those that follow. Lenin, above all a practically minded thinker, is perhaps the central teacher-figure in Brecht's work; here, substance and mode constitute a model unity, a positive example:

> So nützten sie sich, indem sie Lenin ehrten und
> Ehrten ihn, indem sie sich nützten, und hatten ihn
> Also verstanden. (GW 9, 667.)

This indisputable example may by contrast generate criticism of the dominant cult of leadership, in which inflated formulations of praise displaced the practical, active learning process by neutralizing criticism. The same line of argument was identified in 'Der Schuh des Empedokles'.

Lenin is also the guiding figure of the next poem, 'Die unbesiegliche Inschrift' (1934, GW 9, 668), which proceeds from a simple gesture of defiance, developing it into a conceit which illustrates the triumph of materialism. The poem's considerable wit is amplified by its restrained manner, the detachment with which details are described. Such elaboration is a common feature of the joke; it postpones the finish, and increases the tension of expectation. The poem is an appropriately cheerful introduction to a series of poems in which the theme of resistance plays an important part. 'Kohlen für Mike' (1929, GW 9, 669), like most *Chroniken*, was based on material gathered from books and newspapers; originally the poem was intended as an example of solidarity ('Kameradschaft'), and although it retains this sense in 1939, its relevance has been considerably broadened. Solidarity has itself become a form of resistance (since the 'Gleichschaltung' of trade-union organizations in 1933), and conversely, solidarity is essential as the basis for other forms of resistance, which are increasingly dangerous. The poem offers a concrete demonstration of the 'Freundlichkeit' which Walter Benjamin describes as the indispensable condition of the proletarian struggle, the 'moral' of the 'Legende'.

'Abbau des Schiffes Oskawa durch die Mannschaft' (1934/5, GW 9, 670) is open to interpretation as a poem recommending passive resistance and sabotage. This is, on a primary level, what the chronicle describes: it reports in an apparently impartial way, and includes no specific evaluating comment. Within the *Svendborger Gedichte,* however, the poem stands between two unequivocally positive examples of co-operative action, to which the collective destructiveness of the Oskawa's crew is contrasted. This context indicates a reading of the poem as a negative example of inadequate resistance. Brecht here employs the neutral, 'quoting' manner of the *Lesebuch*; but this is a provocative neutrality, which raises questions and elicits corrective responses from the reader. The negative example depends on context, on the clash between the 'Abbau' of this poem, and the 'Aufbau' celebrated in the following one; but there are also indicators within the poem's text. Locally, the strong undercurrent of irony is close to the surface: it is evident, for example, in the reference to the crew's anxiety about their old age, which is repeated three times. This excess of emphasis persuades the reader of the spuriousness of the argument. Similarly, the cargo agent, seeing the load for which he is responsible being destroyed, is justifiably wary of the crew and carries a revolver—to the crew 'ein Zeichen beleidigenden Mißtrauens'. Here, at the very latest, criticism of the crew's entire strategy is generated. The poem does not relate what happened to the crew on arrival in Hamburg, and so does not make judgement of their actions dependent on consequences. The reader is asked to consider the narrative as a closed whole, a tentative parable on the workers' movement, and its problems of organization and action. With discreet insistence it is demonstrated that anarchic, unreflective action is inadequate, unproductive: the irony of the poem's concluding lines demands emphatic rejection of the crew's actions as a model for the proletarian struggle—simple destruction is not enough:

> 'Das Schiff
> Kam auf den Knochenhof. Jedes Kind, meinten wir
> Konnte so sehen, daß unsere Löhnung
> Wirklich zu klein gewesen war.'[24]   (GW 9, 673.)

'Inbesitznahme der großen Metro durch die Moskauer Arbeiterschaft am 27. April 1935' (1935, GW 9, 673) is a conspicuous contrastive example. The sense of boredom and frustration evoked by the preceding chronicle from the capitalist world is highlighted by the swell of excitement, the epic scale and sense of shared achievement evident in this account of collective construction in the socialist world. 'Inbesitznahme' has the significance of a technical term ('appropriation') designating emancipation from alienation:

> Denn es sah der wunderbare Bau
> Was keiner seiner Vorgänger in vielen Städten vieler Zeiten
> Jemals gesehen hatte: als Bauherren die Bauleute!
> Wo wäre dies je vorgekommen, daß die Frucht der Arbeit
> Denen zufiel, die da gearbeitet hatten?   (GW 9, 675.)

Suddenly, labour has become intrinsically worthwhile; volunteer workers emerge 'Lachend aus den Stollen... ihre Arbeitsanzüge/

Die lehmigen, schweißdurchnäßten, stolz vorweisend'. This new quality of labour corresponds to a new quality of product: standards formerly applied to work carried out for a tiny minority are no longer reserved, but socialized, appropriated by the majority—'Für strenge Besteller/ Das Allerbeste' (GW 9, 673).

'Schnelligkeit des sozialistischen Aufbaus' (1937, GW 9, 675) emphasizes in the form of an anecdote that fluidity and a rapid rate of change are characteristic, and positive, features of socialist construction. Socialism is seen as implying the conscious application of the dialectic, not its obsolescence.

The 'Chroniken' section ends with 'Der große Oktober' (1937, GW 9, 675), an ode written for the twentieth anniversary of the revolution in Russia. It is an example of Brecht's use of the grand style, rhetorical and hymnic. Here, the arguments presented in the preceding poems of the section are synthesized; the theoretical lessons of the first six texts are integrated with the practical examples of the following five in this single instance: the turning point of history. This 'Endliches Sichaufrichten der so lange/ Niedergebeugten' provides a positive perspective for the struggle in western Europe, with the Soviet Union as an ally:

Seitdem
Hat die Welt ihre Hoffnung.
Der Kumpel in Wales und der mandschurische Kuli
Und der pennsylvanische Arbeiter, der unter dem Hund lebt
Und der deutsche, mein Bruder, der jenen
Noch beneidet: sie alle
Wissen, es gibt
Einen Oktober. (GW 9, 676.)

Considered in the context in which most of these poems were written and collected, the 'Chroniken' section appears far removed from the one-sidedness which Brecht saw as the unavoidable flaw of the *Svendborger Gedichte*. These poems are artistically complex, characterized by an expansive richness of invention, precisely calculated wit, and often classical lexis and syntax; they constitute a defiant refusal either to accept artistic (thus human) impoverishment, or to retreat into a speciously hermetic world of art, an illusory freedom from politics. Brecht's position shares the qualities he had identified in the Soviet Union—'Fröhlich/ Aber allen Unterdrückern/ Eine Drohung' (GW 9, 677).

The collection's fourth section is a miscellany of poems not united by the consistency apparent in other sections; they may, however, all be classified as theoretical *Lehrgedichte* with a high degree of immediacy. From this point of view, they continue the strand which includes 'Gegen die Objektiven' and 'Wer zu Hause bleibt, wenn der Kampf beginnt'. 'An den Schwankenden' (1934/5, GW 9, 678) is addressed to the disheartened supporters of the anti-fascist struggle; after a strict and honest review of the desperate position of the struggle, the poem formulates questions designed to consolidate this position in spite of everything: 'Was ist jetzt falsch von dem, was wir gesagt haben/ Einiges oder alles?'. These questions, which the addressees are invited to adopt, are finally declared answerable only by their actions; the poem clarifies the problem, but refrains from specific recommendations, assuming the readers' consent in its implication that continued resistance is the only strategy.

As its title suggests, 'An die Gleichgeschalteten' (1935, GW 9, 679) complements the preceding poem in its appeal to sections of the German population which, unlike the organized proletariat, had never contemplated resistance. The immediate object of the poem's interest is the special case of the intellectual, the writer or journalist, whose work is carried out in the public sphere. It is assumed that many such people, pursuing the ideal of integrity, at first refuse to carry out work which implies their assent to a regime which (this, again, is understood) they see as criminal. It is demonstrated that such a position is in fact not one of integrity, but of opportunism, which inevitably leads to increasing compromise in an attempt, finally, to save their own skin. This is all that could be saved, everything else having been abandoned for its sake.

The emphasis on the role of the intellectual may be accounted for by Brecht's own professional interest; the *Tui* complex was conceived in the early thirties—it devotes considerable space to this question.[25] Although it is clear that the intellectual, especially the respected neutral liberal, is capable of doing considerable damage when drawn into complicity by a fascist regime, his is not the only such case. Brecht himself, on reconsidering the poem in 1938, found that it was too exclusively concerned with the 'berufsideologen' and ignored the materially more destructive role played by other intellectual specialists ('kopfarbeiter'), scientists, engineers, and administrators.[26] The poem does refer to these sections briefly, but in its detail touches only the question of public assent.

Brecht's notes on the poem record that he considered its criticisms equally relevant to the petty bourgeoisie, which, like the liberal intellectuals, could resort only to abstract arguments in its opposition to the regime. These wider social sections, Brecht is disturbed to note, find no explicit mention in the text. While he is right to conclude that 'ideological' complicity is the poem's primary and explicit target, Brecht perhaps underestimates its capacity for abstraction:

> Wer mit keiner Wimper zuckt
> Beim Anblick blutiger Verbrechen, verleiht ihnen nämlich
> Den Anschein des Natürlichen. Er bezeichnet
> Die furchtbare Untat als etwas so Unauffälliges wie Regen
> Auch so unhinderbar wie Regen. (GW 9, 679.)

This seems general enough in its appeal to include, not simply the petty bourgeoisie, but the unorganized proletariat, since 1933 equally subject to neutralizing 'Gleichschaltung': it is a refutation of the 'impartial' passive attitude which combines moral scruple with practical complicity. Brecht apparently did not consider the formerly unorganized proletariat comparable with the 'kleinbürger und kopfarbeiter', for whom, in the metaphor of the 'Gleichnis des Buddha vom brennenden Haus', the ground was not yet hot enough, who were unable to see their real material interests in the anti-fascist struggle.

The political problem is also a poetic one; the poem is clear and persuasive in its analysis, and might conceivably have induced its intended addressees to reflect critically on their position. It is not at all clear, however, what action these people might reasonably be expected to take. Recognizing their inability to identify with the proletarian struggle, the poem makes no appeal to material interests, but is content to show the insignificance of any individual moral stance; and it is hard to see what might have been done: public dissent would have been suicidal. Only sabotage seems viable, and it is paradoxically most difficult for the poem's explicit addressee, the intellectual. In the *Svendborger Gedichte* of 1939, even more than when it was broadcast from Moscow in 1935, the poem constitutes a desperate defiant plea.

'Auf den Tod eines Kämpfers für den Frieden' (1938, GW 9,

681), dedicated to the memory of Carl von Ossietzky, provides a contrastive example of open, active opposition. An admonitory epitaph, the poem does not seek to dissipate energy in regret, but to concentrate it in the continuing struggle.

Of the remaining poems of the fourth section, the majority are theoretical *Lehrgedichte,* reminiscent of the songs and choruses from *Die Mutter* and *Die Maßnahme* (in the case of 'Kantate zu Lenins Todestag' quoting them): 'Rede eines Arbeiters an einen Arzt' (1937/8), 'Appell' (1936/8), 'Verhöhnung des Soldaten der Revolution. Seine Antwort' (1937/8), 'Kantate zu Lenins Todestag' (1938), and 'Grabschrift für Gorki' (1936).

'Ansprache des Bauern an seinen Ochsen' (1938, GW 9, 683) is a new version of an Egyptian peasants' song, the chief interest of which lies in the complex symbiotic relationship of the peasants and the ox; their mutual dependence demands that the peasants make considerable sacrifices in order to derive any benefit from their animal. The poem is dominated by the consciousness of the economic imperative, which determines the variations in the terms of the relationship, the surprising transition from the formulaic devotion of the first line—'O großer Ochse, göttlicher Pflugzieher'—to the colloquial wrath of the hard-pressed peasant in the final line—'Willst du etwa/ Vor der Aussaat verrecken, du Hund?'. These contradictory attitudes are the limits which circumscribe the relationship.

The poem is of special interest to Brecht because in its origins it is folk art; the illiterate, down-trodden peasant is enabled to speak out. He does so in a way which is succinct, practical, and informative, and thus exemplifies a mode with which Brecht is himself in sympathy. Nevertheless, the poem's place within the exile collection, its special significance, are problematic. Here too, the problem involves the reconstruction of contemporary sensibilities and expectations, the context in which the text develops its significance. Fortunately, Walter Benjamin's notes of conversations with Brecht offer evidence of this context, which may generally be defined by Brecht's verbal introduction of the poem as his 'Stalin-Gedicht'. This adds a further specific dimension to the poem, and adequately accounts for its inclusion in the collection. Still, as Benjamin's note shows, this area of meaning does not readily reveal itself, even after an explicit indication of its direction:

im ersten Augenblick kam ich nicht auf den Sinn der Sache; und als mir im zweiten der Gedanke an Stalin durch den Kopf ging, wagte ich nicht, ihn festzuhalten. Solche Wirkung entsprach annähernd Brechts Absicht. Er erläuterte sie im anschließenden Gespräch. Darin betonte er, unter anderm, gerade die positiven Momente in dem Gedicht. Es sei in der Tat eine Ehrung Stalins—der nach seiner Ansicht immense Verdienste habe. Aber er sei noch nicht tot. Ihm, Brecht, stehe übrigens eine andere enthusiastischere Form der Ehrung nicht zu; er sitze im Exil und warte auf die rote Armee.[27]

Although the poem is puzzling in the context of *Svendborger Gedichte*, a resolution in this precise direction seems far from automatic; so fine is the contact between the literal and ironic levels of the text that it is practically in code. It was probably only accessible to a small group of readers, like Benjamin, already sensitized in the poem's intended field of reference. The theme of critical interaction with a teacher or leader is a recurring one, and is found in this collection too, in the 'Chroniken', for example. The important (and neglected) prose collection *Me-ti* also includes many models for critical examination of Stalin's role.[28]

'Bei der Geburt eines Sohnes' (1938, GW 9, 684) is also Brecht's version of an ancient poem, and has in common with the previous one its poetic treatment of a mundane subject. This anecdotal poem is one of satire; the social order is such that parents may reasonably hope for an ignorant and lazy son, who might attain the high office and easy life from which learning and intelligence would debar him. This is the familiar topos of the superfluity of virtue in a well-organized society. Since it implies that those in positions of power are likely to be indolent fools, the poem is subversive; but the first premise is open to revision: the resignation of the speaker elicits correction. The establishment of a rational social order demands both industry and intelligence.

The short poem dedicated to Ossietzky is followed by a major poem addressed to the artists: 'Rat an die bildenden Künstler, das Schicksal ihrer Kunstwerke in den kommenden Kriegen betreffend' (1936/7, GW 9, 682). This is approximately parallel with 'An die Gleichgeschalteten', but more clearly conceived in terms of its addressees, who are defined by their profession. The poem makes no explicit distinction between those artists exiled during the thirties and others who remained in Germany. Brecht paints a bleak picture of the fate which will befall their work, and feigns indulgent sympathy with the artists' situation; this sympathy is gradually undermined, as his advice on how works of art may best be preserved from destruction becomes increasingly extreme and complex. In the revised reading which its ironic mode requires, the poem describes their fate as an appropriate end for works of art which were not adequate to the social context in which they were executed; the idea of working only for posterity is attacked (as it had been in 'Über die Bauart langdauernder Werke'), so too is the exaggerated concern for the 'cultural heritage', which takes no account of the essential question of who is to inherit and how. This is the position taken up by Brecht in his speech to the First International Writers' Congress for the Defence of Culture against Barbarism (Paris, 1935):

erbarmen wir uns der Kultur, aber erbarmen wir uns zuerst der Menschen! Die Kultur ist gerettet, wenn die Menschen gerettet sind. Lassen wir uns nicht zu der Behauptung fortreißen, die Menschen seien für die Kultur da, nicht die Kultur für die Menschen! (GW 18, 245.)

Similarly, a later entry in the *Arbeitsjournal*: 'natürlich werden nur die künste gerettet, die an der rettung der menschheit sich beteiligen' (AJ 22.8.42).[29]

The poem argues that autotelic artistic production, not of course confined to the visual arts, is incapable of such participation in humanity's struggle for liberation, and in this sense insufficient: 'Ein paar Stilleben und Landschaften/ Werden die Bombenfliegermannschaften nicht stören'. Measured according to this criterion, there is little to choose between the work of exiled artists, supposed opponents of the regime, and their pro-fascist counterparts; the Popular Front policy of 1935 onwards indulgently avoided any attempt to radicalize such artists (or writers) and Brecht considered it to be fundamentally mistaken. His critique of the liberal, humanist intellectual, begun in the last years of the Weimar Republic, continued with increasing vehemence throughout the exile period. The poem describes a position in clear contrast to that taken up by Brecht himself.

The fifth section of *Svendborger Gedichte* comprises the 'Deutsche Satiren', poems written between 1936 and 1938. These poems belong to the category of 'strafende Satire'; polemic, aggressively destructive, they attack the regime by seizing on its public activities as conspicuous targets. It is a risk which accompanies the satirical mode that a powerful emotional appeal may be made to the detriment of effective, rational argument, so that the work offers a set of impressions which fade quickly. This is a danger which Brecht, while maintaining an angry, satiric intensity, successfully avoids in these minutely calculated poems. The satires are closely related to the epigrams of 'Deutsche Kriegsfibel', with which they share the aim of the destruction of ideology; but where the epigrams are warning epitaphs for those soon to die, the satires are more incisively aggressive:

> Nach schweren Schicksalsschlägen
> Pflegt der Kanzler durch eine große Rede
> Seine Anhänger wieder aufzurichten.
> Auch der Schnitter, heißt es
> Liebt die aufrechten Ähren
> ('Trost vom Kanzler', GW 9, 713.)

The text derives its energy from the tensions it contains—in the ironic quotation of the first line and in the final pair. Here, the metaphor is introduced, with fine *naïveté*, by a conjunction; the casual link increases the force of the final ironic collision. The savage wit of the juxtaposition of such simple, disparate images recalls the 'Fotomontage' technique developed by Brecht's friend John Heartfield; death as the reaper looms over the speech-making Hitler, placing his hysterical rhetoric in a real, material context.

The general plan of this uncharacteristically short satire is typical, both for the other poems of the section, and for many other texts of this period (the 'Deutsche Kriegsfibel' for example). The poem consists of two parts, the second of which provides a turning-point, fixing and often revising the poem's sense; frequently this scorpion action consists in the reductive technique familiar from the primitive materialism of the earliest poetry. In 'Der Dienstzug', for example (GW 9, 696), the narrator assumes the manner of a guide, or news commentator, and maintains it, in spite of an increasing ironic undertow, until the final two lines. Here, following the sustained exercise in fussy particularity, the sudden return to colloquial speech is all the more effective: 'Sie scheißen/ Auf Deutschland'. In 'Schwierigkeit des Regierens', similarly, the final twist is anticipated in the main body of the poem by the enthusiastic pretence of sympathy with the regime: ingenuousness is taken to extremes of ironic exaggeration—

> Ohne die Minister
> Würde das Korn in den Boden wachsen anstatt nach oben.
> Kein Stück Kohle käme aus dem Schacht
> Wenn der Kanzler nicht so weise wäre.
> Ohne den Propaganda-
> minister
> Ließe sich kein Weib mehr schwängern. (GW 9, 697.)

This is satire of high quality, combining attack with poise and artistry; in the next line, this standard is surpassed. Reflecting the model set up in the lines already quoted, the following one is, however, suddenly serious: 'Ohne den Kriegsminister/ Käme niemals ein Krieg'.

The selection of themes in the 'Deutsche Satiren' is not arbitrary; Brecht isolates weak points, contradictions in fascist propaganda on the basis of information on social and economic developments in Germany gained, as Herbert Claas has shown, from the 'Deutschland-Informationen' of the KPD.[30] Besides statistical material, these publications also contained reports of resistance activity within Germany, and of public opinion. Brecht was thus able to proceed from substantial and complex pictures of the situation; in particular, he could adopt and extend lines of argument which were already being explored by his German audience. These poems, though their quality as literary works of art has been emphasized, are also political pamphlets in which a specific argument is delivered with force and sufficient transparency to allow its function as a theoretical model. Method is an integral part of these poems' message. Brecht's contribution to the resistance movement consists in emphatic formulation and consolidation of criticism of the regime. Its propaganda is opposed, firstly by reference to the facts, then, on this basis, by all disposable means of ridicule. This verbal counter-propaganda, written for the 'Deutscher Freiheitssender', and published in *Internationale Literatur* and *Das Wort*, invited appropriation and emulation by its audience.[31] This intellectual act of opposition was the necessary base, and perhaps often the practical limit of resistance. Only in 'Kanonen nötiger als Butter' is there explicit advocacy of more active sabotage:

> Wenn der Artillerie die Munition ausgeht
> Bekommen die Offiziere vorn
> Leicht Löcher im Hinterkopf. (GW 9, 706.)

The metaphor suggests that some equivalent summary response should greet the civil authorities' management of the supply of consumer goods.

The sixth and final section of *Svendborger Gedichte* is evidently more personal in its reference than the preceding ones; most of its poems are explicitly concerned with the theme of exile. It is as if the messages delivered in the poems of the first five sections demanded as support clear information about their source; this idea seems to underlie the epigraph of the collection:

> Geflüchtet unter das dänische Strohdach, Freunde
> Verfolg ich euren Kampf. Hier schick ich euch
> Wie hin und wieder schon die Verse, aufgescheucht
> Durch blutige Gesichte über Sund und Laubwerk.
> Verwendet, was euch erreicht davon, mit Vorsicht!
> Vergilbte Bücher, brüchige Berichte
> Sind meine Unterlage. Sehen wir uns wieder
> Will ich gern wieder in die Lehre gehn. (GW 9, 631.)

This final section does, however, have an epigraph of its own, which modifies the personal orientation by treating it as representative and general. The reader is warned to be vigilant, not to believe that the danger is past; more specifically, the poem may refer to fascism as a leak in the keel of the capitalist world (escape from Germany thus leaving the exile in the same foundering boat): the boat itself is no longer seaworthy, but the immediate task must be to plug the leak.

The first poem, 'Über die Bezeichnung Emigranten' (1936/7, GW 9, 718), provides a careful definition of exile:

> Unruhig sitzen wir so, möglichst nahe den Grenzen
> Wartend des Tags der Rückkehr, jede kleinste Veränderung
> Jenseits der Grenze beobachtend, jeden Ankömmling
> Eifrig befragend, nichts vergessend und nichts aufgebend
> Und auch verzeihend nichts, was geschah, nichts verzeihend.
> Ach, die Stille der Sunde täuscht uns nicht! Wir hören die Schreie
> Aus ihren Lagern bis hierher. (GW 9, 718.)

It ends on the defiant assertion: 'Das letzte Wort/ Ist noch nicht gesprochen'. Following this theoretical exposition, 'Gedanken über die Dauer des Exils' (1936/7, GW 9, 719) takes stock of the complex situation, examining the dialogue between determination and dejection; here, the autobiographical element is conspicuous:

> Tag um Tag
> Arbeitest du an der Befreiung
> Sitzend in der Kammer schreibst du. (GW 9, 720.)

The wish for a speedy return from exile conflicts with the knowledge that this is unlikely; the writer's work in opposition to the regime is carried out in the consciousness that the most he may achieve is not much. The image of the chestnut tree with which the poem closes indicates the time already spent in exile, and anticipates the years which may follow: it also evokes the sense of powerlessness which accompanies the work for liberation. This is both an explanatory statement of Brecht's position, and a prescriptive model; in spite of everything, it declares, the exiled writer must not retire from the struggle.

'Zufluchtsstätte' (1936, GW 9, 720) describes the landscape of exile; its elements are predominantly not natural, but social: the weighted thatch of the roof, the beams of the children's swing, the postman and the ferry. The poem's horizons are modest, domestic; to widen them would have brought the German military machine into view: even the peaceful ferries in the sound remind the poet of his rehearsed escape route. The scene is hospitable, but rests upon a tentative, vulnerable safety, which the delicate rhymes and halting rhythm precisely emphasize.

'Und in eurem Lande?' (1935, GW 9, 720), which was sent to Lion Feuchtwanger in France, takes up the idea suggested by the epigraph ('Du, der du, sitzend im Buge des Bootes'): in countries where fascism has not been established, capitalism, its progenitor, still exists. What was true of the Weimar Republic is also true of the countries of exile:

> Wer die Unwahrheit sagt, wird auf Händen getragen
> Wer dagegen die Wahrheit sagt
> Der braucht eine Leibwache
> Aber er findet keine. (GW 9, 720.)

Brecht's personal and exemplary position as one who spoke the truth is defined in 'Verjagt mit gutem Grund' (1938, GW 9, 721). Exile is explained as the result of Brecht's change of class allegiance, his betrayal of the bourgeoisie to the proletariat.

This final section of *Svendborger Gedichte* is concluded by the major poem 'An die Nachgeborenen' (GW 9, 722). It begins with an impassioned complaint; in such dark times, simplicity and innocence are inadequate. There is no refuge from the intrusion of history, when a moment's diversion betrays friends who need help. Laughter has become rare and conspicuous; it reminds the speaker only of the bad news by which it will inevitably be silenced. Similarly, his own survival has neither reason nor justification, and is viewed in the shadow of the same, poisoning implications. In the extreme logical compression of the poem:

> Aber wie kann ich essen und trinken, wenn
> Ich dem Hungernden entreiße, was ich esse, und
> Mein Glas Wasser einem Verdurstenden fehlt?
> Und doch esse und trinke ich. (GW 9, 723.)

The ancient books of wisdom (Buddhist scripture and the *Tao Tê Ching*, for example) offer no adequate advice; a passive ascetic philosophy is ultimately no protection against involvement in the world's conflict. The first part of the poem is composed in the present tense; in the second, the preterite is dominant, as the speaker reviews his life. The hungry cities where he lived formed a battleground, on which he fought together with the forces of revolt: in this context, the complaint of the poem's first part is reiterated—

> Mein Essen aß ich zwischen den Schlachten
> Schlafen legte ich mich unter die Mörder
> Der Liebe pflegte ich achtlos
> Und die Natur sah ich ohne Geduld. (GW 9, 724.)

The struggle was dangerous, and its outcome far from certain. The refrain 'So verging meine Zeit/ Die auf Erden mir gegeben war' reminds the reader by its liturgical insistence that the poem is addressed to posterity, by a writer whose work will outlive him: the speaker is a ghost. In the third part of the poem, the reader learns that the speaker perished in a flood, and is entreated to consider the faults of the speaker and his comrades with sympathy, remembering the dark times in which they lived. They had fought for mankind, conscious of the fact that their struggle itself excluded them from complete humanity. The poem may thus first appear to be an epitaph, in which the plea for indulgence has most weight.

Such a reading, which registers the emotional impulses of the poem, is far from exhaustive; it creates as many problems as it solves. The fundamental difficulty consists in the need to explain the poem's function in its prominent place, at the end of a collection whose importance for Brecht can scarcely be overestimated. Acceptance of the simple reading outlined above would make 'An die Nachgeborenen' a recantation of Brecht's poetry after 1926, and indeed of the positions adopted in the preceding texts of *Svendborger Gedichte*. The title itself is a difficulty: apparently proclaiming an indeterminate posterity as its only audience, the poem clearly contradicts its title by the fact of its publication in 1939, firstly in the collection, then also in *Die Neue Weltbühne*.[32] It was deliberately addressed to contemporary readers, who are thus permitted to eavesdrop on the poet's autobiographical apologia. The question whether the title then constitutes a simple fiction, a conceit, is perhaps not especially important; in so far as a poem is able to engage the interest of non-contemporary readers, it may be seen as addressed to posterity. Brecht's thinking on this question was explored in the context of the *Lehrgedicht* 'Über die Bauart langdauernder Werke', which proposed (under certain conditions) that poetry should be written with a complex system of reception in mind: given that an enduring work was necessary, it was important to remember that its reception was itself dependent on contemporary factors. In the case of 'An die Nachgeborenen', it appears that a duality of direction is an integral part of its conception: 'Die Kräfte waren gering. Das Ziel/ Lag in großer Ferne'—if this indicates the long-term perspective, in which the lasting work has its function, the poem's publication argues that the author was aware that, unless it was capable of engaging in the immediate struggle, the conditions for its later reception might not be fulfilled at all.

If the poem is more than a plea to a later, happier world for sympathy, where does its additional meaning lie? What does it say to its contemporaries? The first section, probably the last to be written (1938), elicits the reader's concurrence in the exclamation: 'wirklich, ich lebe in finsteren Zeiten!' The repetition of this sentence encloses the first section as if in parentheses, the entire section elaborating on this theme. The terms of this elaboration are emotional, moral, above all general, forming the basis for a wide appeal. This appeal is not merely one for sympathy, on the basis of expressions of regret which the reader is invited to make his own; the section also contains statements of fact, clear positions which are equally compelling. 'Das arglose Wort ist töricht' combines regret with assertive proposition, while the concluding 'alles das kann ich nicht' points to the kind of informed discourse appropriate to the dark times: indirectly, but nonetheless emphatically, the section demands active participation in conflict, insisting that violent struggle may be unavoidable, if wants are to be satisfied. The argument is extremely abstract, its overall movement proceeds from resignation to revolt; this easy abstraction makes the argument more persuasive, more open to adoption.

The second section, written in 1934 (and thus the earliest part), is organized retrospectively; clearly autobiographical, it is, like the preceding section, formulated in such general terms that it appears typical. Here again, a sense of loss and regret is combined with the exposition of historical fact in the poem's tactic of persuasion. The 'dark times' of the first section are situated in their historical context, in the 'Zeit der Unordnung', whose characteristic was hunger. This was, moreover, the 'Zeit des Aufruhrs', in which mankind rose in protest; the two epochal definitions stand in parallel, without explicit logical or grammatical connection, but this reticence itself underlines the parallelism, suggesting an effective connection between the social setting and political revolt. The connection is not made to justify revolt; the accent is on the simple facts and general development. Revolt is not merely a reaction to the symptoms of a world in disorder, but is the collective movement of mankind. Statements of historical fact are made to win the reader's assent by means of a foreground simplicity, which, on closer examination, dissolves, to reveal important implications: adoption of the apparently neutral, factual assertions in fact implies the assumption of a critical, partisan viewpoint. Brecht's argument is gently, discreetly persuasive; again, it depends on the reader's acceptance of extremely general propositions (reinforced here by the generality of history, large-scale, overall movement) whose full premises and consequences are not immediately evident.

The same sense of the magnitude of historical forces, in comparison with which individual actions appear insignificant, is evoked in the concise paradox: 'die Straßen führten in den Sumpf zu meiner Zeit'. The principal highway of human activity leads to nothing more than 'natural' disorder: this is partly a reformulation of a favourite paradox of Brecht's—the production of means of destruction. It is here combined with recognition of the difficulty of remedying the social ill; the streets of history are solidly constructed, forming and also limiting human progression. The speaker's admission: 'ich vermochte nur wenig' is not surprising. Nevertheless, it is in this immediate context that a more explicit declaration of intent is formulated; what had previously been identified as revolt is now made more specific, as an attack on those who wielded power. Protest is thus given clear direction.

The poem's cunningly oblique attitude allows it a breadth of appeal which poems such as 'Lob des Kommunismus' do not attain; the hesitant, non-aligned reader is not repelled by dogmatic argument. At the same time, this subtle tactic, based on repeated assumptions of common ground between speaker and reader, may risk a harmlessly diluted exposition of policy; in this poem, the goal evoked as the shared aim of mankind remains abstract. This is perhaps not so serious a defect as it first appears: the extraordinary reticence of the poem is puzzling, and would probably have surprised many of its contemporary readers. It is likely that this effect was a calculated one. For the reader of *Svendborger Gedichte*, the restrained indications of 'An die Nachgeborenen' would have been readily translatable with the help of the preceding texts. Outside this context, published individually (as in *Die Neue Weltbühne*), the poem would be placed by its author's name, and would both modify and ultimately integrate the reader's expectations, urging him gradually to a position of solidarity. In this process, the poem's persuasiveness, its capacity for overcoming prejudice and suspicion, are of primary importance: the specific details of the allegiance to which the poem persuades are important, but secondary. They are indicated in the poem, but are also assumed as a connotation of the author's name: 'zu dem "wert" eines gedichts gehört das "gesicht" des verfassers' (AJ 5.8.45).

The third section of the poem produces a synthesis of the argument outlined above. Firstly, it provides a system of temporal relationships within which the reader must locate himself in order to make sense of the poem.[33] The first two lines combine future and past tense, reminding the reader that the speaker belongs to the past (for the contemporary reader this was a fiction in which his complicity was assumed); the present is thus placed in a historical context by its relation to the flood which separates the speaker from the 'Nachgeborenen'. This definition of location constitutes a fixed point, to which the previously indeterminate perspectives of the first two sections may be referred.

The flood apparently signifies the war, which Brecht considered inevitable in 1937, when this section was written; in 1939 it seemed imminent to all but the most insensitive. At the same time, the flood, like the biblical deluge, is envisaged as a cathartic catastrophe: those born later will have escaped the dark times of which the poem complains:

> Gedenkt
> Wenn ihr von unseren Schwächen sprecht
> Auch der finsteren Zeit
> Der ihr entronnen seid. (GW 9, 724.)

There follows a summary of the preceding sections: the familiar, tenacious argument for the continuation of the struggle and for an honest understanding of what the struggle costs—'Auch der Zorn über das Unrecht/ Macht die Stimme heiser'.

It would be conceivable that the poem should end here; the fact that it does not, and the lines which ultimately conclude it, alter the third section and thus the entire poem. As if to state unequivocally that the poem does not argue against anger at injustice for the sake of purity of voice, Brecht added four lines which make the introductory exhortation ('Gedenkt...') explicitly conditional:

> Ihr aber, wenn es so weit sein wird
> Daß der Mensch dem Menschen ein Helfer ist
> Gedenkt unsrer
> Mit Nachsicht. (GW 9, 725.)

This implies a fundamental revision of the perspective established at the beginning of the third section: the deluge of the war may not be cathartic enough to end the dark times of disorder, hunger, and unrest, the 'homo homini lupus' of exploitation. The 'Nachgeborenen' to whom the plea for sympathetic criticism may properly be addressed are thus strictly defined as those born when 'die Kriege der Klassen' are no longer necessary: in a post-revolutionary world. The simple future 'wenn es so weit sein wird' allows no doubt concerning the achievement of this goal; it appeals to the category of general, objective movement, historical fact, but only on the basis of the collective struggle to which the poem summons its pre-revolutionary readers. The establishment of an ordered, happier world is made conditional on the actions of these addressees in their respective present times.

The poem's complex perspectives make it flexible enough to engage both immediately contemporary readers and those born later; these groups are, in terms of the poem's final admonitory sentence, virtually contemporary—both are asked to recognize that in spite of everything, it is necessary that the struggle be continued. The emphasis on the persuasive, rather than the informative and didactic, mode which distinguishes 'An die Nachgeborenen' suggests that particular importance was attached to its effectiveness in attracting the sympathetic interest of a specific readership: the exiled and unexiled intellectuals. The poem shares this direction of appeal (which is not exclusive) with its companion poems in the sixth section of *Svendborger Gedichte*, and with others of the collection ('An die Gleichgeschalteten', 'Gleichnis des Buddha vom brennenden Haus').

Though the poem's 'active' aspect is important, its formulations of regret should not be seen as a mere device, a ploy with which to lure suspicious readers. The sense of regret at the difficulty of realizing emancipation as a process (not simply as a distant goal) is real, and honest:

> Ach, wir
> Die wir den Boden bereiten wollten für Freundlichkeit
> Konnten selber nicht freundlich sein. (GW 9, 725.)

Within the system of priorities which the poem sets up, there is room for such elements of sympathetic and generous reflection, in partial anticipation of the full, humane indulgence which will ultimately be practicable.[34]

'An die Nachgeborenen' combines most of the major themes identified as typical of the period 1934–9, a period which the poem itself spans. It is a summary review, which takes account of the principal, general factors: class conflict and alienation in the context of the European crisis; exile and war are special forms of this conflict.[35]

Svendborger Gedichte is less easy to characterize as a collection than *Lieder Gedichte Chöre,* because it is more comprehensive and is organized in a less formal, linear way; it presents a representative selection of poems, as it was to have done in the Malik *Gesammelte Werke.*

The range of poems is wide: from the *Massenlied* to the epigram, from the classical masks of the *Chroniken* to the ironic energy of the satires. The dominant mood is no longer optimistic, but defiant. This widening poetic range accompanies a widening of the target public; this is no longer the small network of organized resistance operating within Germany, nor the audience offered by political and (increasingly, in the late thirties) non-political emigration. These groups are not excluded, but there is a much larger potential audience inside Germany, in the proletariat, and amongst the intellectuals and the petty bourgeoisie. In spite of the extent to which the fascist regime was able to control these sections (Brecht had few illusions here) he considered them too important to be neglected. Many of the poems collected may be construed as attempts to sow and propagate the seeds of doubt, in the hope of undermining the regime's position.

The urgency of this function did not prevent a growing emphasis on the literary aesthetic in *Svendborger Gedichte*: artistry, not only a camouflage but as an integral contribution to the force of the attack. It does not appear that the poems of the collection are hopelessly sterile or one-sided (the sonnets and Chinese poems,[36] their contemporaries, reinforce this conclusion); on the contrary, they represent a rich and differentiated artistic response to a situation which was capable of inducing crippling despair.[37]

Chapter 5
EXILE (3) 1939–1947

THE second half of Brecht's exile was the bleaker. The Second World War had begun; as it continued, Brecht's own position became increasingly threatened. In April 1939 he was forced to leave Denmark for Sweden; in May 1940 a move to Finland was necessary. It was followed, less than a year later, by his departure for the Soviet Union on his way to the United States. The fascist regime, having suppressed the labour movement within Germany, was preparing to attack the Soviet Union; if Brecht's life was at risk, so too was the significance of his work.[1]

Brecht's production of poetry is altered in two ways during this period. There is, firstly, a marked reduction in the volume of poems written, most conspicuously in 1940-1; secondly, a general reduction in the length of individual texts.[2] Besides a large number of epigrams, there are many epigrammatic poems, and many texts comprised of a cycle of short poems ('1940', GW 9, 817 for example).

The general category of the *Lehrgedichte* remains the centre of Brecht's work as a poet, although the predominant coincidence of this category with that of the poetry in free rhythms is now diminished by the greatly increased production of metrical texts. The metrical epigram is a major new development. Not surprisingly, Brecht wrote no *Massenlieder* in this period; political songs like 'Deutsches Miserere' and 'Und was bekam des Soldaten Weib?' were incorporated into the plays. 'Kinderkreuzzug' (1939, GW 10, 833), 'Deutschland' (1941/2, GW 10, 843) and 'Lied einer deutschen Mutter' (1942, GW 10, 854) are examples of the rare mode of ballads and songs with political subjects; it is evident, too, that these poems are less aggressive, more open to lyrical pathos than their precedents in Brecht's writings. A much greater number of metrical lyrics is devoted to more private subjects: 'Die Krücken' (1939, GW 9, 739), 'Ardens sed virens' (1939, GW 9, 750), 'Gemeinsame Erinnerung' (1943, GW 10, 863), and 'Auch das Beschädigte' (1943, GW 10, 857) are love-poems with a strong 'philosophical' element.

A small number of prose poems was produced in the early part of this period, the 'Visionen' (GW 9, 729) are mythical, allegorical *Chroniken* whose grotesque imagery places them in the proximity of the satires. 'Die Hoffnung der Welt' (GW 9, 738) and 'Überall vieles zu sehen' (GW 9, 809) are also prose poems. Within the sub-group of abstract theoretical poems, the metrical *Lehrgedicht von der Natur der Menschen* (GW 10, 895) occupies the most prominent position; its periphery includes most of the theoretical material written at this time. Besides the major poetological complex of the *Messingkauf* poems (1939/40, GW 9, 760) there are other notable exceptions: 'Ich habe gehört' (1939, GW 9, 752), 'Die neuen Zeitalter' (1943, GW 10, 856) and 'Viele sehen es so' (1944, GW 10, 875) are all autonomous texts.

The subgroup of the *Chroniken* is quite large; it includes 'Bericht der Serben' (1941, GW 9, 813), 'Das Pferd des Ruuskanen' (1941, GW 9, 805), and 'Im Zeichen der Schildkröte' (1943, GW 10, 855). These are reportage poems, directly related to the 'Geschichten aus der Revolution' and the anti-fascist chronicles. Other poems, equally concrete in reference, are not reports, but epistles, addresses: 'Briefe der Mutter an ihre Kinder in der Ferne' (1940, GW 9, 799), 'Rede einer proletarischen Mutter an ihre Söhne bei Kriegsausbruch' (1939, GW 9, 750), 'An die deutschen Soldaten im Osten' (1941/2, GW 10, 838) and 'Die gute Tat' (1942/3, GW 10, 853).

Finally, the autobiographical *Chronik* is represented by the cycles 'Finnland 1940' (1940, GW 9, 754) and '1940' (1939/40, GW 9, 817), and by poems such as 'Nachdenkend über die Hölle' (1941, GW 10, 830), 'Die Landschaft des Exils' (1941, GW 10, 830), and 'Sonett in der Emigration' (1941, GW 10, 831).

As the war continued, Brecht was forced into positions of increasing isolation, in which the factor of sheer physical distance was important. Access to Germany was now impossible; even communication between fellow exiles became extremely difficult.[3] The *Arbeitsjournal* is particularly rich in material from this period of enforced introversion; it contains many notes on poems, which were subject to the same, echoless delay as the dramas and prose writings. This practical isolation is apparent in the limitation which is a dominant characteristic of the poetry of this time; limitation here signifies a narrowing of focus, restriction of attention to a small range of subjects (above all, the war), which are treated in concrete detail. There is an increase in the number of poems identifiable as occasional works, and in those which employ personal, autobiographical material. The overall decrease in production and the shift towards shorter forms may be seen as part of this general trend. Such limitation does not, however, imply the production of work of less value or significance.

The Epigram

steff bringt mir den KRANZ DES MELEAGROS, übertragen von august OEHLER. die schönen epigramme erinnern mich an mein sonett RAT AN DIE LYRIKER DER USSR, ÖFFENTLICHE BAUWERKE ZU BESCHRIFTEN. ich mache bei einigen der epigramme änderungen und schreibe selber einige neue, als beispiele. wenn man bedenkt, wieviel die weimarer von den problemen der griechischen epigrammatiker wußten und wieviel wir noch davon wissen, sieht man den furchtbaren abstieg... hier, in diesen griechischen epigrammen, durchdringt die stimmung jene für sich wunderbare gegenständlichkeit und mit ihr den sinn, wie ein besonderer wind (abend- oder früh- oder april- oder schneewind) früchte und blätter eines baums bewegt. (AJ 25.7.40.)

This note documents an interest in the epigram which has been established by reference to the poems; it also indicates with what other concerns this interest is associated. Reference to the sonnet ('Vorschlag, die Architektur mit der Lyrik zu verbinden', GW 9, 551) illustrates the attraction of artistic control and economy; the train of thought is extended by consideration of the related aesthetic of Weimar Classicism. In this admittedly local and singular way, Weimar is regarded as belonging to a Golden Age, Brecht's distance from which constituted a sign of decline. Finally, Brecht praises the effectiveness of the epigram as a mode of poetry which attains both specific solidity ('gegenständlichkeit') and delicate, sensuous precision. Later notes extend this argument:

über die abbreviatur des klassischen stils: wenn ich auf einer seite genügend viel auslasse, erhalte ich für das einzige wort *nacht*, etwa in dem satz 'als die nacht kam', den vollen gegenwert an vorstellung beim leser. die inflation ist der tod jeder ökonomie. am besten, die wörter entlassen ihre gefolge und treten sich gegenüber mit so viel würde, als sie aus sich herstellen können. und ganz falsch zu sagen, daß die klassiker die sinne des lesers vergessen, im gegenteil, sie rechnen damit. unsere sensualisten gleichen rückenmärklern; um irgendein gefühl in die sohlen zu bekommen, müssen sie aufstampfen wie die napoleons. (AJ 9.8.40.)

The epigram's spare, disciplined mode implies an enhancement of the value of individual words, which therefore evoke a clearer and stronger response. It is thus mistaken to suppose that classic control involves sensuous impoverishment; pursuing the economic metaphor, Brecht insists that considered expenditure is more effective than careless squandering, that the readers' senses, far from responding only to undifferentiated cumulative impact, are eminently accessible to precise nuances of pressure and tension.

The specific association of this concept of fine sensitivity with the newly explored possibilities of the epigram should not obscure the general relevance of reflection and control to Brecht's poetry since the early twenties (in particular the major strand in free rhythms). In this sense, Brecht's notes constitute a retrospective theoretical formulation of what has already been practised. The epigram itself, while its dominance at this time is new, has a long history within Brecht's work.

It is only superficially a paradox that the emphasis on the classic mode is intimately connected with a concern for sensuous quality; this concern, which emerges strongly in the late thirties, is both a retention and a critique of elements of primitive materialism which were identified in Brecht's early work. 'wir deutschen haben einen materialismus ohne sinnlichkeit' (AJ 12.8.38); the gross sensual indulgence evoked in the *Baal* complex is subjected to critical appraisal: it is not simply rejected, but modified, made adequate to the demands of Marxist theory.

The epigrams written in Finland in the late summer of 1940, to which Brecht's notes refer, are not the same as those of the 'Deutsche Kriegsfibel' of *Svendborger Gedichte*; the new 'Finnische Epigramme' are not 'reimlose Lyrik mit unregelmäßigen Rhythmen', but metrical poems (iambic pentameters) based on a four-line, rhymed strophe.[4] These epigrams are formally related to the *Kinderlieder* and the metrical lyrics referred to in the introductory survey; they are closer to the sonnets, to whose quatrains they correspond directly. It is not surprising that Oehler's translations of the Greek epigrams remind Brecht of his own sonnet, which combines the formal link with a thematic one; the poem's recommendation of inscriptions and their appropriate lapidary style is in fundamental agreement with the classical texts. Apart from this instance of anticipation (the sonnet was written in 1935), these metrical epigrams constitute a completely fresh area of work;

it seems reasonable to follow the evidence of the *Arbeitsjournal* in attributing this development to the influence of the Oehler translations.

> Es hat an der athena tempelschwelle
> Des meisters theris kunsterfahrne hand
> Den maßstab hier, die schnurgerade elle
> Die starre säge mit gebognem rand
> Die axt, den hobel, leicht der hand sich fügend
> Den bohrer auch, der sich gedreht im kreis
> Zur schau gestellt, dem handwerksbrauch genügend
> Da er geendet seinen alten fleiß. (leonides) (AJ 25.7.40.)

In this quotation from Oehler, the 'gegenständlichkeit' admired by Brecht is evident: the epigram is concise and exact in its treatment of instruments of work, the approving detail of its description evokes the master's skill. A later note of Brecht's further illuminates his admiration:

> in den altgriechischen epigrammen sind die von den menschen verfertigten gebrauchsgegenstände ohne weiteres gegenstände der lyrik, auch die waffen ... es sind in unserer zeit nicht zuletzt moralische hemmungen, welche das aufkommen solcher lyrik der gegenstände verhindern. die schönheit eines flugzeuges hat etwas obszönes. (AJ 28.8.40.)

In the *Arbeitsjournal* entry for the following day, three more examples of Oehler's translations are interposed between photographs of a bomber cockpit and a set of hand-grenades; the contrast between the classical texts and the modern photographs emphasizes the 'obscenity' of modern weaponry. In the 'Finnische Epigramme' Brecht employs primarily domestic material, as if to avoid such brutal intrusion:

> FINNISCHE GUTTSSPEISEKAMMER 1940
>
> O schattige Speise! Einer dunklen Tanne
> Geruch geht nächtlich brausend in dich ein
> Und mischt sich mit dem süßer Milch aus großer Kanne
> Und dem des Räucherspecks vom kalten Stein.
> Bier, Ziegenkäse, frisches Brot und Beere
> Gepflückt im grauen Strauch, wenn Frühtau fällt!
> Oh, könnt ich laden euch, die überm Meere
> Der Krieg der leeren Mägen hält! (GW 9, 820.)

This poem, with the few similar texts for which it stands, marks a new departure in Brecht's poetry. Its first six lines display an unprecedented level of attention to material objects and physical details; in its celebration of colour, sound, smell, taste, and texture the poem generates a sense of richness which may be understood as an antidote to the sterile one-sidedness which Brecht saw as threatening his work. This richness is achieved with a startling economy of means; the poem relies on a predominantly nominal and adjectival diction, especially on the epithet–noun pair. No lexical special effects are employed, no exotic words; the words used stand in autonomous prominence and high definition, to which the syntactic organization of the poem contributes effectively. Syntax operates here in two distinct ways, firstly by its virtual absence (in phrases like: 'schattige Speise!', 'Bier, Ziegenkäse, frisches Brot und Beere'), and secondly by its contrasting complexity in word-order and the use of the genitive: 'einer dunklen Tanne Geruch ... mit dem süßer Milch ... und dem des Räucherspecks'; nominal autonomy is reinforced by such complexity, which obliges the reader to analyse constructions and isolate proper antecedents. Vocal reading of the poem has to be particularly slow and careful; it underlines the poem's sense of static fullness, its evocation of the condition of rest which follows both natural process and human labour—the scent of the pine blown in by the night wind, the berries plucked in the morning dew. Variations in the length of line (lines three and four, for example), and restrained assonance add to the poem's subtle richness.

The poem attains a transcendent kind of simplicity, almost an illusion of simplicity, which only superficially conceals the complex artistry of the text. Its clarity is the result of a high degree of compositional control; strict economy of subject-matter, limitation of focus provoke in the reader's imagination the sense of other objects co-present with those named in the text.

This is not, however, a purely descriptive and idyllic poem, a literary refuge from the dark times; its final lines place it firmly in the context of the war and exile. The poem is virtually divided into two parts which are made to interact: the significance of each part is modified, made relative by the other. As in 'An die Nachgeborenen', Brecht, far from envisaging escape, insists that—however limited its possibilities—work against fascism must be continued, in the full knowledge of what it costs. Both title and text of the epigram emphasize the paradoxical conjunction of its two parts; idyllic elements are anachronistic, inadequate—yet they contain substantially the human completeness which is the goal of the present inhuman struggle. Adoption of the dialectic thus formulated in the epigram equips the reader for his un-idyllic work.

'Finnische Gutsspeisekammer 1940' is clearly distinguished from 'An die Nachgeborenen' by its more generous attention to the alienating aspects of political work; it evokes a more immediate and acute sense of impoverishment, in which the autobiographical elements of the poem play an important role. Besides its more general interests, the poem clearly refers to Brecht's situation; his isolation, both personal and political, contradicts his equally complex enjoyment of the Finnish idyll. The epigram is an attempt to make such contradictions productive in the present dark times. Once again thinking of the history of the German lyric and its decline in the post-Weimar era, Brecht writes of 'die sprachwaschung, die ich mit den finnischen EPIGRAMMEN vornehme' (AJ 22.8.40); the metaphor may be understood in terms of the limitation referred to as characteristic of these poems; brevity, metrical and lexical discipline, concentration, and clarity. This very discipline implies the opposite of aesthetic impoverishment: artistic limitation is the basis of imaginative fullness.[5] In this extended sense, 'sprachwaschung' indicates a partial washing-away of the one-sided, over-emphatic intrusions of the war; in its attention to the pleasures of sensuous detail, the epigram anticipates a more general emancipation from alienation. More strongly than in Brecht's previous mature work, the literary aesthetic is employed as a weapon.

> Der verkrüppelte Baum im Hof
> Zeigt auf den schlechten Boden, aber
> Die Vorübergehenden schimpfen ihn einen Krüppel
> Doch mit Recht ...
>
> In mir streiten sich
> Die Begeisterung über den blühenden Apfelbaum
> Und das Entsetzen über die Reden des Anstreichers.
> Aber nur das zweite
> Drängt mich zum Schreibtisch.
>
> ('Schlechte Zeit für Lyrik' 1939, GW 9, 743.)

The 'Finnische Epigramme' demonstrate that the model presented in 'Schlechte Zeit für Lyrik' is not unique in Brecht's work; once seated at his writing table, Brecht persistently integrates the awareness of pleasurable human experience in politically operative poetry. This materialist aesthetic is implicit in Brecht's poetry from the early thirties onwards; it is especially prominent in the second half of the exile period.

The importance of these epigrams rests on their quality as literary works: they do not otherwise represent a major area of Brecht's production. The degree of aesthetic emphasis attained in these poems was not adopted as a general orientation. In the note already referred to (AJ 29.8.40), the confrontation of Oehler's translations with modern photographs does not only illustrate the 'obscenity' of the weapons shown; it suggests that such poetry is radically inadequate to a situation in which these weapons exist. Brecht's epigrams imply the recognition and attempted rectification of this inadequacy in their own confrontation of the domestic means of reproduction with the distant wholesale destruction of the war; Brecht may nevertheless have considered that traces of inappropriateness remained in these poems, where detail of domestic objects contrasts with only general focus on the war: this set a limit to their political specificity.

If the Finnish epigrams thus remain an impressive literary exercise, related developments in Brecht's poetry suggest that the exercise, though short-lived, was not a dead end. The *Arbeitsjournal* entries begin to be accompanied by photographs cut out from newspapers early in 1940. The entry for 21.9.40 is of particular interest:

die berliner illustrirte ist immer sehr interessant. in der nr. 38 finde ich auf einanderfolgenden seiten das bild des gebombten london und dann *deutsche baumeister.*

As the following page of the journal shows, Brecht cut out the title and pasted it on to the page above the photograph of bomb damage to London, as an ironic headline. The significance of this piece of wit, a simple variation of John Heartfield's classic technique, is made clear by the entry for 15.10.40. Here, photographs from newspapers are provided with texts specially written by Brecht; beneath a picture which shows Hitler shaking hands with an old woman, Brecht writes:

> Die alten Weiber lasset zu mir kommen!
> Daß sie noch sehn, vor sie zur Grube fahren
> Der ihre Söhne in sein Heer genommen
> Als jene noch aus ihren Gruben waren.

This text is clearly related to the Finnish epigrams; in its reference to the photograph it is a 'Gegenstandsgedicht'. It is also a rhymed poem, composed of iambic pentameters in four-line groups. Its subject, however, is no longer primarily domestic, but explicitly political; the experiment in aesthetic emancipation is displaced by the familiar mode of satirical criticism. These 'fotoepigramme', later simply 'fotogramme', bring a new directness and concision to this mode.

Other antecedents of the 'fotogramme' may be identified in the epigrams of the 'Deutsche Kriegsfibel' with which they share their general thematic orientation; an examination of 'Deutsche Kriegsfibel II' reveals a specific point of contact between the free rhythms and the rhymed, metrical epigrams: besides the typical

> Der Bauer pflügt den Acker.
> Wer
> Wird die Ernte einbringen? (GW 9, 734.)

the series includes one text which is conspicuously different:

> Da wird ein Tag sein, wo ihr dies bereut
> Ihr Lauten, die ihr schreit und die ihr schweigt, ihr Stillen!
> Und käm kein solcher Tag, ich weinte um euch heut
> Und wär es nur um eurer Kinder willen. (1939, GW 9, 736.)

Formally, and in its exclamatory tone, this poem is related to the experimental 'fotogramme' of the *Arbeitsjournal*. 'Auf einem Meilenstein der Autostraßen' (GW 9, 736), though in free rhythms, is a 'Gegenstandsgedicht' similar in conception to the 'fotogramme'; it is less literal than the other 'Deutsche Kriegsfibel' poems, which avoid fictional elements.

Closer still to the 'fotogramme' are 'Grabschrift aus dem Krieg des Hitler' (1941, GW 9, 758) and 'Ich lese von der Panzerschlacht' (1940, GW 9, 821). The latter was to be included in the *Steffinische Sammlung*, which also contains three rhymed iambic epigrams later published with photographs as 'fotogramme': 'Gedenktafeln für im Krieg des Hitler gegen Frankreich Gefallene' (1940, GW 9,

821) and 'Gedenktafel für 4000, die im Krieg des Hitler gegen Norwegen versenkt wurden' (1940, GW 9, 822). The earliest example of the short metrical epitaph is a poem written four years earlier: 'Und so beginne ich ihn denn zu suchen' (GW 9, 571), which may be resolved into three quatrains. Brecht had been presented with an edition of Kipling's verse during his stay in London in 1936; this edition contains Kipling's 'Epitaphs of the War', which are so close to Brecht's metrical epigrams that the hypothesis of direct influence seems most plausible.[6]

The complex line of descent of these war-epigrams runs from the sonnet quatrains, via Kipling's epitaphs, Oehler's translations, and the 'Finnische Epigramme', to the 'Grabschriften' of the *Steffinische Sammlung*. The prototypes of the 'fotogramme' included in the *Arbeitsjournal* in October 1940 were followed in the next four years by more than seventy similar texts, the majority of which were published in 1955 under the title *Kriegsfibel*. These poems are immediate responses to aspects of the war simply illuminated in the photographs to which they are appended; the original significance of the picture is modified more or less radically, corrected, or extended by the critical commentary of the epigram. The *Kriegsfibel* epigrams are miniature *Chroniken*; they expose the perverse logic of the war (2; 9; 20), its real basis (22; 35) and social character (32; 33; 57); they extend from satirical attacks on the fascist hierarchy (25-8) to the prescriptive and admonitory mode of numbers 59, 64, 67, 68, and 69.

> Das da hätt einmal fast die Welt regiert.
> Die Völker wurden seiner Herr. Jedoch
> Ich wollte, daß ihr nicht schon triumphiert:
> Der Schoß ist fruchtbar noch, aus dem das kroch. (69; GW 10, 1048.)

Compared with those of *Svendborger Gedichte* these poems are modest and limited; they fulfil their function with clarity and force, generalizing without over-simplifying. Probably Brecht considered the restriction of focus to the public and actual an appropriate solution to the problems of writing described above. The anticipatory artistic emancipation evoked in the 'Finnische Epigramme' is superseded by the austerely political 'fotogramme' of the *Kriegsfibel*, for which the struggle is all. The distance between the practice of poetry and the decisive events of the war is, at least potentially, reduced.[7]

In June 1941 Brecht was forced to leave Finland; he travelled across the Soviet Union and sailed for the USA, where he settled on Santa Monica as his base. This move greatly increased Brecht's physical separation from his country and correspondingly his sense of isolation.

hier lyrik zu schreiben, selbst aktuelle, bedeutet: sich in den elfenbeinturm zurückziehen. es ist, als betreibe man goldschmiedekunst. das hat etwas schrulliges, kauzhaftes, borniertes. solche lyrik ist flaschenpost, die schlacht um smolensk geht auch um die lyrik. (AJ 5.4.42.)

The eccentricity which Brecht saw as afflicting the writing of poetry in the USA is apparently not derived simply from his isolation from Germany: it is specific to the American context itself. Brecht's inability effectively to influence events within Germany was underlined by this foreign social climate, in which the mechanisms of capitalism operated so openly, and with such wide assent, that he at first despaired of finding a public at all:

> Ich fragte mich: warum reden mit ihnen?
> Sie kaufen das Wissen ein, um es zu verkaufen.
> Sie wollen hören, wo es billiges Wissen gibt
> Das man teuer verkaufen kann. Warum
> Sollten sie wissen wollen, was
> Gegen Kauf und Verkauf spricht?
>
> ('Das will ich ihnen sagen' 1941/2, GW 10, 852.)[8]

From this point of view it is less surprising that Brecht, whose poems, like his other writings, had sought to provide helpful suggestions, should suddenly see them as hopeless requests for aid ('flaschenpost'); more than at any previous time, Brecht was aware that, without an audience, his work was worthless. The battles in the Soviet Union would thus decide whether his intended (German) audience would be accessible.

The 'Hollywood-Elegien' (1942, GW 10, 849–50) adopt the satirical mode of 'Verschollener Ruhm der Riesenstadt New York' and 'Lied der preiswerten Lyriker'; they examine the glittering magnificence of Hollywood, finding that it is merely fool's gold. These bitter and aggressive epigrams are only peripherally elegies:

> IV Unter den grünen Pfefferbäumen
>   Gehen die Musiker auf den Strich, zwei und zwei
>   Mit den Schreibern. Bach

Hat ein Strichquartett im Täschchen. Dante schwenkt
Den dürren Hintern.

This reference to Bach and Dante was not lightly made; Brecht saw himself as a poet of equivalent importance and was himself obliged to seek a kind of patronage as a screen writer. 'Hollywood' (1942, GW 10, 848) summarizes his view of this situation:

> Jeden Morgen, mein Brot zu verdienen
> Gehe ich auf den Markt, wo Lügen gekauft werden.
> Hoffnungsvoll
> Reihe ich mich ein zwischen die Verkäufer.

The fantastic and scurrilous exoticism of the 'Hollywood-Elegien' is powerful and rich, in spite of the poems' concision;[9] in the example quoted, the pepper trees suggest an irritant abrasiveness which is appropriate to the grotesque scene of classical composers and poets walking in pairs, waiting for customers.

Brecht knew that much of his most important work was either 'für die schublade' or for the limited circle of German-speaking exiles with whom he was in contact during these years. Nevertheless, he still thought in terms of publication:

könnte ich die VERSUCHE weiterführen, würde ich außer den epigrammen und den lyrischen kurzgedichten in der versart der kriegsfibel doch auch einige szenen aus dem drehbuch von TRUST THE PEOPLE abdrucken. (AJ 18.10.42.)

This note confirms the importance of the epigram in this phase of Brecht's production, and demonstrates that 'epigrammen' signifies the rhymed, metrical poems discussed above (the 'Finnische Epigramme', and above all the 'fotogramme') as distinct from the lyrics in free rhythms (the 'Deutsche Kriegsfibel' of *Svendborger Gedichte,* for example). These 'lyrische kurzgedichte in der versart der kriegsfibel' are not to be confused with the metrical 'foto gramme' later published as *Kriegsfibel*; the epigrams and epigrammatic poems in free rhythms are a distinct, though related strand. It includes 'Der Lautsprecher' (1939, GW 9, 758), 'Im Bade' (1939/40, GW 9, 759), 'Die Maske des Bösen' (1942, GW 10, 850), 'Zeitunglesen beim Teekochen' (1942, GW 10, 846), and the cycles 'Finnland 1940' (GW 9, 754) and '1940' (GW 9, 817).

Further evidence of Brecht's defiantly edition-orientated thinking is provided in the *Arbeitsjournal* (26.9.43). This is the preliminary selection for a new collection of poems under the title formerly given to the final section of *Gesammelte Werke* (1938) IV: 'Gedichte im Exil'. The project reaches its conclusion in December 1944: 'photographische experimente . . . erstes resultat GEDICHTE IM EXIL' (AJ 12.44); the experiments enabled the production of photographic copies, small editions of poems which Brecht sent to friends, including Heinrich Mann.[10] In its several forms, the American 'Gedichte im Exil' collection sought to present a representative sample of poems written between 1938 and 1943; those selected are almost all epigrammatic poems in free rhythms, autobiographical *Chroniken*. In this collection Brecht reflects on the negative potential of the 'sprachwaschung' idea, in so far as it implied lexical limitation:

im grund sind die gedichte in einer art 'basic german' geschrieben. das entspricht durchaus nicht einer theorie, ich empfinde den mangel in ausdruck und rhythmus, wenn ich solch eine sammlung durchlese, aber beim schreiben (und korrigieren) widerstrebt mir jedes ungewöhnliche wort. (AJ 12.44.)

What in the early 'Finnische Epigramme' had been conceived as a means of avoiding aesthetic impoverishment, is later, in the context of poems in free rhythms, regarded as an (albeit unavoidable) instance of such impoverishment. Such near-contradiction illustrates the precarious equilibrium of Brecht's artistic sovereignty in the second half of the exile period.

Landscapes

Natural elements are an important constituent of many poems from the late thirties onward; appearing as singular elements in the 'Gegenstandsgedicht', 'Finnische Gutsspeisekammer 1940', they are unified as landscape in poems of the cycles 'Frühling 1938' and '1940':

II Über dem Sund hängt Regengewölke, aber den Garten
   Vergoldet noch die Sonne. Die Birnbäume
   Haben grüne Blätter und noch keine Blüten, die Kirschbäume hingegen
   Blüten und noch keine Blätter. Die weißen Dolden
   Scheinen aus dürren Ästen zu sprießen.
   Über das gekräuselte Sundwasser
   Läuft ein kleines Boot mit geflicktem Segel.

In das Gezwitscher der Stare
Mischt sich der ferne Donner
Der manövrierenden Schiffsgeschütze
Des Dritten Reiches. (GW 9, 815.)

The conclusions derived from analysis of 'Finnische Gutsspeisekammer 1940' are relevant to this poem, and to its companions in the *Steffinische Sammlung*; the treatment of landscape is not an escapist choice, but a kind of limitation. The landscapes of his exile are the mediating links between the poet and political conflict; in the thematization of landscape, Brecht recognizes his separation from the centres of the struggle. In the poem quoted, the general significance of landscape seems to be the felicitous anticipation identified in the epigram: the beauty of such acute and contrasting detail could be accessible to everyone; it is inappropriate to the war which intervenes, or is the war, seen at a distance, inappropriate to such a world? On closer examination, the naval artillery which interrupts the birdsong also threatens the fisherman, the producer and proletarian ('ein kleines Boot mit geflicktem Segel'); war against the 'Third Reich' is his war. The specific detail of the observed landscape is also important: in the complex dissimultaneity of the weather and the development of the trees, a subtle dialectic is perceived. Political developments too tend to be unequal; this uncertainty leaves room for surprises—blossom may spring from apparently barren branches.

A similar hopeful potential is intimated in 'Der Kirschdieb' (1938, GW 9, 816), in which the poet is surprised by a cheerful and very early act of appropriation. Typically, subject matter of immediate and solid presence is made the focus of much wider reflection.[11]

In 'Vom Sprengen des Gartens' (1943, GW 10, 861) insistent detail invites the reader to look beyond the literal reference of the poem and consider its possible resonances. Culture, restored to its primary sense, is shown to be the result of human labour, acting on natural material. The gardener's function is to liberate productivity, a role which demands generosity ('gib mehr als genug'), and an eye for the potential of the most inauspicious places:

>Und übersieh mir nicht
>Zwischen den Blumen das Unkraut, das auch
>Durst hat. Noch gieße nur

Den frischen Rasen oder den versengten nur:
Auch den nackten Boden erfrische du.

The poem may be seen as an extension of 'Der Pflaumenbaum' and 'Über die Unfruchtbarkeit' in the direction of positive prescription. It evokes, outside the sphere of horticulture, a general emancipation whose slogan 'from each according to his ability, to each according to his needs' may gloss the poem.

'Garden in Progress' (1944, GW 10, 883) was written in praise of Charles Laughton's garden in Hollywood. Interwoven with the long and precise description are a number of locally allegorical strands: the complex, flourishing equilibrium of the garden is produced by work, as much intellectual as physical; but the balanced whole is not static or finished. The law of unequal development applies to the rich variety of this garden, which is not administered by an inflexible dictator: 'Wie der Garten mit dem Plan/ Wächst der Plan mit dem Garten'. At the same time, the gardener is not reluctant to carry out measures of critical intervention: 'Der Herr des Gartens/ Baut mit der scharfen Säge/ Alljährlich ein neues Geäst'.

Brecht's use of landscape as material for parabolic reflection does not reduce this material to the role of invented costume, or mere cipher. These landscapes are real, often specifically identifiable and it is precisely the perceptive seriousness with which they are viewed (for example, as changing products of interaction between human and natural forces) that allows the transition to metaphorical reference. Such transitions are characteristically prepared with extreme subtlety: the reader is invited to consider possibilities of reference, but is never dictated to.

Materialism

The early Finnish epigrams share with these later landscape poems a high level of attention to the specific detail of sense-experience; like the sensuous emancipation evoked in the epigrams, this development is related to the increasing prominence of the theme of materialism in all Brecht's work from 1938. *Leben des Galilei, Herr Puntila und sein Knecht Mätti, Flüchtlingsgespräche,* and the short story 'Eßkultur' all treat this theme.

As the first chapter of the study sought to show, materialism was not a theme which Brecht discovered in the late thirties: its origins are in his earliest work. While the general term usefully indicates this important connection, it obscures the fact that there is no simple continuity between materialist elements in Brecht's work of 1918 and those typical of work produced twenty years later. It is evident that the metrical epigrams and the landscape poems are consciously fundamentally political: theirs is a Marxist materialism.

The complex continuity which is involved here may conveniently be illustrated by reference to the *Baal* complex; the centre of 'primitive' materialism in Brecht's early work, it rose to new prominence in 1938, when Brecht considered the possibility of a new 'Lehrstück' based on this first play: *Der böse Baal der Asoziale*:

baal, der provokateur, der verehrer der dinge, wie sie sind, der sichausleber und der andreausleber. sein 'mach, was dir spaß macht!' gäbe viel her, richtig behandelt. (AJ 11.9.38.)

If Baal, as the 'verehrer der dinge, wie sie sind' denotes the sceptical, reductive vision tending towards resignation, which was shown to be fundamental to the early poetry, the imperative which follows clearly implies a critical attitude with more positive potential. (This aspect of the *Baal* material, to which Brecht attaches his plans for the new project, was itself prefigured in the original text; the 'Choral vom Manne Baal' proclaims: 'Seid nur nicht so faul und so verweicht/ Denn Genießen ist bei Gott nicht leicht!' (GW 8, 250). The intimate connection between pleasure and work is precisely the direction of Brecht's renewed interest in the *Baal* complex.) A later note indicates the development of this idea:

der große irrtum, der mich hinderte, die lehrstückchen vom BÖSEN BAAL DEM ASOZIALEN herzustellen, bestand in meiner definition des sozialismus als einer *großen ordnung*. er ist hingegen viel praktischer als *große produktion* zu definieren. produktion muß natürlich im weitesten sinn genommen werden, und der kampf gilt der befreiung der produktivität aller menschen von allen fesseln. (AJ 7.3.41.)

The liberation of the forces of production is the proletarian revolution.

Such reflections are directly relevant to the poetry; in connection with a dramatic project related to *Baal*, 'Die Reisen des

Glücksgotts', conceived in late 1941, Brecht composed a cycle of songs and poems:

mitunter denke ich nach über einen zyklus LIEDER DES GLÜCKS-GOTTS, ein ganz und gar materialistisches werk, preisend 'das gute leben' (in doppelter bedeutung). essen, trinken, wohnen, schlafen, lieben, arbeiten, denken, die großen genüsse. (AJ 20.7.43.)

Like the new *Baal* project, this was to remain fragmentary, a fact which accounts for the considerable scope and flexibility of the extant material. Not all these poems were written after the formulation of the plan quoted above: 'Siebentes Lied des Glücksgotts' I and II (GW 10, 891-3) may have been produced as early as 1939, while the epigram 'Ich bin der Glücksgott' (GW 10, 894) was written in 1941.

The poems integrate this theoretical dimension in an energetic and colloquial manner which is itself close to the mode of such early poems as 'Beschwerdelied'; in 'Arie des Glückgotts' (GW 10, 889), the mocking, but not unsympathetic god proffers materialism in the shape of agricultural and economic advice: production transforms a life which offers no enjoyment. Much may be accomplished by a minimum of labour. In the invitation of the final lines, there is also a challenge—production must be matched by appropriation: 'Dann komm und hol dir die Äpfel/ Von dem Baum, den du bestellt'. This is a revolutionary slogan.

'Zweites Lied des Glücksgotts', which follows, is an ironic, provocative poem, strongly reminiscent of the early lyrics; but its over-emphatic, resigned acquiescence here demands correction by the reader. The call to action of the first song is here supported *ex negativo,* via the contradiction of such statements as: 'Groß bleibt groß und klein bleibt klein/ Soviel weiß ich noch'.

The third song moves to a simpler and more specific argument:

> Als die Braut ihr Bier getrunken
> Gingen wir hinaus. Der Hof lag nächtlich.
> Hinterm Abtritt hat's gestunken
> Doch die Wollust war beträchtlich. (GW 10, 890.)

From this direct, sensual experience the poem proceeds to emphasize the value of life; its final two lines are a variation on the theme of 'Gegen Verführung': 'Unterm grünen Rasen/ Ist zu wenig Abwechslung'.

'Liebesunterricht' explores further this section of the wide materialist spectrum defined in Brecht's *Arbeitsjournal* note. Besides its particular practical recommendations, the song argues for the abandonment of several traditional distinctions, whose core is the false dichotomy of neo-Platonism, body and soul: 'Fleischlich lieb ich mir die Seele/ Und beseelt lieb ich das Fleisch' (GW 10, 890). Sensuousness is firmly reinstated as a proper constituent of materialism (but is not an exclusive definition, as in the early poems). 'Siebentes Lied des Glücksgotts' I elaborates the position of the pagan (and priapic) subversive deity: he is a low and common god, fundamentally opposed to sterile sublimity.

> Freunde, wenn ihr euch mir verschreibt
> Und das könnte sich lohnen
> Wißt, daß ihr dann nicht geduldet bleibt
> Mehr in den höheren Regionen! (GW 10, 891.)

The implications of this good-natured witty introduction are shown to be wide and radical; the simple pleasures of physical sensation and comfort lead to the more general rhetorical question: 'Und ein Stück Fleisch und ein Dach überm Kopf/ Ist der Mensch etwa dazu geboren?', which provokes an affirmative response. The reader is reminded, to quote other Brecht texts, that 'die Wahrheit ist konkret' (GW 9, 820), or that 'Wenn die Niedrigen nicht/ An das Niedrige denken/ Kommen sie nicht hoch' (GW 9, 633). The song is concluded triumphantly:

> Ich bin der Gott der Niedrigkeit
> Der Gaumen und der Hoden
> Denn das Glück liegt nun einmal, tut mir leid
> Ziemlich niedrig am Boden.

Materialism in its full and complex sense is admitted to be a 'niedrige Gesinnung': the proper, socially conscious 'Gesinnung der Niedrigen'.[12] Collective happiness, the 'good life' are not only metaphorically close to the ground; the fertile earth is also the real material basis of any social development. Its proper use results in sufficient production; the social appropriation of these products is the precondition for the quality of life foreseen by Marx in communism. Just as the materialism proposed by Brecht insists on a continuity between the detail of sensuous pleasure and the complexity of thought of the Marxist dialectic, so too it denies any total separation of the goal from the path.[13] Work for the revolution, far from postponing all emancipation, must integrate as much as possible into the immediate, daily struggle.[14] This major theoretical insight also underlies the early 'Finnische Epigramme' discussed above. Corresponding to theoretical positions adopted by Marx and Engels (and indeed Heine), this generous and ambitious demand was in revolt against the idealist tradition, which Brecht saw as a major contributor to the 'Deutsche Misere'— and perhaps against elements of idealism evident in the theory and practice of Soviet socialism. The 'Gegenstandsgedicht' illuminates the revolutionary character of the 'Glücksgott':

> Ich bin der Glücksgott, sammelnd um mich Ketzer
> Auf Glück bedacht in diesem Jammertal.
> Ein Agitator, Schmutzaufwirbler, Hetzer
> Und hiemit—macht die Tür zu —illegal.   (GW 10, 894.)

The second part of 'Siebentes Lied des Glücksgotts' describes the disciples called to follow this god; a sense of humour is a primary qualification: it takes the form of defiant wit, praised in the *Flüchtlingsgespräche* as characteristic of the dialectic. 'Unter uns, ich nehm gern Partei/ Für die unruhigen Geister'; the subversive god demands rebellious followers, and instructs them in terms reminiscent of the 'Einheitsfrontlied': 'Freunde, duldet nicht nur keinen Herrn/ Sondern auch keinen Sklaven' (GW 10, 893).

The 'Elftes Lied . . .' is an epigram, the only poem of the cycle composed in free rhythms; in the extravagant conceit of the first section, it is proposed that there is no situation in which the struggle for human happiness can be totally suppressed.[15] The final lines exaggerate this point of view, inviting an ironic reading and a reconstruction of the challenge as: 'seid Künstler, Lebende!'—why wait until it is too late?

Finally, another metrical epigram, thematically close to the 'Finnische Epigramme', counterweights the aggressive, abrasive tone of the preceding songs by its evocation of the bucolic idyll: the plebeian god, the materialist and rebel, is at the same time the god of production and plenty—

> Ich bin der Schutzgott der Pflüger und Säer
> Der Lehrer der Pflücker, der Lehrer der Mäher:
> Die schäumende Milch, das duftende Brot
> Traube und Birne war's, was ich bot.   (GW 10, 894.)

Lehrgedicht von der Natur der Menschen

In January 1945 Brecht was once again occupied with 'Die Reisen des Glücksgotts', which he now conceived as an opera (AJ 23.1.45); his main undertaking was, however, the translation of *Galilei*, in which Charles Laughton collaborated. This creative co-operation between dramatist and actor, which Brecht considered of classic significance, was interrupted in February when Laughton was summoned to bread-winning film work:

da LAUGHTON für 8 wochen in einen piratenfilm muß, schaue ich mich nach einer arbeit um und beschließe, das manifest zu versifizieren, in der art des lukrezischen lehrgedichts, als fleißarbeit. (AJ 11.2.45.)

The cool pragmatism of these lines may be deceptive: there is strong evidence that a 'philosophisches Lehrgedicht' was envisaged a decade earlier, and indeed some texts incorporated in the poem of 1945 are dated 1933.[16] Laughton's departure was perhaps less the prime motive of Brecht's decision than a trigger: the disruption of Brecht's plans provided an opportunity for the execution of a major latent project. Moreover, as the continuing text of the *Arbeitsjournal* entry shows, 'fleißarbeit' is not to be understood exclusively as an artistic exercise in imitation and probably far from being a mere surrogate for dramatic work, the poem is a social task:

das manifest ist als pamphlet selbst ein kunstwerk; jedoch scheint es mir möglich, die propagandistische wirkung heute, hundert jahre später, und mit neuer, bewaffneter autorität versehen, durch ein aufheben des pamphletistischen charakters, zu erneuern.

The attempt to produce a classic version of one of Marxism's classic texts contained an element of political actuality; since 1943, as the *Arbeitsjournal* records, Brecht had continually re-examined the question of the possibility of revolt for the German proletariat.[17] His preliminary conclusion was that no uprising could be expected (or expected to succeed) as long as the machinery of terrorist repression was intact. In 1945, when the German defeat was imminent, the overwhelming power of the state appeared susceptible to erosion, and Brecht hoped for news of local rebellion in advance of the Allied conquests. As notes closely contemporary with the 'philosophisches Lehrgedicht' reveal, it was commenced in an attitude which mingled disappointment with expectancy.[18] The new poem was intended as propaganda, for the use of an emergent German proletarian movement, to which the advancing Red Army would lend its 'bewaffnete autorität'. It is not clear precisely when Brecht decided that a *Communist Manifesto* in verse should form the centre-piece of a 'philosophisches Lehrgedicht'; by the end of March 1945 a detailed plan for the work had been formulated.[19] It was to comprise four cantos, of which the second and third were to present versions of the first and second chapters of the *Manifesto* respectively; this core was to be flanked by an account of 'die schwierigkeit ... sich in der natur der gesellschaft zurechtzufinden', together with a brief treatment of contemporary socialist literature, in the first canto, and by the fourth canto, in its exposition of 'die ungeheuerlich gesteigerte barbarisierung'. The second canto was the first to be written: though it produced positive judgements from Brecht's son Stefan, from Helene Weigel, Fritz Kortner, Karl Korsch, and others whose opinion Brecht valued, it was never completed, and the remaining cantos are fragmentary.[20] Hanns Eisler considered the project too ambitious: Brecht seemed to take too much for granted in the demands such a work would make on its intended readers, many of whom, Eisler noted, were not familiar with the *Manifesto* in its original text. Lion Feuchtwanger shared with Eisler the opinion that Brecht's hexameters were unacceptably free, indeed faulty. Brecht apparently was more concerned about the aesthetic argument, and foresaw no insuperable problems of reception. It is unlikely that Brecht's tenacity should have been undermined by this discouraging response alone; the political developments of 1945 emphasized the intrinsic difficulty of this undertaking, and it was put aside, probably in mid 1945. This did not, however, signify the abandonment of the 'Lehrgedicht' project; it was taken up once more in 1947, probably at the instigation of Korsch, who wished to see its publication mark the centenary of the *Communist Manifesto*.[21] Hans Bunge records sporadic work on the poem throughout the fifties, including a final experiment in versification: in 1955, ten lines were written in which the stichic hexameters of all previous versions were transposed into elegiac couplets.

Of the 'kernstück', 'Das Manifest', only the first half has been published; the fragmentary third canto (equivalent to the second chapter of the *Manifesto*) is not represented in the *Gesammelte*

Werke. In the flexible, loose hexameters of the second canto, Brecht presents a version of the 1848 text which is in general close to the original. The overall structure is retained, as are many phrases; Brecht's text is often a direct verse paraphrase.[22] There are occasional alterations in sequence, and Brecht's version is considerably shorter than the original, since it avoids several explanatory and extensive passages. Nevertheless, Brecht included new examples, and was not content to reproduce uncritically what Marx and Engels had written; his poem was produced for a specific readership of the mid twentieth century.

In the 'Preface', beginning 'Kriege zertrümmern die Welt . . .' (GW 10, 911), the actuality obtained by such slight alterations is apparent; where Marx and Engels had affirmed the status of communism as a political force, Brecht takes war as his point of departure. He recognizes the painful dialectic of communist participation in the current war—'riesige Tanks besteigend und fliegend in tödlichen Bombern'—concluding confidently: 'Ehrengast in den Elendsquartieren und Furcht der Paläste/ Ewig zu bleiben gekommen: sein Name ist Kommunismus'. The poem's immediate value is strengthened by its cultivation of the historical dimension: Marxism, too, is history, but is not obsolete.[23] On the contrary, the *Lehrgedicht*, in this central section, undertakes to illuminate the present by means of a careful and critical reappropriation of the classical text. In an attitude reminiscent of the *ad fontes* of Renaissance scholarship, Brecht introduces the main body of the text: 'Viel davon hörtet ihr. Dies aber ist, was die Klassiker sagen.' The appeal to authority in this sentence is made relative by the critical inquiry which it implies as its condition; and the contemporary significance of the 'Klassiker' is proclaimed by the use of the present tense.

Economy dictates that the present study should concentrate on distinctive features of Brecht's poem; a more complete account would demand detailed treatment of the *Communist Manifesto* itself.

Brecht's first major departure from the original text is the passage 'Zwar, es handeln . . .' to 'Sturz in das Chaos' (GW 10, 912–13). This expansion of the argument is devoted to the application of the fundamental theory of history as 'zuvörderst Geschichte der Kämpfe der Klassen'; contrasting two forms of the bourgeois state,

Brecht illuminates the rise of fascism in Europe. Some parliamentary democracies were able to maintain business as usual, without resorting to terrorist dictatorship and war economy:

> Hier eine Klasse vor allem den großen Despoten benutzend
> Dort die despotische Vielfalt der Kammern, und eine den Vorteil
> Suchend durch blutige Kriege, und eine gemach durch Verträge.[24]

War is characteristically accompanied by a blurring of class conflict, but is nonetheless an extension of it:

> Burgfrieden gab es zuweilen. Die Klassen kämpften verbündet
> Gegen den äußeren Feind und stellten den eigenen Kampf ein;
> Doch den von beiden erfochtenen Sieg gewann dann nur eine...
> Tiefer nämlich und dauernder ist als der Krieg noch der Völker
> Den die Geschichtsschreiber schwatzhaft berichten, der Kampf
>   doch der Klassen.

In the context of the imminent conclusion of war against Germany, this extensive theoretical discourse contains a challenge equivalent to the topos: 'endlich die Gewehre in die richtige Richtung gerichtet!'

Another addition is made for professional reasons: the account of the displacement of use-value by exchange-value in capitalist economy is enriched by examples from the field of artistic production. The analysis is familiar from poems such as 'Lied der preiswerten Lyriker' and 'Die Literatur wird durchforscht werden':

> Und was hat der Künstler zu tun für sein Essen?
> Schön porträtiert er das Antlitz der Bourgeoisie mit dem adelnden Pinsel
> Kundig des Kunstgriffs massieret der Dame erschlafftes Gemüt er.
> So denn verwandelt die Bourgeoisie in ihre bezahlten
> Kopflanger alle die Dichter und Denker. (GW 10, 915.)

A similar motivation is discernible in a further interposed section; noting that the development of the means of production leads to conflict between these forces and the existing mode of production, Brecht argues that the economic forces tend to modify property relations, and thus the law in general. Similar modifications follow in other areas of the superstructure, religion, philosophy, and the whole of intellectual life. The relationship between base and superstructure is not treated as an automatic, mechanical one; the latter is described in terms of a specificity which implies a degree of autonomy. In the field of ideas, religion, and political discourse, old dominances may be dissolved as a consequence of economic change, but may, alternatively, be retained in more or less unaltered form:

Heilige Tempel, die tausend Frühlingen trotzten, zerfallen
Lautlos in Staub über Nacht, vom Tritt der Sieger erschüttert
Und in den stehengebliebenen wechseln die Götter ihr Antlitz;
Wundersam gleichen die alten jetzt plötzlich den jetzigen Herrschern.
(GW 10, 918.)[25]

In connection with the subject of the cyclical crises typical of capitalism, Brecht touches on the unemployment which results from such crises, and proceeds to an examination of the alienated and alienating character of commodity production (GW 10, 920–2). This is also an original text: it is based on a core from the *Manifesto*.

Nicht zum Wohnen bestimmt ist das Haus, das Tuch nicht zum Kleiden
Noch ist das Brot nur zum Essen bestimmt; Gewinn soll es tragen.

The theme of unemployment was crucial in Brecht's attempt to address contemporary issues in his poem: he wrote to Korsch, in March 1945: 'einiges im manifest habe ich so vorsichtig wie mir möglich geändert, anstelle der verelendungstheorie die unsicherheit durch die konstitutionelle arbeitslosigkeit gesetzt usw. halten Sie das für richtig?'. To this Korsch replied that he was not able to recall any passage in the *Manifesto* which expounded the immiseration theory.[26] Korsch had no copy of the German text at the time; had one been available, he could have experienced little difficulty in locating the text, in the penultimate paragraph of the first chapter, which begins:

Der moderne Arbeiter dagegen, statt sich mit dem Fortschritt der Industrie zu heben, sinkt immer tiefer unter die Bedingungen seiner eigenen Klasse herab. Der Arbeiter wird zum Pauper, und der Pauperismus entwickelt sich noch schneller als Bevölkerung und Reichtum.[27]

This passage corresponds to an inserted text in Brecht's poem, 'Berge von Maschinerie . . .' (GW 10, 929); at a similar location near the end of the canto, this text concerns unemployment.

The immiseration theory is a crux of Marxist economic theory; in so far as Marx's work is concerned, it has been argued that the idea of the absolute impoverishment of the proletariat was not proposed, but opposed. None the less, the theory was supported by some economic authorities, including those of the Soviet Union, as recently as 1955. The theory originated with Malthus, and was adopted by Lasalle; it is true that the above quotation from Marx and Engels has a strong Malthusian tone, which may have led Brecht to read it as an exposition of the immiseration thesis. Nevertheless, the text is problematic, and certainly open to other interpretation; 'der Arbeiter wird zum Pauper' is a generalization which may signify that increasing numbers of workers are condemned to poverty through age, accident, sickness, or—unemployment. This reading would make Brecht's avoidance of the immiseration theory appear not as a modification or correction, but as a straightforward interpretation.

With the exception of the instances discussed above, and other minor alterations, the second canto of Brecht's *Lehrgedicht von der Natur der Menschen* remains very close to the original: 'daß ich mich im übrigen eher schülerhaft an den text der klassiker hielt, finde ich richtig'.[28] Significantly, Brecht's version of the *Manifesto* (Chapter 1) ends not with the confident, sober prognosis of the original, but with a challenge. The text is compounded of materials from the concluding paragraphs of Chapter 1, together with extracts from the end of Chapter 2:

> Seine ist die Bewegung der Mehrzahl, und würde es herrschen
> Wär es nicht Herrschaft mehr, sondern die Knechtung von Herrschaft.
> Nur Unterdrückung wird da unterdrückt, denn das Proletariat muß
> Unterste Schicht der Gesellschaft, um sich zu erheben, den ganzen
> Bau der Gesellschaft zertrümmern mit all seinen oberen Schichten.
> Abschütteln kann es die eigene Knechtschaft nur abschüttelnd alle
> Knechtschaft aller.[29]   (GW 10, 930.)

Lehrgedicht von der Natur der Menschen: this title, besides echoing that of Lucretius' poem, proposes a question—what is the nature of man? It is clear from Brecht's letter to Korsch that such a concept would be formulated in opposition to 'die unnatur der bürgerlichen verhältnisse'; following Marx and Engels, Brecht proceeds from reflection on the present to an examination of its genesis. The account offered is a materialist one, which takes as its first object of inquiry human beings in action: work. This perspective allows both a subtle and dynamic definition of human 'nature' and a contrasting picture of the present unnatural, inhuman conditions under which most people live.

Dieses Natürliche, die Arbeit, das, was
Erst den Menschen zur Naturkraft macht, die Arbeit
Dieses wie schwimmen im Wasser, dieses wie essen das Fleisch
Dieses wie begatten, dieses wie singen
Es geriet in Verruf durch lange Jahrhunderte und
Zu unserer Zeit. (GW 10, 895.)

The following description of alienated labour, of man confronted by the products of human labour in the shape of fossilized, 'reified' economic and social relations, introduces a fundamental theme of Marxist theory, and the central concern of the first canto of Brecht's poem. The difficulty of finding one's way in the 'nature' of society, which was announced as the theme of this canto, may be analysed in terms of this alienation; the difficulty is both practical (making a living) and theoretical (knowing what to do in a society where many are denied the possibility of making a living). The proletarian who is a mere instrument, and object of others' plans, cannot remedy his position unless he makes himself the conscious subject of his work; much of the first canto is devoted to the learning process which is the indispensable precedent of such an attack on alienation. (The practical recommendations of Marxism—organization of the proletariat and deliberate pursuit of the class struggle—were better known and less problematic than its theoretical elements, to which Brecht here draws his readers' attention.)

'Nicht von Erscheinungen schlechthin noch Anschauung sei hier die Rede'—this passage (GW 10, 896-7) insists that inquiry should not simply seek the truth, but endeavour to produce what Brecht had previously referred to as the 'praktikable Wahrheit':

wenn man erfolgreich die Wahrheit über schlimme Zustände schreiben will, muß man sie so schreiben, daß ihre vermeidbaren Ursachen erkannt werden können. (GW 18, 229.)

The point is underlined in 'Über das Begreifen des Vorhandenen' (GW 10, 898): 'daß alles Begreifen zu wenig war'; practice constitutes a control on theory. In the same spirit of rigorousness, the construction of elaborate theoretical models is criticized because such models characteristically neglect the dynamic, fluid quality of the historical dimension—'Gleichermaßen gefährlich und nützlich ist auch das Machen/ Einleuchtender Bilder' (GW 10, 902-3).[30]

Beyond such basic provision, the materialist conception of history is expounded with careful precision; 'Da sie aber bedrückt sind vom Kapitalismus' (GW 10, 899–900) corrects the misconception of history as a series of 'free' decisions, some of which are found to be mistaken. It proposes that history be recognized as the product of human activity, which nevertheless confronts men as a solid mass, limiting their actions and their understanding. Choice is thus possible within narrow confines; and there can be no retracing of historical steps: 'Denn der Korn und Zinsen tragende Acker/ Hat die Menschen verändert' (GW 10, 900). The tendency of thinking to become abstract, to content itself with terminological processes rather than real ones, is countered by a strict, sceptical materialism:

> Auch war die Art, die Industrie aufzubauen doch nicht
> Einfach die falsche, sondern die wirkliche. Diese Maschinen
> Wurden gebaut und betrieben so, wie es möglich war.

If the idea of history as the simple exercise of the human will is thus rejected, so too by implication are the still less concrete notions of 'necessity' or 'historic mission' as governing principles. Reference to practical, material limits offers a theory of greater efficiency, economy, and elegance. Such abstract idealist notions, it is suggested, are themselves unanalysed products of a society based on dominating and dominated classes; history is seen as a succession of orders and instructions: 'aber in Wirklichkeit waren die Herrn nicht so herrlich'.

In a text dated 1933, the political implications of materialist theory are explored—'Da sie nun glauben, der Gedanke allein könne sie einen' (GW 10, 902). Besides the general insistence on material interest as a powerful determinant which underlies political organization and conflict, the passage contains a more specific critique of elements of fascist ideology ('Volksgemeinschaft' above all). Even under the institutional chauvinism of its fascist phase, capitalism could not establish a community of interests between Krupp and 'his' workers. 'Über Ungleichheit. Schwierig, sie zu entdecken' (GW 10, 901), examines the inequality characteristic of a class society.

'Wenn sie so jammern' (GW 10, 898) was included in the story *Die Trophäen des Lukullus* of 1939, where these lines were fictionally attributed to Lucretius. Proceeding from the humanist theme of fear of death, Brecht here describes the ruinous and pervasive alienation which accompanies the suppression of use-values; as in the visions of the *Dreigroschenroman*, society is perceived as a system of exploitation, in which persuasion, if ineffective, will give way to violence:

Wer könnt in solcher Welt den Gedanken des Todes ertragen?
Zwischen 'Laß los!' und 'Ich halt's!' bewegt sich das Leben und beiden
Dem der da hält und dem der entreißt, krümmt die Hand sich zur Klaue.[31]

The texts associated with the first canto are connected by their treatment of forms of alienation which constitute the general condition of bourgeois society. Amongst the texts which the *Gesammelte Werke* edition attributes to the fourth canto, 'Über die geistige und materielle Kultur' (GW 10, 903) is most closely related to the themes of the introductory canto. Taking up a central topic of the 'Glücksgott' songs, Brecht argues against the persistent and damaging division of mind and body, thought and feeling, the traditional idealist attitude which Brecht had criticized publicly and privately during the thirties.

Generally, the texts of the fourth canto realise the planned portrayal of the 'ungeheuerlich gesteigerte barbarisierung' in their description of war. Itself a primary locus of human alienation, war was, in 1945, an unavoidable and urgent theme; historically, too, it appears as a characteristic of modern capitalism: Germany had seen three major wars since the first publication of the *Communist Manifesto*.

'Die apokalyptischen Reiter' (GW 10, 904) attempts, in its mythic vision, to extract the positive significance of the horrors of war. The biblical motif itself suggests that this interpretation must lie in the direction of war as purification; if Brecht here seems surprisingly close to the proclamations of quasi-religious affirmation with which writers had greeted the 1914–1918 war (and which Ernst Jünger and others echoed two decades later), the context of the passage at least locates Brecht's expectations in an area far removed from chauvinistic self-sacrifice and idealism in general. The war, however barbarous, means the defeat of the fascist regime in Germany, and thus offers the possibility of a rational conclusion of the final struggle: the establishment of socialist democracy. The 'Weiblein' of the text is reminiscent of the 'blutbeschmierte alte Vettel' which Galilei had envisaged as the shape of the new age;[32] at the same time, her encounter with the horsemen of the apocalypse contains a slight, but distinct, idyllic element, and is related to the short text 'Intervention' (GW 10, 907) which, however, lacks any apocalyptic dimension.

The text which begins 'Viele sprachen vom Krieg wie von Ungewitter und Meerflut' (GW 10, 905) illuminates a central concept of Brecht's poem: nature. It was suggested above that the poem's title announces a fundamental opposition between a postulated true human nature, social and unalienated, and the unnatural and inhuman condition in which mankind still exists. Outside this paradigm, the situation is more complicated; following man's emergence from the primary nature of prehistory, he had increasingly modified nature and himself by his own activity. The social structures produced as a consequence of this process themselves appeared as natural, externally imposed (by gods or ancestors), and unchanging. This 'second nature' was above all an artefact. Under capitalism, human alienation and the displacement of use-value by exchange-value ('das nackte Interesse . . . die gefühllose "bare Zahlung"') had reduced this second nature to a system which was able to contain only a more and more restricted humanity. Still, the social artefact was perceived as natural, even when it led to wholesale and open destruction of human life: the ideology of war as an expression of mankind's nature, his warlike spirit, is the subject of this text's critical discussion. 'Bericht von einem hundertjährigen Krieg 2' (GW 10, 907) defines the terrible paradox: war as an ordinary day's work—no longer a natural disaster, it simply appears as natural:

> Nicht mehr wie ein Erdbeben erschien der Krieg
> Nicht mehr wie ein Taifun, sondern
> Wie ein Sonnenaufgang. Wie man Brot backte
> So führte man Krieg.

Alienation, the dehumanization of humanity both objective and subjective, approaches completion.

Amongst the texts collected as belonging to the poem's fourth canto 'Denk nicht: es sah dich nicht, der dies schrieb' (GW 10, 909–10) is the most directly reflexive: it thematizes the problematic actuality of the poem. Even the published fragments are sufficient proof that the *Lehrgedicht von der Natur der Menschen* project represents the culmination of the theoretical-didactic strand in Brecht's poetry; the production of this extensive and demanding work may appear eccentric in the context of the urgent practical problems of the German situation. It is this question which the text addresses:

Denk nicht, es sah dich nicht, der dies schrieb, als er schrieb, als er solches
Weit Entferntes besprach, so Schwieriges, so nur Gedachtes
So als hätte er Jahre noch Zeit, um zu Ende zu denken
Du aber hast nur mehr Stunden, und wenn jetzt die Kälte noch zunimmt
Kann dir bald keiner mehr sagen, was tun, um dem Tod zu entrinnen.

It was Brecht's view that immediate, pragmatic responses to these real and desperate needs should not replace or exclude the more radical and long-term undertaking to which the poem is devoted, and which alone promised a real solution.

Wo die Not am größten, ist die Hilfe am fernsten.
Ebenso kalt wie der Wind ist die Lehre ihm zu entgehen
Ebenso dürftig wie deine Nahrung der Rat sie endlich zu mehren.
Also gibt dich der Lehrende auf?

This relentless honesty recalls the attitude of the *Lesebuch* text 'Wenn ich mit dir rede'; but in this later work strictness is combined with a more conspicuous sympathy in the defiant challenge of the final question.

The *Lehrgedicht von der Natur der Menschen* in its published form is so far from completion that it is impossible to construct a reliable detailed picture of its intended shape. The attribution of individual texts to the four cantos cannot be regarded as conclusive; several published texts in free rhythms (GW 10, 906-7) are perhaps more properly seen as paralipomena than as integral texts. Only a critical edition would solve such philological problems.

The enigmatic third canto was to be based on an Engels text contemporary with the *Manifesto*; it was to consist of questions which Marx and Engels would answer. Examination of the original 'catechism' suggests such fundamental and controversial questions as the policy of 'socialism in one country', which Engels had dismissed;[33] had Brecht intended to follow the original text closely, this would have demanded a treatment of the Trotskyist opposition, which offered a critique of Stalin's policies. Similarly, the section of canto 1 intended to provide a critical appraisal of contemporary socialist literature (Ch. III of the *Manifesto*) is not represented by published material, and may not have been written.

It too would have implied discussion of the contributions made by Trotsky, and perhaps those of Rosa Luxemburg; the Frankfurt School might have attracted energetic criticism, as might the elements of Soviet policy which were questioned implicitly in the first canto's rigorous historical materialism. The *Arbeitsjournal* records Brecht's criticisms of the *Geschichte der KPdSU (B)* (1938), to which Stalin had contributed:

> der verfasser dieser geschichte ist sozusagen klar und undeutlich, er haut seine sätze mit der axt zu und schreibt sich dauernd in den finger. die revolutionen werden aus der metaphysik abgeleitet, sie gehen vor, weil das alte dem neuen weicht und 'unwiderstehlich nur ist, was entsteht und sich entwickelt'. alles hängt von allem ab, und die entwicklung geschieht in wunderbaren sprüngen. (AJ 29.1.40.)

The history of this strand of criticism reaches back over several years: Walter Benjamin's notes of 25 July 1938 record a significant remark—

> gegen Abend fand mich Brecht im Garten bei der Lektüre des 'Kapital', Brecht: 'Ich finde das sehr gut, daß Sie jetzt Marx studieren — wo man immer weniger auf ihn stößt und besonders wenig bei unsern Leuten'.[34]

Similarly, the *Arbeitsjournal* on the Soviet Union:

> literatur und kunst scheinen beschissen, die politische theorie auf dem hund, es gibt so etwas wie einen beamtenmäßig propagierten dünnen blutlosen proletarischen humanismus. (AJ 1.39.)

And, more soberly, in what may be a later essay:

> der Faschismus mit seiner grotesken Betonung des Emotionellen und vielleicht nicht minder ein gewisser Verfall des rationellen Moments in der Lehre des Marxismus veranlaßte mich selber zu einer stärkeren Betonung des Rationellen.
>
> ('Über rationellen und emotionellen Standpunkt' GW 15, 242.)

Against this background, the 'Renaissance' attitude which underlies the project is more clearly defined. The theoretical generosity of the undertaking is central to its critical function; for all its consciousness of the urgency of action, of the opportunity to be seized, the poem retains a firm hold on the insights of 'Lob des Zweifels' and 'Lob des Lernens':

Scheue dich nicht zu fragen, Genosse!
Laß dir nichts einreden
Sieh selber nach!...
Du mußt die Führung übernehmen. (GW 9, 463.)

Directives and exhortations were clearly no substitute for a method of critical inquiry and understanding. The poem's *ad fontes* gesture was part of its actuality, of the specific 'propagandistische Wirkung' which Brecht sought to renew.

As scrutiny of the published material shows, the *Lehrgedicht von der Natur der Menschen* is a work of primary importance. It is both theoretically and artistically impressive, especially in those texts which approximate most closely to completion. Hannah Arendt's characterization of the poem as 'curiously baroque . . . an almost total failure' is not confirmed by a reading of its text; since she makes no attempt to understand the work historically, her judgement is in any case both abstract and arbitrary.[35] The considerable demands which this poem makes on its intended (and unintended) readers result partly from Brecht's 'Aufheben des pamphletistischen Charakters'; his poetic treatment produces a degree of difficulty which, paradoxically, reinforces the immediate significance of the work. The reader learns that only close attention, careful analysis, and occasional repetition render the poem accessible. In its promotion of critical and deliberate use, the poem as a literary object underlines a fundamental element of its argument. It is, like the original *Manifesto,* an illuminating and polemical work: it can be read with enjoyment.

Satires

Brecht wrote few poems between 1945 and 1947; the negative criticism of satire is their dominant element. 'Was ist geschehen?' (1945, GW 10, 931) and its contemporary 'Gestank' (GW 10, 931-2) examine the situation in Germany following its unconditional surrender: the terms of the post-fascist dialectic may be defined by the juxtaposition of lines from these poems—'die Revolution hat ihre erste Schlacht gewonnen', but 'Ganz Deutschland stank wie der Waffenrock von Fridericus Rex/ Der sich niemals wusch'. Two poems probably written in 1946, 'Der Nürnberger Prozeß' (GW 10, 939) and 'Der Krieg ist geschändet worden' (GW 10, 939), indicate that considerable obstacles stood in the way of continued revolutionary progress. In 'Der anachronistische Zug, oder Freiheit und Democracy' (GW 10, 943–9), written early in 1947, Brecht defined the obstacles specific to the western sectors of Germany. Inspection of the economic and political aims of the western allies led Brecht to the conclusion that a bourgeois restoration was likely: this was the real basis to which the slogan 'freedom and democracy' would correspond. Bourgeois democracy signified capitalist freedom, which Marx had described as anarchy; Shelley's satirical ballad obligingly adopts the term albeit in a different sense—'The Mask of Anarchy'. Brecht had translated part of his work in 1938, and referred to it in the essay 'Weite und Vielfalt der realistischen Schreibweise' (GW 19, 340 ff.). The concept of anachronism which Brecht's title introduces connects the poem to the general analysis of fascism which Brecht had constructed in the course of the preceding fifteen years; fascism was the last resort of German capitalism, its most advanced and liberated form.[36] After the defeat of fascism, it made little sense (except from the viewpoint of capital) to return to the pre-fascist status quo, by restoring the economic structure. In this strictly rational sense, Brecht's earlier assertion was a valid hypothesis: 'nach dem Faschismus... kann nur der Kommunismus kommen, nichts anderes' (GW 20, 240; 1935?), though he neglected to define the historical scale on which the prognosis was conceived. From this heroically rational standpoint, the bourgeois restoration appeared anachronistic: it reintroduced an economic and social mode which had been tested to destruction two decades before. If the Weimar Republic had contained the seeds of fascism, a new bourgeois republic would retain its roots:

> Doch dem Kreuz dort auf dem Laken
> Fehlen heute ein paar Haken
> Da man mit den Zeiten lebt
> Sind die Haken überklebt. (GW 10, 944.)

Sufficiently fundamental changes would not be made: cosmetic measures had been chosen as a profitable surrogate. The angry criticisms of the ballad anticipate Brecht's subsequent decision not to take up residence in the western-occupied zones of Germany.

Chapter 6

THE POST-EXILE POETRY 1948-1956

BRECHT left the USA in October 1947; in the course of the next year, while based in Zürich, he travelled to Berlin, Salzburg, and Prague. In October 1948 he took up residence in Berlin, thus concluding his exile from Germany.

Brecht and Germany

Brecht was no supporter of nationalism; he retained a critical attitude towards the nation-state, viewing it as a historical formation, an entity defined by political, linguistic, and geographical boundaries, which was clearly distinguishable from the populace and its constituent social groupings. The adoption of nationalistic policies by the KPD, and later by the SED, was in Brecht's view 'ein entsetzlich opportunistischer quark'; as 'Über Deutschland' (GW 9, 752) declared, his home was the region to which his revolutionary hopes applied.[1] This perspective was the dominant theme of Brecht's reflections in 1945, as he worked on the *Lehrgedicht von der Natur der Menschen*; six months after his cautious examination of the possibility of revolt against the fascist regime, Brecht was convinced that the revolutionary moment had passed. Germany was 'ein völlig zu boden geworfener kapitalistischer staat':

eine arbeiterregierung könnten nur die russen einsetzen, etwa wenn sie allein hitlerdeutschland niedergerungen hätten, aber selbst dann könnte sich so etwas nur sehr schwer zu einem sozialismus entwickeln.

(AJ 3.8.45.)

This note was written after the conclusion of the Potsdam Conference and thus was based on the assumption that Germany would at least be unified: even so, its prognosis for German socialism was gloomy. In the following months Brecht explored theoretically amongst Germany's political ruins, seeking out those elements which might be useful on the path to socialism:

im deutschen fall wäre es lohnend, einmal ernsthaft die sozialistischen elemente aufzuspüren, die der national'sozialismus' pervertiert zum operieren brachte. (AJ 26.3.47.)

As the division of Germany into Eastern- and Western-occupied zones solidified, Brecht criticized the fatal limitation of economic and political measures: 'weitermachen ist die parole . . . alles fürchtet das einreißen, ohne das das aufbauen unmöglich ist' (AJ 6.1.48, p. 814); the re-education and denazification policies were examples of such piecemeal procedure: bureaucratic exercises, rather than effective changes.[2] Brecht deplored the slow decay of political conflict, the 'katalaunische geisterschlacht', but was determined that the cultural arena at least should promote more decisive, radical action:

die literatur kann sich nicht hinter die elbe zurückziehen und lediglich eine von den russen militärisch (und polizeilich) verteidigte musterprovinz aufbauen helfen. das übrige deutschland kann nicht durch eine mustermesse zur revolution gebracht werden. die literatur muß sich engagieren, sich in den kampf bringen über ganz deutschland hin und einen revolutionären charakter haben, ihn auch äußerlich, in den formen, zeigen.

(AJ 11.12.48.)

Brecht had decided that the Soviet-controlled sector of Berlin offered the most promising opportunities for such an undertaking.

New Poems

The general decrease in Brecht's lyric production which was described as a feature of the later exile period is more strongly marked after Brecht's return to Germany. This reduction in quantity neither logically nor in fact implies any qualitative reduction.[3]

In the post-exile period, the formal distinction between metrical texts and those composed in free rhythms reasserts itself more clearly; among the many metrical poems are the new *Massenlieder*, 'Aufbaulied', 'Zukunftslied', 'Lied vom Glück', 'Friedenslied'; an extensive cycle of children's poems, 'Kinderlieder 1950', and a related set of short 'classical' lyrics, 'Als ich kam in die Heimat', 'Sprüche', 'Vom Glück des Gebens', 'Frühling'. Poems in free rhythms still constitute the majority, however, and here, as in the second half of the exile period, shorter texts predominate. The epigrammatic lyrics of the late period are distinct both from the metrical 'fotogramme' and from the free epigrams of 'Deutsche Kriegsfibel'; poems such as those of the *Buckower Elegien* collection recall the longer epigrammatic texts of the *Steffinische Sammlung*. There is a small number of poems which take up the 'fotogramm' strand: the 'Friedensfibel' poems (GW 10, 1026-7; 1028), and 'Inschrift für das Hochhaus an der Weberwiese'.

In terms of the categories evolved in the treatment of the exile poetry, the structure of Brecht's late poetry may be analysed thus: though the general category of the *Lehrgedicht* is still valid as a comprehensive grouping, its specific subgroups are no longer dominant areas of production; the abstract *Lehrgedicht,* the *Chronik* and its autobiographical form, are now comparatively rare as distinct types: individual texts increasingly integrate their particular elements, and are thus more complex, concentrated formations. At the same time, the metrical poems tend to coincide in theme and attitude with the epigrammatic poems in free rhythms, combining elements of autobiography, historical and exemplary documentation, and abstract reflection; the earlier correspondence between formal and attitudinal categories (free rhythms as the form of the *Lehrgedicht*) is thus dissolved.

One of the major attractions of Berlin's eastern sector in 1948 was its position as a cultural centre; the arts received considerable official support, and Brecht formulated new plans for the publication of his poetry. The first project was given the title *Gedichte im Exil,* which had previously introduced two collections of poetry (in 1937 and 1943-4), neither of which ultimately was published; the new collection, conceived late in 1948, was no more fortunate. This edition was planned as a representative one; a substantial volume was to introduce Brecht's poetry to the German readership from which he had been almost totally isolated for fifteen years. It was thus planned as a parallel edition, in which the Munich publisher, Kurt Desch, was to have primary rights, while the Aufbau-Verlag in Berlin would be responsible for publication in the eastern sector. By January 1949 the original plan had been altered: four volumes were to replace the large single edition, and would present a larger selection of poems. Brecht seems to have made these changes in order to achieve slim, pocket-sized volumes, inviting easy and convenient use; for the Aufbau edition, at least, he envisaged a departure from standard format, for the same reason.[4] Though the Aufbau edition had apparently reached an advanced stage of preparation, neither it nor its western companion was published; Wieland Herzfelde, who was the editor of the project, produced a different, but also substantial selection of poems under the title *Hundert Gedichte* (Aufbau, Berlin), which appeared in 1951. The abandonment of *Gedichte im Exil* (1948) remains unexplained. In 1955 the publication of the 'fotogramme' under the title *Kriegsfibel* (Eulenspiegel-Verlag, Berlin (DDR)) was carried out in spite of official opposition. The anti-militarist position of Brecht's epigrams may have appeared inopportune in the context of rearmament.

In addition to such major undertakings, a number of smaller collections were published; the poems made known through *Hundert Gedichte* were widely anthologized, and others appeared in periodicals (above all in *Sinn und Form*, under the editorship of Peter Huchel), as well as in newspapers.[5] Brecht had gradually regained, and finally surpassed the prominence he had enjoyed during the last years of the Weimar Republic; he was occupied by new opportunities for dramatic work, and by many commitments in the field of cultural politics. In this context Brecht wrote new *Massenlieder*, which the two earliest examples, 'Aufbaulied' (GW 10, 955) and 'Zukunftslied' (GW 10, 956), may adequately represent. Both songs were written in December 1948.

> Keiner plagt sich gerne, doch wir wissen:
> Grau ist's immer, wenn ein Morgen naht
> Und trotz Hunger, Kält und Finsternissen
> Stehn zum Handanlegen wir parat.
> Fort mit den Trümmern
> Und was Neues hingebaut!
> Um uns selber müssen wir uns selber kümmern
> Und heraus gegen uns, wer sich traut!

It is apparent from this strophe that the 'Aufbaulied' does not aspire to artistic sophistication: it is an effective work of craftsmanship.[6] The poem recognizes honestly the enormity of the material problems facing the emergent socialist state and insists that only one course offers a solution: to build. This refers not only to the production of new buildings but to the equally necessary construction of a new political apparatus, a state. It is here, indeed, that the song's weight lies: the path to socialism is obstructed by external forces (as the defiant challenge of the chorus implies) and by internal ones (as strophes 3 and 4 suggest), which add to the fundamental difficulties of reconstruction. The state is an instrument for the organization of large-scale communal undertakings, and for regulating conflict; but if reconstruction was impossible without a state, it would lose much of its value for German socialism if this state were not radically different from its antecedents. The fifth strophe is the final and most important one; it thematizes the contradiction between the new *state* and the *new* state:

> Besser als gerührt sein ist: sich rühren
> Denn kein Führer führt aus dem Salat!
> Selber werden wir uns endlich führen:
> Weg der alte, her der neue Staat!

Here, as in the second strophe, the emphasis is firmly on 'neu', Brecht argues that if democracy depends on socialism, socialism depends on democracy. More specifically, the song is addressed to the German proletariat, and proceeds from the negative model of the fascist state to recommend the general rejection of administration from above: the new state must be democratic.

Brecht was a critical observer of the Soviet Union, where the first attempts to construct a socialist state had been made: he was no admirer of the state as a social ideal.[7]

kleines lied für die FREIE DEUTSCHE JUGEND gemacht (AUFBAULIED). bin unzufrieden, daß der 'neue staat' hereinkommt, ist aber nötig, damit der materielle aufbau verknüpft werden kann mit dem politischen. (AJ 21.12.48.)

Brecht was not the only one to have reservations about the 'Aufbaulied'; the Berlin group leader of the FDJ had objected to another line—'kein Führer führt...':

denn hitler interessiere niemand mehr, da er olle kamellen sei (aber kamellen verwandeln sich, wenn unbeobachtet, leicht in olle lorbeern), und dann gebe es eine führung durch die partei. ich kann aber nicht entsprechen, die strophe ist auf das motiv des sich-selbst-führens aufgebaut, und das ganze lied dazu. (AJ 2.1.49.)

Brecht's refusal to amend the song is not that of the arrogant or self-righteous poet; he considers the objections offered, and rejects them. The decision is as much a political as a poetic one.

If there is an admonitory gesture underlying the 'Aufbaulied', the same is true of the 'Zukunftslied', in which the chorus extracts from the historical details of the strophes the following simple observation: 'Über der Getreidekammer hob sich hoh/ Eine wunderbare Fahne, die war rot'. A note in the *Arbeitsjournal* reveals that this refrain is not the straightforward celebration which it may seem to be, but rather an urgent propagandistic appeal:

schreibe das ZUKUNFTSLIED, da alle erziehung hier zu lokal betrieben wird (und die rote fahne geradezu im verruf ist, worauf man eingeht).
(AJ 22.12.48.)

The song reconstructs the historical context of the Soviet occupation, presenting it as the positive point of departure for socialism in Germany. The Soviet forces were not generally seen as liberators, nor was the SED viewed as a party of liberation; Brecht sought to persuade his readers that the future depended on their assent to the SED and its allies, and presented the difficult historical understanding on the basis of which such assent would be possible.

'Aufbaulied' was a commissioned poem, while 'Zukunftslied' appears to have been a spontaneous contribution; this distinction could hardly be deduced from purely textual evidence, however, and it is clear that Brecht assumed a social commission even when none had been expressly formulated by officers of party or state. Both songs are specific and limited in their intentions; they combine brisk, cheerful movement with elements of colloquial diction to produce what Brecht described as their 'vulgarität und primitivität' (AJ 29.12.48). This is by no means self-condemnatory: such effects are commensurate with the songs' intended functions. Later reflections confirm Brecht's confident attitude to the problems of commissioned poetry: 'im allgemeinen sind die harfen weniger zerbrechlich, als ihr klang vermuten läßt und, verstimmt, können sie neu gestimmt werden' (AJ 7.7.51). Nevertheless, this proposition is followed by a warning:

die gelegenheitsarbeit ist es, die den künstler zum professionellen macht, aber mitunter auch zum kunstgewerbetreibenden ... es kommt alles darauf an, daß man aus einem stoff und auftrag nicht mehr macht, als drin ist. nötig kunstverstand.

This opposition between the professional and the craftsman is significant: it implies that the craftsman, the skilled specialist,

THE POST-EXILE POETRY 1948–1956 189

practises an outmoded manner of production, and that this special position may condemn him to the production of more or less decorative work to the specifications of powerful patrons. The professional recognizes the limits of commissioned work and executes it accordingly; this 'modernity' preserves a much greater degree of autonomy. Brecht's independent formulation of what, at various times, he perceived as his commission is evidence of such professionalism.

'Schlechte Zeiten' (GW 10, 963) was written in 1949; it recalls the reflective elegiac mode as well as the characteristic imagery of 'Über die Unfruchtbarkeit', 'Schlechte Zeit für Lyrik' and 'Der Pflaumenbaum':

> Der Baum erzählt, warum er keine Früchte gebracht hat.
> Der Dichter erzählt, warum die Verse schlecht geworden sind.
> Der General erzählt, warum der Krieg verloren wurde.

In the context of such apparent parallels, each statement is made distinct, specific; its relation to its companion becomes problematic. The barren tree and the frustrated poet may perhaps correspond, on the model of earlier poems: but the third example, while primarily congruent, in fact illustrates an opposite case. In Germany, in 1949, the war whose loss the generals explained was the fascist war; its loss (perhaps in spite of what the generals declared) was not a matter for regret.

This first triad sets up the structural pattern on which the poem rests, and introduces its dominant theme: the careful drawing of distinctions, the rejection of apparent correspondences. The calm restraint of this first strophe gives way to impassioned exclamation in the second, which presents new instances of loss and futility; here in each case failure appears as unachieved communication— the fault lies in the process of transmission and reception. These examples are concrete and particular, but develop more general reference; the loss of contact which they illustrate is especially relevant to the poet, but also applies to the wider social field, where the third line suggests an analogous disturbance: 'großes Verhalten, von niemandem beobachtet!'. The melancholy indignation with which the third strophe contemplates varieties of damage is confronted by the more positive and decisive attitude of the following strophe; here, concrete, practical examples are proposed:

Lob denen, die aus den baufälligen Häusern ausziehen!
Lob denen, die dem verkommenen Freund die Türe verriegeln!
Lob denen, die den undurchführbaren Plan vergessen! (GW 10, 963.)

These explicit lines conclude the critical exercise to which the first four strophes are devoted; the following strophes demand less strenuous reflection, they are sober, direct propositions. The poem's field of reference is more precisely defined by the fifth strophe; it is located in the Soviet-governed territories of post-war Germany. The practical point of view of the lines quoted above is endorsed with a seriousness which takes account of the limits of the possible. The house which was so urgently needed was built as it had to be, with the materials at hand. The sixth strophe underlines this insistence on the factors limiting production: the quality and quantity of the materials available, the conditions of production, distribution, and consumption and, above all human factors:

Gegeben wurde den Bedürftigen.
Gesprochen wurde mit den Anwesenden.
Gearbeitet wurde mit den Kräften, der Weisheit und dem Mut, die zur Verfügung standen.

This is an appeal for the recognition and continuation of the work of reconstruction: it is founded on an honest and critical appreciation of the real, material limits within which such work could be carried out, and derives its authority from this fact.

This appeal is qualified in the final strophe, which warns against complacent acquiescence—'mehr wäre möglich gewesen'; the concluding pair of lines emphasizes that expressions of regret are not sufficient, that only constructive action can produce a way out of the 'Schlechte Zeiten' of the poem's title.

It is evident from this text that the dialectic is not abandoned in the poetry of this period: the poem's reticence and complexity persuade the reader to weigh its propositions with critical care. There remain, after all, enough objective contradictions which demand the application of critical analysis; the Marxist poet does not become a laureate, singing the praises of his patron state:

allenthalben macht sich in dieser großen stadt, in der immer alles in bewegung ist, wie wenig und provisorisch auch immer dies alles geworden sein mag, die neue deutsche misere bemerkbar, daß nichts erledigt ist, wenn schon fast alles kaputt ist. die mächtigen impulse werden von den russen gegeben, aber die deutschen tummeln sich mehr in dem strudel, der dadurch entsteht, daß die andern besatzungsmächte sich der bewegung widersetzen. die deutschen rebellieren gegen den befehl, gegen den nazismus zu rebellieren; nur wenige stehen auf dem standpunkt, daß ein befohlener sozialismus besser ist als gar keiner ... es ist dabei nicht nur so, daß die deutschen arbeiter im augenblick nicht erkennen, daß ihre eigene diktatur 'drinnen' ist, sondern daß sie wirklich nicht bereit scheinen, sie zu übernehmen. die volksherrschaft in der form der diktatur (nach außen *und* innen) leuchtet ihnen nicht ein.[8]   (AJ 9.12.48)

This analysis informs 'Wahrnehmung' (1949, GW 10, 960):

> Als ich wiederkehrte
> War mein Haar noch nicht grau
> Da war ich froh.
>
> Die Mühen der Gebirge liegen hinter uns
> Vor uns liegen die Mühen der Ebenen.[9]

The last two lines were an expression of Brecht's fundamental attitude; they were to have formed the motto of the 'Neue Gedichte' volume planned in 1949. In this poem Brecht employs his own persona, recording the thoughts of the poet on his return from exile. He notes with satisfaction that he has returned before growing old, and the very possibility of his return indicates that the major task, the defeat of the fascist regime, has been accomplished. This range of significance does not exhaust the poem; each of its sections generates distinct, complementary senses. If the troubles of the plains demand less intensity of exertion than the troubles of the mountains, they are nonetheless troubles, and require continued exertion. Similarly, the poet's gladness at his comparative youth may rest on the knowledge that he still has much to do. The poem's general attitude is positive: the remaining troubles are to be met on a level road. This is the central point of orientation: recognition of what had already been achieved and of what still demanded action.

Brecht's poems of this period offer a catalogue of the difficulties encountered on the new level; the most apparent are economic.

> Außer diesem Stern, dachte ich, ist nichts und er
> Ist so verwüstet.
> Er allein ist unsere Zuflucht und die
> Sieht so aus.   (1949, GW 10, 959.)

In this reflection on the extent of destruction suffered in the course of the war, the recognition of material fact struggles against a sense of disbelief and unreality in the long, thoughtful lines which halt in mid-sentence. Other poems treating the same theme attempt to convert the sense of despair evoked by the ubiquity of ruin into a more positive attitude; this is the function of the naïve mode in 'Als ich kam in die Heimat' (1948, GW 10, 959), where Brecht insists that there can be no easy escape from such fundamental problems.

> Als ich kam in die Heimat
> Und sah den Rest so stehn
> Da bekam ich einen Schrecken
> Und wollte schneller gehn.
>
> Doch wär ich auch schneller gegangen,
> So schnell wie nie, uns bangt:
> Aus solcher Trümmerstätte
> Wär ich nicht hinausgelangt.

The necessary economic response to such devastation is described in a contemporary poem:

> Als unsere Städte in Schutt lagen
> Verwüstet durch den Krieg des Schlächters
> Haben wir begonnen, sie wieder aufzubauen
> In der Kälte, im Hunger, in der Schwäche. (GW 10, 960.)

As the preceding notes from Brecht's *Arbeitsjournal* show, such economic problems were accompanied by equally serious political difficulties. The admonitory stance evident in 'Aufbaulied' and 'Zukunftslied' ('kein Führer führt aus *dem* Salat') is a response to the problematic context within which political reconstruction was necessarily begun; the German proletariat had suffered two major defeats—first by, then with the National Socialist regime:

> Als wir zogen gegen Osten, ach, besiegt von unsern Herrn
> Die uns gegen Brüder warben, haben die mit Tank und Wagen
> Uns im Kaukasus geschlagen. ('Zukunftslied', GW 10, 957.)[10]

Similarly, in 'An meine Landsleute' (1949, GW 10, 965):

> Ihr Männer, greift zur Kelle, nicht zum Messer!
> Ihr säßet unter Dächern schließlich jetzt
> Hättet ihr auf das Messer nicht gesetzt
> Und unter Dächern sitzt es sich doch besser.
> Ich bitt euch, greift zur Kelle, nicht zum Messer!

THE POST-EXILE POETRY 1948–1956

The fascist regime had brought about systematic political deprivation, the effects of which were now painfully apparent; besides new organizations, a new political consciousness was an urgent necessity. Economic ruin was perhaps more easily remedied than this destruction of political life; such reflections illuminate one sense of the concise proposition of 'Schlechte Zeiten': 'der Umsturz wurde gemacht mit den Umstürzlern, die vorhanden waren'. In the light of such an analysis, Brecht's occasional chiding proselytism is comprehensible; from his position of solidarity with the SED, Brecht formulated impatient invitations whose urgency gave them the character of imperatives, directives from above: the act of social appropriation appeared not as liberation and emancipation, but as a series of dictated administrative measures. Even in this reconstructed context, such poems as 'Nimm Platz am Tisch' (1948/9, GW 10, 961) are problematic; 'Heute mittag um zwölf Uhr/ Beginnt das goldene Zeitalter' appears, in retrospect, exaggerated. It remains hard to decide how much irony Brecht had applied to these lines—he may well have assumed that on a first reading they would meet with scornful dismissal in the face of the overwhelming 'Mühen der Ebenen': the following lines attempt to evoke a sense of the new possibilities which might provide valid foundations for such a euphoric perspective. Contemporary readers of the poem were perhaps expected to follow this movement from ironic reading in the first strophe, to critical assent in the final one, where the 'golden age', no longer an isolated challenging slogan, becomes a serious, rational concept:

> Mutter, dein Sohn soll essen.
> Der Krieg ist abgesagt worden. Wir dachten
> So sei es dir recht. Warum, fragten wir uns
> Das goldene Zeitalter noch aufschieben?
> Wir leben nicht ewig.[11]

Once such assent could be obtained and translated into political as well as economic activity, the coincidence of invitation with direction would itself become redundant. Even the mere beginnings of the golden age would then share its illuminating character.

> Traue nicht deinen Augen
> Traue deinen Ohren nicht
> Du siehst Dunkel
> Vielleicht ist es Licht.

('Sprüche' 1949, GW 10, 966.)

This epigram revives the theme of such poems as 'Lob des Zweifels' and 'Der Zweifler': scepticism as an element of the dialectic capable of generating hope. 'Frühling' (1950/51, GW 10, 969) proposes a similar idea:

> An einem dürren Ast
> Ist eine Blüt' erblüht
> Hat sich heut nacht bemüht
> Und nicht den Mai verpaßt.
> Ich hatt' so kein Vertraun
> Daß ich ihn schon verwarf
> Für Anblick und Bedarf.
> Hätt ihn fast abgehaun.

Understood quite literally, the poem advances a warning against premature negative assumptions: experience has shown that considered expectations may suddenly be surpassed. The very simplicity and clarity of the poem produce an effect of transparency, encouraging an immediate transition from the particular and anecdotal, to the level of metaphoric correspondence. The notion of unexpectedly quick fruition, after all hope seemed vain— this is not only a philosophic generality; it is directly relevant to social and political conditions in Germany. It was suggested that these conditions allowed no good prima facie case for revolutionary hopes, and yet here, as in 'Der Kirschdieb', Brecht contemplates the possibility of a surprise: new exertions might mean that the spring of socialism in Germany would not be missed—by which sections of the population remains, significantly, an open question.[12]

Like the preceding epigram, this text is rhymed and has a metrical base: its lyric style is distinctly classical. These characteristics are typical of a small number of poems written between 1949 and 1951; 'Vom Glück des Gebens' (1950, GW 10, 968) and 'Wenn es im Geahnten ist' (1950/51, GW 10, 969) are further examples, and the 'Neue Kinderlieder' of 1950 form a related group.

'Kinderlieder 1950' and Warnings of Crisis

Brecht's poems for children (GW 10, 970-8) are not directed exclusively to their declared audience; implying recognition of the probable mode of reception (the delivery of the text by adult readers), these poems consistently engage the interest of adults. The element of play is an important constituent here; the poems invite the enjoyment of rhyme and rhythmic melody: they are also instructive. In the delicate conceit of 'Drachenlied'—'Knecht der sieben Windsgewalten/ Zwingst du sie, dich hochzutreiben'—the dialectic is prefigured subliminally but emphatically. 'Liedchen aus alter Zeit', 'Aberglaube', and 'Eines nicht wie das andere' promote a gently critical approach to aspects of childhood experience while 'Stürme schmettern', 'Über die Berge', 'Mailied', 'Neue Zeiten', and 'Vom kriegerischen Lehrer' are more energetically didactic in their treatment of solidarity, nationalization, and the problems of the Prussian tradition. If many of these poems would be suitable for collective use as songs, they equally provide the basis for dialogues in which the questions provoked may be examined in detail. 'Die Vögel warten im Winter vor dem Fenster' may be read as a simple didactic lyric which encourages sympathy, friendliness, and generosity: but the specificity of the three cases presented, and the insistence of the chorus on payment for work carried out, modify this primary reading. The three functions demand critical comparison as useful activity, and together are contrasted with the figures of the raven and the vermin, to which, it is implied, no such sympathy should be extended. This latter distinction is a fundamental one, but within the range of activity viewed with approval there is no clear order of priority: the usefulness of the thrush's song may be different in kind, but not in degree.[13]

Amongst the 'Kinderlieder 1950' two poems stand out: 'Kinderhymne' and 'Die Pappel vom Karlsplatz'.

> Anmut sparet nicht noch Mühe
> Leidenschaft nicht noch Verstand
> Daß ein gutes Deutschland blühe
> Wie ein andres gutes Land.

Simultaneity of passion and reason, effort and grace, is made a precondition for the construction of 'ein gutes Deutschland'; the artificial syntax of the first line stresses 'Anmut' very strongly, as if to compensate for the weight which everyday experience gave to 'Mühe': in the poem it is presented, not without wit, as an apologetic afterthought. Following this surprising imperative, the second line proposes an admittedly less sharply graded priority of passion over reason. The poem supports the construction of socialism in Germany, but at the same time is critical of its restricted basis; Brecht implicitly refers to the Marxist conception of emancipation as a complex process, in which necessary labour itself becomes pleasurable. An immediate reduction in the degree of alienation is proposed: emphasis on 'Anmut' and 'Leidenschaft' indicates that the social and political spheres are seen as areas where such emancipation has still to be grasped.[14]

'Die Pappel vom Karlsplatz' is closely connected to the argument of the 'Kinderhymne' by its rejection of an exclusively economic point of view. The Berliners who, despite the extreme cold and the shortage of fuel, refuse to fell the surviving tree provide an example of the potential scope of emancipation; their action constitutes a defiant rehabilitation of the aesthetic, in the context of a dominant austerity, and demonstrates that the numbing and blinkering effect of material deprivation can be overcome.

'fertige in kleinen büscheln kinderlieder für eisler an. silberschmiedekunst' (AJ 10.6.50)—this may well be more than a neutral description; it recalls Brecht's contrastive use of 'professionalism' and 'craftsmanship' in an earlier note, and suggests that the new 'Kinderlieder' seemed dangerously close to mere decorativeness. It was argued that these poems are not merely self-indulgent, but clearly instructive, even gently critical. Perhaps this very delicacy motivated the comparison with 'silberschmiedekunst': the poems may have appeared too slight and conciliatory, too harmless to achieve any useful effect. Brecht's doubts about the adequacy of 'Kinderlieder 1950' need not have focused exclusively on the poems themselves, which might also be regarded as formulating demands which anticipate social and political developments: in so far as such developments could be viewed as 'overdue', the poems themselves would only be as inadequate as objective conditions. Brecht's awareness of the difficulty of realizing immediate and omnilateral emancipation had been memorably articulated in 'An die Nachgeborenen': 'Ach, wir, die wir den Boden bereiten wollten für Freundlichkeit/ Konnten selber nicht freundlich sein'; but the problem develops new poignancy in the context of the newly founded DDR, where the ground has, at least partly, been prepared.

ich blättere in lorcas gedichten . . . ich lese mit genuß, halte aber verschiedentlich ein, nachzudenken, wie unsere werktätigen zu solchem genuß kommen könnten, und ob sie dazu kommen sollten. man kann einwenden: die lage, die phase läßt dies nicht zu! keine räusche bei klettertouren! aber die klettertouren selber erzeugen räusche, und die literatur, wie einige andere künste,—[entry incomplete, P.W.]. (AJ 29.12.50.)[15]

Brecht's doubts concerning the appropriateness of the 'Kinderlieder' may run parallel with such reflections.

There is no evidence of any such doubt in the case of the contemporary work 'Die Erziehung der Hirse' (GW 10, 979-92). This long epic is unique in Brecht's poetry, though it is related to the *Chronik* strand: its loose iambo-trochaic lines present an exemplary narrative taken from the history of the Soviet Union. The poem's clear didactic line is accompanied by a strong idyllic element:

> Kamen Gäste, griff zum Netz der Alte
> Ging zum Uil und holte silberschuppigen Fisch.
> Denn es lehrt und lernt sich doch bei weitem besser
> Hat man etwas Gutes vor sich auf dem Tisch   (GW 10, 982.)

This is an attempt to evoke the emancipatory perspective of fullness and plenty which the 'Glücksgott' songs and the 'Finnische Epigramme' had introduced; but here the more modest terms of the evocation carry less conviction. Occasionally the idyllic mode appears as a device for enriching a narrative which is often bland and trite:

> Laßt uns so mit immer neuen Künsten
> Ändern dieser Erde Wirkung und Gestalt
> Fröhlich messend tausendjährige Weisheit
> An der neuen Weisheit, ein Jahr alt.
>   Träume! Goldnes Wenn!
>   Laß die schöne Flut der Ähren steigen!
>   Säer, nenn
>   Was du morgen schaffst, schon heut dein Eigen!
>   (GW 10, 992.)

There are important points of emphasis in this strophe, which the complaisant tone smuggles across. The poem as a whole combines a historical lession with a call to increase production: it seems to be a simple mouthpiece for economic policy. It is therefore significant, though easily overlooked, that the preliminary impulse of the story comes, not from any central instruction, but from one inventive peasant. Brecht argues for the continuing dialectic, which cannot be dictated, and against the fossilization of theory as ideology. 'Fröhlich' recalls the idyllic tenor in its suggestion of work as unalienated pleasurable activity. Taking up the theme of 'Nimm Platz am Tisch', the refrain proposes that appropriation should not be postponed, but anticipated. This is no longer a purely economic argument, but a social and political one of immediate importance in the DDR.

A similar bucolic strain is evident in other contemporary poems, though it is never a dominant feature. In 'Glückliche Begegnung', 1952 (GW 10, 1000), a rural setting contributes to the picture of felicitous simultaneity in which familiar distinctions (labour and leisure, manual and intellectual work, town and country) are eroded. The 'Liebeslieder' of 1950 (GW 10, 993–4) present a private idyll in which natural elements play an important part. 'Glücklicher Vorgang' (1952, GW 10, 1004) belongs to this group of poems too:

> Das Kind kommt gelaufen
> Mutter, binde mir die Schürze!
> Die Schürze wird gebunden.

In this small-scale study of successful communication, demand and response are harmoniously matched; it is not by chance that the relationship of mother and child was taken as a model. As its title indicates, 'Unglücklicher Vorgang' (1952, GW 10, 1004) forms a contrastive pair with the poem quoted above; once again, the 'process' observed has a substantial communicative element. The coincidence of invitation and instruction identified in 'Nimm Platz am Tisch' is also evident in the first half of this poem:

> Hier ist ein Haus, das für euch gebaut ist.
> Es ist weit. Es ist dicht.
> Es ist gut für euch, tretet ein.

Here, however, the response is also recorded; indeed, this is where the 'Unglücklicher Vorgang' really begins, since this response is far from simple, happy mutuality. Those to whom the invitation was addressed approach hesitantly, but whether they ultimately accept it remains unclear. Attention is focused on the disturbance of communication, which the specific designations of the final two lines ironically intensify: those who hesitate to approach the house are the builders themselves. In the domestic scene of the first poem, mother and child are 'at home': in the second poem, those who had built the house perceive it as inhospitable. This inhospitality is capable of precise definition; it is characteristic of capitalism. Parallel descriptions are abundant: 'Die Weber gehen von den Webstühlen in Lumpen' (GW 5, 2072); or 'Daß ihr müd seid, Häuser zu bauen und/ Nicht darin zu wohnen' ('Nimm Platz am Tisch', GW 10, 961). The location of such observations in the transitional society of the DDR constitutes a criticism of prime importance; however effective the act of appropriation may be legally and economically, traces of capitalist society remain until the extension of appropriation to the social sphere finally eradicates them. This critical point of view includes political implications, which rest on the problematic conjunction of imperative and invitation; the fundamental fault is not contained in the workers' hesitation after being summoned, but rather in the fact that the summons was issued, in its origins, and in the manner of its delivery. A contemporary fragment, which recalls the argument of 'Lob des Zweifels', illuminates this crux:

Dem, der das Kommando gibt, sag:
Kommando muß sein, bei so vielen, in so großen Unternehmungen
Mit so wenig Zeit
Aber kommandiere so
Daß ich mich selber mitkommandiere!

('An einen jungen Bauarbeiter der Stalinallee', 1952, GW 10, 1003–4.)

The 'Aufbaulied' of 1948 had insisted that political reconstruction should take the form of 'sich-selbst-führen'; the failure to achieve this level of emancipation is at the centre of the 'Mühen der Ebenen'. By 1952 it is evident that Brecht's critical summary of the political scene, 'der Umsturz wurde gemacht mit den Umstürzlern, die vorhanden waren' ('Schlechte Zeiten') may operate as a double-edged sword; if at first it refers to the debilitation of the proletariat, it becomes increasingly applicable to another distinct type of 'Umstürzler', the SED and the government of the DDR. They had failed in one of their principal tasks: the effective promotion of proletarian self-government, of the democracy without which socialism is restricted to a matter of economic form.

'Das Brot des Volkes' (1953, GW 10, 1005) is directed against this malaise; its central metaphor, biblical in its simplicity and presence, connects and distinguishes the economic and the sociopolitical spheres. Following the proposition of the first line, the literal and metaphorical planes (bread and justice) are repeatedly and conspicuously separated and recombined to produce cumulative emphasis: the poem, in its extreme clarity and pedestrian repetitions, is almost a sermon. Brecht's argument is insistent, indeed aggressive:

> Weg mit der schlechten Gerechtigkeit!
> Der lieblos gebackenen, der kenntnislos gekneteten!
> Der Gerechtigkeit ohne Würze, deren Kruste grau ist!
> Der altbackenen Gerechtigkeit, die zu spät kommt!

These are evidently radical propositions; the continuing text suggests that they are inescapably necessary:

> Wenn das Brot gut und reichlich ist
> Kann der Rest der Mahlzeit verziehen werden.
> Nicht alles kann es gleich in Fülle geben.
> Vom Brot der Gerechtigkeit genährt
> Kann die Arbeit geleistet werden
> Von der die Fülle kommt.

The poem's unequivocal conclusion is that those whose work is the motive power of the economy must also actively control the social and political machinery:

> So wie das andere Brot
> Muß das Brot der Gerechtigkeit
> Vom Volk gebacken werden.

Far from accepting that such proletarian appropriation should be postponed until some more opportune moment, Brecht defines it as an immediate necessity, the *sine qua non* of further emancipation. The SED and the government of the DDR were not prepared to envisage, still less to encourage, such developments. They must be seen as the chief focus of the criticisms formulated in 'Das Brot des Volkes'.[16]

The complex malaise described reached its crisis in mid June 1953; Brecht was a witness to the events in East Berlin. The most detailed account of his understanding of the crisis is offered by the *Arbeitsjournal* (20.8.53):

alles kam darauf an, diese erste begegnung voll auszuwerten. das war der kontakt. er kam nicht in der form der umarmung, sondern in der form des faustschlags, aber es war doch der kontakt. — die partei hatte zu erschrecken, aber sie brauchte nicht zu verzweifeln.... aber nun, als große ungelegenheit, kam die große gelegenheit, die arbeiter zu gewinnen. deshalb empfand ich den schrecklichen 17. juni als nicht einfach negativ.[17]

In the context of the political and emotional confusion of 1953, this analysis displays exemplary dispassion and assurance; the proletariat had momentarily grasped its political power, and this, despite the disorganized character of its actions, was a welcome development. The SED, confronted for the first time by the class it sought to represent, as a body capable of spontaneous action, might have achieved much, had it recognized this positive element: but it failed to see that the blows which threatened the party's role of absolute leadership did signify contact, the potential of a dialogue whose possibility had seemed remote. It is conceivable that the party was incapable of such rigorous and painful application of the dialectic, that it was overtaken by events. In the following months, however, the party did not attempt to remedy its mistakes—indeed, they were compounded; blows were answered by the more powerful blows of the state; contact with the proletariat as an active political force was not encouraged, but prevented by more effective insulation of the party. Brecht's analysis leaves the question of the party's response open to subsequent correction, though the overall prognosis following the loss of this inopportune opportunity was not good; presumably the next instance of contact would be more painful.

It is significant that Brecht sees the position of party and government as politically mistaken; he apparently did not consider that the interests of the party had been so divorced from those of the proletariat that promotion of a real political dialogue was precisely what it must seek to prevent. Brecht's solidarity with the proletariat is never in doubt; in 1953 it is evident that he extended his solidarity as a critical Marxist to the SED.

Buckower Elegien

'buckow. TURANDOT. daneben die BUCKOWER ELEGIEN. der 17. juni hat die ganze existenz verfremdet' (AJ 20.8.53).

The *Buckower Elegien* of the summer of 1953 were Brecht's last collection of poems; including the motto, there are twenty-two published texts which belong to the cycle, and two further texts recently released for publication.[18]

> Ginge da ein Wind
> Könnte ich ein Segel stellen.
> Wäre da kein Segel
> Machte ich eines aus Stecken und Plane.   (GW 10, 1009.)

This epigraph is written in a 'basic german', from which only the syntactic inversion deviates; on the literal level, the poem is almost excessively clear, so that metaphorical significance is indicated. At the same time, metaphor is here so tenuously grounded that doubt and hesitancy are placed in tension with a primary sense of calm, resolute confidence. Formulating the wish that some motive force were present, the poem expresses a willingness to improvise in order to take advantage of it: there is a faint echo of 'Schlechte Zeiten' here. The use of natural metaphor for social phenomena is a characteristic of Brecht's writing; while 'Das Lied vom Klassenfeind' operates provocatively on this basis, later poems are sometimes content to employ metaphor simply and persuasively: the 'Lied vom Glück' for example—

> Die Arbeit ist nicht Fluch
> Für die nicht Sklaven sind
> Ist Milch und Tuch und Schuh und Buch
> Und wie dem Segler Wind.   (GW 10, 998.)

'Wind' in the epigraph need not be identified dogmatically as the proletariat; it may be read, more abstractly, as productive human activity, freed from restraint.[19] The total sense of the urge to move forward is dominant. This may seem an optimistic attitude, but it is important that the poem's sense of calm derives partly from its unresolved conditional clauses, which suggest precisely the absence of any effective motive force, and thus sharpen the poem's voluntary aspect in a critical, challenging, and potentially elegiac way.

'Der Radwechsel' (GW 10, 1009) is apparently more concrete and autobiographical than the reflective, abstract motto. The poem's first person is, however, not necessarily confined to individual reference: indeed, the speaker becomes a representative persona. Like the motto, this text employs the metaphor of travel; here, a journey has been interrupted by a breakdown and the

THE POST-EXILE POETRY 1948-1956 203

traveller is forced to wait while repairs are carried out. His leisured view from the roadside allows him time to reflect that both his point of departure and his destination hold sufficient unpleasantness for him: he should be able to enjoy the interruption. Paradoxically (the last pair of lines invite a tone of bemused humour) the traveller is impatient to continue his journey. Again, the metaphor is relatively open; its significance is defined by the fact of Brecht's authorship, and by the experience of the historical situation which he shared with his readers.

The poem's minimal style has an intensifying effect, highlighting individual words and the relationships between them; the word which receives the highest prominence is the final one: 'Ungeduld'. This, with the question-mark which follows, suggests a slightly doubtful optimism. Impatience, one of the relativistic virtues of revolutionary socialism, the urge to progress, is here confronted by the knowledge of an unpleasant past and of a future so arduous and problematic that it is no more hospitable. Impatience outweighs such considerations, and the poem seems to ask whether this is not justified by the necessity to proceed.

It is tempting at first to translate the 'Radwechsel' in terms of the events of June 1953; this is a restriction which is not supported by the text. Rather it defines the location of the DDR historically between the era of capitalism and that of transitional societies; if the breakdown corresponds to any specific caesura, it is surely the 'Stunde Null' of 1945. The period in which the major driving force is out of action lasts too long. Brecht, whose own position of ambivalent privilege as an intellectual is evoked in the poem's first line, insists that there can be no return to the age of Weimar; the restoration in progress in the BRD offered no better prospects than socialist construction in the DDR. The third line may be read literally, and personally: rather East Berlin than Augsburg. On the basis of this statement of principle, an appraisal of probable developments in the DDR is presented: it offers no grounds for hope. Impatience, defiant and almost irrational, is directed to goals which lie further ahead than preliminary destinations; it recognizes that the sooner these are reached, the sooner they may be left behind.[20]

The poem invites its readers to adopt the honest and critical point of view which it presents, to agree that revolutionary impatience must have the last word.

'Der Blumengarten' (GW 10, 1009) is a metrical poem, the only one of the cycle which is also strophically arranged. The first strophe of the epigram describes a picture of sheltered richness, a static idyll whose location may be understood as the vicinity of Brecht's summer house in Buckow.[21] Its indication of the co-operation of human praxis and natural process ('Mauer und Gesträuch') places the poem in a long series of related texts, from 'Über die Bauart langdauernder Werke' to 'Garden in Progress' and 'Kalifornischer Herbst': observation of landscape leads to social reflection. The transition is partly metaphorical, but also metonymic: a 'worked' landscape is a microcosm of all culture. Brecht again adopts his public voice: the poet would gladly write with only his readers' pleasure in mind; as things are, however, this cannot be his dominant concern. The concluding lines formulate this dual proposition:

> [Ich] wünsche mir, auch ich mög allezeit
> In den verschiedenen Wettern, guten, schlechten
> Dies oder jenes Angenehme zeigen.

'Auch ich . . .' indicates that this statement is derived from the preceding observations; the sheltered garden offers such abundant enjoyment because it is so wisely arranged. Translated via the garden-as-society metaphor into the language of the conclusion, this causal clause defines the poem's argument clearly: the society in which the poet lives is not so wisely arranged that he is able consistently to offer pleasure.[22] The poet's wish thus implies a recommendation that the requisite wisdom be applied. Within the limits of this long perspective, the lines quoted also stand as a simple and immediate declaration: even before all necessary conditions have been fully satisfied, while no shelter against unfavourable weather exists, it may be possible to anticipate the pleasures of the later happy state.

The phrase 'hier in der Früh' seems to integrate two levels of discourse, describing both the time of day at which the real garden is visited, and Brecht's situation in the problematic early phase of socialism. The pleasurable aspect of the real garden is contrasted with the painful difficulties of the social garden. Potential is confronted by reality. 'Nicht allzu häufig' assures the reader that the real garden, and the reflections provoked by it, are not simply a refuge from society; the poet has other occupations, including (it may be supposed) the treatment of matters less pleasant.[23] This is a corollary of the poem's final sentence, and is confirmed in practice by other poems of the same collection.

'Große Zeit, vertan' (GW 10, 1010) recalls 'Unglücklicher Vorgang'; it is an 'open' poem, which records attitudes and opinions without clearly attributing them—thus making the points of view themselves a centre of interest. The speaker declares his sense of dissociation from such fundamental undertakings as urban construction, and explains it by characterizing these projects as statistically, rather than historically significant. The separate concluding pair of lines may be read as a continuation of this argument, or indeed as its confirmation from another source. It provides a more substantial explanation of the speaker's lack of interest: 'Was sind schon Städte, gebaut/ Ohne die Weisheit des Volkes?'; these lines suggest that those who recognize no proper significance in the building of new cities are precisely those whose knowledge and experience are excluded from the undertaking.[24] The poem thus includes an *a posteriori* attribution: to the people themselves; and the unhappy process described is aggravated by the fact that these cities, nominally and in fact, were built for the people.

The poem does not admit a reading which assumes opposition to the building of cities: the necessity of this task is understood as a basic premise; nor is it easily interpretable as a call for the rejection of large-scale planning, which follows on the above premise. The principal emphasis rests on the question cited above, concerning the mode of planning and execution. This may be seen as one specific aspect of the central problem defined above as the coincidence of socialism with democracy; in the terms of the poem, the problem appears as a contradiction: projects undertaken for, and partly by, the people none the less fail to appear as such. This paradox includes an important subjective factor, but clearly extends into the objective sphere with the provocative assertion that these projects are not undertaken *with* the people, whose productivity is thus accurately felt to be restricted. Construction is capable of both literal and metaphorical application, as the 'Aufbaulied' demonstrates.

The wasted opportunity to which the title refers is immediate human emancipation: the responsibility for its loss (which need not be permanent) remains an open question. As a corrective challenge, the poem is addressed to proletariat and party alike.

A similar sense of loss and failure is described in 'Böser Morgen' (GW 10, 1010), where the subjective element is emphasized to produce a surprising intensity of emotion. The autobiographical stance is particularly strong. The speaker has had a bad dream, the effects of which are slow to fade; as he surveys his familiar surroundings, their pleasant features appear spoiled: 'Der See/ Eine Lache Abwaschwasser, nicht rühren!'. The poem is hinged on the question 'warum?', which demands that the painful dream be recounted. Broken, hard-worked fingers had pointed at the speaker in disgust: his retort ('Unwissende!') is modified by the subsequent admission of responsibility. The ignorance with which he charges his injured accusers is partly his fault. However strongly a directly personal reference may be implied here, the poem by no means excludes more general understanding: what applies to Brecht is applicable to other Marxist intellectuals, and, significantly, to the SED. The violence and damage which form the poem's implicit background are perhaps simple reminders of the events of 17 June: the broken fingers of the poem correspond to contact 'in der form des faustschlags'. The party and its allies were better equipped than the proletariat to prevent their contact adopting this painful form: their failure may appear more substantial.

As the poems discussed above indicate, the *Buckower Elegien* are not exclusively concentrated on the crisis of 1953, tending rather to include it in wider critical reflections. Other texts of the collection insist more explicitly on the importance of historical context:

> In der Frühe
> Sind die Tannen kupfern.
> So sah ich sie
> Vor einem halben Jahrhundert
> Vor zwei Weltkriegen
> Mit jungen Augen.   ('Tannen', GW 10, 1012.)

The natural continuity on which the poet's sudden recognition depends is finally confronted by the discordant recollection of the unnatural destruction and disturbance of human life in the same period: two world wars have been fought in the time taken for a man to grow old.

The proximity of the Second World War is the subject of two poems, 'Der Einarmige im Gehölz' and 'Vor acht Jahren' (both GW 10, 1013). The first text records a brief episode which demonstrates the problematic character of Brecht's attitude towards the German population: Brecht is here representative of many Marxists, above all those who had been exiled.[25] 'Schweißtriefend bückt er sich...'—the poem's observations are at first sympathetic to the disabled man, gathering fuel. This innocent view, in which the wood-gatherer appears as a victim (probably of the war) is suddenly transformed in the final sentence: a simple movement betrays him as a former oppressor—at least to the poem's implied observer. The suspicion is not confirmed, merely stated as a possibility; the episode indicates that the fascist past intrudes on the present, and is indeed continuous with it, at least at a personal level. (It is unimportant whether the man observed had really belonged to the SS, or whether the observer's suspicions—themselves a kind of war wound—persist, still reacting to the slightest cue.)

'Vor acht Jahren' also explores the paradoxical presence of history: like the previous poem, it allows no easy solution—the first lines 'Da war eine Zeit/ Da war alles hier anders' may be read as an approving comparison by the poet, or as his adoption of a remark overheard. The following lines tend to demand the latter reading: the first sentence is exhibited as a quotation, whose correctness the poet admits, but within a set of values not necessarily shared by those quoted. The primary difference between 1945 and 1953 was constituted by the defeat of the fascist regime, which divided the bourgeois republic from the transitional society of the DDR; in this positive sense, all had changed. The commentary provided in the remainder of the text introduces an opposite understanding of the statement, a sense in which it was probably often heard: the problems of the present are unfavourably contrasted with the 'order' of the past. Like the wood-gatherer of 'Der Einarmige im Gehölz', the postman of this poem is a threatening figure, a reminder of slaughter and oppression. Does his retention of a military posture signify his eagerness to quit the tameness of a civilian occupation and return to arms? Does the butcher's wife (is she his widow?) think longingly of the profiteering which is no longer possible? The poem argues that the past and thus fascism in particular, are not finished, even in the DDR; specifically, it suggests that the petty bourgeoisie may still be accessible to the arguments of capitalism: 'wir haben unseren eigenen Westen bei uns!', Brecht remarked in August 1953.[26]

This Hegelian theme is pursued more generally in 'Gewohnheiten, noch immer' and 'Heißer Tag' (both GW 10, 1011); the first poem employs a favourite area of imagery in Brecht's writings: food and eating. Its attractiveness rests on its materialism and potential for realism; it allows easy transition from biological to economic and social fact. The first section of the poem describes a conspicuous contradiction: 'Mit schriller Stimme/ Ertönt das Kommando: Zum Essen!'; satisfaction of the most fundamental human needs is made the subject of an artificial command. This is a crass perversion of human behaviour; where earlier poems of the post-exile period had described (and themselves exhibited) the problematic coincidence of invitation and order, this text shows a dominance of the imperative which leaves little room for invitation. Eating does not appear as necessary and pleasurable, simply as an instruction from above; this moment of alienation is located in the DDR of 1953—hence the implication of the title, that such phenomena should belong only to the past. The three lines of the poem's second section define this perversion as belonging to the Prussian tradition. Read metaphorically, the poem presents incisive criticism of social and political conditions in the DDR. Government by bureaucratic dictate is neither itself democratic, nor does it promote the development of democracy.

'Heißer Tag' is an anecdotal poem which shares the penetrating wit of 'Die Lösung'; the sight of the child, labouring to transport the oppressive weight of the surfeited nun and her dubious, equally leisured companion, appears to the poet as a symbol of previous societies based on exploitation. The repeated exclamation 'wie in alten Zeiten!' reminds the reader that the literal element of the symbol is situated in the present. A satiric perspective is thus opened, but not explored: is it only the trivial scene itself which provokes the poet's anger, or does it also represent a real, and wider present malaise comparable with the exploitative burden of the church? The poem insists by its silence that none but the reader can decide whether such a double analogy is fully applicable.

'Der Himmel dieses Sommers' and 'Die Kelle' (both GW 10, 1015) transfer the sense of threat which informs these poems to a more concrete perspective: the risk of renewed war. The first poem has an undercurrent of irony: like fledglings waiting for food, those left alive after the previous war ('Kinder', 'Frauen', 'ein Greis') look up to see—a warplane. Here again, the food metaphor is employed to define a central contradiction: the aircraft, supreme achievement of industry and science, does not bring nourishment but destruction. This is not a decidedly pacifist poem: it opens dialogue and refrains from tendering slogans. 'Die Kelle' relates a dreamed episode in which the work of construction is interrupted by violence; here, too, considerable restraint is observed: no blame is apportioned, but it is gently suggested that destructive aggression must be resisted.

In both 'Der Himmel dieses Sommers' and 'Die Kelle', the category of production stands in positive contrast to the destructive potential of which the poems warn; production was shown to be a category of emancipation. 'Der Rauch' (GW 10, 1012) and 'Laute' (GW 10, 1014) are reminders of the necessarily human character of emancipation:

> Das kleine Haus unter Bäumen am See.
> Vom Dach steigt Rauch.
> Fehlte er
> Wie trostlos dann wären
> Haus, Bäume und See.[27]

The poem may at first appear to illustrate that nature is only hospitable when there are guests to claim her hospitality. This 'humanist' idea is also a Marxist postulate—communist society as 'the accomplished union of man with Nature, the veritable resurrection of Nature, the realized naturalism of man and the realized humanism of Nature'.[28] The poem does indeed touch on this central theme; but its title is not simply 'Das Haus', as a dominance of this theme would tend to demand. Such primary emphasis on the smoke indicates that the dominant concern of the poem penetrates beyond the general interaction of man and nature, to the internal (and economic) detail of human society. The natural landscape is not simply inhabited; it is properly lived in. The mere presence and occupation of a house is not sufficient assurance of human life: full appropriation is a continuous human activity.

'Laute' provides a more general statement of the same position; recognizing the place of plant and animal life in a familiar landscape (and, implicitly, its aesthetic value for human observers), the poem modifies this point of view, with its potential emphasis on the picturesque, by confronting it with its human equivalent. The sounds of people, however mundane, are not resented as disturbances of natural peace, but are accepted with the same modest approval as the natural sounds which belong to the area.

Like 'Die Lösung' (GW 10, 1009), 'Die Wahrheit einigt' (GW 10, 1011) is a relatively explicit poem; it is presumably for this reason that Dieter Thiele insists on a restrictively specific reading of these two poems, as directed exclusively to Brecht's fellow-writers.[29] It is true that the first example refers directly to Kuba (Kurt Barthel); but it is unlikely that Brecht would have considered a purely individual criticism worthwhile. Kuba had provided a clear example of the general malaise of political disjunction between the party and the proletariat; his attitude of moralistic condescension, his rebukes delivered from a position of assumed infallible authority were not his personal failings; they were typical, and were at the focus of Brecht's critical comments on the role of the party in the catastrophe of 1953. Thiele's apologetic indulgence towards the SED of that period fails to take account of the critical insight for which Brecht argued, and which was (at least theoretically) invited by the party itself: 'wenn Massen von Arbeitern die Partei nicht verstehen, ist die Partei schuld, nicht die Arbeiter!'[30]

'Die Wahrheit einigt' demands precisely such openness to self-criticism, the honest examination of facts, without which effective action is impossible. To understand this fundamental and urgent appeal as directed to the literary intelligentsia alone is absurd; the detail of Brecht's argument contradicts such a reading.

The subjunctives of the first sentence suggest that the friends addressed are far removed from the productive realism which the poem recommends; this is confirmed by the argument *ex negativo* in the second sentence: 'nicht wie fliehende müde Cäsaren: Morgen kommt Mehl!' This imperial manner is equivalent to the authoritarian tradition described in 'Gewohnheiten, noch immer'; it is significant that the authoritarian mode is accompanied by a crude emphasis on the economic factor. Lenin's exhortation to collective action is presented as a contrastive example: here there is no contemplation of piecemeal palliative measures. The poem's positive recommendations imply serious criticisms of the SED.

> Im Traum heute Nacht
> Sah ich einen großen Sturm
> Ins Baugerüst griff er
> Den Bauschragen riß er
> Den eisernen, abwärts.
> Doch was da aus Holz war
> Bog sich und blieb.   ('Eisen', GW 10, 1012.)

As in 'Die Kelle' and 'Böser Morgen', the poem is nominally the record of a dream; dreams enjoy the privilege of immunity from censorship, both internal and external. The simplicity and concentration of the imagery, together with the cue provided by the first line ('im Traum'), encourage a symbolic or allegorical reading: the poem is an illustration of the sentence from 'Legende von der Entstehung des Buches Taoteking'—'das Harte unterliegt'. The poem warns against excessive inflexibility, against rigid authority and unquestionable doctrine: what fails to bend may be broken by overwhelming force. The iron of the title is apparently a chiffre for Stalinism. (The poem also modifies the slogan 'steel stood' to which Brecht repeatedly referred.)[31]

With the exception of the introductory pair of lines, the poem is composed as a loose pastiche of the elegiac couplet; rather than make this gesture openly, Brecht chooses to suggest it delicately by taking the caesurae as additional line-endings. The classical tone of the poem, above all the frequent dactyls, suggest a classic authority: authority based on long experience and common assent.

The great storm to which 'Eisen' refers is ambivalent; it may seem destructive, a threat to the work of construction—yet it appears that any damage done is clearly the consequence of unsuitable scaffolding, that the storm would normally have been weathered without difficulty. 'Bei der Lektüre eines sowjetischen Buches' (GW 10, 1014) describes forces of similar ambivalence and complexity. Here, the point of departure is not a dream, but the work of another writer: 'Die Wolga, lese ich, zu bezwingen/ Wird keine leichte Aufgabe sein'. These lines define the tone of the poem's first section (as far as the dash: '— aber, lese ich'). The blank simplicity of the first sentence suggests ironic understatement, criticism of a hubristic undertaking; in contrast, the following sentences, which describe the heroic might of the river system, adopt increasingly inflated and discordant language: 'Dieses erfinderische Genie, mit dem teuflischen Spürsinn/ Des Griechen Odysseus'. This epic crescendo might be satire; but of what? A single book hardly seems a sufficient object.

The local ironies do not coalesce to indicate any simple and coherent inversion of sense; in spite of the apparent departure from irony in the second section, the poem as a whole remains a disproportionate text, a puzzle incapable of resolution within its own terms. If this second section may be understood literally, what is the function of the preceding lines?

Besides litotes and hyperbole as ironic markers, there is the repeated distancing interjection 'lese ich', which suggests that the understatement and exaggeration, though discovered and juxtaposed by the poet, are not his work, but 'quotation'; this may also account for the sharp contrast between the excited confusion of the first section, and the reflective sobriety of the second. This encompassing irony appears to offer a coherent solution to the poem's problems, to the sense of disjunction produced when it is read as an expression of opinion, a direct commentary on a Soviet book; a secondary reading allows the poem to exhibit elements of the book, inviting the reader to reproduce the poet's critical reflections. The role of the book as a literary work is perhaps of subsidiary importance here: it may conveniently define the distinction between words and actions. The poem does not inquire whether the book is satisfactory as literary art, but principally whether its attitudes and statements are adequate to the reality to which they refer.

The central question which this 'reading of a Soviet book' provokes thus concerns the reality of the Soviet transitional society. The construction of a dam appears, in an immediate and economic sense, as a positive step—though at the level of imagery it is clearly ambivalent: dams prevent disastrous floods, but also block rivers.[32] In reality, too, social and economic factors may contradict the building of a dam (it may simply be unnecessary). The non-material areas of reality, the political sphere above all, offer additional complications and here the Soviet book, as an indicator of the problematic connections of consciousness and reality, gains special relevance. A dam may be objectively, economically, necessary and may at the same time appear to those affected by or engaged in its construction not as productive, but as destructive, not as emancipation, but as oppression. The interplay of 'objective' economic factors with 'subjective' political ones is a dominant social dialectic: if it is here illustrated from a Soviet book, it is of equal significance in the context of the DDR. It is, for example, the base of the dialectic of 'Gewohnheiten, noch immer', in which appropriation appears as a directive from above.

The poem demands considerable intellectual efforts from its readers, offering in return not a set of conclusions but a model of critical thought, dialectic in its manipulation of contradictory possibilities, materialist in its insistence that reality is more important than its verbal treatment—though it too is real. The reader, after extracting this model from the poem, must also apply it.

'Rudern, Gespräche' (GW 10, 1013) presents an image which is the polar opposite of the scene described in 'Heißer Tag'; in the evening (after their day's work?) two young men are observed across the water in canoes. Their nakedness excludes any question of social specificity, and suggests an easy confidence that they will need no protection. Talking as they row side by side, the two canoeists are in contact; their activity is co-operative and coherent, without restricting independent movement. They form a complex, changing unity whose felicity depends on its unforced mutuality, responsiveness and even transience: a slight change of pace would be sufficient to interrupt the conversation and the canoes themselves can be dismantled—they are perhaps improvised craft. The young men are equal participants in free association; their thought and speech and their physical exertion enjoy the same equality: reflection and action are combined, united in a collective movement which is itself a goal.[33] With an elegance derived from subtlety and concision, the poem develops a positive and genuine utopian vision; the limits of this vision are defined by its abstraction from the immediate experience of the mundane present.

> Selbst die Sintflut
> Dauerte nicht ewig.
> Einmal verrannen
> Die schwarzen Gewässer.
> Freilich, wie wenige
> Dauerten länger!
> ('Beim Lesen des Horaz', GW 10, 1014.)

Here once again the reader is confronted by the poet's response to a text unknown to the reader; it is not clear whether the poem is to be understood as quotation or commentary, though the 'bei' of the title seems to indicate the latter possibility. In either case this is presented as an autonomous text, in which the relation to a source is not of dominant importance.

The poem begins with what is evidently a response (possibly, not necessarily, to some specific text of Horace); its attitude is concessive, as if admitting the validity of a reassuring assertion that present difficulties will not last for ever: in its categorical extension (as if to say that nothing lasts for ever) this is also a corrective response—the concession is ironic. This irony and the corrective potential based upon it are not immediately apparent and the second sentence seems to accept unequivocally that there is comfort in the idea of transience. This sense of patient hope is, however, brusquely deflated by the final sentence, which fully mobilizes the ironic potential of the first two lines in its new and devastating turn: a statement in parallel with the first sentence (people do not live for ever), this is also its effective contradiction. By pursuing a comforting argument to its practical consequences the poem shows the inadequacy of the argument and demands its inversion; far from the attitude of resignation and passivity at first implied, only active intervention promises that problems will be solved. The poem is not, however, dogmatic in its reversal of the argument for patience; it is not denied that problems *may* be outlasted, simply implied that this is probably not a productive attitude. Here, as in 'Bei der Lektüre eines sowjetischen Buches', Brecht does not seek to promote fixed conclusions but rather to develop a dialectic whose specific and actual terms the reader must define. In the context of the DDR in 1953 the argument in favour of immediate, wide, and active participation is surely predominant: there had been sufficient patient endurance practised in Germany since 1933. Socialism meant democracy. 'Beim Lesen des Horaz' may thus recall 'Gegen Verführung', in a modified specific sense: 'Laßt euch nicht vertrösten!/ Ihr habt nicht zu viel Zeit!'.[34]

'Bei der Lektüre eines spätgriechischen Dichters' (GW 10, 1016), like 'Beim Lesen des Horaz', is conceived as the poet's reply to another poem (in this case a translation from Cavafy). The substantial part of the text may be read as a précis of that poem, whose significance is defined by the concluding sentence—'auch die Troer also'. This is a clear invitation to the reader to compare the situation described with his own observations; Brecht implies that such a comparison is valid. The concise analysis identifies the Trojans' position as precarious: powerful enemies surrounded them. While some had already given up all hope, others carried out minute improvements to the main defences, believing that this would save them. It is argued that the DDR, in a similarly vulnerable position, was equally content with piecemeal measures

THE POST-EXILE POETRY 1948-1956 215

(specifically, perhaps, expansion of the Deutsche Grenzpolizei and the Kasernierte Volkspolizei, which had been a major cause of the economic malaise in 1952-3) and that the assurance derived from these measures was illusory. The poem's first line is a reminder that for the Trojans all had been decided; their defeat had been planned even before their defences were strengthened: they were to be defeated from within. No military measures could save them. If the poem's final line is read as a simple statement, it appears to proceed from criticism of the policies of the DDR, to the conclusion that all is already lost; such defeatism is, however, not part of a credible reading and the sentence may equally be read ironically, provoking a decision on the reader's part: to what extent is the comparison really valid? If all were lost, Brecht's poem would have no function.

It is reasonable to conclude that the poem seeks to identify a major fault of policy: the tendency to take refuge in administrative measures, to think economically and militarily, but not politically. The extension of the comparison with Troy thus appears as a provocative warning, as from Cassandra: but the relevance of the warning rests on the assumption that in the DDR it is *not* too late to remedy the malaise, thus averting the real danger of defeat from within. The Trojan horse was already within the walls ('wir haben unseren eigenen Westen bei uns') and only internal, political strength, real democracy, would suffice to prevent defeat. The poem's urgent warning may be seen as an instance of what 'Die Wahrheit einigt' had recommended: 'Freunde, ein kräftiges Eingeständnis/ Und ein kräftiges WENN NICHT!'.[35]

Buckower Elegien is a cycle, a collection of poems related in theme and style; but the collection is neither thematically nor technically divorced from the main body of poetic production of this period. The cycle is an informal series, in which specific order is not decisive: the overall context of the series is important, however, and its individual texts illuminate one another. These poems represent the central strand of the late poetry: they are characteristically (but not exclusively) texts of remarkable compression, oblique in mode and thus reticent. They demand considerable intellectual exertion on the part of the reader, and many poems, having promoted such a high level of conscious activity in the process of literary reception, clearly indicate that it is the reader's task to extend such activity to the wider social and political sphere. Such poems as the motto, 'Der Radwechsel', 'Große Zeit, vertan' and 'Beim Lesen des Horaz' are model exercises in critical praxis; they state their own limits as literary works. The title of the series thus appears as ironic; like the concealed hexameters of 'Beim Lesen des Horaz' it even suggests a joke: these are critical poems, melancholy satires rather than elegies—but, depending on their reception, on the development of emancipation, they may *become* elegies.

The *Buckower Elegien* do not reflect Brecht's determination to write for the whole of Germany: this intention had been overtaken by events. These poems are focused on the socialist state and were addressed to the proletariat and its allies within this context. Paradoxically, the difficulty of the texts contributes substantially to their effectiveness; in a phase of over-heated and ideological argument their call to action is preceded by the demand for careful thought. This same difficulty may also have protected the poems from the crude censorship to which Brecht's letter to Ulbricht on 17 June had fallen victim.[36] Six poems from the collection were published in 1953 in *Sinn und Form*, and in *Versuche, 13* in 1954.[37]

The Last Poems

After 1953 the production of poetry decreases further; the *werkausgabe* lists only thirty-eight poems (not including those incorporated in dramatic projects) for the period between 1953 and Brecht's death in 1956. Amongst them are poems of major importance. 'Nicht in die Schlacht wirf, Feldherr, alle!' (GW 10, 1019, 1954) is a representative text; it consists of three sections in the epigrammatic style of the *Buckower Elegien*. The poem's title, with which the first section also begins, is a general precept: the metaphorical commander is warned not to deploy all his forces in battle; there is other work to be done ('das Fleisch einholen'), on which the battle itself may depend. The battle must be won without those properly employed elsewhere.

The second section moves from this abstract and enigmatic proposition to consider concrete examples; on the evening following an unsuccessful battle, when all hope seemed lost, a common soldier restored Alexander's will to live, by pointing out a quail. This simple act is revealed as a kind of extravagance in the following lines—a quail is more than reason enough:

> Um das Leben zu schätzen
> Meinte der Soldat
> Genügt ein Stück Käse.

These two sections combine to synthesize the argument that a battle is, at best, the unavoidable means to an end; it should never be allowed to mask that end by its own demands. Life should not be taken lightly. The great general is reminded of the proper status of life by an anonymous man from the ranks, a man in possession of the 'Weisheit des Volkes', and one perhaps not averse to watching the sky.

The military setting may represent structures of power in general: the poem would then plead for critical reference to the purpose which such structures claim to serve. It appears, however, that this setting has intrinsic significance too; the poem is concerned with the specific risks which accompany military structures (above all, their potential for the destruction of life). Though the need for battle is conceded in the first section ('schaff uns den Sieg!'), it is all but forgotten in the emphatic affirmations of life which follow. The poem may be regarded as a sequel to the antimilitary attitude of 'Bei der Lektüre eines spätgriechischen Dichters'. In its historical context this appears as a critical poem; but its positive moments carry more weight: the third section adds new reasons to the soldier's modest proposition.

> Die gelben frühen, neugedruckten Bücher
> Das Autofahren, Fliegen, Blumenpflanzen
> Die abendlichen Berge, nicht gesehenen Städte
> Die Männer, die Frauen.

The potential for pleasurable life is clearly inexhaustible; it is the realization of this potential which is the goal. Human emancipation must not be obscured, still less impeded, by the means of its attainment: it should be conceived as a process rather than a final state which continuously recedes into the future. 'Das Leben zu schätzen' is an immediate demand, rich in implications.

At the centre of this complex text is the materialism found to be characteristic of the poetry written in the second phase of exile, between 1939 and 1947. Closely linked to the concept of full human emancipation, this materialism was also derived from the fundamental orientation of the early poetry, which it both dissolved and recrystallized in a new dimension. Some early texts thus reappear in these last poems; 'Man sollte nicht zu kritisch sein' (1922/23, GW 8, 118) is perceptible in texts such as the third section of 'Nicht in die Schlacht wirf, Feldherr, alle!', and in many others so closely related that they are virtually extensions and elaborations of this poem: '1954: Erste Hälfte' (1954, GW 10, 1022); 'Einmal, wenn da Zeit sein wird' (1954/55, GW 10, 1027); 'Fröhlich vom Fleisch zu essen' (1954/55, GW 10, 1031); and, preeminently, 'Vergnügungen':

> Der erste Blick aus dem Fenster am Morgen
> Das wiedergefundene alte Buch
> Begeisterte Gesichter
> Schnee, der Wechsel der Jahreszeiten
> Die Zeitung
> Der Hund
> Die Dialektik
> Duschen, Schwimmen
> Alte Musik
> Bequeme Schuhe
> Begreifen
> Neue Musik
> Schreiben, Pflanzen
> Reisen
> Singen
> Freundlich sein.   (1954/5, GW 10, 1022.)

This may seem to be a static, complacent poem, a purely private utterance, or at most an example to be admired. Here, as often, the fact of Brecht's authorship acts as an obstacle in the way of a primary reading, provoking its revision; the poem does not offer explicit recommendations of a moral character, but is content to list objects and activities which give the poet pleasure. This direct experience is the basis of the dialogue which the poem promotes: it invites the reader to consider to what extent he is able to share its observations; his answers amount to a measure of his emancipation.[38] Realized as a universal programme (and not an individual example) the poem defines the concrete utopia of communism. Its operation as a provocative model does not exclude the poem's more immediate celebration of material, sensuous pleasures; the cumulative progression of the text eradicates distinctions between mind and body, reflection and action, intellect and emotion, which all belong to pleasurable human life—a unity greater than the sum of its parts.

The concept of the proper function of death corresponds to that of full and enjoyable life. Death is viewed as an event of minor importance, which does not itself require any special marker: 'Ich benötige keinen Grabstein'. 'Als ich im weißen Krankenzimmer der Charité' (1956, GW 10, 1031) summarizes one of the central arguments of Lucretian (Epicurean) materialism in support of its thesis that death should be envisaged with equanimity, as part of a continuous process:

> Schon seit geraumer Zeit
> Hatte ich keine Todesfurcht mehr. Da ja nichts
> Mir je fehlen kann, vorausgesetzt
> Ich selber fehle. Jetzt
> Gelang es mir, mich zu freuen
> Alles Amselgesanges nach mir auch.

This is a positive and rational point of view: it recalls the more energetically expressed, but very similar assertion of the 'Großer Dankchoral': 'Es kommet nicht auf euch an/ Und ihr könnt unbesorgt sterben'.

'Ach, wie sollen wir die kleine Rose buchen?' (1954/5, GW 10, 1020) is a poem of primary importance; in this delicate philosophizing lyric the image of the rose which produces an unexpected bud is made to contain a rich complexity of significance. The poem's genesis and preliminary meaning may well be banal; but the final two lines proceed from observation to theoretical abstraction:

> Ach, wie sollen wir die kleine Rose buchen?
> Plötzlich dunkelrot und jung und nah?
> Ach, wir kamen nicht, sie zu besuchen
> Aber als wir kamen, war sie da.
>
> Eh sie da war, ward sie nicht erwartet.
> Als sie da war, ward sie kaum geglaubt.
> Ach, zum Ziele kam, was nie gestartet.
> Aber war es nicht so überhaupt?

Following a strong lyric tradition in which the red rose is a symbol of love, this too is a love-poem, which celebrates the incalculable potential of the smallest social unit: two people; it also celebrates the corresponding (and equally incalculable) productive potential of larger social structures. This is less a parallel reading of the love-poem than its linear extension into the sphere of general social relations. Love and revolution are intimately linked in Brecht's works; love as '[eine] große Produktion' as spontaneous, autotelic (in short: unalienated) human activity, is a microcosm of the complete liberation of all productive forces.[39] The hopeful paradox of the penultimate line is anticipated in the conceit of the first line: 'buchen'; its primary sense is here 'enter' or 'record'—it is a commercial term. The sudden proximity of the rose defies reduction to an item on a register: it is not capable of definition in accounting terms. But 'buchen' also means 'book', arrange in advance, or reserve, thus signifying administrative measures—which the autonomous spontaneity of the rose simply negates and transcends. Productivity, in its fullest emancipation, may outstrip all plans and calculations.

Direct contemporary evidence of this correspondence between love and politically productive activity is provided by the song 'Wie der Wind weht' (1955, GW 10, 1027). The first two strophes argue that in love as in politics it is wise to be informed of the disposition of the parties involved; the third strophe, clearly distinguished from the preceding lines, is an epigrammatic quatrain: a commentary—

> (Wenn so der Dichter Führen und Verführen
> In einem Atem nennt, als sei es eins
> Denkt er an Völker, die sich nicht recht rühren
> Und wollen ihr Vergnügen so, als wär es keins.)

Political direction and seduction, it is implied, coincide at one critical point: both are poor substitutes for unrestricted, cooperative, mutually responsive activity. Such activity is pleasurable, and to a large extent, autotelic.

The poem expresses the wish that the wind should blow more strongly; it translates the natural metaphor quite specifically, recommending that the passivity which allows 'Führen und Verführen' should be abandoned in favour of appropriate (and appropriating) collective action. Love, in so far as it has relinquished the pattern of seducer and seduced, may serve as a model for the praxis of social emancipation. 'Wie der Wind weht' might have been titled 'Gegen Verführung'; it recalls the motto of *Buckower Elegien*—'Ginge da ein Wind'—the positive example of 'Rudern, Gespräche', and the 'Aufbaulied' of 1948: 'besser als gerührt sein, ist: sich rühren'.[40]

Anticipatory, immediate emancipation, a theme of 'Vergnügungen', 'Fröhlich vom Fleisch zu essen' and 'Ach, wie sollen wir die kleine Rose buchen?', is a central concern of the late poetry; it does not displace the critical attitude. 'Dauerten wir unendlich' (1956, GW 10, 1031), 'Und ich dachte immer' (1956, GW 10, 1030) and 'Der schöne Tag, wenn ich nutzlos geworden bin' (1955, GW 10, 1028) are admonitory poems. It was shown that attitudes characteristic of the early poetry recur in the poetry of 1947–56: thus, for example, the lines 'Wenn ich sage, was ist/ Muß jedem das Herz zerfleischt sein', which would not appear out of place in a text dated 1918. If the political 'Gegenlied zu "Von der Freundlichkeit der Welt"' (1956, GW 10, 1032) is primarily destructive in its treatment of one early text, it stands in full agreement with another: 'Denn Genießen ist bei Gott nicht leicht!' (GW 8, 250). The 'Gegenlied . . .' is reflective, critical and energetic: a typical and adequate lyric last word:

> Soll das heißen, daß wir uns bescheiden
> Und 'so ist es und so bleib es' sagen sollen?
> Und, die Becher sehend, lieber Dürste leiden
> Nach den leeren greifen sollen, nicht den vollen?
>
> Soll das heißen, daß wir draußen bleiben
> Ungeladen in der Kälte sitzen müssen
> Weil da große Herrn geruhn, uns vorzuschreiben
> Was da zukommt uns an Leiden und Genüssen?
>
> Besser scheint's uns doch, aufzubegehren
> Und auf keine kleinste Freude zu verzichten
> Und die Leidenstifter kräftig abzuwehren
> Und die Welt uns endlich häuslich einzurichten!

APPENDIX

(1) So wie die Oberen ihren Krieg rüsten
Rüsten auch die Unteren ihren Krieg.
In der Dürre erinnert sich der
Durstende an jene
Die ihm geraten haben
Wasserlöcher zu graben.
Aus dem Frieden wird Krieg
Wie aus der Saat Ernte wird.
Ihr Krieg tötet nur
Was ihr Frieden übriggelassen hat.
Viel Mut ist nötig
Aus dem Krieg wegzugehen.
Sein Leben zu retten
Ist ein gefährliches Unternehmen.
('Deutsche Kriegsfibel 36', GW Supp. IV, 330-1.)

(2) Die Oberen sagen: Friede und Krieg
Sind aus verschiedenem Stoff.
Aber ihr Friede und ihr Krieg
Sind wie Wind und Sturm.

Der Krieg wächst aus ihrem Frieden
Wie der Sohn aus der Mutter
Er trägt
Ihre schrecklichen Züge.

Ihr Krieg tötet
Was ihr Friede
Übriggelassen hat.

('Deutsche Kriegsfibel', in *Svendborger Gedichte*, GW 9, 635.)

These two texts invite comparison: there is some doubt about whether they are versions of the same poem (1 as a study for 2), and the editor of the *Supplementbände III* and *IV*, Herta Ramthun, edited poem 1 precisely because its claim to be presented as an autonomous text seemed strong. It nevertheless appears reasonable to proceed on the assumption that the texts stand in close relationship to one another, beyond that indicated by similarity of technique and title.

Brecht did not select poem 1 for publication, and it is possible to identify some of the characteristics which may well have motivated his decision:

(i) The poem is diffuse: the relationship between its component sections is tenuous (between the first and second, and the second and third, for example).

(ii) As a consequence of (i), the poem's argument is ultimately unclear; the final four-line group may be read simply as an incitement to desertion, to saving one's own skin—a very different proposition from that of the first six lines, which present the familiar topos of arms appropriated for the proper struggle against 'die Oberen'. Or do the first lines indicate that this is exactly what no longer occurs? Does the 'ihren' in l. 2 refer to 'die Oberen'?(!)

The second poem is at once perceived as a more unified and tightly organized text. (One hesitates to say that it is more 'polished', though there may be something of this: perhaps 'tuned' would be a better metaphor.) Here certainly there is no doubt about the poem's argument, no ambiguity. The poem takes up the idea of the central pair of line-groups in the first text, and builds a self-contained text upon it. By beginning with less (four lines out of fourteen), the second poem achieves much more.

The first line adopts the same pattern of opposition as the other 'Deutsche Kriegsfibel' poems, and indeed as the first text above: 'die Oberen: die Unteren'. Yet *what* those in high places are alleged to say is familiar enough—war and peace are different things; on the face of it, it would be hard to find anyone who would disagree. As the poem is reread, however, it emerges that these first two lines can also be understood as illustrating a fundamental materialist thesis: 'Die herrschenden Ideen einer Zeit waren stets nur die Ideen der herrschenden Klasse.' The remainder of the poem is devoted single-mindedly to the destruction of the simple distinction referred to.

It is evident that l. 3-8 in the second poem are related to the line 'Wie aus der Saat Ernte wird' in the first. It is no less clear that they show a striking improvement when compared with it. Potentially, the clash between the 'positive' natural process (seed to ripeness) and the growth of war out of peace might be most effective: but a glance at the fourth line of the second text demonstrates its superiority. 'Wie Wind und Sturm' is less clever, but simpler and therefore more forceful; conceptually, it brings war and peace closer together—there is no qualitative difference, only one of degree.

Once this point has been made, the natural simile is reinstated, though in a new guise: 'Wie der Sohn aus der Mutter', and this is effectively underlined by the next lines, which insist on their resemblance, and recall the first line group in their reminder that peace is no guarantee of good life, or even survival.

This is the link with the final line-group; the poem ends with a terse, direct indictment. These three lines are almost identical with 'Ihr Krieg tötet nur/ Was ihr Frieden übriggelassen hat'. Firstly, 'nur' is dispensed with. It is a relatively weak word, though its position at the end of a line gives it pivotal emphasis in the first poem; still, the second text shows that it can very well be done without. (It is a correction of the sort urged upon T. S. Eliot by Ezra Pound: 'Damn "perhaps"!') Secondly, and most significantly, the line-divisions are altered, and here the hand of a master is in evidence: the insertion of a slight pause after 'Friede' provides a gap across which the reader's imagination sparks into contact with the last words. Against this version, the two lines of the first poem seem prosaic, almost offhand. The third adjustment is a minor one, but plays its part in reinforcing the second change—'Friede' replaces 'Frieden'. This may well not have been a conscious alteration, but the 'open' ending on the vowel both lengthens the pause, and points forward in the text. Small changes combine to make a great difference.

Some of the minor changes noted were made at a relatively late stage; the 1939 *Svendborger Gedichte,* in common with all the typescripts between 1936 and 1939 had a three-line final section which read as follows:

> Ihr Krieg tötet *nur*
> Was ihr Friede*n*
> Übrig gelassen hat

Each line includes a minor deviation from the text of GW, which is first approached in a typescript probably of the late 1940s (bba 598/25). Here the only remaining difference from GW is the splitting of 'übriggelassen', a difference which is retained in the early editions of *Hundert Gedichte* too.

NOTES

Notes to Introduction

1. Cf. Hans Georg Gadamer, quoted in *Rezeptionsästhetik,* ed. Rainer Warning (Munich, 1975), pp. 120 f.

   Auslegung ist nicht ein zum Verstehen nachträglich und gelegentlich hinzukommender Akt, sondern Verstehen ist immer Auslegung, und Auslegung ist daher die explizite Form des Verstehens.
2. Martin Esslin, *Brecht. A Choice of Evils* (London, 1959), and Hannah Arendt, *Men in Dark Times* (Harmondsworth, 1973).
3. Klaus Schuhmann, *Der Lyriker Bertolt Brecht 1913–1933,* 2nd edn. (Munich, 1967), pp. 389 ff.
4. Walter Benjamin, *Versuche über Brecht* (Frankfurt am Main, 1966), p. 50; and compare Brecht, AJ 9.8.43:

   'o sprengen des gartens, das grün zu ermutigen'. und 'die vaterstadt, wie finde ich sie doch?'. aber ein lyrisches gesamtwerk muß eine (innere) geschichte haben, die in harmonie oder kontrast stehen mag zur äußeren geschichte. ich denke an so etwas wie die 'phasen' der maler, in unserer zeit etwa des picasso. so ungeordnet die eindrücke, so willkürlich die eingriffe in diesen jahren auch sind—was ich an gedichten schreibe, behält doch immer den versuchscharakter, und die versuche ordnen sich in einer gewissen beziehung zueinander an, und die lektüre kann kaum adäquaten genuß verschaffen, wenn etwa solch ein gedicht wie das erstere nicht auch in seiner neuheit innerhalb der gesamten produktion genossen werden kann, als domesticum.

   (All *Arbeitsjournal* dates are quoted as in the text.)
5. Schuhmann, *Der Lyriker*; Silvia Schlenstedt, *Die Chroniken in den 'Svendborger Gedichten': eine Untersuchung zur Lyrik Brechts* (Diss. Berlin (DDR), 1959); Steffen Stettensen, *Bertolt Brechts Gedichte* (Copenhagen, 1972); Peter Paul Schwarz, *Lyrik und Zeitgeschichte. Brecht: Gedichte über das Exil und späte Lyrik* (Heidelberg, 1978). This is a largely anecdotal treatment, in which frequent quotation tends to displace discussion and argument, Christiane Bohnert, *Brechts Lyrik im Kontext. Zyklen und Exil* (Königstein im Taunus, 1982): this is a much more useful work, which will be referred to as appropriate below. The subtitle is problematic, however, since it is by no means clear that the collections analysed in the main body of

the book (*Lieder Gedichte Chöre, Svendborger Gedichte*, 'Gedichte im Exil' 1944) are cycles at all. Paradoxically, Bohnert specifically excludes consideration of what she refers to as 'open' types of cycle, *Aus einem Lesebuch für Städtebewohner, Die drei Soldaten, Studien*, and *Buckower Elegien*, which appear to be cycles in the normal sense of the term. Bohnert comments 'diese Zyklen stehen dem bürgerlichen Zyklus (?) in ihrer formalen Konstruktion relativ nahe' (p. 15). In so far as she is able to explain her application of the term at all, it is apparently derived from the work of J. Müller and H. Mustard, whose historical studies are neither new nor anti-bourgeois. Brecht scarcely uses the word 'Zyklus', preferring 'Zusammenstellung' or 'Auswahl'. In spite of this curious theoretical muddle, the detailed attention to individual texts produces some illuminating discussion.

Notes to Chapter 1

1. Schuhmann, op. cit., pp. 9–30.
2. Peter Paul Schwarz, *Brechts frühe Lyrik 1914–1922* (Bonn, 1971).
3. Knopf, *Bertolt Brecht: ein kritischer Forschungsbericht* (Frankfurt am Main, 1974), p. 138.
4. Carl Pietzcker, *Die Lyrik des jungen Brecht. Vom anarchischen Nihilismus zum Marxismus* (Frankfurt am Main, 1974).
5. *Lyrik des jungen Brecht*, p. 299.
6. K.-D. Müller offers a summary of the common ground of these poems, though he does not support it by detailed reference. He is concerned to describe Brecht's view of history, which the early poems significantly generally do not document. His concise account is, however, based on close attention to the texts themselves:

es gibt keine Transzendenz und damit auch keine verbindliche und gültige Sinngebung, weder für soziale Gebilde noch für das Menschsein. Mit dem Verlust seiner vermeintlichen Sonderstellung in der Welt steht der Mensch auf einer Stufe mit allen Lebewesen und selbst mit der Vegetation: sinnfällig wird das im Prozeß der Verwesung, durch den alles Leben in den ewigen Kreislauf der Natur eingefügt ist. Damit ist vom Tode her jedes Menschenleben auf sich selbst gestellt und muß sich in der Immanenz erfüllen. . . . Erst der Asoziale ist frei und kann in dieser Freiheit seine Kreatürlichkeit voll ausleben: er kann sich seinen Trieben hingeben. Die Gesellschaft als Raum der Geschichte ist in diesem Denken nur Fessel und wird darum negiert. Der ewige Kreislauf der Natur schließt Geschichte aus, reine Natur ist Geschichtslosigkeit, ist

NOTES

Anarchie (*Die Funktion der Geschichte im Werk Bertolt Brechts* (Tübingen, 1972), p. 15). This analysis will be shown to be substantially correct. Müller, like Schwarz, understands these poems as implying a 'philosophical' view, a way of looking at existential questions. The texts give at least one explicit pointer in this direction: 'Lied der müden Empörer' has the alternative title of 'Philosophisches Tanzlied' (GW 10, Anmerkungen 4).

7. 'Soldatengrab' quoted in *Brecht in Augsburg*, edited by W. Frisch and K. W. Obermeier (Frankfurt am Main, 1976), p. 277.
8. Compare Schuhmann, pp. 35 f.
9. Michael Morley, 'The Light that shineth more and more', *MLN* 88 (1973), p. 566 n.
10. J. K. Lyon, *Bertolt Brecht und Rudyard Kipling* (Frankfurt am Main, 1976), p. 65.
11. Schuhmann, pp. 40-1.
12. Ibid. pp. 163-4.
13. See Heinz Brüggemann, *Literarische Technik und soziale Revolution: (Versuche über das Verhältnis von Kunstproduktion, Marxismus und literarischer Tradition in den theoretischen Schriften Bertolt Brechts)* (Reinbek, 1973), pp. 65-6.
14. Bertolt-Brecht-Archiv (=bba) 800/01-16.
15. bba 800/11. Excerpt quoted in Hans Otto Münsterer, *Bert Brecht: Erinnerungen aus den Jahren 1917-1922* (Zürich, 1963), p. 99.
16. Schuhmann, op cit., p. 166.
17. A full account of the genesis and history of the *Hauspostille* collection is provided by Klaus Schuhmann, *Untersuchungen zur Lyrik Brechts: Themen, Formen, Weiterungen* (Berlin (DDR) and Weimar, 1973), ch. 1. For details concerning the publication of these and later poems see Walter Nubel, 'Bertolt Brecht-Bibliographie', in *Sinn und Form*, Sonderheft Bertolt Brecht II (1957).
18. Compare Hans Mayer, 'Die Gelegenheitsdichtung des jungen Brecht', *Sinn und Form* (1958), p. 280.
19. Bernard Guillemin, 'Was arbeiten Sie? Gespräch mit Bertolt Brecht', *Die Literarische Welt* (30.7.1926). Letter to Alfred Döblin, GW 18, 64 (Oct. 1928).
20. Cf. Schuhmann, *Der Lyriker*, pp. 172-3.
21. Hans Mayer, 'Gelegenheitsdichtung', p. 280: 'ein genau durchkonstruiertes und komponiertes Buch'.
22. Hans Sträter, *Die Gedichte der Hauspostille* (Diss. Tübingen, 1966), p. 7.
23. A. C. Baumgärtner, 'Vom Baalischen Weltgefühl', in R. Hirschenauer and A. Weber (eds.), *Interpretationen zur Lyrik Brechts* (Munich, 1971), p. 9.

24. Regine Wagenknecht, 'Bertolt Brechts Hauspostille', in *Text+Kritik*, Sonderband Bertolt Brecht II (Munich, 1973). Cf. also Ulla Lerg-Kill, *Dichterwort und Parteiparole* (Bad Homburg, Berlin and Zürich, 1968), p. 227 n. 48, E. Rotermund, *Die Parodie in der modernen deutschen Lyrik* (Munich, 1963), p. 139, and Bohnert, *Brechts Lyrik*, pp. 21–6. This new attempt to identify a principle underlying the organization of Brecht's first collection (here, the 'Zyklus' *Taschenpostille*) takes issue with Wagenknecht concerning the relative 'seriousness' of the 'Anleitung'. The present writer finds Wagenknecht's view in general more plausible, but is still convinced that the individual 'Lektionen', their titles, and their contents are characterized by a deliberate, even calculated, anarchic arbitrariness which cannot yield any unifying plan, and which is part of a large-scale ironic structure, almost a joke, embracing the entire collection, and surviving in all its versions.
25. Wagenknecht, 'Hauspostille', p. 27.
26. This reading of the poem is substantially in agreement with that presented in considerable detail by Klaus Schuhmann, *Der Lyriker*, pp. 193–4.
27. Compare Münsterer, *Erinnerungen*, p. 73 and Klaus Völker, *Bertolt Brecht: eine Biographie* (Munich, 1976), pp. 17–18.
28. 'Von einem Maler' has the alternative title 'Psalm an einen Maler', see Bertolt-Brecht-Archiv, *Bestandsverzeichnis des literarischen Nachlasses*, ii (Berlin, 1970), bba no. 6583=(452/88).
29. Compare Brecht AJ 3.8.38:

in der lyrik habe ich mit liedern zur gitarre angefangen und die verse zugleich mit der musik entworfen. die ballade war eine uralte form, und zu meiner zeit schrieb niemand mehr balladen, der etwas auf sich hielt. später bin ich in der lyrik zu anderen formen übergegangen, weniger alten, aber ich bin mitunter zurückgekehrt und habe sogar kopien alter meister gemacht, villon und kipling übertragen. der *song*, der nach dem krieg wie ein volkslied der großen städte auf diesen kontinent kam, hatte, als ich mich seiner bediente, schon eine konventionelle form. ich ging aus von dieser und durchbrach sie später. aber die massenlieder enthalten formale elemente dieser faulen, gefühlsseligen und eitlen form. ich schrieb dann reimlose verse mit unregelmäßigen rhythmen. ich glaube, ich wandte sie zuerst im drama an. jedoch gibt es ein paar gedichte aus der hauspostillen-zeit, die elemente dazu zeigen, die psalmen, die ich zur gitarre sang.

Similarly GW 19, 395–403; GW 19, 413–4; GW 19, 502–7.
30. Ernst Schumacher, *Die dramatischen Versuche Bertolt Brechts 1918–1933* (Berlin (DDR), 1955), p. 33.

31. Compare Brüggemann, *Literarische Technik,* p. 73:

   der 'grobe', der 'niedrige Materialismus' des Frühwerks hat so den Boden gebildet, auf dem eine differenzierte gesellschaftliche Thematik und eine Geschichtsauffassung, die zur umfassenden Theorie der historischen Entwicklung sich ausweitete, erwachsen konnte.

   Brüggemann proceeds (following the example of Walter Benjamin) to place the early poems in their social and historical context; he interprets their portrayal of death and decay as figurations of social decline:

   Vereinzelung, Kampf um Daseinsgenuß, der Mitmensch als Konkurrent und Opfer—all das wird gerade darum mit angeblich so zynischer, in Wahrheit aber prätendierter Kälte vorgetragen, weil eben jene historischen Gewalten, die die zwischenmenschlichen Beziehungen zu solchen des Marktes verzerrt haben, auch von einem Vereinzelten in historischer Ohnmacht erfahren werden und daher als übermächtige, als scheinbare Naturgewalten in Brechts literarische Produktion eingehen.

   This is a legitimate *interpretation,* which develops much of the poems' potential; but Brüggemann and Benjamin are too ambitious in their attempts to read the poems as texts calculated necessarily to provoke critical analysis of an anarchy implicitly grasped as social, rather than natural and absolute. A reading which attributes to these poems the 'prätendierte Kälte' and the analytical penetration which such a provocative technique presupposes, situates the *Hauspostille* of 1927 in advance of the experimental *Lesebuch* poems. This improbable hypothesis would assume as its precondition a complex system of stable irony; the free, 'unstable' irony, the 'irresponsibility' identified as characteristic of the early poems appears more likely to obtain in the context of the 1927 collection: the intellectual leap required if this irresponsibility is to be read as historical, as the exhibition of a symptom, is excessively long, and draws no apparent impetus from the texts themselves, nor from the 'Anleitung', whose incipient seriousness is rapidly eroded. Cf. Walter Benjamin, *Versuche über Brecht* (Frankfurt am Main, 1966), pp. 50–65.

32. As indicated at p. 227, n. 17, above, Schuhmann offers a detailed study of the edition-history. More recently, John Willett, as editor of *Brecht. Poems 1916–1956,* (2nd edn., London, 1979) has provided a clear summary (pp. 487 ff.). His account differs from Schuhmann's in points of detail, and the most recent study (Bohnert, pp. 21 ff.) covering the same ground, differs from both. Willett, given his close acquaintance with the archive materials over a long period, must be

regarded as the most reliable witness, though there is clearly still room for disagreement.

33. This poem, which seems to proclaim a sudden change of focus, is itself an example of Brecht's use of material imagery; the direct concrete realism of 'faulige Tapeten' and 'die wäßrigen Gemüse' here stands beside the imaginative exaggeration of an image familiar from the earlier poems: the vulnerable body—'es regnet hinein in ihn' (GW 8, 157).

Notes to Chapter 2

1. See Schuhmann, *Untersuchungen*, p. 43, and frontispiece of Brecht, *Gedichte 1* (Frankfurt am Main, 1960), pp. 2–3.
2. Compare GW 18, 14:

   Als ich mir überlegte, was Kipling für die Nation machte, die die Welt 'zivilisiert', kam ich zu der epochalen Entdeckung, daß eigentlich noch kein Mensch die große Stadt als Dschungel beschrieben hat. Wo sind ihre Helden, ihre Kolonisatoren, ihre Opfer? Die Feindseligkeit der großen Stadt, ihre bösartige, steinerne Konsistenz, ihre babylonische Sprachverwirrung, kurz: ihre Poesie ist noch nicht geschaffen.

   11. September, 1921.

   The city is a theme pursued in a substantial number of unpublished poems:

   > die städte die wir da bauen
   > dauern nicht lange
   > wenn mit dem bauen aufgehört
   > wird
   > fallen sie ein.   (bba 819/20.)

   > jung+hilflos in die städte gekommen
   > abkommandiert zu denen opfern die
   > geopfert werden
   > geb ich rasche antwort auf
   > jegliche frage
   > sagte: ich gehe+ging
   > oder: ich bleibe+blieb
   > heute weiß ich:
   > was ich sage+tue das
   > ist nicht dasselbe
   > allzu oft sah ich mich.
   > (ich lasse nicht in der kette aus/ein glied)

wenn ich sag(t)e: dies schmeckt mir
sogleich wurd mir die speise bitter im
mund. (bba 823/40a-41.)

die städte mit den schwarzen blattern
sind voll von aas bis oben hin
+um l essen zu ergattern
wandelt mancher seinen sinn. (bba 819/40.)

GW supp. III, p. 203 'Anrede' was originally published as a *Lesebuch* text, though it appears to bear a much closer relationship to poems like 'Gedicht vom unbekannten Soldaten unter dem Triumphbogen'. Other texts also edited for the first time in the Supplementband might be related to the *Lesebuch*-complex:

Nimm willig
Aus unserer Hand dein Brot.
Hier ist die Decke, hier dein Lager, Freund!
Aber nicht ganz nur durch uns
Lebe, nicht von bestimmten Händen allein
Lebe!

Daß du uns brauchst, das
Bekräftigt deinen Anspruch.

Nimm willig
Dein Brot aus Menschenhand
Decke, Lager und Anzug
In fertigem Zustand. Arbeite weiter
An deinem Platz mit unserm Handwerkszeug
An dem Stück, das wir schon bearbeitet haben.
Vor es fertig ist, liefere es ab.
Unsere Ansichten
Übernimm, füge neue hinzu, wir werden sie
Ergänzen, Freund. (GW Supp. III, 231-2.)

and:

Folgendes habe ich sagen hören
In euren Städten ( )
Mancherlei Rat, auch gutgemeinten
Aber keinen
Der einen Sinn ergab, wenn man nicht wußte
Wir ihn wem gab

Welche Leute mögen solches sprechen
Was für Städte sinds, in denen solche
Reden gehen

> Wie verschieden wohl sind ihre Interessen
> Wie verschieden zu sein ist gut für solche
> Und ich sagte, völlige Verwirrung
> Herrscht in ihnen
> z.b. ein Metzger scheint zu seinem Kalb zu sprechen
> (einer rät einem andern religiöse Passivität...)
> (GW Supp. III, 245.)

These represent developments from the starting point of the *Lesebuch*, in the direction of the *Lehrgedicht*.

3. Compare Völker, *Biographie*, pp. 60 ff., *Brecht in Augsburg*, pp. 220-1 and TAA, pp. 185-6.
4. bba 4/25, quoted in Sträter, pp. 38-9.
5. See GW 10, 'Anmerkungen' 6; p. 143 n.
6. See Helfried W. Seliger, *Das Amerikabild Brechts* (Bonn, 1974), pp. 109 ff.
7. See Golo Mann, *The History of Germany since 1789* (London, 1968), pp. 201, 204.
8. See Elisabeth Hauptmann, 'Notizen über Brechts Arbeit 1926', in *Sinn und Form*, Sonderheft Bertolt Brecht II (1957), pp. 241 f.
9. See Völker, *Biographie*, p. 87.
10. Guillemin, 'Was arbeiten Sie?'.
11. Schuhmann, *Der Lyriker*, pp. 174 f.
12. Compare Knopf, *Kritischer Forschungsbericht*, pp. 89-90.
13. Hauptmann, 'Notizen'.
14. See Nubel, 'Bibliographie': c 192 'Aus einem Lesebuch für Städtebewohner', in *Berliner Börsen-Courier* (1.1.1927); c 180 'Behauptung', in *Das Tagebuch* (31.7.1926); c 184 'Vom fünften Rad', in *Berliner Börsen-Courier* (7.11.1926); c 187 'An Chronos', in *Berliner Börsen-Courier* (5.12.1926); c 198 'Anleitung für die Oberen', in *Neue Bücherschau* (1927); and Schuhmann, *Der Lyriker*, p. 213.
15. The *Bestandsverzeichnis*, vol. ii, shows that many of the *Lesebuch* poems also belong to the *Fleischhacker* drama: (6486) 'Verwisch die Spuren!', (6454) 'Über die Städte 2', (6493) 'Vier Aufforderungen'. Under nos. 5799-809 a similar overlap between *Happy End* and *Der Brotladen* is recorded.
16. See previous note.
17. Benjamin, *Versuche*, pp. 66-9. Marx and Engels wrote: 'die Arbeiter haben kein Vaterland', *Manifest der kommunistischen Partei* (Berlin, 1945), p. 64. There are parallels to 'Verwisch die Spuren!' in *Mahagonny*:

> Paul   Wenn man an einen fremden Strand kommt
>   Ist man immer zuerst etwas verlegen.

Jakob Man weiß nicht recht, wohin man gehen soll.
Heinrich Wen man anbrüllen darf!
Joseph Und vor wem man den Hut zieht. (GW 2, 508.)

and in *Der Brotladen*:

Dieser da hat recht!
Er sagt nichts!
Er fragt nichts!
Und er gibt nichts!
Denn er kennt seine Lage! (GW 7, 2932.)

18. P. V. Brady, 'On a Brecht essay in obliqueness', *GLL* 26 (1973), p. 166.
19. Schuhmann's detailed analysis of these poems, which devotes considerable space to the isolation of rhetorical features, does not identify their provenance. *Der Lyriker*, pp. 213–18, and pp. 233–6.
20. Brady, pp. 161–2.
21. Walter Benjamin's remarks on the *Dreigroschenroman* are apposite here: 'was da steht, hat noch nie jemand ausgesprochen, und doch reden sie alle so', *Versuche*, p. 90.
22. Jürgen Jacobs, 'Wie die Wirklichkeit selber: zu Brechts Lesebuch für Städtebewohner', in *Brecht-Jahrbuch 1974* (=*Brecht heute*) (Frankfurt am Main, 1975), p. 91.
23. Cf. the following extracts:

Die Arbeit produziert Wunderwerke für die Reichen, aber sie produziert Entblößung für den Arbeiter. Sie produziert Paläste, aber Höhlen für den Arbeiter. Sie produziert Schönheit, aber Verkrüppelung für den Arbeiter.

Zu Hause ist er, wenn er nicht arbeitet, und wenn er arbeitet, ist er nicht zu Haus. Seine Arbeit ist daher nicht freiwillig, sondern gezwungen, *Zwangsarbeit*. Sie ist daher nicht die Befriedigung eines Bedürfnisses, sondern sie ist nur ein *Mittel*, um Bedürfnisse außer ihr zu befriedigen.

Eine unmittelbare Konsequenz davon, daß der Mensch dem Produkt seiner Arbeit, seiner Lebenstätigkeit, seinem Gattungswesen entfremdet ist, ist die *Entfremdung des Menschen* von dem *Menschen*. Wenn der Mensch sich selbst gegenübersteht, so steht ihm der *andre* Mensch gegenüber.

Das unmittelbare, natürliche, notwendige Verhältnis des Menschen zum Menschen ist das *Verhältnis* des *Mannes* zum *Weibe*. In diesem *natürlichen* Gattungsverhältnis ist das Verhältnis des Menschen zur Natur unmittelbar sein Verhältnis zum Menschen, wie das Verhältnis zum Menschen unmittelbar sein Verhältnis zur Natur, seine eigne *natürliche* Bestimmung ist. In diesem Verhältnis *erscheint* also *sinnlich,* auf ein anschaubares *Faktum* reduziert, inwieweit dem Menschen das menschliche Wesen zur Natur oder die Natur zum menschlichen Wesen des Menschen geworden ist. Aus diesem Verhältnis kann man also die ganze Bildungsstufe des Menschen beurteilen.

(Karl Marx, *Ökonomisch-philosophische Manuskripte* (Leipzig, 1974) pp. 154, 155, 159, 183.)

24. Alexander Mitscherlich, *Auf dem Weg zur vaterlosen Gesellschaft: Ideen zur Sozialpsychologie* (Munich, 1963), p. 380-1. This anticipatory line of argument might be further pursued by reference to later formulations by Brecht:

'Eine kühne und schöne Architektur der Sprachformen verfremdet den Text.' (GW 15, 345.)

'Me-ti sagte: Der Dichter Kin-je darf für sich das Verdienst in Anspruch nehmen, die Sprache der Literatur erneuert zu haben.... Er wandte eine Sprachweise an, die zugleich stilisiert und natürlich war. Dies erreichte er, indem er auf die Haltungen achtete, die den Sätzen zugrunde liegen.' (GW 12, 458.)

The paradoxical statement of the second passage seems to converge with and illuminate Benjamin's remark quoted in n. 21 above.

25. Schuhmann, *Der Lyriker,* p. 221.
26. Ibid., p. 231.
27. Ibid., p. 224.
28. Ibid.
29. Klaus Völker (*Biographie,* p. 144) notes that this poem also had a more private function: it was addressed to Elisabeth Hauptmann.
30. Brady, pp. 171, 172 n. 2 and Schuhmann, op cit., p. 229.
31. Brecht, *Versuche 1* (Berlin, 1930), introductory note.
32. Brecht, TAA (19.12.1921), p. 182.

Notes to Chapter 3

1. Hauptmann, 'Notizen' (8.6.1926).
2. Schuhmann, *Der Lyriker,* pp. 266-70.
3. See Nubel, 'Bibliographie', c 236, c 245, and Schuhmann, op. cit., pp. 409-10.
4. Compare Reinhard Kühnl, *Der deutsche Faschismus in Quellen und Dokumenten* (Cologne, 1975), pp. 189-90.
5. Edgar Marsch, *Brecht: Kommentar zum lyrischen Werk* (Munich, 1974), pp. 184-5.
6. Münsterer, *Erinnerungen,* p. 57, also notes the connection between Swift's *Modest Proposal* and *Die drei Soldaten.*

7. Cf. GW Supp. IV, 286 ff., 'Proletariat, die Hoffnung der Welt', an extensive series of poems, some of which were to be incorporated in the 'Koloman-Wallisch-Kantate' (GW Supp. IV, 385–95) of 1945. The poems are of special interest here because, in the range of attitudes exhibited, they link the *Lesebuch* poems referred to above, and *Die drei Soldaten* with the later *Deutsche Satiren*. See in particular p. 290:

> Neulich hörte ich
> Daß große Ehrungen für sie geplant sind.
> Es heißt, die Herrschenden
> Werden ihnen ihr Lob aussprechen. . . .
> Wenn diese Ehrungen erfolgen sollten
> Dann wird unter den Hungrigen
> Große Freude sein.

8. From 1932 onward, the NSDAP made inroads in areas previously committed to the SPD and KPD; Brecht takes account of this development, recognizing it as a consequence of serious political mistakes made by both parties. Cf. Kühnl, *Der deutsche Faschismus*, p. 239. Lion Feuchtwanger records the same phenomenon in the 'Beefsteak' metaphor (brown outside, but red within) which illustrates the ambiguous position of many 'supporters' of national socialism after 1933; see *Die Geschwister Oppenheim* (Amsterdam, 1933), p. 374.
9. 'Langdauernd', since it is linked to the dual significance of 'Werk' (process/product), itself acquires a double sense: duration *and* endurance.
10. The special interests of literature are also represented in this struggle, which is, indeed, the precondition for the development of all forces of production: artistic as well as material. This is a dominant theme of Marxist theory throughout the 1930s: it emerges in the notes to *Mahagonny*, in Walter Benjamin's essay *Der Autor als Produzent* (*Versuche*, pp. 95–116), in 'Kein Platz für fortschrittliche Musik' (GW 18, 219–21), and *Interview* (GW 20, 262–5).
11. This reading of the poem accords to a great extent with that offered by Klaus Schuhmann (*Der Lyriker*, pp. 344–7), though he is perhaps too concerned to clarify the anti-reformist stance of the poem (important though it is), and thus neglects its clearly dialectical structure: the poem surely argues for immediate assistance at the same time as defining the limits of such 'first aid'.
12. See Hans-Albert Walter, *Deutsche Exilliteratur 1933–1950* (Darmstadt and Neuwied, 1972), ii, *Asylpraxis und Lebensbedingungen in Europa*.
13. *Komintern und Faschismus: Dokumente zur Geschichte und*

Theorie des Faschismus, edited by Th. Pirker (Stuttgart, 1965), see especially pp. 156, 171, 175. Cf. Kühnl, *Der deutsche Faschismus*, pp. 188-90, 398-9.
14. Compare Walter, *Deutsche Exilliteratur*, ii. 185-7.
15. Nubel, 'Bibliographie', c 247, c 248, c 249, c 250, c 251, c 253, lists the following examples: previews from *Lieder Gedichte Chöre* appeared in *Neue Deutsche Blätter* ('Hitler-Choräle'), *Unsere Zeit* ('Die Ballade vom Baum und den Ästen'), *Der Gegenangriff* and *Die Neue Weltbühne*. Under b 118, Nubel records that 'Lob der illegalen Arbeit' and 'Wiegenlieder' I and II were included in the camouflaged book *Deutsch für Deutsche* produced by the Schutzverband Deutscher Schriftsteller (Paris) in 1935, Brecht noted (AJ 16.2.43) that his 'gedichte über den anstreicher' [='Hitler-Choräle'?] were known inside Germany, and were recited even in Brandenburg Prison (!). Similarly 'Das Saarlied' (GW 9, 542), which was published in *Unsere Zeit*, attained wide distribution in the Saar region: see Werner Hecht, H.-J. Bunge, K. Rülicke-Weiler, *Bertolt Brecht: Sein Leben und Werk* (Berlin, 1969), pp. 107, 113-14. On the possibility of distribution by other means, see Willy Haas, *Bert Brecht* (Berlin, 1958), p. 85, where it is suggested that the BBC broadcast material written by Brecht. Ernest Bornemann, 'Ein Epitaph für Bertolt Brecht' in *Sinn und Form,* Sonderheft Bertolt Brecht II, p. 153, offers equally vague information on radio and leaflet distribution. Brecht's letters throw some light on these questions: Brief 193 for example, 'In Paris habe ich einen Band mit Gedichten fertiggestellt.... Ein großer Teil der Ausgabe geht nach Deutschland.' (Dec. 1933.) Also Brief 231: 'Wie wirst du zurückfahren? Wenn übers Saargebiet, dann schick ich Dir die letzten Arbeiterlieder von mir und Eisler mit Musik. (Sehr einfach, Marschlieder.)' Nov. 1934; 'Warum rempelst Du das "Saarlied" an? Es ist in 10 000 Exemplaren im Saargebiet verbreitet, stand in allen antifaschistischen Zeitungen, auch in englischen, und hat mehr Wichtigkeit als ein halbes Dutzend Dramen.' (Brief 237, late 1934/ early 1935.) Finally, from Brief 252, Moscow, April 1935: 'Heute abend spreche ich zum zweiten Mal im Radio...'
16. See Schuhmann, *Der Lyriker*, p. 165.
17. Compare *Braunbuch über Reichstagsbrand und Hitler-Terror* (Basle, 1933), p. 30: 'sie [the NSDAP] versprachen allen Alles: den Arbeitern höhere Löhne, den Unternehmern höhere Gewinne, den Mietern niedrigere Mieten, den Hausbesitzern höhere Mieten, den Bauern höhere Preise, den Kleinbürgern wohlfeilere Lebensmittel'. Similarly, Walter Benjamin, *Das Kunstwerk im Zeitalter seiner technischen Reproduzierbarkeit* (Frankfurt am Main, 1963), p. 48: 'der Faschismus versucht, die neu entstandenen proletarisierten

Massen zu organisieren, ohne die Eigentumsverhältnisse, auf deren Beseitigung sie hindringen, anzutasten. Er sieht sein Heil darin, die Massen zu ihrem Ausdruck (beileibe nicht zu ihrem Recht) kommen zu lassen'.
18. Compare Karl Marx, *Ökonomisch-philosophische Manuskripte* (Leipzig, 1974), p. 184 (=MEGA i. 3, p. 114): 'er [der Kommunismus] ist das aufgelöste Rätsel der Geschichte und weiß sich als diese Lösung'.
19. Compare Roman Jakobson, 'Der grammatische Bau des Gedichts "Wir sind sie" von Bertolt Brecht', *alternative*, 65 (1969), pp. 62–74.
20. See Ulla Lerg-Kill, *Dichterwort und Parteiparole: Propagandistische Gedichte und Lieder Brechts* (Bad Homburg, Berlin, Zürich, 1968), p. 272 n. 24.
21. The KPD did not share Brecht's implicit analysis of the events of 1933, preferring to cling to the myth of 'tactical withdrawal' and insisting that the revolution was imminent; see, for example, Gustav Regler, *Das Ohr des Malchus: eine Lebensgeschichte* (Frankfurt am Main, 1975), pp. 208–9. Bohnert (*Brechts Lyrik*, pp. 41–2) insists that Brecht shared the official prognosis of the KPD. This view does not bear comparison with the evidence of the poems themselves, nor with Brecht's other writings in 1933. Brief 193 for example: 'Die Zeit der glänzenden Aufrufe, Proteste usw. ist bis auf weiteres vorüber. Nötig ist jetzt eine geduldige, zähe, mühsame Arbeit der Aufklärung, auch des Studiums'. Brecht steadfastly refused to admit its finality, but he was in no doubt at this time about the fact of the defeat of potentially revolutionary forces in Germany. Bohnert does emphasise a different and perhaps equally important point which the present work also raises: that historical processes were not seen by Brecht as automatic, inevitable, or 'necessary' (p. 51).
22. Eighteen hundred to two thousand is the total (i.e. not only up to 1934) given for writers in exile by Gerhard Roloff, *Die Erforschung der deutschen Exilliteratur: Stand — Probleme — Aufgaben* (Hamburg, 1973), p. 110. Bohnert (*Brechts Lyrik*, p. 68), in her discussion of the likely addressees of the collection, envisages a similar dual appeal, principally to the proletariat, but also to sections of the intelligentsia (in the final section). Her summary supports the present account of *Lieder Gedichte Chöre*: '(die) Gesamtkonzeption ist . . . darauf angelegt, einen Solidarisierungseffekt zu erzeugen, der zum Sieg über den Faschismus führen soll' (p. 72).
23. See 'Als der Faschismus immer stärker wurde', GW 8, 400; and Schuhmann, *Der Lyriker*, pp. 376–7.
24. Compare W. Alff, *Der Begriff Faschismus und andere Aufsätze zur Zeitgeschichte* (Frankfurt am Main, 1971), and R. Kühnl, *Formen bürgerlicher Herrschaft: Liberalismus—Faschismus* (Reinbek, 1971).

25. Brecht's critique of the intelligentsia in the *Tui-Komplex* is here anticipated. Compare GW 20, 189:

> warum ist es erschreckend, daß es dem geistigen Arbeiter erst gesagt werden muß, daß das Verbot von 14 kommunistischen Zeitungen ihn zu einem Wutschrei veranlassen müßte? Es ist erschrekkend, weil er hier, wo die Stätte der Wahrheit und der Entwicklung geschlossen wurde, niemals gesehen worden war, und daß, als die Wahrheit verboten wurde, nichts verboten wurde, was er je gesagt hätte oder je sagen würde.

and GW 12, 672:

> die Tuis wanderten in die Gefängnisse . . . In dieser Behandlung erblickten die Tuis eine große Ungerechtigkeit. Waren sie nicht zu allem bereit gewesen? Wann je hatten sie versagt? Was hatten sie nicht verraten? Welche Gemeinheit hatten sie verweigert? Warum also wurden sie jetzt übergangen? Sollten sie wirklich nicht ausgereicht haben, das Eigentum der Herrschenden zu schützen?

26. Compare GW 20, 242:

1. Nach Angabe der linken Emigration bedroht der Faschismus die bürgerliche Welt. In Wirklichkeit versucht er, sie zu retten (versucht sie, sich in ihn hinein zu retten).
2. Nach Angabe der Linken läßt sich die bürgerliche Welt ohne Faschismus und also ohne Aufgabe der bürgerlichen Kultur, etwa durch Reformen, konservieren. In Wirklichkeit ist die bürgerliche Welt nur unter Aufgabe der bürgerlichen Kultur zu retten.

27. Benjamin, *Das Kunstwerk*, pp. 48–51.
28. See Herbert Claas, *Die Politische Ästhetik Bertolt Brechts vom Baal zum Caesar* (Frankfurt am Main, 1977), p. 262 n. 332, and Jürgen Thöming, 'Kontextfragen und Rezeptionsbedingungen bei Brechts frühen Geschichten und Kalendergeschichten', in *Text+Kritik*, Sonderband Bertolt Brecht II, pp. 75–6, also AJ 16.8.38: 'die vielfalt kann nur im ganzen entstehen, durch zusammenbau in sich geschlossener werke'. In the case of *Lieder Gedichte Chöre*, Bohnert's analysis of the thematic development of the collection is convincing, and coincides to a large extent with the findings of the present study, except where the term 'Zyklus' is concerned. There is no sense of the sort of specific unity of theme and style which constitutes the customary working definition of the term.

Notes to Chapter 4

1. Compare Nubel, 'Bibliographie', c 248–91; and Lerg-Kill, p. 280 n. 37: bba note 'der Deutsche Freiheitssender auf Welle 29,8 sendet neuerdings politische Gedichte von Bert Brecht'. Similarly, p. 281 n. 39: 'Ankündigung. Moskauer Radiostunde für deutsche Arbeiter und Spezialisten, Unionsender RCS, Welle 1107 m. 271 kHz. 22.05 Uhr. Am 13. April hören Sie "Bert Brecht liest revolutionäre Gedichte"' (in *Deutsche Zentral-Zeitung*, 12.4.34).
2. Compare GW 12, 483: 'einige Leute, welche die Klassiker ungenau studiert haben, sagen, die Arbeiter hätten eine Mission gegenüber der Menschheit. Das ist ein sehr schädliches Gewäsch.'
3. The essay has a complex history: first published (as a shorter work, describing three difficulties) in Paris in 1934, it was later printed in a camouflaged edition (though under its present title) for distribution within Germany. Compare Nubel, 'Bibliographie', c 263, c 266, and a 111.
4. 'Why I am a Marxist', paragraph 2, quoted in *alternative*, 41 (1965), p. 69; compare also Marx's motto, 'De omnibus dubitandum'.
5. See GW 19, 287–382, and GW 19, Anmerkungen 1–4. Knopf, *Kritischer Forschungsbericht*, p. 195 n. 665 lists secondary works relevant to these debates.
6. This may be an implicit criticism of the literary programme of such writers as Johannes R. Becher and the 'Bund proletarisch-revolutionärer Schriftsteller'. This suggestion gains support from Brief 140:

   Auch ein Kongreß wird es nicht fertigbringen, was ihre Produktion nicht fertigbringt, nämlich beweisen, daß sie wirklich in Betracht kommende Feinde der bürgerlichen Klasse sind. Sie sind nur Feinde der bürgerlichen Schriftsteller (...) In ihrem eigenen Schoß erzeugt die beherrschte Klasse nur bürgerliche Kultur, und die proletarische erzeugt sie im Schoß der bürgerlichen Klasse.
   (Sept./Oct. 1928).

   Brecht's final formulation in this dismissal of the BPRS coincides to some extent with Trotsky's views expressed in 'Literature and Revolution'.
7. Compare GW 20, 90: 'die Basis unserer Einstellung zur Kultur ist der Enteignungsprozeß, der im Materiellen vor sich geht. Die Übernahme durch uns hat den Charakter einer entscheidenden Veränderung.' Brecht described one mode of such decisive alteration in the programmatic remarks of 'Über die gestische Sprache in der Literatur' (from *Me-Ti*, GW 12, 458). This brief declaration encompasses fundamental elements of Brecht's literary

theory, especially the aesthetic—the 'kühne und schöne Architektur der Sprachformen' (GW 15, 345) which was identified as one means of producing the *Verfremdungseffekt*, and thus allowing a realistic, operative use of language. Both Klaus Baumgärtner, 'Interpretation and Analyse. Brechts Gedicht "Die Literatur wird durchforscht werden"', *Sinn und Form*, 12 (1960), pp. 395–415, and Martin Walser, 'Über die verständlichen Gedichte', in *Ausgewählte Gedichte Brechts mit Interpretationen*, edited by W. Hinck (Frankfurt am Main, 1978) pp. 72–8 provide readings of this poem which accord with that given above.

8. See for example the superb contemporary sonnets 'Das achte Sonett' and 'Liebesgewohnheiten' (GW Supp. IV, 282; 284) and the later 'Empfehlung eines langen, weiten Rocks' (GW 10, 888).

9. The history of this collection is representative: following *Lieder Gedichte Chöre*, new poems were collected under the title 'Gedichte im (aus dem) Exil' (1937). This new collection was to form part of *Gesammelte Gedichte*, the fourth volume of Brecht's *Gesammelte Werke* (London, 1938), published by Wieland Herzfelde's Malik-Verlag. The first two volumes of the four volume collected edition appeared in March 1938; the second two were at the proof stage, and may even have been printed and bound, when the Sudeten area of Czechoslovakia (where the binding was to be carried out) was occupied by German troops. The editions were apparently then destroyed. Elisabeth Hauptmann (who was in the USA at the time, and thus excluded from first-hand knowledge of these events) states that it was then decided to publish the 'Gedichte im Exil' separately, under the title *Svendborger Gedichte*; compare GW 10, Anmerkungen 17. This account does not appear acceptable; it fails to accommodate the following facts: though the *Svendborger Gedichte* were finally printed in Copenhagen, a Prague printing had been planned, and the galley proofs are in the possession of the Bertolt-Brecht-Archiv (bba 999/1–119). Brecht refers to the *Svendborger Gedichte* (AJ 10.9.38) before the occupation of the Sudeten area. It therefore seems reasonable to conclude that this collection was planned as a special edition in the summer of 1938, not as a replacement for the *Gesammelte Gedichte* volume, but as its parallel. Similar 'Sonderdrucke' of *Die Gewehre der Frau Carrar, Dreigroschenoper*, and *Furcht und Elend des dritten Reiches* were produced by Malik in 1938, and the final edition of *Svendborger Gedichte* carried the prefatory note: 'Vorabdruck aus Brecht, "Gesammelte Werke", Bd. 4'. In the *Arbeitsjournal* (23.4.39), Brecht explicitly distinguishes between the *Svendborger Gedichte* and the *Gesammelte Gedichte*, and in a letter to Wieland Herzfelde in Prague he refers to 'die sonderausgabe der gedichte (SVEND-

BORGER GEDICHTE)' which is 'besonders dringend'. This letter is quoted in: *Der Malik-Verlag 1916-1947*, edited by the Deutsche Akademie der Künste (Berlin (DDR), 1966). In April 1939, following the occupation of Prague, Brecht may have abandoned any residual hopes concerning the fate of the third and fourth volumes of *Gesammelte Werke*; publication of the special edition of new poems may then have seemed more urgent than ever. Brief 369 provides confirmation of the above account:

> Außerdem habe ich einen Band neuer Gedichte fertiggestellt, die unter dem Titel 'Svendborger Gedichte' ebenfalls im Malik-Verlag erscheinen sollen (...) Gleichzeitig redigiere ich für die Maliksche Gesamtausgabe den IV. Band, der meine 'Gesammelten Gedichte' enthalten soll.
>
> (Sept. 1938).

Brief 393, dated June 1939, is also addressed to the American Guild for German Cultural Freedom, and informs them of the fate of the final volumes of the collected edition, as well as the ultimate production of *Svendborger Gedichte* by subscription. Lerg-Kill reports (p. 281 n. 41) that Wieland Herzfelde estimates the edition at one thousand, with an additional thirty signed copies.

10. Benjamin, *Versuche*, pp. 73-4.
11. Compare Brecht's use of a 'popular' expression in 'Legende vom toten Soldaten', GW 19, 422, and similarly the theoretical statement from *Volkstümlichkeit und Realismus* (GW 19, 325): '*volkstümlich* heißt: den breiten Massen verständlich, ihre Ausdrucksform aufnehmend und bereichernd/ ihren Standpunkt einnehmend, befestigend und korrigierend'.
12. GW 20, 191: 'in Zeiten, wo die Täuschung gefordert und die Irrtümer gefördert werden, bemüht sich der Denkende, alles, was er liest und hört, richtigzustellen.'
13. Compare Jürgen Kuczynski, *Die Geschichte der Lage der Arbeiter unter dem Kapitalismus* (Berlin, 1964), vi, pp. 151-62.
14. AJ 14.6.40: 'so war die kriegsrüstung tatsächlich die lösung des arbeitslosigkeitsproblems auf dem kapitalistischen feld'. Similarly, AJ 19.2.39: 'hitler ist nun konsequent: die grenzen, welche von den waren nicht überschritten werden können, werden von den tanks überschritten, welches auch waren sind (sowie die sie bedienenden arbeitskräfte)'.
15. Compare GW 20, 156: 'die "Notwendigkeit" des gegebenen geschichtlichen Prozesses ist eine Vorstellung, die von der Mutmaßung lebt, für jedes geschichtliche Ereignis müsse es zureichende Gründe geben, damit es zustande kommt. In Wirk-

lichkeit gab es aber widersprechende Tendenzen, die streitbar entschieden wurden, das ist viel weniger'.
16. Benjamin's notes (*Versuche*, p. 73) indicate that this poem was to have been included in the 'Deutsche Kriegsfibel' section, and this is confirmed by Bohnert (*Brechts Lyrik*, pp. 82–3). It is not clear why the poem did not appear in the 1939 *Svendborger Gedichte*, but Bohnert writes that it was to be reinstated in the 1948 plan for 'Gedichte im Exil'.
17. A similar reading is offered by Bohnert (p. 90).
18. See Schuhmann, *Der Lyriker*, p. 324. See also GW 19, 328:

Arbeiterchöre sprachen kompliziert rhythmisierte Verspartien ('wenn's Reime wären, dann ging's runter wie Wasser, und nichts bliebe hängen') und sangen schwierige (ungewohnte) Eislersche Kompositionen ('da ist Kraft drin'). Aber wir mußten bestimmte Verszeilen umändern, deren Sinn nicht einleuchtete oder falsch war. Wenn in Marschliedern, die gereimt waren, damit man sie schneller lernen konnte, und die einfacher rhythmisiert waren, damit sie besser 'durchgingen', gewisse Feinheiten (Unregelmäßigkeiten, Kompliziertheiten) waren, sagten sie: 'da ist ein kleiner Dreh drinnen, das ist lustig'. Das Ausgelaufene, Triviale, das so Gewöhnliche, daß man sich nichts mehr dabei denkt, liebten sie gar nicht ('da kommt nichts bei raus'). Wenn man eine Ästhetik brauchte, konnte man sie hier haben...

and GW 18, 223:

die Zeiten der äußersten Unterdrückung sind meist Zeiten, wo viel von großen und hohen Dingen die Rede ist. Es ist Mut nötig, zu solchen Zeiten von so niedrigen und kleinen Dingen wie dem Essen und Wohnen der Arbeitenden zu sprechen.

19. Cf Benjamin, *Versuche*, pp. 75–6.
20. See ibid., pp. 133–5.
21. The careful arrangement of poems in the 'Chroniken' section was noted by S. Schlenstedt, *Die Chroniken in den "Svendborger Gedichten". Eine Untersuchung zur Lyrik Brechts* (Diss. Berlin, 1959), pp. 67 ff., and also by K.-D. Müller, *Die Funktion der Geschichte im Werk Bertolt Brechts. Studien zum Verhältnis von Marxismus und Ästhetik*, 2nd edn. (Tübingen, 1972), pp. 103–4.
22. Benjamin, *op. cit.*, pp. 79–83.
23. Benjamin, p. 83. Martin Esslin, *Brecht. A Choice of Evils* (London, 1959), p. 235, presents, in referring to this poem, a reading which is at once perverse and representative of a cold-war trend of 'neutralizing' interpretation: 'This Taoist attitude of yielding to the flow of things, while recognizing its absurdity, coexisted in Brecht's mind

NOTES 243

with, and below, the doctrine of the class struggle and the gospel of the violent transformation of the world. This is in fact the passive attitude, the yielding to emotion, the abandonment of reason he so feared in his youth, transformed into a profound and mellow philosophy . . . he preaches the wisdom of patient non-violence.'

24. This analysis contradicts that offered by Michael Morley, 'The source of Brecht's "Abbau des Schiffes Oskawa durch die Mannschaft"', *Oxford German Studies*, 2 (1967), pp. 149 ff. Morley writes that 'Brecht has fashioned a classic example of the class struggle' (pp. 152–3) and interprets the example thus: 'although Brecht does not comment on the actions of the sailors, it is obvious that he approves of them' (p. 153). In view of this direction of interpretation, to which Morley clings resolutely, it is not surprising that the poem's ironic indicators create difficulties for his analysis: this is precisely their function. Unfortunately Morley fails to respond by revising his first reading of the poem as a positive case; after noting the difficulty of his undertaking (p. 159) Morley proceeds to construct a grotesque conclusion: 'but if . . . Brecht is here introducing a note of deliberate irony, it must be intended to set the reader pondering on the wider implications—i.e. how can one bring home to the bourgeois public [sic!] the significance of such events, and is a society tolerable in which they are not forcibly brought to the public's awareness?' (p. 160). In fact, the poem argues for the proper conduct of the class struggle, and is not primarily addressed to a 'bourgeois public'; in so far as non-proletarian readers may be envisaged, the significance of the poem surely lies in its implicit rejection of indiscriminate destructiveness as a model. The aim of revolution is not the destruction, but the appropriation of the means of production. Morley's view of the poem is shared by Bohnert, who does not, however, refer to his article. She writes: '(das Gedicht) beschreibt . . . die Destruktion des kapitalistischen Systems durch die Weigerung des Proletariats, es noch länger zu stützen . . . die Mannschaft besitzt die richtige Denkhaltung, und den Mut zur geeigneten Aktion' (p. 107). It is a feature of Bohnert's work that she is too often content to assume a particular reading, to take for granted what requires demonstration; this is especially dangerous in Brecht's case.

25. See *Brechts Tui-Kritik* (=*Das Argument*, Sonderband II), edited by Herbert Claas and Wolfgang Fritz Haug (Karlsruhe, 1976).
26. See AJ 22.7.38.
27. Benjamin, *Versuche*, pp. 131–3. Here too, Bohnert offers a divergent view, which is almost an inversion of the reading provided here: 'Das Regime entspricht also dem Bauern, während der Angesprochene — der Ochse — sein Werkzeug ist' (*Brechts Lyrik*, p.

112). She proceeds to read the poem as describing the disjunction between the regime's public posturing and its real attitude towards the proletariat in Germany. No reference is made to Iring Fetscher's article, 'Es gibt keine Götter—auch Stalin: ein Ochs', *Merkur,* 23 (1969), Heft 9, p. 888, which accords with the present account.
28. See especially GW 12, 467, 535, 538–9.
29. Compare GW 20, 90: 'was von der Kultur also verteidigen wir? Die Antwort muß heißen: Jene Elemente, welche die Eigentumsverhältnisse beseitigen müssen, um bestehenzubleiben'. Similarly, GW 18, 249:

> wenn dem so ist, wenn die Kultur etwas von der gesamten Produktivität der Völker Untrennbares ist, wenn ein und derselbe gewalttätige Eingriff den Völkern die Butter *und* das Sonett entziehen kann, wenn also die Kultur etwas so Materielles ist, was muß dann getan werden zu ihrer Verteidigung?
> Was kann sie selbst tun? Kann sie sich schlagen? Sie schlägt sich, also: sie kann es.

30. Claas, *Politische Ästhetik,* pp. 93–9.
31. See Nubel, 'Bibliographie', pp. 552–3: c 277 *Internationale Literatur,* 7. no. 10 (1937); c 280 *Das Wort,* 7. No. 12 (1937); c 282 *Das Wort,* 3. no. 1 (1938); c 284 *Das Wort,* 3. no. 5 (1938). Not all critics share this positive view of the 'Deutsche Satiren'; Esslin is scornful: '(they) are interesting as experiments in an extremely free kind of free verse, but they have worn badly. Today they appear not only dated but politically naive.' (*A Choice of Evils,* p. 59). He refers to the 'inevitable mediocrity' of this kind of writing. Characteristically, Esslin does not consider it necessary to demonstrate the accuracy of his view by giving examples of this mediocrity. Hans-Albert Walter presents an opposite assessment of the quality of the satires ('Der Dichter der Dialektik. Anmerkungen zu Brechts Lyrik aus der Reifezeit', *Frankfurter Hefte,* 18 (1963), Heft 8, pp. 532–43), and bases his account on detailed attention to the texts.
32. *Die Neue Weltbühne,* 35, no. 24 (15.7.1939), pp. 745 f.
33. A similar temporal structure is evident in a much earlier poem: 'Diese babylonische Verwirrung' (GW 8, 149–50), and compare also 'Die Literatur wird durchforscht werden' with its post-revolutionary perspective.
34. Compare also GW 19, 316: 'natürlich entfaltet der Kampf um das volle Menschentum in den kämpfenden Menschen wieder die Menschlichkeit, aber das ist ein komplizierter Prozeß, und er findet eben nur bei den Kämpfenden statt'.
35. This reading of the poem contradicts that of W. Muschg, whose analysis may be taken as generally representative of a large body of

critical opinion, including Arendt and Esslin: 'die Krone aller seiner Selbstdarstellungen ist aber das Triptychon "An die Nachgeborenen" mit dem er sich schon 1938 hinter dem Rücken der Partei nicht an den Westen, sondern an die Nachwelt wandte. Schon das schlechte Gewissen dieser Verse ist keine Maske mehr. Hier spricht einer, der sich schuldig fühlt und resigniert auf sein Leben zurückblickt' (*Von Trakl zu Brecht* (Munich, 1961), 363.) Esslin (*A Choice of Evils,* p. 61) concurs with the line of interpretation adopted by Muschg: 'An die Nachgeborenen' is 'perhaps Brecht's most personal poem ... in which he begs the generations of a happier age to forgive him for the harshness of his writing.' Bohnert does not pursue this argument in her study of the poem (*Brechts Lyrik,* pp. 137–40), but does insist too exclusively on the poem's being addressed to future generations: it was shown that this, in Brecht's terms, is too simple a view.

The present writer is in general agreement with the comments of E. Fried in *Ausgewählte Gedichte Brechts mit Interpretationen,* edited by W. Hinck (Frankfurt am Main, 1978) pp. 92–7. Fried's own poem, eloquently titled 'Noch vor der Zeit', is an illuminating gloss on Brecht's text:

> Ich lese den Nachgeborenen
> das Gedicht Bertolt Brechts
> AN DIE NACHGEBORENEN vor
> aus der Zeit vor dem Zweiten Weltkrieg
>
> Schon den ersten Teil
> der anfängt und aufhört mit den Worten
> 'Wirklich, ich lebe in finsteren Zeiten!'
> muß ich den Nachgeborenen nicht erklären
>
> Sie nicken voll Verständnis bei jeder Einzelheit
> mit der der Dichter die Finsternis seiner Zeiten
> beschrieben hat. Sie finden sein Gedicht
> ihrer eigenen Zeit auf den Leib geschrieben
>
> Diese unmittelbare Verständlichkeit
> hätte den Dichter, obwohl er sonst immer bestrebt war,
> verstanden zu werden,
> eher traurig gemacht.

36. See Anthony Tatlow, *Brechts chinesische Gedichte* (Frankfurt am Main, 1973).
37. Compare AJ 16.8.38: 'die GEDICHTE AUS DEM EXIL sind natürlich einseitig'; and AJ 10.9.38:

> diesem werk [*Hauspostille*] gegenüber bedeuten die späteren SVENDBORGER GEDICHTE ebensogut einen abstieg wie einen

aufstieg. vom bürgerlichen standpunkt aus ist eine erstaunliche verarmung eingetreten. ist nicht alles auch einseitiger, weniger 'organisch', kühler, 'bewußter' (in dem verpönten sinn)? meine mitkämpfer werden das, hoffe ich, nicht einfach gelten lassen. sie werden die HAUSPOSTILLE dekadenter nennen als die SVENDBORGER GEDICHTE. aber mir scheint es wichtig, daß sie erkennen, was der aufstieg, sofern er zu konstatieren ist, gekostet hat. der kapitalismus hat uns zum kampf gezwungen. er hat unsere umgebung verwüstet. ich gehe nicht mehr 'im walde vor mich hin' sondern unter polizisten. da ist noch fülle, die fülle der kämpfe. da ist differenziertheit, die der probleme.

Notes to Chapter 5

1. 'mit jedem siegesrapport hitlers verliere ich an bedeutung als schriftsteller' (AJ 20.4.41); 'die schlacht um smolensk geht auch um die lyrik' (AJ 5.4.42).
2. The following notes bear witness to this tendency:

    mich in einigen epigrammen versucht (DIE REQUISITEN DER WEIGEL, DIE PFEIFEN, FINNISCHE GUTSSPEISEKAMMER). ganz unfähig, dramatisches zu arbeiten. dabei wäre es so nötig, den GUTEN MENSCHEN fertigzustellen; es handelt sich nur noch um details. in solchen zeiten des stockens wäre journalistiche oder theaterarbeit nötig, beides ist jetzt gehindert. (AJ 30.7.40).

    im augenblick kann ich nur diese kleinen epigramme schreiben, achtzeiler und jetzt nur noch vierzeiler (AJ 19.8.40).
3. es ist interessant, wie weit die literatur, als praxis, wegverlegt ist von den zentren der alles entscheidenden geschehnisse (AJ 16.9.40).

    The above analysis did not prevent Brecht from undertaking new attempts at communication, though they were envisaged within a military context, as in the poem 'An die deutschen Soldaten im Osten' (GW 10, 838 ff.). This extensive propaganda poem follows the recommendation of the sonnet 'Vorschlag, für den Kreig mit Hitler schießbare Radioempfangsgeräte zu bauen' (GW 9, 737, 1938):

    > Ach, eines Tages, euer Bau'n zu stören
    > Wird sie ihr Peiniger doch auf euch treiben
    > Sie peitschend, daß sie ihm nicht stehenbleiben:
    > Sorgt, daß sie nicht nur *seine* Stimme hören!
    >
    > Ich wollt, ihr spracht zu ihnen vor den Schlachten
    > Und bautet für sie die Empfangsgeräte

Die man wirft unter sie, als ob man säte
Und fragtet Tag und Nacht sie, was sie machten.
Schlagt ihnen vor, sie sollen sich mit euch verbünden!
die Gründe sagt! Beschießt sie mit den Gründen!
So mancher mag getroffen werden und sich zu euch wenden.
Denn manchen fängt man nur mit einem Strick
Doch manchen fängt man auch mit Argumenten:
Ich denk an die aus Grube und Fabrik.

See also AJ 9.1.42. Kühnl, *Der deutsche Faschismus*, p. 428 f, quotes from a comparable declaration made by German exiles in the Soviet Union:

Soldaten der Wehrmacht! Macht Schluß mit dem verbrecherischen Eroberungskrieg! Hört nicht auf eure Offiziere! Schießt nicht auf die russischen Arbeiter und Bauern! *Schafft in allen Truppenteilen Soldatenkomitees zum Kampf gegen den Krieg und gegen Hitler!* Kehrt eure Waffen um gegen den Feind im eigenen Lande, gegen den Volksfeind Hitler und sein mörderisches Regime! Geht mit der Waffe in der Hand auf die Seite der Roten Armee über! (January 1942.) On the *Arbeitsjournal*, compare Herbert Claas, 'Brechts "Buch der Vertagungen": Anmerkungen zum "Arbeitsjournal" anläßlich der Besprechung durch Bruno Frei', *Das Argument*, 85 (1974), pp. 220–7.

4. 'Finnische Epigramme' refers, properly, to the second section of the *Steffinische Sammlung* (GW 9, 819–22), and thus denotes the metrical epigrams in general. The collection in fact includes epigrams of the type represented by 'Finnische Gutsspeisekammer 1940' and those which appear as antecedents of the *Kriegsfibel* fotogramme ('Ich lese von der Panzerschlacht' and the 'Gedenktafeln', which were included in *Kriegsfibel*). In the present text, however, 'Finnische Epigramme' is intended to refer primarily to poems of the first type, thus excluding the war epitaphs. The sensuous mode of 'Finnische Landschaft', 'Die Pfeifen', and 'Finnische Gutsspeisekammer 1940' appears closer to the dominant attitudes of the *Steffinische Sammlung* and to the defiant aesthetic of its motto.

Dies ist nun alles und ist nicht genug
Doch sagt es euch vielleicht, ich bin noch da.
Dem gleich ich, der den Backstein mit sich trug
Der Welt zu zeigen, wie sein Haus aussah. (GW 9, 815.)

See GW 10, Anmerkungen 19 on *Steffinische Sammlung*.

5. Significantly, a loss of sensuousness is seen as an indicator of the

decline of poetry in both the descendent branches (George and Kraus) identified by Brecht (AJ 22.8.40). The following note pursues a related theme.

> gerade in dieser entmenschten situation kann
> 'a lovely apparition, sent
> to be a moment's ornament'
> die erinnerung wachrufen an menschenwürdigere situationen... ein kriterium für ein kunstwerk kann sein, ob es noch die erlebnismöglichkeiten irgendeines individuums bereichern kann. (unter umständen: eines individuums, das, wenn voraus, von der masse eingeholt werden kann, bei der vorauszusehenden wegrichtung.) (AJ 24.8.40.)

6. See J. K. Lyon, *Bertolt Brecht und Rudyard Kipling*, pp. 113f. P. V. Brady presents an account of Brecht's application of photographic material in the *Arbeitsjournal* which supports and extends the argument of the present study. 'From cave-painting to "fotogramm". Brecht, Photography and the "Arbeitsjournal"', Forum for Modern Language Studies, 14 (1978), pp. 270–82.

7. See also AJ 20.6.44:

> arbeite an neuer serie der fotoepigramme. ein überblick über die alten, teilweise aus der ersten zeit des kriegs stammend, ergibt, daß ich beinahe nichts zu eliminieren habe (politisch überhaupt nichts), bei dem ständig wechselnden aspekt des kriegs ein guter beweis für den wert der betrachtungsweise. es sind jetzt über 60 vierzeiler, und zusammen mit FURCHT UND ELEND DES DRITTEN REICHES, den gedichtbänden und vielleicht FÜNF SCHWIERIGKEITEN BEIM SCHREIBEN DER WAHRHEIT gibt das werk einen befriedigenden literarischen report über die exilszeit.

Apparently the *Kriegsfibel* collection, published by the Eulenspiegel Verlag, Berlin, was the subject of some controversy, and its publication followed only after considerable exertions by Brecht himself. Compare Lerg-Kill, p. 285 (n. 78). Nubel, 'Bibliographie', records publication of a number of the 'fotogramme' in 1944, in the *Austro-American-Tribune* (New York), (c 312). Bohnert, on the basis of her study of the *Kriegsfibel* material, dissents from the view of Lerg-Kill (and of Esslin, p. 83–4): she asserts that there were no external hindrances to the early publication of the collection (*Brecht's Lyrik*, p. 245).

8. Compare:

> eine besondere chance, die der marxismus in europa hatte, fällt hier weg. die sensationelle enthüllung der geschäfte des bürgerlichen staats gab dem marxismus diesen aufklärungseffekt, der hier nicht möglich ist. hier hat man einen direkt vom bürgertum eingerichteten

staat vor sich, der sich natürlich keinen augenblick schämt, burgerlich zu sein. das parlament ist mehr oder weniger eine agentur und handelt und spricht als eine solche. das ist kaum korruption, da kaum eine illusion besteht. (AJ 18.2.42.)

Similarly, AJ 18.4.42: 'dieses land zerschlägt mir meinen TUIROMAN. hier kann man den verkauf der meinungen nicht enthüllen, er geht nackt herum'.

9. 'dies sind volle gedichte, sie enthalten ihrer lakonik wegen nicht weniger als ein langes gedicht' (AJ 3.10.42).
10. Compare GW 10, Anmerkungen 18; and *Gedichte*, 6, p. 209. More recently, detailed information on this and other collections is provided in *Bertolt Brecht: Poems 1913–1956*, edited by John Willett and Ralph Manheim (London, 1976).
11. Bohnert reads this poem in a similar way: 'er nimmt sich, was er braucht von den—im doppelten Sinne—Früchten des Intellektuellen' (*Brecht's Lyrik*, p. 149–50). She also points out that the speaker's role in this act of appropriation is a passive one.
12. Compare GW 12, 560, 'Über niedrige Gesinnung'. There is an echo of the 'Beschwerdelied' in 'Siebentes Lied des Glücksgotts (1)':

> Wer nicht nach Sternen langt, ist ein Schwein
> Wer da lacht, der ist niederträchtig. (GW 10, 892.)

> Wollt ihr Sterne langen
> Müßt ihr rennen sehr.
> Denn ihr tragt an Stangen
> Schnell sie vor euch her. (GW 8, 16.)

13. Compare GW 16, 567: 'der Begriff des richtigen Wegs ist weniger gut als der des richtigen Gehens'.
14. Compare GW 12, 576, 'Tu will kämpfen lernen und lernt sitzen':

Tu sagte: Wenn man immer danach strebt, die bequemste Lage einzunehmen und aus dem Bestehenden das Beste herauszuholen, kurz, wenn man nach Genuß strebt, wie soll man da kämpfen? Me-ti sagte: Wenn man nicht nach Genuß strebt, nicht das Beste aus dem Bestehenden herausholen will und nicht die beste Lage einnehmen will, warum sollte man da kämpfen?

15. AJ 16.11.41:

in chinatown für 40 cts einen kleinen chinesischen glücksgott gekauft. überlegte ein stück DIE REISEN DES GLÜCKSGOTTS. der gott derer, die glücklich zu sein wünschen, bereist den kontinent. hinter ihm her eine furche von exzessen und totschlag. bald werden die behörden aufmerksam auf ihn, den anstifter und mitwisser mancher verbrechen. er muß sich verborgen halten, wird illegal. schließlich denunziert, verhaftet, im prozeß überführt, soll er getötet werden. er erweist sich als unsterblich. lachend sitzt er gemütlich zurückgelehnt im elektrischen stuhl, schmatzt, wenn er gift trinkt usw. völlig erschöpft ziehen die verstörten henker, richter, pfaffen usw ab, während die menge vor dem totenhaus, die von furcht erfüllt zur exekution gekommen war, von neuer hoffnung erfüllt, weggeht ...

Cf. the later account in 'Bei Durchsicht meiner ersten Stücke' (1954, GW 17, 947-8). It is noticeable that the story quoted above contains (in a new transformation) many elements of the life of Christ.

16. The *Bestandsverzeichnis*, volume 2, offers the following datings:

(9113) 'Über das Begreifen des Vorhandenen' (=GW 10,898) and (10740) 'Da sie nun glauben ...' (=GW 10, 902) are found in notebooks of 1933. Hans-Joachim Bunge, '"Das Manifest" von Bertolt Brecht: Notizen zur Entstehungsgeschichte', *Sinn und Form*, 15 (1963), p. 187, dates the following texts to 1939: 'Viele sprachen vom Krieg wie von Ungewitter' (=GW 10, 905), 'Und jetzt erfährst du als erstes ...' (=GW 10, 910), 'Nicht von Erscheinungen schlechthin ...' (=GW 10, 896). He also notes that these texts were found in the same file as material from the 'Glücksgott' project, which was partly contemporary with the 'philosophisches Lehrgedicht'. Additional evidence of early consideration of the 'philosophisches Lehrgedicht' is provided by Benjamin, *Versuche*, p. 126 (27.9.34); and also by Brüggemann, *Literarische Technik*, pp. 285-6 (n. 187):

Hanna Kosterlitz, eine Freundin Korschs, erinnert sich: 'KK gab Kurse im Hause der Karl Marx Schule, Neukölln. Danach lange Sitzungen im Cafe Adler am Alexanderplatz. Dort auch Vorträge und panel Diskussionen von KK und andern....Aus diesen Diskussionen entsprang die Idee zum Komm. Man. in Versform'.

Evidence of Brecht's interest in Lucretius tends to support such an early dating: the first reference occurs in the essay *Fünf Schwierigkeiten beim Schreiben der Wahrheit*, of which the first version was written in 1934. See GW 18, 233.

The poems recently published include a few texts which may be related to the *Lehrgedicht von der Natur der Menschen:*

Immer verrät, wer vom Wesen spricht, ob er nun froh spricht
Oder anscheinend verzweifelt, den Wunsch, es möchte dies Wesen
Immer so bleiben, und klagt er auch noch so: er gibt zu erkennen
Er jedenfalls weiß kein Mittel zu ändern, was da eben Wesen ist!
(GW Supp. IV, 295.)

Und es verwandelte sich in Eis das Innre des Menschen

Und auf dem Eis erschienen in hungrigen Rudeln die Wölfe.
Schnell erzwang sich Gehör das Gesetz der Dschungel, das vorschreibt
Daß der Bruder den Bruder erschlägt und bei Strafe verbietet
Daß die Mutter das Kind säugt. (GW Supp. IV, 397.)

17. zu meinem entsetzen vertritt auch der skeptische und linke gorelik die vansittartthese. 'warum haben die deutschen arbeiter nicht protestiert gegen die greuel in rußland?' (es ist hier üblich, daß hochbezahlte schreiber, die den verstand der amerikanischen massen vergiften, mitunter proteste gegen dies und das unterschreiben.) der grad der faschistischen und besonders der nazistischen unterdrückung ist hier unvorstellbar. (AJ 8.8.43.)

Similarly AJ 10.8.43

AJ 20.8.43: 'man hört von streiks, nicht nur in milano, auch in berlin. mitunter, für einen augenblick, scheinen sich die schlachtfelder, kriegsschauplätze, geographischen reliefs europas zu bevölkern. es sind menschen in milano und in hamburg...'

AJ 15.8.44: 'da sind immerzu die fragen, warum die deutschen noch kämpfen. nun, die bevölkerung hat die SS auf dem genick, außerdem hat sie keine politische willensrichtung, der paar parlamentarischen institutionen zweifelhafter art beraubt und ökonomisch unter dem stiefel der besitzenden, wie immer....mit einem satz: die deutschen kämpfen noch, weil die herrschende klasse noch herrscht'.

18. AJ 25.2.45

während der ganzen zeit ist mir das hier so erzürnt kommentierte ausbleiben von aufständen gegen hitler in d(eutschland) vollkommen verständlich. zum erstenmal sehe ich jetzt möglichkeiten (aus der ferne), wenn ich höre, daß im reich eine schere entstanden ist: mangel an arbeitskräften für die kriegsindustrie und zugleich arbeitslosigkeit, weil es an rohstoffen fehlt, das transportwesen niederbricht und die fabriken gebombt sind. in petersburg rebellierten 1917 die arbeiter der putilow-werke, als die bourgeoisie sie aus den munitionsfabriken aussperrte.

Cf 10.3.45: 'zwischen dem LEHRGEDICHT und den schrecklichen zeitungsberichten aus deutschland. ruinen und kein lebenszeichen von den arbeitern'.

19. See *alternative,* 41 (1965), p. 45: Letter from Brecht to Korsch dated end of March 1945 (=Brief 494). Further information is provided in Bunge, '"Manifest"', and in Gerhard Seidel, *Die Funktions- und Gegenstandsbedingtheit der Edition* (Berlin, 1970), pp. 89–90, 245.

20. See Bunge, '"Manifest"', pp. 197–9; also AJ 3.3.45, June–July 1945.

Cf. Bunge, *Fragen Sie mehr über Brecht: Hanns Eisler im Gespräch* (München, 1970), p. 91ff.
21. See *alternative*, 105 (1975), pp. 254–8 (257–8): Letter from Korsch to Brecht, 18.4.47.
22. Bunge, "'Manifest'", p. 184: 'bei der Versifizierung folgte er im allgemeinen dem Wortlaut von Marx und Engels, häufig unter Benutzung ihrer Formulierungen. Einige Absätze stellte Brecht um. Hier und da straffte er die Darstellung. Andrerseits fügte er Beispiele neu hinzu. Wo es ihm notwendig schien, aktualisierte Brecht das klassische Dokument behutsam.'
23. Robert H. Spaethling, 'Bertolt Brecht and the "Communist Manifesto"', GR, 37 (1962), arrives at a different conclusion. He describes the 'epic' character of Brecht's treatment, and proceeds to examine its consequences; recognizing that the *Manifesto* is treated as a historical document, Spaethling concludes that Brecht's poem (the literary quality of which he concedes) demonstrates the obsolescence of Marxism:

by applying his 'epic technique', Brecht created a distance between himself and the 'classical' precepts of Marx and Engels. The Masters' dogmas do not, in these instances, 'speak for themselves', but they are viewed historically and, knowingly or unknowingly, Brecht submitted them thereby to the same revaluation to which he subjected all 'einmalige, vorübergehende, mit bestimmten Epochen verbundene Vorgänge' (p. 290),

and 'it appears that Brecht has fallen into the dilemma of having to reconcile his need for a permanently valid doctrine with his need and desire for critical thinking' (p. 290). This is crude sophistry: no Marxist would deny that the critique of political economy is capable of being made obsolete—it is made obsolete by the completed revolution. Brecht's *Manifest* declares explicitly (and precisely in the form of one of the 'epic' interruptions on which Spaethling bases his case) and implicitly that Marx's findings and method are still urgently relevant: 'dies aber ist, was die Klassiker sagen'. The assertion that Brecht disapproves this point *malgré soi* is a feeble attempt to bolster up an argument which lacks foundation: Spaethling fails to grasp that Brecht did not comprehend Marxism as a creed, or set of immutable principles, whose discussion is equivalent to its refutation.
24. Cf.: 'sie haben nichts begriffen von der Methode des Faschismus, den Klassenkampf in Rassenkämpfe zu verwandeln. Sie selber brauchen ihre eignen Klassenkämpfe noch nicht zu verwandeln. Sie können noch Parlamente haben, da sie noch die Mehrheit in den Parlamenten haben' (GW 20, 245).
25. Cf. the thematically related texts (GW 10, 863 ff.) which may belong

NOTES

to the periphery of the *Lehrgedicht von der Natur der Menschen*. In particular: 'Die Verwandlung der Götter' and 'Über den bürgerlichen Gottesglauben'.

26. See *alternative*, 41, p. 54: Letter from Korsch to Brecht (15.4.45).
27. Cf. Ernest Mandel, *Marxist Economic Theory* (London, 1968), pp. 150–4.
28. *alternative*, 41, p. 45.
29. Comparison with the corresponding texts of Marx and Engels illuminates both the general fidelity of Brecht's treatment and the syncretic character of his approach; the lines quoted combine the following *loci:*

Alle bisherigen Bewegungen waren Bewegungen von Minoritäten oder im Interesse von Minoritäten. Die proletarische Bewegung ist die selbständige Bewegung der ungeheuren Mehrzahl im Interesse der ungeheuren Mehrzahl. Das Proletariat, die unterste Schicht der jetzigen Gesellschaft, kann sich nicht erheben, nicht aufrichten, ohne daß der ganze Überbau der Schichten, die die offizielle Gesellschaft bilden, in die Luft gesprengt wird (*Manifest*, ch. I, p. 56); and

Wenn das Proletariat im Kampfe gegen die Bourgeoisie sich notwendig zur Klasse vereint, durch eine Revolution sich zur herrschenden Klasse macht und als herrschende Klasse gewaltsam die alten Produktionsverhältnisse aufhebt, so hebt es mit diesen Produktionsverhältnissen die Existenzbedingungen des Klassengegensatzes, die Klassen überhaupt, und damit seine eigene Herrschaft als Klasse auf. (*Manifest*, ch. II, p. 68).

30. Compare GW 12, 463: 'Kein Weltbild machen'.
31. See especially GW 13, 910–12: 'Kämpfe ringsum'.
32. Compare Ernst Schumacher, *Drama und Geschichte: Bertolt Brechts 'Leben des Galilei' und andere Stücke* (Berlin (DDR), 1968), p. 37. Compare also the stories 'Für die Suppe' and 'Die zwei Söhne', (GW 11, 240; 363–6).
33. See *MEW*, iv (Berlin (DDR), 1972), pp. 361–80: 'Grundsätze des Kommunismus'.
34. Benjamin, *Versuche*, p. 132.
35. Hannah Arendt, *Men in Dark Times* (Harmondsworth, 1973), p. 235.
36. Compare AJ 14.4.41: 'er [Hitler] ist die feinste blüte, die der k(apitalismus) hervorbracht hat, das "bisher letzte wort", die gereinigte, verbesserte ausgabe, die alles enthält und neues dazu ...'.

Notes to Chapter 6

1. See AJ 10.11.43 and 20.2.47: similarly GW 12, 489, 534 and 725 f. On 'Über Deutschland' see GW 14, 1455: 'der Sinn ist, man sollte es erobern, es würd sich lohnen'.
2. Compare AJ 1.1.48: 'das deutsche Bürgertum "entnazen" heißt, es entbürgern'.
3. Hannah Arendt asserts 'that the few poems of his last years, published posthumously, are weak and thin' (Arendt, p. 210). It is characteristic of Arendt that this is only an assertion, unsupported by argument or demonstration. Esslin agrees with Arendt's assessment: 'the poems he wrote in this period show a deep feeling of guilt, malaise, and a nostalgic, tender yearning for the Augsburg of his youth. Was it this tiredness that kept him from writing anything of major significance after his return to East Berlin? Was it the oppressive lack of freedom?' (A Choice of Evils, p. 86.) Strange to say, that here again, a wide generalization is based upon not a single cited instance!
4. See AJ 3.1.49, 10.2.49 and 12.2.49. Compare *Bestandsverzeichnis*, vol. 2, section 1: 'Sammlungen'.
5. See Nubel, 'Bibliographie', c 338–407.
6. Lerg-Kill notes (p. 257 n. 248) that all extant versions carry a note in Brecht's hand: 'ANONYM'. Horst Bienek writes (in a letter to Lerg-Kill, 6.4.61; see p. 287 n. 96): 'mir ist bekannt, das das Aufbaulied im Auftrag entstanden ist'.
7. See AJ 1.1.40, 26.1.40 and 19.8.48; also Benjamin, *Versuche*, p. 128 (28.6. 38) and p. 132 (25.7.38).
8. See AJ 6.1.48 (p. 813).
9. These final lines are reminiscent of the earlier 'Reglement für den Soldaten M.S.' from, the 'Lieder des Soldaten der Revolution':
   Was kein Soldat vergißt
   Sondern worauf er sich immer besinnt:
   Wenn die Schwierigkeit
   Der Gebirge überwunden ist
   Ist es so weit
   Daß die Schwierigkeit der Ebenen beginnt.   (1937, GW 9, 598.)
10. 'freilich wir, die mit hitler nicht gesiegt hätten, sind mit ihm geschlagen' (AJ 3.8.45). Compare GW 20, 323: 'die nahezu beispiellose Doppelniederlage, die das deutsche Volk erlitten hat, wirkt sich immer weiter aus. Zuerst vernichtend geschlagen von Hitler, dann, zusammen mit Hitler, von den Alliierten, findet es sich nun im Abgrund der Erschöpfung zusammen mit seinen Unterdrückern, die nur das eigene Volk besiegen konnten'. This sober appraisal of political conditions in Germany was shared by such divergent

NOTES 255

contemporaries as J. R. Becher, W. Girnus, and R. Havemann; see Hans-Dietrich Sander, *Geschichte der schönen Literatur in der DDR* (Freiburg, 1972), p. 84, n. 43 (Havemann) and pp. 88-90 (Becher). Girnus's recollections are recorded in *Sinn und Form*, 29 (1977), pp. 289, 293. Wolf Biermann summarizes the analysis in *Deutschland. Ein Wintermärchen:*

>Die ganze rote Richtung war
>Nach zwölf Jahren Faschismus
>Ein unwillkommenes Geschenk.

(*Nachlaß 1*, (Cologne, 1977), p. 105.)

11. Compare 'Der Letzte' (GW 10, 934, 1945) which begins by insisting that there must be no further postponement: 'Der Kampf ist gekämpft, zu Tisch jetzt!/ Auch die schwarzen Zeiten nehmen ein Ende'; and similarly the later poems 'Beim Lesen des Horaz' and 'Dauerten wir unendlich'.

12. In 'Der Kirschdieb' (GW 9, 816) the thief is described as 'ein junger Mann mit geflickter Hose', which sufficiently defines his social position.

13. See Gerlinde Wellman-Bretzigheimer, 'Brechts Gedicht "Die Vögel warten im Winter vor dem Fenster"', *Basis*, 6 (1976), pp. 97-114.

14. It is significant that the first manuscript of the 'Versuch einer Nationalhymne' has a different first line: 'Arbeit sparet nicht noch Mühe...' (bba 74/49; quoted in Seidel, p. 203). Brecht's revision of this line clearly sought to illuminate more strongly the poem's emancipatory perspective. Lerg-Kill (p. 116-7) notes that the poem's metre recalls that of the 'Deutschlandlied'; Hans-Georg Werner believes that Schiller's 'Freude, schöner Götterfunken' is likewise referred to: '"Gestische Lyrik": Wirkungsabsicht und literarische Technik in den Gedichten Brechts', *Etudes Germaniques* (1973), p. 493.

15. 'Genuß' is a central concept in all Brecht's work and gains increased prominence in the post-exile period; see, for example, AJ 10.6.50: 'lese eine arbeit über gorki und mich, von einer arbeiterstudentin in leipzig verfaßt. ideologie, ideologie, ideologie. nirgends ein ästhetischer begriff; das ganze ähnelt der beschreibung einer speise, bei der nichts über den geschmack vorkommt. wir müßten zunächst ausstellungen und kurse für geschmacksbildung veranstalten, dh für lebensgenuß'. Similarly, GW 20, 331-2, 'Philosophen und Bevölkerung über Vergnügungen': 'der Satz: *Das Ziel eines Menschen ist, sich zu vergnügen* ist deshalb schlecht, weil es dem guten Satz: *Das Ziel der Menschheit ist, sich zu vergnügen* ins Gesicht schlägt', and GW 20, 333, 'Schule der Ästhetik'.

16. The shift of critical focus from people to government is illustrated by a comparison of 'Du bist erschöpft von langer Arbeit' (1952/3, GW

10, 1005) with two similarly conceived poems, 'Höre beim Reden'
(1953, GW 10, 1017) and 'Frage' (1953, GW 10, 1018):
> Der Redner wiederholt sich
> Er spricht lang, er spricht mühsam
> Vergiß nicht, Müder:
> Er spricht die Wahrheit. ('Du bist erschöpft'.)
> Sag nicht zu oft, du hast recht, Lehrer!
> Laß es den Schüler erkennen!
> Strenge die Wahrheit nicht allzusehr an:
> Sie verträgt es nicht. Höre beim Reden!
> Wie soll die große Ordnung aufgebaut werden
> Ohne die Weisheit der Massen? Unberatene
> Können den Weg für die vielen
> Nicht finden. ('Frage')

The second text quoted above is revealed in *Supplementband IV* (1982) to be part of a longer text 'Lehrer, lerne! Lehre, Lernender!' (GW Supp. IV, 435)

17. Cf. also Brecht's long and detailed letter in answer to an enquiry from Peter Suhrkamp, Brief 728, which underlines with considerable emphasis what Biermann referred to as the 'gefährlicher Januskopf' of the events of June 1953–from a Marxist point of view. The justified protests had been infiltrated by, and increasingly dominated by, participants whose aim, far from being the acceleration of socialism, had been the restoration of capitalism. Brecht concludes that only the timely intervention of the occupying Soviet forces prevented the escalation of conflict in the direction of open war.

18. Both these texts have been easily available since 1980, when Gerhard Seidel published them in *Sinn und Form*, Heft 5, p. 1091; they now also appear in GW Supp. IV, 428.

19. Compare Jürgen Link, *Die Struktur des literarischen Symbols: Theoretische Beiträge am Beispiel der späten Lyrik Brechts* (Munich, 1975), pp. 51–52, where 'Wind' is read as 'Arbeiterbewegung' or 'Massenbewegung'.

20. More recently the same argument was adopted by Biermann:
> Und das beste Mittel gegen
> Sozialismus (sag ich laut)
> Ist, daß ihr den Sozialismus
> AUFBAUT!!! Aufbaut! (aufbaut).

From 'Warte nicht auf beßre Zeiten', in *Nachlaß 1*, pp. 73–4.
F. N. Mennemeier presents a reading of the poem which adopts a different emphasis, especially where the poem's key-word 'Ungeduld' is concerned.

Brecht konfrontiert den Leser mit einem Paradox; die scheinbar nichtssagende alltägliche Geschichte zeigt plötzlich ihren Parabel-Charakter. Die Antwort, durch jene Frage provoziert, liegt keineswegs auf der Hand. In einfacher Lesart mag man die Aufforderung zur Geduld hier ausgesprochen finden, Geduld — immerhin auch eine Tugend des Revolutionärs. Doch erlaubt der parabolische Text, einen Schritt weiterzugehen. Der zweiten, schwierigeren Lesart zufolge impliziert die Frage den Hinweis auf das Problem des Fortschritts, anspruchsvoll geredet: den Hinweis auf dessen empirisch nicht ohne weiteres einleuchtendes, transzendentales Wesen. Die Dialektik des Fortschritts zwischen Beharrenwollen und Weitermüssen wird in dem Gedicht zur 'Diskussion' gestellt. Mit der Frage der beiden letzen Zeilen weist es über sich hinaus. Seine Vollendung geschieht im Leser, dann nämlich, wenn dieser aus der 'These' ('Ich bin nicht gern, wo ich hinfahre') und aus der 'Antithese' (Trotzdem 'sehe ich den Radwechsel mit Ungeduld') die Synthese erzeugt.

Mennemeier here identifies the poem's mode of operation quite clearly: nonetheless, the poem seems to speak more of *Weiterwollen* than he allows–the impatience, however surprising in the circumstances, is still felt ('Bertolt Brecht als Elegiker', *Der Deutschunterricht*, Heft 1 (1971) p. 68-9)

21. See AJ 30.8.52: 'vor meiner tür ist eine ecke, gebildet von einem demolierten gewächshaus und einer andern mauer. es gibt gras und tannen, wilde rosenstöcke an den mauern'; and the poem 'Das Gewächshaus' (GW 10, 1023).

22. The metaphor may be derived from the conclusion of Voltaire's *Candide*. 'Der Blumengarten' also recalls (albeit indirectly) the motif of 'Über die Unfruchtbarkeit' and 'Der Pflaumenbaum'; 'Herrn Keuners Krankheit' (GW 12, 411) may summarize the theme:

'Warum bist du krank?' fragten Herrn Keuner die Leute. 'Weil der Staat nicht in Ordnung ist', antwortete er.

23. Compare 'Herr K. und die Natur' (GW 12, 381-2): '(Herr K. sagte auch: "Es ist nötig für uns, von der Natur einen sparsamen Gebrauch zu machen")'.

24. 'Die Weisheit des Volkes' is a recurrent formulation in Brecht's late work; compare GW 19, 555; GW 20, 326; and the similar direction of argument in 'Die Volkskammer' (GW 20, 329-30).

25. Compare AJ 12.9.53, 7.7.54; Stefan Heym describes this attitude in the words of his principal character Witte (a communist of long standing and member of the SED):

das ist nun leider eine der Freuden unseres Lebens. Zuerst dachte ich, ich würde es nicht aushalten, immer wieder mit Menschen zu tun zu haben, die mich gestern mit Handkuß umgebracht hätten und mich morgen mit ebensolchem Vergnügen umbringen würden, wenn sie nur könnten. Aber man gewöhnt sich.

From *Fünf Tage im Juni* (Copenhagen, 1974), p. 19.
26. In a letter to Paul Wandel, mid-Aug. 1953; quoted in Völker, *Biographie*, p. 396 (=Brief 733).
27. The image appears in two earlier poems: 'Heimkehr des Odysseus'— 'Dies ist das Dach. Die erste Sorge weicht./ Denn aus dem Haus steigt Rauch: es ist bewohnt' (GW 9, 563, 1936). If the general significance of the 'Rauch' image is anticipated here, its specific character in the Buckow poem is made clear in 'Überall vieles zu sehen' (GW 9, 809) of 1941:

> Ich habe ein Haus gesehen, das war so baufällig, daß es nur durch einen Hügel aufrecht gehalten wurde; aber so lag es den ganzen Tag im Schatten. Ich kam zu verschiedenen Stunden vorbei, und niemals stieg aus dem Kamin Rauch, als ob Essen gekocht würde. Und ich sah Leute, die dort wohnten.

A. Bergstedt offers a similar analysis in 'Bemerkungen zur dialektischen Struktur von Brechts Gedicht "Der Rauch"', *Weimarer Beiträge*, 24, Heft 9 (1978), p. 163.
28. MEGA I/3, pp. 115-6, quoted and translated in Bottomore, Rubel, *Karl Marx*, p. 251.
29. See Dieter Thiele, 'Brecht als Tui?', in *Brechts Tui-Kritik*, pp. 227, 233.
30. 'Beschluß des ZK der SED, 21.VI.53: "Über die Lage und die unmittelbaren Aufgaben der Partei"', quoted in Arnulf Baring, *Der 17. Juni 1953* (Cologne, Berlin, 1965), p. 181.
31. Compare the direction of changes in 'Morgendliche Rede an den Baum Griehn' made in 1956 (in preparation for the *Gedichte* editions). The previous version of this poem (that which would have been printed in *Gesammelte Gedichte* in 1938), was longer; strophes two and three of bba 123/17-18 were cut and modified to produce the second strophe of the text printed in GW (8, 186).

> Ich bekenne einfach, daß ich mich geirrt habe:
> Sie haben den bittersten Kampf Ihres Lebens gekämpft.
> Es interessierten sich Geier für Sie.
> Sie wissen jetzt, was Sie wert sind, Green.
> Heute glänzt die gelbe Sonne in Ihren nackten Ästen.
> Aber Sie schütteln noch immer Zähren ab, Green?
> Sie leben ziemlich allein, Green?
> Ja, wir sind nicht für die Masse...
> (bba 123/17-18.)

The revised text includes two completely new lines: 'Und ich weiß jetzt: einzig durch Ihre unerbittliche/ Nachgiebigkeit stehen Sie heute morgen noch gerade' (GW 8, 187); this may be read as a gloss on the poem 'Eisen'. The 'Steel stood' motif occurs in Brecht's early writings (in GW 20, 21;=TAA, p. 205), and in *Fünf Schwierigkeiten beim Schreiben der Wahrheit* (GW 18, 228-9). Brechts attitude towards the Soviet Union had long been 'positiv kritisch' (AJ Jan. 1939); this emerges in the early fifties too, in poems like 'Eisen' and 'Die Musen' where Stalinism is apparently referred to specifically (if implicitly), but it is part of a strand which was shown to appear in the *Lehrgedicht von der Natur der Menschen,* and indeed in *Svendborger Gedichte.* The *Supplementbände* edit a number of poems which complement the brief notes Brecht made following the Twentieth Party Congress in Feb. 1956. (GW Supp. IV, 437-8);

(1) Der Gott ist madig.
Die Anbeter schlagen sich auf die Brust
Wie sie den Weibern auf den Hintern schlagen
Mit Wonne.

(2) Der Zar hat mit Ihnen gesprochen
Mit Gewehr und Peitsche
Am Blutigen Sonntag. Dann
Sprach zu ihnen mit Gewehr und Peitsche
Alle Tage der Woche, alle Werktage
Der verdiente Mörder des Volkes.

Die Sonne der Völker
Verbrannte ihre Anbeter.
Der größte Gelehrte der Welt
Hat das Kommunistische Manifest vergessen
Der genialste Schüler Lenins
Hat ihn aufs Maul geschlagen.

Aber jung war er tüchtig
Aber alt war er grausam
Jung
war er nicht der Gott.
Der zum Gott wird
Wird dumm

(3) Die Gewichte auf der Waage
Sind groß. Hinaufgeworfen
Wird auf die andere Skala die Klugheit
Und als nötige Zuwaag
Die Grausamkeit.

> Die Anbeter sehen sich um:
> Was war falsch? Der Gott?
> Oder das Beten?
> Aber die Maschinen?
> Aber die Siegestrophäen
> Aber das Kind ohne Brot?
> Aber der blutenden Genossen
> Ungehörter Angstschrei?
> Der alles befohlen hat
> Hat nicht alles gemacht.
> Versprochen worden sind Äpfel
> Ausgeblieben ist Brot.

32. Scrutiny of the large body of related texts cannot itself indicate conclusively how this poem should be read: it may, however, illuminate the possibilities. The river image is frequently used; in 'Die Ballade vom Wasserrad' (GW 3, 1007), as in the phrase 'Der Fluß der Dinge', it signifies the course of history, the dialectic of flux. 'Über die Gewalt' (GW 9, 602) explores one aspect of the image in its argument that the violent force of the torrent (like revolutionary violence) is not spontaneous and arbitrary, but the consequence of real conditions:

> Der reißende Strom wird gewalttätig genannt
> Aber das Flußbett, das ihn einengt
> Nennt keiner gewalttätig.

From a literal, rather than metaphorical, point of view the control of rivers is presented as productive: see GW 14, 1486, 1505, and 1514; also GW 16, 671, 673 (paragraphs 22 and 25); 'Über die kritische Haltung', (GW 9, 773) summarizes this point:

> Die Regulierung eines Flusses
> Die Veredelung eines Obstbaumes
> Die Erziehung eines Menschen
> Der Umbau eines Staates
> Das sind Beispiele fruchtbarer Kritik.

Such critical control may appear as force:

> Der Damm schreit im Frühjahr:
> Der Fluß gebrauchte Gewalt!
> Aber der Fluß antwortet ihm: und was
> Gebrauchst du das ganze Jahr?

('Briefe der Mutter an ihre Kinder in der Ferne', GW 9, 801); compare GW 20, 344: 'zuinnerst der Sphäre der Produktion und allüber die Sphäre der Produktion herrschte die Gewalt, sei es die offene des

Flusses, der die Dämme zerreißt, oder die geheime der Dämme, die den Fluß niederhalten'. This complex and contradictory set of interpretative possibilities points to one general conclusion: there can be no simple comprehensive judgement of particular actions, nor of historical phases. In the case of 'Bei der Lektüre eines sowjetischen Buches' judgement must depend on questions such as these: what sort of river is to be dammed? Who is to build the dam? What will its function be? ('Die Wahrheit ist konkret').

'Lied der Ströme' (1954, GW 10, 1024) argues that not all forcible control is productive:

> Mächtige Flüsse hat die Erde
> Daß sie viele schöne Früchte tragen muß
> Aber wir, das Proletariat, sind
> Dieser Erde fruchtbarster Fluß.
> Freunde, er ist auch der stärkste
> Und ist für ihn kein Damm:
> Über die Erde ergießt er sich
> Unaufhaltsam.

'Über die Große Methode' ('Schwierigkeit der Geschichtsschreibung') (GW 12, 459) examines precisely the interpretative difficulty which the poem and its context illustrate: the solution to this theoretical problem may lie in the conscious avoidance of the simple 'Entweder–Oder': in the use of the dialectic. Only this method of critical analysis is adequate to a complex reality where, as in 'Gewohnheiten, noch immer', emancipation and oppression coincide: 'Die Widersprüche in Su' examines a similar case:

Me-ti sagte von Su: Der Entschluß des Vereins in Su, die *Große Ordnung* zu verwirklichen, liegt wie ein Alpdruck auf dem Volk von Su. Die fortschrittlichen Tendenzen bringen die Leute zum Stolpern. Das Brot wird mit solcher Wucht ins Volk geworfen, daß es viele erschlägt. Die segensreichsten Einrichtungen werden von Schurken geschaffen, und nicht wenige tugendhafte Leute stehen dem Fortschritt im Wege. (GW 12, 524)

Rather than presenting any fixed message, the poem invites the reader to learn this method of enquiry and analysis. This reading of the poem finds no support in other studies; Jürgen Link comments

Schon der Titel stellt es dem Gedicht 'Beim Lesen des Horaz' komplementär gegenüber. Das wird durch den Inhalt bestätigt: in der UdSSR wartet man nicht mehr passiv auf das Verrinnen von

Überschwemmungen, man beseitigt die Katastrophen vielmehr präventiv durch 'Studium' und Fünfjahrpläne.
(*Die Struktur des literarischen Symbols* (Munich, 1975), p. 66)

It is slightly surprising that Link should content himself with so simple a reading; possibly his inability to apply his system of symbolic analysis here reduced his interest in the poem. Klaus-Bernd Vollmar, who appears strangely ignorant of Link's provocative study, reads the poem in almost the same way, though he does suggest that besides celebrating the 'Sowjetmenschen' as 'rational und progressiv', the poem carries a 'Warnung vor den Fähigkeiten der Reaktion' (*Ästhetische Strukturen und politische Aufklärung* (Frankfurt and Berne, 1976)). It is ironic that Vollmar, whose brief study bears the ambitious subtitle 'Ein Versuch, die materialistische Literaturtheorie auf den Boden des Textes zu stellen', generally seems content to dispense with any serious confrontation with his chosen texts.

One further reference to another Brecht-locus may be illuminating: In a poem of 1938, which might equally be titled 'Beim Lesen eines Schillerschen Gedichts', Brecht appears to adopt the same critical distance from his text:

> *Ich les,* daß Feuer eine Wohltat ist
> Solang der Mensch es zähmet und bewacht
> Daß es ihn aber, ungezügelt, frißt.
> *Ich frage mich: an was hat der gedacht?*
> Was ist es, das er euch zu zähmen bittet?
> Dies Element, das er so nützlich nennt
> Gesittung fördernd, selber nicht gesittet–
> Was für ein Element ist wohl dies Element?
> Dies Feuer, diese Tochter der Natur
> Die, ihrer Zügel los, durch eure Gassen wandelt
> Mir roter Mütze auf, wer ist das nur?
> Das ist nicht mehr die gute alte Magd!
> Ihr habt wohl die Person zu mild behandelt?
> Ich seh, sie hat euch nach dem Lohn gefragt.

('Über Schillers Gedicht "Die Glocke"' from 'Studien', GW 9, 610. [My emphases–P. W.]).

It is tempting to place this poem beside 'Bei der Lektüre eines sowjetischen Buches' and apply the question of l. 4 to the 'quoted' material of the later poem; perhaps here too, natural forces are a cipher for social ones, control over which may well be an urgent concern of those who rule. But–in the context of the Soviet book, who rules whom?

33. Compare GW 20, 327 ('Zum 17. Juni 1953'): 'die Produktion der Künstler wie die der Arbeiter hatte den Charakter eines Mittels zum Zweck und wurde in sich selbst nicht als erfreulich oder frei angesehen. Vom Standpunkt des Sozialismus aus müssen wir, meiner Meinung nach, diese Aufteilung, *Mittel* und *Zweck, Produzieren* und *Lebensstandard* aufheben. Wir müssen das Produzieren zum eigentlichen Lebensinhalt machen und es so gestalten, es mit so viel Freiheit und Freiheiten ausstatten, daß es an sich verlockend ist'.

34. The six lines of 'Beim Lesen des Horaz' are capable of resolution into two dactylic hexameters; on one hand this lends the poem an air of discreet, lightly borne authority, on the other it suggests a piece of wit: the short lines are brisk (thus underlining the poem's argument), scorning the reflective *sub specie aeternitatis* of the epic line.

Michael Morley, 'Brecht's "Beim Lesen des Horaz"', *Monatshefte*, 63 (1971) has identified one probable source of the poem as *Epistles*, I, 2; but his interpretation of Brecht's poem is unsatisfactory. Morley (p. 377) reads the first two lines, not as part of a reply to some (probably official) plea for patience, but as a direct retort to Horace's poem. A quibble is thus postulated as the centre of Brecht's text: Horace talks of rivers flowing for ever; Brecht of a finite flood. The imputation of this curiously restricted reference ignores a major problem: the majority of Brecht's readers could not be expected to be as well acquainted with Horace as Morley's specialist informant—to them, presumably, the opening lines of the poem would mean nothing? This postulate leads Morley into further complexities: he argues that Brecht, having sought to correct Horace, is ultimately forced to concede that the flood might as well have been eternal, since so few survived. Here (thus Morley, p. 375) Brecht resigns in a mood of pessimistic brooding, intending the poem to recommend consoling patience, and to 'justify his refusal to take a stand' (in 1953; p. 377). Such recourse to vague speculation indicates that Morley's interpretation is faulty.

If Brecht's poem is read as suggested in the present account, as directed against the policy of postponement, a fuller and more coherent picture emerges: following the highly ironic assertions of the first four lines, the poem demonstrates that resigned passivity is a poor way of solving problems. Viewed in this light, the poem is indeed in agreement with Horace, not in the limited and reluctant sense suggested (the implied preliminary disagreement is itself only verbal, not substantial), but in the central theme which emerges in both texts: 'sapere aude/ incipe' ('Entschließ dich zur Einsicht!/ Fange nur an!'). This reading locates the text plausibly in the context of the late poetry, and realizes the potential of Morley's valuable source-research.

Link, pp. 63-5, gives an account which supports the above interpretation; 'der Versuch, der Geschichte zu entfliehen und das Ende der historischen Katastrophen passiv "abzuwarten", bringt in den meisten Fällen die Gefahr mit sich, dabei unterzugehen—das sagt Brecht in ironischer Form: nur sehr wenige überleben den Versuch'. Here, as in many other instances, Link arrives at general conclusions which are considerably more convincing and reliable than his fashionable method.

The following texts from *Me-ti* may be read as glosses to the poem: 'Über die Vergänglichkeit' (GW 12, 469) and 'Gefahren der Idee vom Fluß der Dinge' (GW 12, 525).

Finally, compare Wolf Biermann's treatment of the same theme (and the same source?):

> Wartet nicht auf beßre Zeiten
> Wartet nicht mit eurem Mut
> Gleich dem Tor, der Tag für Tag
> An des Flusses Ufer wartet
> Bis die Wasser abgeflossen
> Die doch ewig fließen
>   die doch ewig fließen.   (*Nachlaß 1*, p. 74)

35. See Link, pp. 69-70; and more particularly, Theodore Fiedler, 'Brecht and Cavafy', *Comparative Literature*, 25 (1973), p. 245.
36. Compare Link, p. 114; and Klaus-Bernd Vollmar, p. 63: 'die "Dunkelheit" des Stils ist hier Schutzmittel'. The notorious letter to Ulbricht is Brief 725.
37. Link, p. 112, and especially p. 124 n. 54 ('an eine Veröffentlichung war damals nicht zu denken') is mistaken in his belief that none of the *Buckower Elegien* was published during Brecht's lifetime.
38. See the essay by K. O. Conrady in *Ausgewählte Gedichte Brechts mit Interpretationen*, pp. 139-46, in which a similar reading of 'Vergnügungen' is envisaged.
39. See 'Kin-jeh über die Liebe', GW 12, 571-2.
40. Cf. AJ 19.12.47; the source of Brecht's title is again amongst the classical doctrines of China.

BIBLIOGRAPHY

(a)
BRECHT, BERTOLT, *Gesammelte Werke in 20 Bänden* (Frankfurt am Main, 1967).
—— *Gesammelte Werke Supplementbände III, IV* (=*Gedichte aus dem Nachlaß 1, 2*) (Frankfurt am Main, 1982).
—— *Gedichte*, vols. 1-10 (Frankfurt am Main, 1960-76).
—— *Bertolt Brechts Hauspostille* (Berlin, 1927).
—— (with Hanns Eisler), *Lieder Gedichte Chöre* (Paris, 1934).
—— *Gesammelte Werke*, 2. vols (London, 1938).
—— *Svendborger Gedichte* (London, 1939).
—— *Kriegsfibel* (Berlin (DDR), 1955).
—— *Versuche*, Hefte 1-15, 2nd rep. edn. (Frankfurt am Main, 1978).
—— *Arbeitsjournal 1938-1955*, 2 vols., with notes in a separate volume (Frankfurt am Main, 1973).
—— *Tagebücher 1920-1922: Autobiographische Aufzeichnungen 1920-1954* (Frankfurt am Main, 1975).
—— *Briefe*, with notes in a separate volume (Frankfurt am Main, 1981).
Bertolt-Brecht-Archiv: Bestandsverzeichnis des literarischen Nachlasses, 4 vols. (Berlin (DDR) and Weimar, 1969-73).

(b)
Aktionen Bekenntnisse Perspektiven: Berichte und Dokumente vom Kampf um die Freiheit literarischen Schaffens in der Weimarer Republik (Berlin (DDR), 1966).
ALFF, W., *Der Begriff Faschismus und andere Aufsätze zur Zeitgeschichte* (Frankfurt am Main, 1971).
alternative, Heft 41 (Berlin, 1965, April), 'Karl Korsch: Lehrer Bertolt Brechts'
——, Heft 105 (Berlin, 1975, December), 'Brecht/Korsch: Aus dem unveröffentlichten Briefwechsel im Exil'.
ARENDT, H., *Men in Dark Times* (Harmondsworth, 1973).
BARING, A., *Der 17. Juni 1953* (Cologne and Berlin, 1965).
BAUMGÄRTNER, K., 'Interpretation und Analyse: Brechts Gedicht "Die Literatur wird durchforscht werden"', *Sinn und Form*, 12 (1960), pp. 395-415.
BENJAMIN, W., *Versuche über Brecht* (Frankfurt am Main, 1966).
——, *Das Kunstwerk im Zeitalter seiner technischen Reproduzierbarkeit* (Frankfurt am Main, 1963).

BERGSTEDT, A., 'Bemerkungen zur dialektischen Struktur von Brechts Gedicht "Der Rauch"', *WB*, 24 (1978), Heft 9, p. 163.
BIERMANN, W., *Nachlaß I* (Cologne, 1977).
BIRKENHAUER, K., *Die eigenrhythmische Lyrik Bertolt Brechts: Theorie eines kommunikativen Sprachstils* (Tübingen, 1971).
BLUME, B., 'Motive der frühen Lyrik Bertolt Brechts: 1. Der Tod im Wasser: 2. Der Himmel der Enttäuschten', *Monatshefte*, 57 (1965), pp. 97-112, pp. 273-81.
BOHNERT, CHRISTIANE, *Brechts Lyrik im Kontext. Zyklen und Exil* (Königstein im Taunus, 1982).
BRADY, P. V., '"Aus einem Lesebuch für Städtebewohner": On a Brecht Essay in Obliqueness', *GLL*, 26 (1972/3), pp. 160-72.
——, 'From cave-painting to "fotogramm". Brecht, Photography and the "Arbeitsjournal"', *FMLS*, 14 (1978), pp. 270-82.
BRANDT, HEINZ, *Ein Traum, der nicht entführbar ist: Mein Weg zwischen Ost und West* (Munich, 1967, repr. Berlin, 1977).
BRANDT, HELMUT, 'Sozialkritischer Umgang mit dem Erbe: Bertolt Brecht', in *Schriftsteller und literarisches Erbe: Zum Traditionsverhältnis sozialistischer Autoren*, edited H. Richter (Berlin (DDR) and Weimar, 1976).
BRANDT, T. O., *Die Vieldeutigkeit Bertolt Brechts* (Heidelberg, 1968).
Braunbuch I: Braunbuch über Reichstagsbrand und Hitler-Terror (Basle, 1933).
BRIDGEWATER, P., 'Arthur Waley and Brecht', *GLL*, 17 (1963-4), pp. 216-32.
BRONNEN, A., *Tage mit Bertolt Brecht: Geschichte einer unvollendeten Freundschaft* (Berlin, Munich, Basle, 1960).
BROWN, T. K., 'Brecht and the 17th June 1953', *Monatshefte*, 63 (1971), pp. 48-55.
BRÜGGEMANN, H., *Literarische Technik und soziale Revolution: Versuche über das Verhältnis von Kunstproduktion, Marxismus und literarischer Tradition in den theoretischen Schriften Bertolt Brechts* (Reinbek, 1973).
BUNGE, H.-J., 'Das "Manifest" von Bertolt Brecht: Notizen zur Entstehungsgeschichte', *Sinn und Form*, 15 (1963), pp. 184-203.
——, *Fragen Sie mehr über Brecht: Hanns Eisler im Gespräch* (Munich, 1972).
CLAAS, H., *Die politische Ästhetik Bertolt Brechts vom Baal zum Caesar* (Frankfurt am Main, 1977).
—— and HAUG, W. F. (eds.), *Das Argument: Argument-Sonderband AS 11.* (Karlsruhe, 1976) (=*Brechts Tui-Kritik*).
DEBIEL, G., *Verfremdung in der Sprachgestaltung Bertolt Brechts* (Diss. Bonn, 1960).
DIETZ, G., 'Bertolt Brechts dialektische Lyrik', *DU*, 18 (1966), pp. 66-77.

ENGBERG, H., *Brecht auf Fünen: Exil in Dänemark 1933–1939* (Wuppertal, 1974).
ERCK, A. and GRÄF, K., 'Bertolt Brechts Gedicht "Die Nachtlager"', *WB*, 13 (1967), pp. 228–45.
ESSLIN, M., *Brecht. A Choice of Evils* (London, 1959).
EWEN, F., *Bertolt Brecht: His Life and Times* (New York, 1967).
FANKHAUSER, G., *Verfremdung als Stilmittel vor und bei Brecht* (Tübingen, 1971).
FETSCHER, I., 'Es gibt keine Götter — auch Stalin: ein Ochs', *Merkur*, 23 (1969), Heft 9, p. 888.
FEUCHTWANGER, LION, *Die Geschwister Oppenheim* (Amsterdam, 1933).
FIEDLER, T., 'Brecht and Cavafy', *Comparative Literature*, 25 (1973), pp. 240–6.
FRISCH, W. and OBERMEIER, K. W. (eds.), *Brecht in Augsburg* (Frankfurt am Main, 1976).
FUEGI, JOHN, 'The Soviet Union and Brecht. The Exile's Choice' in *Brecht heute. Brecht Today* (=Jahrbuch der Internationalen Brecht-Gesellschaft), edited by J. Fuegi, ii (Heidelberg, 1972), pp. 209–22.
GEISSLER, R., 'Zur Struktur der Lyrik Brechts', *WW*, 8 (1957–8), pp. 347–52.
GIBBS, T. S., 'A Study of certain Key-Words in the Poetry of Bertolt Brecht' (unpub. diss., Belfast, 1973).
GIRNUS, W., 'Nationalbewußtsein in Brechts Lyrik', *Sinn und Form*, 16 (1964), pp. 681–91.
GRIMM, R., *Bertolt Brecht und die Weltliteratur* (Nuremberg, 1961).
———, *Bertolt Brecht: Die Struktur seines Werkes* (Nuremberg, 1968, 1st edn. 1959).
———, 'Marxistische Emblematik: Zu Brechts "Rad der Fortuna"', *GQ*, 46 (1973), pp. 548–65.
———, 'Bertolt Brechts "Kriegsfibel"', in R. v. Heydebrand and K. G. Just (eds.), *Wissenschaft als Dialog: Studien zur Literatur und Kunst seit der Jahrhundertwende*, (Stuttgart, 1969), pp. 351–79.
———, *Bertolt Brecht* (3rd edn., Stuttgart, 1971).
HAAS, W., *Bert Brecht* (Berlin, 1958).
HARTINGER, CHRISTEL, 'Von der "unnatur der bürgerlichen verhältnisse". Ein Lehrgedichtfragment Bertolt Brechts', *WB*, 24 (1978), Heft 2, pp. 64–100.
HAVEMANN, ROBERT, *Fragen Antworten Fragen: Aus der Biographie eines deutschen Marxisten* (Reinbek, 1972).
HECHT, WERNER, HANS-JOACHIM BUNGE, and KÄTHE RÜLICKE-WEILER. *Bertolt Brecht. Sein Leben und Werk* (Berlin (DDR), 1969).
HELWIG, W., 'Bertolt Brechts Poesie und Politik: Zur gesellschaftlichen Aufgabe seiner Gedichte', *Merkur*, 16 (1962), pp. 933–43.

HERZFELDE, W., (ed), *Der Malik-Verlag 1916-1947: Ausstellungskatalog der Deutschen Akademie der Künste* (Berlin (DDR), 1966).
HESELHAUS, C., *Deutsche Lyrik der Moderne von Nietzsche bis Yvan Goll: Die Rückkehr zur Bildlichkeit der Sprache* (Düsseldorf, 1961).
——, 'Brechts Verfremdung der Lyrik', in W. Iser (ed.) *Immanente Ästhetik: Ästhetische Reflexion: Lyrik als Paradigma der Moderne*, (Munich, 1966) pp. 307-26.
HEYM, S., *Fünf Tage im Juni* (Copenhagen, 1974).
HILDEBRAND, A., 'Bert Brechts Alterslyrik', *Merkur*, 20 (1966), pp. 952-62.
HINCK, W., *Die deutsche Ballade von Bürger bis Brecht* (Göttingen, 1968).
——, *Von Heine zu Brecht: Lyrik im Geschichtsprozeß* (Frankfurt am Main, 1978).
——, (ed.) *Ausgewählte Gedichte Brechts mit Interpretationen* (Frankfurt am Main, 1978).
HIRSCHENAUER, P., and WEBER, A. (eds.), *Wege zum Gedicht* (Munich, 1968).
—— —— (eds.), *Interpretationen zur Lyrik Brechts* (Munich, 1971).
HOEFERT, S., 'Brechts Nachdichtung von Mao Tse-Tungs "Schnee"', *Neophilologus*, 53 (1969), pp. 48-55.
HOLTHUSEN, H. E., *Kritisches Verstehen: Neue Aufsätze zur Literatur* (Munich, 1961).
HULTBERG, H., *Die ästhetischen Anschauungen Bertolt Brechts* (Copenhagen, 1962).
JACOBS, J., 'Wie die Wirklichkeit selber: Zu Brechts "Lesebuch für Städtebewohner"', *Brecht-Jahrbuch 1974* (= *Brecht heute*) (Frankfurt am Main, 1975), pp. 77-91.
JAKOBSON, R., 'Der grammatische Bau des Gedichts von Bertolt Brecht "Wir sind sie"', *alternative*, 12 (1969), Heft 65, pp. 62-74.
JENS, W., 'Protokoll über Brecht', *Merkur*, 10 (1956).
——, *Statt einer Literaturgeschichte* (Pfullingen, 1958)
——, *Deutsche Literatur der Gegenwart* (Munich, 1961).
——, 'Der Lyriker Bertolt Brecht', in *Zueignungen* (Munich, 1962).
KAUFMANN, H., 'Brecht: Die Entfremdung und die Liebe: Zur Gestaltung der Geschlechterbeziehungen im Werk Brechts', *WB*, 11 (1965), pp. 84-101.
KILLY, W., *Wandlungen des lyrischen Bildes* (Göttingen, 1967).
KLOTZ, V., *Bertolt Brecht: Versuch über das Werk* (Bad Homburg, Berlin and Zürich, 1967).
KNOPF, J., *Bertolt Brecht: ein kritischer Forschungsbericht: Fragwürdiges in der Brecht-Forschung* (Frankfurt am Main, 1974).
KRAFT, W., *Augenblicke der Dichtung* (Munich, 1964).
KRUSCHE, D., 'Dialektik des Wissens: Die Lehr- und Lerngedichte Bertolt Brechts', *DU*, 23 (1971), pp. 23-35.

KUCZYNSKI, J., *Die Geschichte der Lage der Arbeiter unter dem Kapitalismus* (Berlin, 1964), vi.

KÜHNL, R., *Der deutsche Faschismus in Quellen und Dokumenten* (Cologne, 1975).

——, *Formen bürgerlicher Herrschaft: Liberalismus-Faschismus* (Reinbek, 1971).

KUHNERT, H., 'Zur Rolle der "Songs" im Werk von Bertolt Brecht', *NDL*, 11 (1963), pp. 77–100.

LEHMANN, HANS-THIES, and LETHEN, HELMUT (eds.), *Bertolt Brechts 'Hauspostille'. Text und kollektives Lesen* (Stuttgart, 1978).

LERG-KILL, U. C., *Dichterwort und Parteiparole: propagandistische Gedichte und Lieder Bertolt Brechts* (Bad Homburg, Berlin, and Zürich, 1968).

LINK, J., *Die Struktur des literarischen Symbols: theoretische Beiträge am Beispiel der späten Lyrik Brechts* (Munich, 1975).

LYON, JAMES K., 'Bertolt Brecht's love poetry for Margarete Steffin' in *Perspectives and Personalities* (Festschrift Claude Hill), edited R. Ley (Heidelberg, 1972).

——, *Bertolt Brecht und Rudyard Kipling* (Frankfurt am Main, 1976).

——, 'Bertolt Brechts "Bericht vom Zeck": Eine Berichtigung', *Études germaniques*, 23 (1968), pp. 275–79.

——, 'The Source of Brecht's Poem "Vorbildliche Bekehrung eines Branntweinhändlers"', *MLN*, 84 (1969), pp. 802–6.

MANDEL, ERNEST, *Marxist Economic Theory* (London, 1968).

MANN, GOLO, *The History of Germany since 1789* (London, 1968).

MARNETTE, H., 'Bertolt Brecht: "Lob des Kommunismus"', *DU*, 16 (1963), pp. 573–7.

MARSCH, E., *Brecht: Kommentar zum lyrischen Werk* (Munich, 1974).

MARX, K. and ENGELS, F., *Werke*, edited by the Institut für Marxismus-Leninismus beim ZK der SED, 36 Vols (Berlin (DDR), 1957–).

——, *Marx-Engels Gesamtausgabe* (MEGA), edited by the Marx-Engels Institute, Moscow (Moscow, 1927–).

Karl Marx: Selected Writings in Sociology and Social Philosophy, ed. T. B. Bottomore and M. Rubel (Harmondsworth, 1963).

MAYER, H., 'Gelegenheitsdichtung des jungen Brecht', *Sinn und Form*, 10 (1958), pp. 276–89.

——, *Bertolt Brecht und die Tradition* (Munich, 1965).

——, 'Über Brechts Gedichte', *Études germaniques*, 20 (1965), pp. 269–74.

MCLEAN, S. K., *The 'Bänkelsang' and the work of Bertolt Brecht* (The Hague/Paris, 1972).

MEIER-LENZ, D. P., 'Brecht und der Pflaumenbaum', *NDH*, 18 (1971), pp. 40–8.

MENNEMEIER, F. N., 'Bertolt Brecht als Elegiker', *DU*, 23 (1971), pp. 59-73.

——, 'Brechts Faschismustheorie', in *Literaturwissenschaft und Geschichtsphilosophie—Festschrift für W. Emrich* (Berlin, 1975), pp. 561-74.

METSCHER, T. W. H., 'Brecht and Marxist Dialectics', *Oxford German Studies*, 6 (1971-72), pp. 132-44.

MIHM, A., 'Linguistische Beschreibung des Verfremdungseffekts', in *Literaturdidaktik*, ed. Vogt (Gütersloh, 1972), pp. 84 ff.

MITSCHERLICH, A., *Auf dem Weg zur vaterlosen Gesellschaft: Ideen zur Sozialpsychologie* (Munich, 1963).

MITTENZWEI, W., *Brechts Verhältnis zur Tradition* (Berlin (DDR), 1972).

——, 'Die Brecht-Lukács Debatte', *Sinn und Form*, 19 (1967), pp. 235-71.

MORLEY, M., '"Progress is the Law of Life": Brecht's Poem "Die Internationale"', *GLL*, 23 (1969-70), pp. 255-68.

——, 'Brecht's "Beim Lesen des Horaz": An Interpretation', *Monatshefte*, 63 (1971), pp. 372-9.

——, 'Invention breeds invention. Brecht's chronicle of the dialectical principle in action' in *Brecht heute. Brecht today*, ii (Heidelberg, 1972). pp. 105-20.

——, 'An Investigation and Interpretation of two Brecht-Poems', *GR*, 46 (1971), pp. 5-25.

——, 'The Source of Brecht's "Abbau des Schiffes Oskawa durch die Mannschaft"', *Oxford German Studies*, 2 (1967), pp. 149-62.

——, 'The Light that shineth more and more: Another look at Kipling's influence on Brecht', *MLN*, 88 (1973), pp. 562-73.

MOTEKAT, H., 'Bertolt Brecht: "Von der Freundlichkeit der Welt"', *OL*, 19 (1964), pp. 145-51.

MÜLLER, H., *Formen moderner deutscher Lyrik* (Paderborn, 1970).

MÜLLER, J., 'Bertolt Brecht und sein lyrisches Lebenswerk', *Universitas*, 19 (1964), pp. 479-92.

——, 'Zu einigen späten Spruchgedichten Brechts', *OL*, 20 (1965), pp. 66-81.

MÜLLER, K.-D., *Die Funktion der Geschichte im Werk Bertolt Brechts: Studien zum Verhältnis von Marxismus und Ästhetik* (Tübingen, 1967, 2nd edn. 1972).

MÜLLER-SEIDEL, W., *Probleme der literarischen Wertung* (Stuttgart, 1965).

MÜNSTERER, H. O., *Bert Brecht: Erinnerungen aus den Jahren 1917-22* (Zürich, 1963).

MUSCHG, W., *Von Trakl zu Brecht: Dichter des Expressionismus* (Munich, 1961).

OEHLER, D., '"Assommons les pauvres!": Dialektik der Befreiung bei Baudelaire: Mit einer Parallele zu Brechts "Die drei Soldaten"', *GRM*, 56 (=NF 25) (1975), pp. 454-62.

BIBLIOGRAPHY

PASCAL, R., 'The graceful claw', *TLS*, 17 Sept. 1976, pp. 1171-2.
PIETZCKER, C., *Die Lyrik des jungen Brecht: Vom anarchischen Nihilismus zum Marxismus* (Frankfurt am Main, 1974).
PIRKER, TH., (editor), *Komintern und Faschismus: Dokumente zur Geschichte und Theorie des Faschismus* (Stuttgart, 1965).
PONGS, H., *Das Bild in der Dichtung* (Marburg, 1969).
——, *Dichtung im gespaltenen Deutschland* (Stuttgart, 1966).
QUALMANN, E., *Klangformanalyse der Lyrik von Bertolt Brecht, an ausgewählten Beispielen dargestellt* (Diss. Greifswald, 1968).
RASCH, W., 'Brechts marxistischer Lehrer: Zu einem ungedruckten Briefwechsel zwischen Brecht und Korsch', *Merkur*, 17 (1963), pp. 988-1003.
REGLER, G., *Das Ohr des Malchus: Eine Lebensgeschichte* (Frankfurt am Main, 1975).
REY, W. H., 'Hohe Lyrik im Bordell: Bertolt Brechts Gedicht "Die Liebenden"', *Monatshefte*, 63 (1971), pp. 1-18.
RICHTER, H., 'Bertolt Brechts Bemerkungen zur Lyrik', *WB*, 12 (1966), pp. 765-85.
RIES, W., 'Herrscher und Dichtung: Notizen zu Bertolt Brechts Gedicht "Briefe über Gelesenes" und sein römisches Vorbild', *WW*, 25 (1975), pp. 323-31.
RIHA, K., *Moritat, Song, Bänkelsang: Zur Geschichte der modernen Ballade* (Göttingen, 1965).
ROLOFF, G., *Die Erforschung der deutschen Exilliteratur: Stand—Probleme—Aufgaben* (Hamburg, 1973).
ROSENBAUER, H., *Brecht und der Behaviourismus* (Bad Homburg, Berlin and Zürich, 1970).
ROTHSCHILDT, T., 'Metaphorik und Rezeption: Zu drei Gedichten von Bertolt Brecht', *DVjS*, 49 (1975), pp. 356-71.
RÜCKERT, G., 'Die Epistel als literarische Gattung: Horaz—Mörike—Brecht', *WW*, 22 (1972), pp. 58-70.
SACHS, H., '"Entdeckung an einer jungen Frau": Ein Sonett von Bertolt Brecht', *NDH*, 10 (1963), pp. 60-4.
SANDER, H.-D., *Geschichte der schönen Literatur in der DDR* (Freiburg, 1972).
SCHLENSTEDT, D., 'Beispiel einer Rezeptionsvorgabe: Brechts Gedicht "Der Rauch"', in M. NAUMANN (ed.), *Gesellschaft, Literatur, Lesen*, (Berlin (DDR) and Weimar, 1975, 1st edn. 1973), pp. 354-380.
SCHLENSTEDT, SILVIA, *Die Chroniken in den 'Svendborger Gedichten': eine Untersuchung zur Lyrik Brechts* (Diss. Berlin, 1959).
——, 'Brechts Übergang zum sozialistischen Realismus in der Lyrik', *WB*, Sonderheft Bertolt Brecht (1958), pp. 59-64.
——, 'Kinderkreuzzug 1939', *WB, Brecht-Sonderheft* (1968), pp. 12-38.

―― 'Lyrik im Gesamtplan der Produktion. Ein Arbeitsprinzip Brechts und Probleme der Gedichte im Exil', *WB*, 24 (1978), Heft 2, pp. 5–29.

SCHMIDT, D., *"Baal" und der junge Brecht: eine textkritische Untersuchung* (Stuttgart, 1966).

SCHÖNE, A., *Über politische Lyrik im 20. Jahrhundert* (Göttingen, 1965).

――, 'Bertolt Brecht: "Erinnerung an die Marie A."', in B. v. Wiese (ed.), *Die deutsche Lyrik: Form und Geschichte*, (Düsseldorf, 1964), ii.

SCHUHMANN, K., *Der Lyriker Bertolt Brecht 1913–1933*, (2nd edn., Munich, 1967).

――, *Untersuchungen zur Lyrik Brechts: Themen, Formen, Weiterungen* (Berlin and Weimar, 1973).

SCHULTE, HANS H., 'Kinderlieder bei Brecht', *WW*, 27 (1977), pp. 149–59.

SCHULTZ, H., *Vom Rhythmus der modernen Lyrik* (Munich, 1970).

SCHUMACHER, E., *Die dramatischen Versuche Bertolt Brechts 1918–1933* (Berlin (DDR), 1955).

――, *Drama und Geschichte: Bertolt Brechts 'Leben des Galilei' und andere Stücke* (Berlin (DDR), 1968).

SCHWARZ, PETER PAUL, *Brechts frühe Lyrik 1914–22: Nihilismus als Werkzusammenhang der frühen Lyrik Brechts* (Bonn, 1971).

――, 'Legende und Wirklichkeit des Exils: zum Selbstverständnis der Emigration in den Gedichten Brechts', *WW*, 19 (1969), pp. 267–76.

――, *Lyrik und Zeitgeschichte. Brecht: Gedichte über das Exil und späte Lyrik* (Heidelberg, 1978).

SEIDEL, G., *Die Funktions- und Gegenstandsbedingtheit der Edition: untersucht an poetischen Werken Bertolt Brechts* (Berlin (DDR), 1970).

――, *Arbeitsweise und Edition. Das literarische Werk als Prozeß* (revised and extended edition of above work) (Stuttgart, 1977).

――, 'Brecht und die Söhne McCarthys', *Sinn und Form*, 32 (1980), Heft 5, pp. 1086–91.

――, 'Intentionswandel in der Entstehungsgeschichte. Ein Gedicht Bertolt Brechts über Karl Kraus historisch-kritisch ediert', *ZfdPh.*, 101 (1982)=Sonderheft: Probleme neugermanistischer Edition, pp. 163–88.

SELIGER, H. W., *Das Amerikabild Bertolt Brechts* (Bonn, 1974).

SHERRY, PEGGY M., '"Vom armen B.B." as signature: between text and speaking subject', *MLN*, 94 (1979), pp. 455–74.

Sinn und Form, Sonderheft Brecht (Berlin (DDR), 1949).

――, *2. Sonderheft Brecht* (Berlin (DDR), 1957).

SÖLLE, D., 'Bertolt Brechts Weihnachtsgedichte interpretiert im Zusammenhang seiner lyrischen Theorie', *Euphorion*, 61 (1967), pp. 84–103.

SPAETHLING, R. H., 'Bertolt Brecht and the "Communist Manifesto"', *GR*, 37 (1962), pp. 282–91.

STEFFENSEN, STEFFEN, *Bertolt Brechts Gedichte* (Copenhagen, 1972).

STRÄTER, H. H., *Die Gedichte der 'Hauspostille': Untersuchungen zur frühen Lyrik Bertolt Brechts* (Diss. Tübingen, 1968).
SUBIOTTO, A. V., 'A "mathematical" note on Verfremdung and Brecht', *GLL*, 17 (1963–4), pp. 233–7.
TATLOW, A., *Brechts chinesische Gedichte* (Frankfurt am Main, 1973).
——, 'Towards an Understanding of Chinese Influence in Brecht: An Interpretation of "Auf einen chinesischen Teewurzellöwen" and "Legende von der Entstehung des Buches Taoteking"', *DVjS*, 44 (1970), pp. 363–87.
Text+Kritik, Sonderband Bertolt Brecht (Munich, 1972).
——, *Sonderband Bertolt Brecht II* (Munich, 1973).
THOLE, B., *Die 'Gesänge' in den Stücken Bertolt Brechts: Zur Geschichte und Ästhetik des Liedes im Drama* (Göppingen, 1973).
TRACY, G. L., '"Das Gestische" and the Poetry of Brecht', in M. S. Batts and M. G. Stankiewicz (eds.), *Essays in German Literature in honour of J. Hallamore*, (Toronto, 1968), pp. 218–35.
TROST, P., 'Verse von Brecht', in *To honour R. Jakobson* (The Hague, 1967), iii.
——, 'Interpretation eines Gedichts von Brecht: "Einst"', *Germanistica Pragensia*, 2 (1962).
VÖLKER, K., *Bertolt Brecht: Eine Biographie* (Munich, 1976).
——, *Brecht-Chronik* (3rd edn., Munich, 1975).
——, 'Brecht und Lukács: Analyse einer Meinungsverschiedenheit', *Kursbuch*, 7 (1966), pp. 80–101.
VOLLMAR, K.-B., *Ästhetische Strukturen und politische Aufklärung: ein Versuch, die materialistische Literaturtheorie auf den Boden des Textes zu stellen* (Frankfurt and Berne, 1976).
WALTER, H.-A., 'Der Dichter der Dialektik: Anmerkungen zu Brechts Lyrik aus der Reifezeit', *Frankfurter Hefte*, 18 (1963), pp. 532–43.
——, *Deutsche Exilliteratur 1933–50* (Darmstadt and Neuwied, i, 1972; ii, 1972; vii, 1974).
WEINRICH, HARALD, 'Eisen', in *Ausgewählte Gedichte Brechts mit Interpretationen*, ed. W. Hinck, (Frankfurt am Main, 1978), pp. 134–8.
WEISBACH, R., *Das Paradigma des Gedichts in 'Bertolt Brechts Hauspostille'· ein Beitrag zum Verhältnis des jungen Brecht zur Tradition und zum Expressionismus* (Diss. Berlin, 1966).
WEISSTEIN, W., '"Apfelböck oder Die Lilie auf dem Felde": Zur Interpretation eines Gedichtes aus Bertolt Brechts "Hauspostille"', *GQ*, 45 (1972), pp. 295–310.
WELLMANN-BRETZIGHEIMER, G., 'Brechts Gedicht "Die Vögel warten im Winter vor dem Fenster"', *Basis*, 6 (1976), pp. 97–114.
——, 'Brechts Gedicht "Als ich im weißen Krankenzimmer der Charité": Die Hilfe des Sozialismus zur Überwindung der Todesfurcht', in *Brecht-Jahrbuch 1977* (Frankfurt am Main, 1977), pp. 30–51.

WERNER, H.-G., '"Gestische Lyrik": zum Zusammenhang von Wirkungsabsicht und Literarischer Technik in Gedichten Bertolt Brechts', *Études germaniques*, 28 (1973), pp. 482-500.

WHITE, J. J., 'A Note on Brecht and Behaviourism', *FMLS*, 7 (1971), pp. 249-58.

WILLETT, JOHN, *The Theatre of Bertolt Brecht. A Study from Eight Aspects* (London, 1959; 3rd edn., rev., 1979).

——, 'The Poet beneath the skin', in *Brecht heute. Brecht today*, ii (Heidelberg, 1972), pp. 88-104.

——, (ed. with Ralph Manheim), *Bertolt Brecht Poems 1913-1956* (London, 1976; 2nd edn., rev., 1979).

——, '"Honoured Murderer": Brecht's Stalin Poems' *New Statesman*, 15 June 1979, pp. 869-70.

——, *Brecht in Context. Comparative Approaches.* (London and New York, 1984).

WITZMANN, P., *Antike Tradition im Werk Bertolt Brechts* (Berlin (DDR), 1965).

WOODS, B. A., 'The Function of Proverbs in Brecht', *Monatshefte*, 61 (1969), pp. 49-57.

——, 'Perverted Proverbs in Brecht and "Verfremdungssprache"', *GR*, 43 (1968), pp. 100-8.

——, 'Unfamiliar Quotations in Brecht's Plays', *GR*, 46 (1971), pp. 26-42.

COPYRIGHTS

Bertolt Brecht, *Gesammelte Werke*: Copyright Suhrkamp Verlag, Frankfurt am Main, 1967
Supplementbände III, IV: Copyright Stefan S. Brecht, 1982
Arbeitsjournal: Copyright Stefan S. Brecht, 1973
Tagebücher. Autobiographische Aufzeichnungen: Copyright Stefan S. Brecht, 1975
Briefe: Copyright Stefan S. Brecht, 1981
Baal: Copyright 1953, Suhrkamp Verlag, Berlin
Der kaukasische Kreidekreis: Copyright 1955, Suhrkamp Verlag, Berlin
Der Brotladen: Copyright Stefan S. Brecht, 1967
Prosa I: Copyright Stefan S. Brecht, 1965
Me-ti/Buch der Wendungen: Copyright Stefan S. Brecht, 1965
Der Tui-Roman: Copyright Stefan S. Brecht, 1967
Dreigroschenroman: Copyright 1934, Allert de Lange, Amsterdam
Flüchtlingsgespräche: Copyright Suhrkamp Verlag, Frankfurt am Main, 1961
Schriften zum Theater: Copyright Suhrkamp Verlag, Frankfurt am Main, 1963, 1964
Schriften zur Literatur und Kunst: Copyright Stefan S. Brecht, 1967
Schriften zur Politik und Gesellschaft: Copyright Stefan S. Brecht, 1967

Copyright in the poems is as follows:
From *Gedichte* 1 and 2: Copyright Suhrkamp Verlag, Frankfurt am Main, 1960
From *Gedichte* 3 and 4: Copyright Suhrkamp Verlag, Frankfurt am Main, 1961
Lieder Gedichte Chöre: Copyright 1934 by Éditions du Carrefour, Paris VI
Die drei Soldaten: Copyright Suhrkamp Verlag, Frankfurt am Main, 1959
Svendborger Gedichte: Copyright 1939 by Malik-Verlag, London
'Chinesische Gedichte' from *Versuche Heft 10*: Copyright 1950 by Suhrkamp Verlag, late S. Fischer Verlag, Berlin
'Studien' from *Versuche Heft 11*: Copyright 1951 by Suhrkamp Verlag, Berlin
'Gedichte aus dem Messingkauf' from *Versuche Heft 14*: Copyright 1955 by Suhrkamp Verlag, Berlin
From *Gedichte* 5, 6 and 7: Copyright Suhrkamp Verlag, Frankfurt am Main, 1964
Gedichte im Exil: Copyright by Stefan S. Brecht, 1964
From *Gedichte* 8 and 9: Copyright Stefan S. Brecht, 1965
Buckower Elegien: Copyright Stefan S. Brecht, 1964
'Neu aufgenommene Gedichte': Copyright Stefan S. Brecht, 1967

COPYRIGHTS

Poems first published in this edition: Copyright by Stefan S. Brecht, 1985; printed by kind permission of the Bertolt-Brecht-Erben and the Suhrkamp Verlag.

All other Brecht texts printed by kind permission of the Suhrkamp Verlag.

INDEX

'Abbau des Schiffes Oskawa durch die Mannschaft', 131-2
'Aberglaube', 195
'Achttausend arme Leute kommen vor die Stadt', 39, 63
'Ach, wie sollen wir die kleine Rose buchen?', 219-20, 221
'Adresse an den Genossen Dimitroff', 81
alienation, 50-1, 52, 56, 61, 148, 178
'Als der Faschismus immer stärker wurde', 79
'Als ich im weißen Krankenzimmer der Charité', 219
'Als ich ins Exil gejagt wurde', 79
'Als ich kam in die Heimat', 184, 192
'An Chronos', 46, 49
'An den Schwankenden', 134
'An die deutschen Soldaten im Osten', 151
'An die Frauen', 88-9, 90
'An die Gleichgeschalteten', 134-5, 137, 148
'An die Kämpfer in den Konzentrationslagern', 81, 87-8
'An die Nachgeborenen', 142-8, 155, 156
'An einen jungen Bauarbeiter der Stalinallee', 199
'An meine Landsleute', 192
'Ansprache des Bauern an seinen Ochsen', 136-7
'Apfelböck oder die Lilie auf dem Felde', 14
'Appell', 136
'Ardens sed virens', 150
Arendt, Hannah, 1, 181, 245 n. 35, 254 n. 3
'Arie des Glücksgotts', 166
'Auch das Beschädigte', 150
'Auch der Himmel', 115
'Aufbaulied', 184, 186-7, 188, 192, 199, 205, 220
Aufbau-Verlag, 185
'Auf den Tod eines Kämpfers für den Frieden', 135-6
'Auf einen Emigranten', 107
'Auf einem Meilenstein der Autostraßen', 158
Aufstieg und Fall der Stadt Mahagonny, 14, 21, 78
Aus einem Lesebuch für Städtebewohner, 39-61
'Auslassungen eines Märtyrers', 26-7, 29, 62
'Ausschließlich wegen der zunehmenden Unordnung', 98, 113
'Außer diesem Stern', 191

Baal, 4, 19, 153, 165-6
'Ballade vom 30. Juni', 99
'Ballade vom Mazeppa', 14, 15
'Ballade vom Stahlhelm', 63-4
'Ballade vom Tropfen auf den heißen Stein', 65
'Ballade vom Weib und dem Soldaten', 12
'Ballade von der Billigung der Welt', 93-4, 96
Barthel, Kurt, 210
Becher, J. R., 239 n. 6, 255 n. 10
'Begräbnis des Hetzers im Zinksarg', 81, 88
'Bei den Hochgestellten', 116
'Bei der Geburt eines Sohnes', 137
'Bei der Lektüre eines sowjetischen Buches', 211-13, 260-2 n. 32
'Bei der Lektüre eines spätgriechischen Dichters', 214-15, 217
'Beim Lesen des Horaz', 213-14, 216, 263-4 n. 34
Benjamin, Walter, 2, 43, 96, 116, 125, 128-9, 131, 136-7, 180
'Bericht anderswohin', 57
'Bericht der Serben', 151
'Berichtigungen alter Mythen', 126
'Bericht über den Tod eines Genossen', 91
'Bericht über einen Gescheiterten', 107-8
'Bericht vom Zeck', 10
'Bericht von einem hundertjährigen Krieg 2', 178
Berliner Requiem, 97

INDEX

Bertolt Brechts Hauspostille, 1, 18–38, 82; *Taschenpostille*, 19; 'Anleitung', 20; 'Psalmen', 9, 21, 24, 228 n. 28; 'Exerzitien', 15, 17, 21, 22; 'Chroniken', 21
'Besuch bei den verbannten Dichtern', 129
'Bidis Ansicht über die großen Städte', 33–4
Biermann, Wolf, 255 n. 10, 256 n. 17, 264 n. 34
'Böser Morgen', 206, 211
Brady, P. V., 46, 59
'Brief an einen Freund', 25
'Briefe der Mutter an ihre Kinder in der Ferne', 151
Buckower Elegien, 185, 201–16; 'Motto', 202, 220

'Caspars Lied mit der einen Strophe', 12
Cavafy, 214
Chronik: as category, 24, 99, 110, 113–14, 126–33, 148, 151, 185; definition, 62
Chronik: autobiographical, as category, 62, 99, 151, 185; definition, 62
Claas, Herbert, 140

'Da das Instrument verstimmt ist', 112
'Dankgedicht an Mari Hold', 115
'Das Beschwerdelied', 5–8, 18, 21, 60–1, 166
'Das Brot des Volkes', 200
'Das Entsetzen, arm zu sein', 31–2.
'Da sie aber bedrückt sind vom Kapitalismus', 176
Das Kapital, 37
'Das Lied der Eisenbahntruppe von Fort Donald', 6
'Das Lied vom Anstreicher Hitler', 81
'Das Lied vom Geierbaum', 15
'Das Lied vom Klassenfeind', 81, 85, 202
'Das Lied vom SA-Mann', 81, 85
'Das Lied von der Suppe', 89
'Das Manifest', 170–4
'Das Neujahr der Verfolgten', 102
'Das Pferd des Ruuskanen', 151
'Das Saarlied', 99
'Das Schiff', 14
'Das will ich ihnen sagen', 160

Das Wort, 140
'Dauerten wir unendlich', 221
'Da wird ein Tag sein', 158
'Denk nicht: er sah dich nicht, der dies schrieb', 178–9
'Der anachronistische Zug, oder Freiheit und Democracy', 182
'Der Anstreicher spricht von kommenden großen Zeiten', 117
'Der Bauer pflügt den Acker', 158
'Der belgische Acker', 11
'Der Blumengarten', 203–5
Der böse Baal der Asoziale, 165
'Der brennende Baum', 25
'Der Choral vom Manne Baal', 15, 62, 221
'Der Dichter, der ihn manchmal geliebt', 23–4, 25, 95
'Der Dienstzug', 139
'Der Einarmige im Gehölz', 206–7
'Der Fluß lobsingt die Sterne im Gebüsch', 17
'Der Führer hat gesagt', 64
'Der Gedanke in den Werken der Klassiker', 100–2
'Der gordische Knoten', 62
'Der Gottseibeiuns', 124
'Der große Oktober', 68, 133
Der gute Mensch von Sezuan, 107
'Der Herr der Fische', 21
'Der Himmel dieses Sommers', 208–9
Der kaukasische Kreidekreis, 107
'Der Kirschdieb', 163, 194
'Der Kommunismus ist das Mittlere', 99–100
'Der Krieg, der kommen wird', 118
'Der Krieg ist geschändet worden', 181–2
'Der Lautsprecher', 161
'Der Lernende', 108
'Der letzte Wunsch', 113
'Der Nürnberger Prozeß', 181–2
'Der Nachgeborene', 25, 115
Der Ozeanflug, 78
'Der Pflaumenbaum', 122–3, 164, 189
'Der Radwechsel', 202–3, 216
'Der Rauch', 209
'Der Schneider von Ulm', 122
'Der schöne Tag, wenn ich nutzlos geworden bin', 221
'Der Schuh des Empedokles', 126–8, 131
'Der Tod im Wald', 11

INDEX

'Der Zweifler', 109, 111, 194
Desch, Kurt, 185
'Deutsche Kriegsfibel', 115–19, 139, 153, 158, 185, 222
'Deutsche Satiren', 138–41
'Deutsches Lied', 120
'Deutsches Miserere', 150
'Deutschland', 96
'Deutschland' (1941), 150
'Deutschland, du blondes, bleiches', 25, 96
'Die apokalyptischen Reiter', 177–8
Die Ausnahme und die Regel, 7, 107
'Die Auswanderung der Dichter', 102–3
'Die Ballade vom Baum und den Ästen', 81
'Die Ballade vom Liebestod', 14
'Die Bolschewiki entdecken...', 79
'Die da wegkönnen', 72
'Die dialektische Dramatik', 7
Die drei Soldaten, 63, 65–71, 93, 118, 122, 124
'Die Erziehung der Hirse', 197–8
'Die Geburt im Baum', 11
'Die gute Tat', 151
Die heilige Johanna der Schlachthöfe, 21
'Die Hoffnung der Welt', 151
Die Horatier und die Kuriatier, 105
'Die Internationale', 79
'Die Käuferin', 113, 114
'Die Kelle', 208–9, 211
'Die Krücken', 150
'Die Landschaft des Exils', 151
'Die Legende der Dirne Evlyn Roe', 9
'Die Literatur wird durchforscht werden', 112–13, 172
'Die Lösung', 208, 210
'Die Macht der Arbeiter', 113
'Die Maske des Bösen', 161
Die Maßnahme, 81, 88
'Die Moritat vom Reichstagsbrand', 99
Die Mutter, 81, 88
'Die Nachtlager', 79
'Die neuen Zeitalter', 151
Die neue Weltbühne, 144, 146
'Die Oberen sagen', 117–18, 222
'Die Pappel vom Karlsplatz', 195, 196
'Die Reisen des Glücksgotts, 164–8, 169, 197
'Die rote Rosa', 84
'Diese Arbeitslosigkeit', 64
'Diese babylonische Verwirrung', 36

'Die sechzehnjährige Weißnäherin Emma Ries vor dem Untersuchungsrichter', 113
'Die Sendlinge', 124
'Die Städte sind für dich gebaut', 53–4
'Die Teppichweber von Kujan-Bulak ehren Lenin', 130–1
Die Trophäen des Lukullus, 176
'Die unbesiegliche Inschrift', 131
'Die Vögel warten im Winter vor dem Fenster', 195
'Die Wahrheit einigt', 210
Die Wiederherstellung der Wahrheit, 117
Dimitrov, G., 88
'Dimitroff', 79
'Drachenlied', 195
Dreigroschenoper, 121
Dreigroschenprozeß, 59, 78
Dreigroschenroman, 98, 103–4, 177
'Dreihundert ermordete Kulis berichten an eine Internationale', 63
'Drei Paragraphen der Weimarer Verfassung', 64
'Du, der das Unentbehrliche...', 58, 72

'Ein Bericht', 81, 87
'Eines nicht wie das andere', 195
'Einheitsfront', 118
'Einheitsfrontlied', 121–22, 125
'Einmal, wenn da Zeit sein wird', 218
'Ein pessimistischer Mensch', 25
'Eisen', 210–11
Eisler, Hanns, 64, 97, 121, 170
'Elftes Lied des Glücksgotts', 168
Engels, F., 100, 168, 171, 174, 179
epigram, 99, 115–19, 152–9, 161–2, 184–5, 186, 194
'Epistel', 25
'Er ging die Straße hinunter', 49
'Es gibt kein größeres Verbrechen als Weggehen', 79
'Es ist Nacht', 119
'Eßkultur', 164
Esslin, M., 1, 242 n. 23, 244 n. 31, 245 n 35, 254 n. 3
'Es war leicht, ihn zu bekommen', 52
'Exil', 103

Fascism, 85, 86, 87, 103, 119, 172, 182, 238 n. 26, 252 n. 24
Fatzer, 37
FDJ, 187

INDEX

Feuchtwanger, L., 142, 170
'Finnische Epigramme', 153–9, 197, 247 n. 4
'Finnische Gutsspeisekammer', 154–6, 162, 163
'Finnland 1940', 151, 161
Flüchtlingsgespräche, 107, 164, 168
'Fragen eines lesenden Arbeiters', 126
'Friedensfibel', 185
'Früher dachte ich...', 60
'Friedenslied', 184
'Fröhlich vom Fleisch zu essen', 218, 221
'Frühling', 184
'Frühling 1938', 162
Fünf Schwierigkeiten beim Schreiben der Wahrheit, 104–5, 111, 117, 125

'Garden in Progress', 164, 204
'Gebt keinen euresgleichen auf', 110–11
'Gedanken über die Dauer des Exils', 141–2
'Gedenktafel für 4000, die im Krieg des Hitler gegen Norwegen versenkt wurden', 159
'Gedenktafel für im Krieg des Hitler gegen Frankreich Gefallene', 158
Gedichte im Exil (1948), 185–6
'Gedicht vom unbekannten Soldaten unter dem Triumphbogen', 39, 81, 97
'Gegen die Objektiven', 106, 134
'Gegenlied zu "Von der Freundlichkeit der Welt" ', 221
'Gegen Verführung', 10–11, 13, 17, 166, 220
'Gemeinsame Erinnerung', 150
George, Stefan, 38
'Gesang des Soldaten der roten Armee', 12
'Geschichten aus der Revolution', 151
Geschichten vom Herrn Keuner, 'Der hilflose Knabe', 68
'Gestank', 181
'Gewohnheiten, noch immer', 207–8, 210, 212
'Gleichnis des Buddha vom brennenden Haus', 129–30, 135, 148
'Glückliche Begegnung', 198
'Glücklicher Vorgang', 198
Goethe, J. W. v., 78
'Grabschrift aus dem Krieg des Hitler', 158
'Grabschrift für Gorki', 136
'Grabschrift 1919', 81
'Großer Dankchoral', 11–12, 13
'Große Zeit, vertan', 205, 216
Grosz, Georg, 65
Gustav Kiepenheuer Verlag, 82

'Hätten Sie die Zeitungen aufmerksam gelesen wie ich', 68
Hauptmann, Elisabeth, 7, 37, 39, 40, 115, 234 n. 29, 240 n. 9
Havemann, R., 255, n. 10
Heartfield, John, 139, 157
Heine, Heinrich, 168
'Heißer Tag', 208, 213
'Herr Doktor', 64
Herr Puntila und sein Knecht Matti, 164
Herzfelde, Wieland, 114, 186
'Hitler-Choräle', 81, 86–7, 89, 114, 116
Hölderlin, 78
'Hollywood', 161
'Hollywood-Elegien', 160
Horace, 91
Hundert Gedichte, 186
'Hymne an Gott', 12

'Ich beginne zu sprechen vom Tod', 18
'Ich bin der Glücksgott', 166
'Ich bin im Dreck', 49, 52
'Ich habe gehört', 151
'Ich habe ihm gesagt, er soll ausziehen', 52
'Ich habe lange die Wahrheit gesucht', 79
'Ich lese von der Panzerschlacht', 158
'Ich merke, ihr besteht darauf', 57
'Ich sage ja nichts gegen Alexander', 62
'Ich weiß, was ich brauche', 43–4, 45, 49, 52
'Im Bade', 161
'Ich will nicht behaupten', 55
Im Dickicht der Städte, 37
'Immer wieder', 52
'Im Überfluß', 102
'Im Zeichen der Schildkröte', 151
'Inbesitznahme der großen Metro durch die Moskauer Arbeiterschaft am 27. April 1935', 132–3
'In finsteren Zeiten', 105–6
Inflation, 37
'Inschrift für das Hochhaus an der Weberwiese', 185
Internationale Literatur, 140

INDEX

'Intervention', 178
Irony, 8, 18, 20–1, 27, 30, 31, 53, 68, 83, 84, 105, 116, 117, 120, 124, 129–30, 132, 138, 139, 148, 157, 193, 211–12

Jacobs, J., 48, 53
'Jene verloren sich selbst aus den Augen', 25, 35
'Jetzt ist alles Gras aufgefressen', 35
Joe Fleischhacker, 35, 36, 37, 69
Jünger, Ernst, 177

'Kalifornischer Herbst', 204
'Kanonen nötiger als Butter', 140–1
'Kantate zu Lenins Todestag', 136
'Karfreitag', 12
'Karl Hollmanns Sang', 18
'Keinen Gedanken verschwendet an das Unänderbare!', 72
'Keiner oder alle', 121
'Kinderhymne', 195
'Kinderkreuzzug', 150
Kinderlieder, 99, 122–6, 194–7
'Kinderlieder 1950', 184
Kipling, R., 7, 24, 159 ('Epitaphs of the War')
Klampfenfibel, 18–19
'Kleines Bettellied', 122
Klopstock, F. G., 78, 91
Knopf, J., 4
'Kohlen für Mike', 39, 131
KPD, 65, 80, 90, 91, 92, 103, 104, 140, 183, 235 n. 8, 237 n. 21
Korsch, Karl, 109, 170, 173, 174
'Kranlieder', 122
Kriegsfibel, 159, 186, 248 n. 7
Kuhle Wampe, oder Wem gehört die Welt?, 64–5

'Larrys Ballade von der Mama Armee', 12
'Laßt eure Träume fahren', 60
Laughton, Charles, 164, 169
'Laute', 209
Leben des Galilei, 107, 109, 164
Leben Eduards des Zweiten, 37
'Legende vom toten Soldaten', 12, 23, 42, 63, 81, 82, 114
'Legende von der Entstehung des Buches Taoteking auf dem Weg des Laotse in die Emigration', 128–9, 211
Lehrgedicht: as category, 60–1, 99, 110, 150, 185; definition, 60, 62

Lehrgedicht von der Natur der Menschen, 63, 124, 151, 169–81
Lenin, V. I., 100, 103, 130, 131, 210
Lerg-Kill, U., 22, 91, 96
'Liebeslieder', 198
'Liebesunterricht', 167
'Lied am schwarzen Samstag', 16
'Liedchen aus alter Zeit', 195
'Lied der Galgenvögel', 15
'Lied der preiswerten Lyriker', 94–6, 112, 160, 172
'Lied der Schwestern', 12
'Lied der Starenschwärme', 120
'Lied des Stückeschreibers', 21
'Lied einer deutschen Mutter', 150
Lieder Gedichte Chöre. 1, 79–97, 98, 103
'Lied gegen den Krieg', 120–1
'Lied vom Glück', 184, 202
'Lied von den Kavalieren der Station D', 19
'Liturgie vom Hauch', 23, 62, 67
'Lob der Dialektik', 91–2, 105, 109
'Lob der illegalen Arbeit', 91
'Lob der Partei', 90, 110
'Lob des Dolchstoßes', 72
'Lob des Kommunismus', 89–90, 100, 146
'Lob des Lernens', 89, 180
'Lob des Revolutionärs', 91
'Lob des Zweifels', 109–10, 122, 180, 194, 199
Luxemburg, Rosa, 81, 84, 180

'Mahagonnygesänge', 23
'Mailied', 195
Malik-Verlag, 114, 148, 240–1 n. 9
Mann, Heinrich, 162
Mann, Thomas, 96
Mann ist Mann, 37
'Man sollte nicht zu kritisch sein', 27–30, 218
'Maria', 126
Marsch, E., 67
Marx, Karl, 50, 57, 100, 103, 167, 168, 171, 173, 174, 179, 182
Marxism, 39, 40, 90, 101, 109, 127
Materialism, 8–18, 29, 164–8, 217–18
Mayer, Hans, 19, 21
'Mein Bruder war ein Flieger', 124
Messingkauf, 151
Me-ti, 'Unrecht tun und Unrecht dulden', 68, 101, 137

'Me-tis Strenge', 101
Müller, K.-D., 30, 226–7 n. 6
Münsterer, O., 19
Münzenberg, Willi, 'Éditions du Carrefour', 80

'Nachdenkend über die Hölle', 151
'Neue Zeiten', 195
'1954: Erste Hälfte', 218
'1940', 150, 151, 161–2
'Nicht in die Schlacht wirf, Feldherr, alle', 216–17, 218
'Nimm Platz am Tisch', 193, 198, 199

'O Falladah die du hangest', 23, 63
'Oft in der Nacht träume ich', 51
Ossietzky, C. v., 136, 137

Pietzcker, C., 5
'Prometheus', 15
Propyläen-Verlag, 82

'Rapport von Deutschland', 113
'Rat an die bildenden Künstler, das Schicksal ihrer Kunstwerke in den kommenden Kriegen betreffend', 137–8
'Rede einer proletarischen Mutter an ihre Söhne bei Kriegsausbruch', 151
'Rede eines Arbeiters an einen Arzt', 136
'Reden Sie nichts von Gefahr!', 49
'Resolution der Kommunarden', 121
Rilke, R. M., 38
Rotermund, E., 22, 228 n. 24
'Rudern, Gespräche', 213, 220

Satire, 82, 83, 87, 94, 114, 130, 137, 138–40, 149, 158, 160, 181, 208, 216
'Schlechte Zeiten', 189–91, 193, 202
'Schlechte Zeit für Lyrik', 156–7, 189
Schlenstedt, S., 3
'Schnelligkeit des sozialistischen Aufbaus', 133
Schumacher, Ernst, 30
Schuhmann, Klaus, 2, 4, 19, 38, 40, 52–3, 57, 58, 59
Schwarz, P. P., 4
SED, 183, 188, 193, 199–201, 206, 210
'Seht ihr nicht, daß ihr zu viele seid?', 115
'Setzen Sie sich!', 54–5, 60

'Siebentes Lied des Glücksgotts' I, 166, 167; II, 166, 168
'Sintflut', 115
'Sokrates', 126
'Soldatengrab', 5
'Solidaritätslied', 64–5
'Sonett in der Emigration', 151
'Sonett vom Erbe', 112
'Sonnenburg', 81, 87
sonnets, 99, 113, 149, 153, 240 n. 8
SPD, 65, 70, 71, 90, 92, 93
'Sprüche', 184, 193–4
'Stärke des Dritten Reiches', 114
Stalin, J. V., 137, 179, 180
Stalinism, 180–1, 211, 212, 259–62 nn. 31–2; cult of personality, 127, 131, 136–7; 'socialism in one country', 179; 'necessity', 'historic mission', 102, 176, 239 n. 2, 241–2 n. 15
Steffensen, Steffen, 3
Steffinische Sammlung, 158, 159, 163, 185, 247 n. 4
Sträter, Hans, 21–2
'Stürme schmettern', 195
Svendborger Gedichte, 1, 39, 110, 114–49, 240–1 n. 9, 245–6 n. 37
Swift, Jonathan, *Modest Proposal*, 54

'Tannen', 206
'Tarpeja', 25
Tao Tê Ching, 143
'Tödliche Verwirrung', 114
'Tritt an! Warum kommst du so spät?', 53–4
Trommeln in der Nacht, 19
Trotsky, L. D., 180
Tui complex, 134

'Überall vieles zu sehen', 151
'Über das Begreifen des Vorhandenen', 75
'Über das Lehren ohne Schüler', 103
'Über das Mißtrauen des Einzelnen', 56–7
'Über dem Sund hängt Regengewölke', 162–3
'Über den Einzug der Menschheit in die großen Städte zu Beginn des dritten Jahrtausends', 35, 36
'Über den enthaltsamen Kanzler', 114
'Über Deutschland', 183
'Über die Anstrengung', 13–14, 15

INDEX

'Über die Bauart langdauernder Werke', 72, 75–8, 101, 106, 110, 111, 138, 144, 204
'Über die Berge', 195
'Über die Bezeichnung Emigranten', 141
'Über die geistige und materielle Kultur', 177
'Über die Städte', 33–4
'Über die Städte (2)', 52
'Über die Unfruchtbarkeit', 123, 164, 189
'Über rationellen und emotionellen Standpunkt', 180
Über reimlöse Lyrik mit unregelmäßigen Rhythmen, 112
'Über Ungleichheit. Schwierig, sie zu entdecken', 176
Ulbricht, Walter, 216
'Unbezahlbar ist', 55
'Und ich dachte immer', 221
'Und immer wieder gab es Abendröte', 1?
'Und in eurem Lande?', 142
'Und so beginne ich ihn denn zu suchen', 159
'Und was bekam des Soldaten Weib', 150
'Und wenn wir's überlegen', 17–18, 115
'Unglücklicher Vorgang', 198–9, 205
'Unsere Erde zerfällt', 35

Verfremdung, 51, 61, 123, 234 n. 24
'Vergnügungen', 218, 220–1
'Verhalten in der Fremde', 79
'Verhöhnung des Soldaten der Revolution. Seine Antwort', 136
'Verjagt mit gutem Grund', 142
'Verschollener Ruhm der Riesenstadt New York', 94, 160
Versuche, 39, 40, 59, 65, 78
'Verwisch die Spuren', 42–3, 44, 45–6, 49, 51, 54, 60
'Viele sehen es so', 151
'Viele sind für die Ordnung', 100
'Viele sprachen vom Krieg wie von Ungewitter und Meerflut', 178
'Vier Aufforderungen an einen Mann zu verschiedenen Zeiten von verschiedener Seite', 39, 50
Villon, F., 24
'Visionen', 151

Völker, Klaus, 37
'Volksfront', 118, 138
'Vom armen B. B.', 34–5, 62
'Vom Brot und den Kindlein', 9–10
'Vom François Villon', 15
'Vom fünften Rad', 49, 54
'Vom Glück des Gebens', 184, 194
'Vom Kind, das sich nicht waschen wollte', 122
'Vom Klettern in Bäumen', 16
'Vom kriegerischen Lehrer', 195
'Vom Mitmensch', 15
'Vom schlechten Gebiß', 16, 19
'Vom Schwimmen in Seen und Flüssen', 16
'Vom Sprengen des Gartens', 163–4
'Von allen Werken', 72–4, 75, 78
'Von dem Gras und Pfefferminzkraut', 15, 17
'Von den Osseger Witwen', 120
'Von den Sündern in der Hölle', 19
'Von der Freundlichkeit der Welt', 13, 15
'Von der "Judenhure" Marie Sanders', 120
'Von der Kindesmörderin Marie Farrar', 9, 23, 62
'Von der zermalmenden Wucht der Städte', 35
'Von des Cortez Leuten', 25
'Von einem Maler', 24–5
'Vor acht Jahren', 206–7
'Vorschlag, die Architektur mit der Lyrik zu verbinden', 116, 152

Wagenknecht, Regine, 22
'Wahrnehmung', 191
'Warum esse ich Brot', 40–2, 55
'Was ist geschehen?', 181
'Was nützt die Güte?', 106–7
'Was zersetzt', 113
Weill, Kurt, 97
'Weite und Vielfalt der realistischen Schreibweise', 182
'Wenn es im Geahnten ist', 194
'Wenn es zum Marschieren kommt', 118
'Wenn ich mit dir rede', 47–9, 50, 60, 101, 179
'Wenn sie so jammern', 176–7
'Wer aber ist die Partei?', 90, 101–2
Werfel, F., 38
'Wer keine Hilfe weiß', 71

'Wer sich wehrt', 71, 100
'Wer zu Hause bleibt, wenn der Kampf beginnt', 106, 134
'Wie der Wind weht', 220
'Wiegenlieder', 81, 84–5, 88, 103
'Wie ich genau weiß', 25
'Wir haben einen Fehler begangen', 72
'Wir hören, Du willst nicht mehr mit uns arbeiten', 72
'Wozu Märkte erobern...', 119

'Zeit meines Reichtums', 79
'Zeitunglesen beim Teekochen', 161
'Zitat', 106
'Zufluchtsstätte', 142
'Zukunftslied', 184, 186, 188, 192
'Zu Potsdam unter den Eichen', 81, 84
'Zweites Gedicht vom unbekannten Soldaten unter dem Triumphbogen', 81
'Zweites Lied des Glücksgotts', 166